INTRODUCTION TO CRIMINAL JUSTICE

LAWRENCE F. TRAVIS, III
University of Cincinnati

anderson publishing co.
2035 reading road
cincinnati, ohio 45202
(513) 421-4142

Introduction to Criminal Justice

Copyright © 1990 by Anderson Publishing Co., Cincinnati, OH

ISBN 0-87084-845-3
Library of Congress Catalog Number 89-80457

Kelly Humble *Managing Editor*

Cover Design by Scott Burchett

Acknowledgments

Writing a book has never been a solitary experience for me, although it has sometimes been a lonely one. This book would not have been completed without the encouragement and support of many people, too numerous to mention by name. Nonetheless, some of those who helped me to complete this text deserve special recognition.

I begin by thanking my colleagues at the University of Cincinnati, whose comments, suggestions and support were invaluable. The high level of scholarly productivity of my colleagues here in Cincinnati was just enough to give me the proper amount of anxiety and compulsion to complete the manuscript. Ed Latessa, the department head, and Bob Langworthy deserve recognition for the support--material, moral and otherwise, which they afforded to me. Frank Cullen deserves mention as principal nag. It gives me pleasure to report that I completed the manuscript more closely to deadline than Frank has ever done.

From Anderson Publishing, Mickey Braswell can never be fully thanked for his attention to detail and painstaking editorial commentary. His wife, Susan, of course, was the true driving force and actually did most of the work. To paraphrase an old saying, before every great woman stands some man.

Speaking of great women leads me to thank my wife Pat, who kept me on schedule, understood the long hours, tolerated my compulsiveness and generally kept me sane throughout the process of writing this book. My children, to whom the book is dedicated, also did their best to encourage and support my efforts. Should I actually earn royalties, they have already spent them. Further, it was in earnest hope that this book would provide their sole knowledge of the justice system, that I wrote the manuscript. There is still a chance that this hope may be realized.

The idea for the book, and much of the rationale for the approach I have taken, stems from what I have learned from my students over the years. I thank them for teaching me about teaching criminal justice, and I hope that this text will make the learning for future generations a more pleasant experience. I must also thank those who taught me about the criminal justice system, notably Don Newman, Rita Warren, Leslie Wilkins and Vincent O'Leary. While I did not always appreciate their lessons at the time, I come to respect their knowledge and expertise more with each passing year.

A final debt of gratitude is owed to my colleagues in the field of criminal justice, on whose research I rely and whose comments and suggestions form the content of this book. I also rely on them to use the book. If they are not all cited within the following pages, I apologize and promise to do better with the next edition.

While I have written the book, and am ultimately responsible for any errors that it contains, I deny responsibility. Any mistakes are undoubtedly the result of my trusting nature and the failure of those named above.

Lawrence F. Travis, III
Cincinnati, Ohio

FOR MY SONS

LARRY, CHRIS AND GREG

CONTENTS

1 Criminal Justice Perspectives

Imagine that you are standing on a busy street corner. You look at the people around you. What do you see?

A woman drops a postcard in a mailbox.

Across the street, a man carrying a small suitcase steps off of a bus.

Several feet away from you a couple is arguing over something.

A police car slowly passes through the intersection.

Half a block away, someone is "jaywalking" while a small child nearby is reading a street sign.

A man deposits money in a nearby parking meter.

A stranger approaches you and asks that you sign a petition in support of seatbelt legislation.

What you probably do not see is that the mix of pedestrian and vehicular traffic is orderly. You do not notice that almost everyone watches the police car, at least briefly. You do not realize that all of these strangers at the intersection are going about their own business, apparently unaware of each other. Yet, in a well-rehearsed routine, they stop and go on cue from the traffic light. You probably do not see a crime (with the possible exception of the jaywalker).

Without realizing it, you have observed the criminal justice system in action. What you did not know is that the postcard was a monthly report the woman was sending to her probation officer. Nor was it clear that the man with the suitcase just left the state penitentiary on parole. The arguing couple may be tonight's (or last night's) domestic disturbance. The slow-moving police car is searching for the small child, who is reading the street signs because he is lost. The jaywalker crossed the street to avoid walking past a group of teens gathered on the sidewalk. The man at the parking meter wants to avoid a citation. The person with the petition hopes to insure that motorists wear their seatbelts.

The entire street corner scene just described, and all of the individuals in it, are affected by the workings of the criminal justice system. Interestingly, the individuals also directly affect the workings of that system. Should the argumentative couple become too boisterous, the shopper fail to deposit the correct coins in the parking meter, the woman not mail the postcard, etc., you would expect some sort of official response from the justice system. Thus, criminal justice is an integral part of our society and social living.

Sociologists often speak of the purposes of social institutions as "functions" (Parsons, 1966). Functions are the goals served by a social institution. For instance, schools serve the function of education. Institutional functions can be classified as either *manifest* or *latent*. Manifest functions are the stated purpose of the institution and latent functions are the unstated or hidden goals. For example, schools serve the manifest function of education through teaching students various academic subjects. They also meet the latent functions of providing child care and controlling the work force by otherwise occupying millions of young people.

A primary function of criminal justice is social control. The components of the justice process are police, courts and corrections. These components have the manifest function of controlling different kinds of deviance which are defined as crime. It is to be noted that "crime" is only a small part of the total activities and behaviors which are the targets of social control. Most social control works through "informal" mechanisms such as shunning or ostracizing the person who is rude, insensitive or bothersome. Other forms of deviance are defined as mental illness and handled through the mental health system. In 1924 Roscoe Pound (1929:4) remarked, "Law does but a part of this whole task of social control; and the criminal law does but a part of that portion which belongs to the law."

Criminal justice then is the formal social institution designed to respond to a narrowly defined set of social control needs. Crime control is the primary purpose of the criminal justice system, but there are other latent functions also served by criminal justice. As we shall see, police, courts and corrections do much more than merely fight crime. Nonetheless, our examination of the criminal justice process cannot progress until we understand this central purpose. Whatever other functions it may serve, and whatever methods it may employ to achieve its ends, the justice system can be measured (or judged) as an institution of social control.

Focusing upon the social control function of criminal justice (the control of crime) makes it easier to study and understand criminal justice practices and policies. We assess the value of a policy or procedure, or proposed changes in them, by how well they meet the objective of crime control. Theoretically, it seems easy enough to maintain an "objectives" perspective, but it is often very difficult to do so in practice. In his discussion of objectives-based analysis, Frederic Kellogg (1976:50) has observed:

> It has never made much of an impact on the administration of criminal justice, most likely because there is so little agreement as to the "objectives" of criminal justice, the purposes of punishment, and the most appropriate strategy to reduce crime.

The disagreement to which Kellogg refers concerns the *means* by which the justice system is expected to achieve crime control. While it is true that criminal justice practices may be controversial in particular instances, the overriding interest in controlling crime is a constant goal. Although we may disagree over the use of the death penalty, wiretaps, plea bargaining or probation, we can agree that what we want to do is reduce the incidence of crime. Unfortunately, criminal justice practices too often become focal points for debates which are stated in terms of the purposes of the justice system. The President's Commission on Law Enforcement and Administration of Justice aptly illustrated this confusion in its report (1967:70):

> Any criminal justice system is an apparatus society uses to enforce the standards of conduct necessary to protect individuals and the community. It operates by apprehending, prosecuting, convicting, and sentencing those members of the community who violate the basic rules of group existence. The action taken against lawbreakers is designed to serve three purposes beyond the immediately punitive one. It removes dangerous people from the community; it deters others from criminal behavior; and it gives society an opportunity to attempt to transform lawbreakers into law-abiding citizens.

A debate may arise over whether deterring others from criminal behavior or transforming violators into law-abiding citizens is the best *means* of achieving the objective of social control, but the objective itself is not questioned. This confusion of means and ends is not limited to disagreements over specific practices such as capital punishment, but also includes ideological conflicts. Not only do people disagree over the appropriate forms of capital punishment (beheading, burning at the stake, electrocution, poison gas, lethal injection), but also the use of capital punishment (the sanctity of life, "an eye for an eye"). Yet, what would happen to these debates if the justice system could eliminate murder?

To further complicate an already complicated picture, the justice system is not the only social control institution in operation. The mental health system deals with those "rule violators" deemed inappropriate subjects for the justice system. Families, churches, schools, social organizations and the media all serve social control purposes by informing us of what is and is not acceptable behavior. The usefulness of the justice system must be understood within the total context of social control institutions. These other social control devices are often very effective (perhaps more effective than the criminal law), as is illustrated in Box 1.1.

For example, the fact that most of the pedestrians and vehicles in the illustration which opens this chapter obey the traffic lights and signs is evidence of social control. How are these individuals controlled? Some may be controlled by fear of a citation (justice system); others may react as a result of learning traffic safety at home, in school, or from the media. All of these sources of social control converge at this intersection to produce an orderly and predictable flow of traffic. To what extent is this level of conformity attributable to the justice system?

Box 1.1
Social Control Institutions in America

Social control is achieved in many ways: through lessons learned by the individual about what is appropriate or inappropriate behavior, through structured opportunity that does not allow the individual the chance to deviate, through the exercise of coercive force to limit behavior. Nearly all social life affects social control, but the principal institutions in our society achieve social control in the following ways:

LESSONS	serve to teach us what behaviors are acceptable.
STRUCTURES	limit our opportunities for misbehavior.
COERCION	forces us to behave correctly, or prevents us from misbehaving.

LESSONS

The Family	Children learn to respect others' property and opinions, how to resolve conflict peacefully.
Schools	Students learn appropriate behavior, work habits, and respect for others.
Churches	Members learn rules for behavior (e.g., the Ten Commandments).
Social Groups	Members learn tolerance, rules for personal relations and behavior (e.g., majority rule).
Recreation	Players learn rules and discipline, ways of behaving (e.g., sportsmanship).
Employment	Workers learn discipline, work habits, "chain of command."

| *Mental Health* | Patients learn coping skills and ways of behaving (e.g., through token economies). |
| *Law* | Defendants and observers learn rules of behavior (laws) through their application. |

STRUCTURE

The Family	Children are supervised, must abide by constraints on behavior (e.g., curfews).
Schools	Students follow fairly regimented academic schedules, are supervised by teachers.
Churches	Members participate in legitimate activities (e.g., weekly services, "Sunday School," service projects).
Social Groups	Members engage in activities (e.g., formal meetings).
Recreation	Players participate in organized activities and competitions.
Employment	Workers engage in defined activities and meet performance standards (e.g., production quotas).
Mental Health	Patients participate in organized activities (e.g., group meetings).
Law	Statutes require certain behaviors (e.g., providing care to children, maintenance of rental property).

COERCION

| *The Family* | Children are punished for wrongdoing (e.g., "grounding," spankings). |
| *Schools* | Students who misbehave are punished (e.g., detention, suspension from school, written assignments). |

Churches	Offending members are penalized (e.g., excommunication, threat of eternal damnation).
Social Groups	Offending members are sanctioned (e.g., ridicule, expulsion from the group, ostracism).
Recreation	Wrongdoers are punished (e.g., game forfeiture, penalties, loss of eligibility).
Employment	Misbehavior is penalized (e.g., loss of pay, dismissal, demotion).
Mental Health	Behavioral problems are controlled (e.g., passive restraint, sedation, forcible restraint).
Law	Offenders are sanctioned (e.g., fines, incarceration, execution, assessment of damages).

One need only consider two examples of traffic behavior to realize the complex interaction of the many sources of social control. First, compare the orderliness of most street traffic to the relative "free-for-all" chaos characteristic of most partially filled shopping mall parking lots. Second, think of the number of times you (as driver or passenger) have waited at a stoplight on a deserted street. The presence or absence of others does not completely explain the differences in behavior. Rather, it may be the public nature of the road as opposed to the private nature of the parking lot. The criminal justice system is addressed to the issue of public social behavior. However, in cases of a public nature, the justice system is not the only working mechanism of social control.

The study of criminal justice involves the study of social control, which itself is a complex topic. Further, the justice process serves a number of conflicting and often contradictory purposes while achieving social control. Finally, the justice process is characterized by a wide variety of agents, agencies, and structures. Criminal justice, as a topic of study, involves a high level of complexity. The immediate task is to develop a perspective which allows us to integrate many components into a cohesive framework.

PERSPECTIVES ON CRIMINAL JUSTICE

The study of criminal justice is akin to moving a fifty-pound watermelon; you are sure you could lift the melon, if only you could get a firm grasp on it. Our "grasp" on the study of the justice process comes from an analytic perspective. A variety of different approaches have been used to study criminal justice, and we will examine five of these: disciplinary, comparison, process, thematic and systems analyses of criminal justice.

Disciplinary Analyses

The total criminal justice process, as well as aspects of the process, have been topics of study in a variety of social science disciplines. How any particular decision in the process is viewed depends upon whether the analyst is trained as a sociologist, psychologist, lawyer, political scientist, economist, or something else.

An arrest may be an interpersonal interaction, the product of the police officer's perceptions, an exercise of legal authority, a power relation, a rational decision, or something different. In fact, most arrests probably result from a combination of these factors. The study of criminal justice operations in the United States is perhaps best described as *multidisciplinary* or *interdisciplinary*.

A discipline is a branch of study or learning. Thus, sociology or political science are branches of a more generic area of learning that could be called "human behavior." The fact that programs in criminal justice at colleges and universities tend to include courses in psychology, sociology, law, political science, social work, and other disciplines illustrates the multidisciplinary nature of criminal justice study. That is, justice issues may be approached from a number of specialties. Box 1.2 briefly describes the approaches that analysts trained in different social science disciplines might prefer in studying justice topics.

The number and variety of different disciplines which provide a perspective for the study of justice issues raises the possibility that these issues are interdisciplinary. For example, a full understanding of arrests, criminal penalties or other parts of criminal justice is achieved through the application of several disciplinary approaches. Thus, in studying the arrest decision, the analyst should be aware of the legal, political, rational, perceptual, organizational and personal factors in operation.

Recent observers have commented upon both the multidisciplinary and interdisciplinary nature of criminal justice (Toder, 1987). Orsagh (1983) suggested that economics has much to offer the study of crime and crime control. In discussing the combination of economics and what he termed "traditional criminology," he stated, (1983:395) "Taken together, they significantly broaden and enrich the study of crime and criminal justice." Others have noted that an effect of interdisciplinary approaches would appear to be a lack of theory (Williams, 1984; Willis, 1983). They argue that the use of many disciplines yields descriptive data without a clear theoretical, interpretative scheme.

Box 1.2
Disciplinary Approaches to Criminal Justice

As the table below indicates, criminal justice professors (and researchers) come from a variety of disciplinary backgrounds. These backgrounds prepare them to approach justice topics and issues from different perspectives:

Sociologists look to the social organization of groups and interactions among people to explain how things occur.

Historians look to larger social and intellectual movements over time to explain how things occur.

Psychologists look to individual motivations and perceptions to explain how things occur.

Political Scientists look to the processes of influence and the distribution of power to explain how things occur.

Lawyers look to established legal principles, statutes and rules to explain how things occur.

Economists look to costs and benefits as an explanation of how things occur.

Distribution of Graduate Degree Fields
of Criminal Justice Faculty 1980*

Field	Percent of Faculty
Criminal Justice	28.42%
Social Science	26.43%
Education	13.71%
Public Administration	10.97%
Other	10.22%
Law	9.99%

Totals do not equal 100% due to rounding.
*SOURCE: Richard Pearson, et al. (eds.) (1980), *Criminal Justice Education: The End of the Beginning.* New York: John Jay Press, pp. 158-59.

Multidisciplinary approaches remind one of the old story about the blind men meeting an elephant. Each man feels a different part of the beast and concludes that it is different things. The man touching the trunk believes he has a snake, the one with the tail feels it is a horse, the one at the leg believes he faces a tree, etc. The result is several interpretations of the same phenomenon, each colored by the unique perspective of the observer. Critics of the interdisciplinary approach believe that the sighted observer will describe a large gray or brown beast with a snakelike frontal appendage, a tail, and four large legs. That is, he will be able to describe the elephant, but not know what it is.

Disciplinary approaches to the study of criminal justice provide important interpretations of criminal justice, but interpretations which are necessarily limited. Multidisciplinary approaches often yield conflicting information, while interdisciplinary approaches may provide accurate descriptions yet lack true understanding or valid interpretations. Thus, while useful and necessary, studies of criminal justice based on disciplinary perspectives may be unduly restricted.

Comparison Analyses

As the title suggests, these strategies for the study of criminal justice establish standards to which actual practices of justice agencies or an entire justice system are compared. Perhaps the best known example of this approach was suggested by Herbert Packer (1968) through the application of "ideal types" of justice systems (either due process or crime control). In this approach, the analyst first constructs a model or ideal justice system to which the actual justice system will be compared.

As illustrated in Box 1.3, Packer suggested that two conflicting goals characterize the American criminal justice process. On the one hand, we seek to control crime so that we can expect the justice system to quickly respond to criminal acts. On the other, we seek to preserve liberty so that we can expect the justice system to be highly constrained in interfering with suspected individuals.

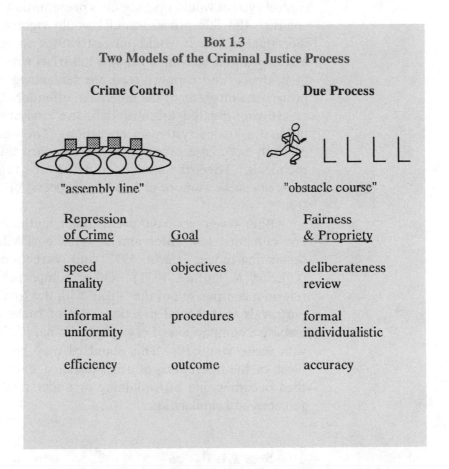

Box 1.3
Two Models of the Criminal Justice Process

Crime Control		Due Process
"assembly line"		"obstacle course"
Repression of Crime	Goal	Fairness & Propriety
speed finality	objectives	deliberateness review
informal uniformity	procedures	formal individualistic
efficiency	outcome	accuracy

The first step in this type of analysis is to envision the "perfect" justice system if only one of these goals is dominant. The crime control model would support efficiency with an emphasis on speedy processing of cases. We would expect an enhancement of police powers to search and arrest, and a relaxation in the rules of evidence to allow relevant information to be presented in court. The emphasis on speed would support plea bargaining and prosecutorial discretion, as well as mandatory sentences to hasten the disposition of cases. While consistent with the basic tenets of a democratic society (no coerced confessions), the crime control system would operate on a presumption of guilt. In contrast, the due process model would vigorously protect individual rights. It would put restrictions on searches and arrests without warrants, require full trials with strict rules of evidence and support separate sentencing hearings to protect the interests of the individual offender.

Having created these models, the analyst would next observe a justice system in operation. The analyst would carefully note case processing, and compare this reality to the ideals. Then, the analyst would be able to classify the justice process as more or less "due process" or "crime control."

Other observers have used similar methods to classify and compare law enforcement agencies (Wilson, 1968), sentencing judges (Levin, 1972) and correctional agencies (O'Leary & Duffee, 1971). Other comparison strategies rely on a comparison of the "ideal" with the "real," or media portrayals with actual practice. All of these approaches employ a comparison of observed criminal justice practices with some standard. This standard may be an artificial ideal, or the operations of other justice agencies. The task then becomes one of explaining or understanding the differences and similarities.

Process Analyses

Another perspective on the justice system can be found in analyses which focus on case processing. These approaches focus less on the outcome of the system and more on how the system "runs." Rather than viewing due process or crime control as guides for the entire system, this perspective traces the flow of cases from detection of crime through ultimate disposition. It focuses on the decision-making of actors in the justice process. Plea bargaining, for example, does not represent a commitment to "crime control" as much as it does a concession to heavy caseloads.

The American Bar Foundation provided perhaps the best illustration of this approach. Beginning in the 1950s, the foundation undertook massive case studies of the justice process in three states. The results of these studies of the justice process were published in five volumes describing investigation (Tiffany, McIntyre & Rotenberg, 1967), arrest (LaFave, 1965), prosecution (Miller, 1970), conviction (Newman, 1966) and sentencing (Dawson, 1969).

As the titles of the books indicate, the focus of this analysis was on the decisions of justice system actors at the major stages of the process. The studies investigated how the justice system "processed" cases to determine what factors influenced decisions to pass a case further along the system or to divert a case from further processing. This perspective describes the ways police, courts and corrections handle different cases. The task is one of explaining or understanding deviations from the "normal" processing routine.

Thematic Analyses

Still others studying the justice process examine one or more issues as they apply across the entire system. For example, Remington, et al (1969), suggested such an approach using the themes of evidence sufficiency, consent, fairness and propriety, effectiveness, and discretion. Newman (1978) applied functions such as the punitive, deterrent, community protection, corrective and due process functions of criminal justice.

This approach compares different points or aspects of the justice process with each other regarding the theme.

Thus, arrest and sentencing might be compared in terms of how much evidence (evidence sufficiency) is required to justify each type of decision. Similarly, granting bail, probation, or parole release may be compared and contrasted with reference to how well each serves the corrective function, the deterrent function, or both.

As with the process approaches, this technique is based on the various decisions which comprise the justice system. Here, however, the focus is on the characteristics of the decision (e.g., level of evidence required, degree of consent involved) or the effects of the decisions (e.g., deterrent effect, punitive effect, etc.) This approach results in descriptions of common themes or purposes of criminal justice decisions rather than the decisions themselves.

For instance, if we compared process and thematic approaches applied to the decision to buy a new car, process analysts focus on the decision to buy or not, while thematic analysts look at why people come to their decisions. Thus, the process analyst might determine that 50% of shoppers actually purchase a new automobile. The thematic analyst will look at new car buyers and might determine that a rebate program increases car sales by 10%. The process analyst might next look at the decision to buy a new refrigerator, while the thematic analyst will study the effect of rebate programs on sales of refrigerators.

Systems Analyses

The final perspective which we will examine is the "systems approach." This perspective views the criminal justice process as a whole comprised of the separate, but interrelated, parts of law enforcement, courts, and corrections. These parts work together to achieve the goal of crime control in our society.

Although the roots of what is called *General Systems Theory* can be traced back hundreds of years (Van Gigch,

1974:49-52), it was best espoused by Ludwig von Berta-lanffy in 1950 and later expanded by him in 1968. The heart of systems theory is an emphasis on *context*. Whatever the phenomena under study, systems analysts strive to see the "big picture." They are concerned with how their units of study fit into a larger environment.

A *system* is a set or collection of interrelated parts working together to achieve a common goal. Systems seek balance and operate in an equilibrium. As a result, a system will react and adapt to pressures in such a manner as to maintain or reestablish equilibrium. The disruption of a system's balance affects each of its component parts and alters its total operation. Therefore, systems are generally resistant to change.

The systems analyst attempts to understand both how and why decisions are made, and looks for reasons or explanations which are internal to the justice process, as well as for those arising from the larger environment. The systems approach compels the analyst to see the big picture and to determine whether the parts are interconnected. This perspective also sensitizes the analyst to the complexity of the criminal justice system. For example, the analyst not only attempts to understand how police decide to arrest offenders, but also to learn how this arrest decision affects prosecutors, judges, and correctional authorities.

CHOOSING A PERSPECTIVE

Having briefly reviewed these perspectives on the analysis of criminal justice, we must now choose the one we will use. At this point, we still have a fifty-pound watermelon to move. This book will rely on the systems approach to criminal justice because of its flexibility.

The major shortcoming of the other approaches to the study of criminal justice is that they are too restrictive. Indeed, what often occurs is that an analyst employing one of these perspectives actually holds a "systems" view of the justice process. To explain different levels of discretion, evidence sufficiency, deterrent value or community protection, the analyst must seek reasons outside the narrow realm of his or her approach. This also is true of those who employ a process approach or disciplinary perspective.

The process approach yields excellent descriptions of how cases move along the justice system, but often fails to provide adequate explanations for deviations from normal operation. To explain why a particular case or set of cases receives special treatment, these analysts frequently refer to external (environmental) factors. So too, those using a comparative approach often must refer to environmental factors to explain their observed deviations from the ideal, or to explain differences between models. The systems approach is multidisciplinary and grounded in the context or environment of the justice system. It includes not only the capacity to seek external causes for practices of the justice process, but also requires the analyst to search for the causes.

The systems approach is broad enough to allow the analyst to employ any (or all) of these other perspectives within it. That is, the systems approach is flexible enough to include many different disciplinary backgrounds and approaches to the study of the justice process. The analyst might concentrate on the psychological motivations of prosecutors in plea bargaining with offenders, but do so with reference to the organizational needs of the courts, police and prosecutor's office, as well as sensitivity to the evidentiary standards of arrest, charging, and conviction.

The systems approach forces the analyst to remember that many factors influence each decision and decision-maker in the justice process. The analyst is able to consider not only how a change in the criminal law might affect police enforcement behavior, but also to consider how changes in that behavior may be reacted to by prosecutors, judges and correctional authorities.

In comparison to other possible approaches to the study of criminal justice, the systems approach provides a "picture window" through which to view criminal justice as compared to the "portholes" available with other perspectives. For this reason, we will adopt a systems perspective on criminal justice for the remainder of this book. We hope to see the big picture, as well as its component parts.

SYSTEMS THEORY
AND THE SYSTEMS APPROACH

The properties of systems are easily understood within the common-sense meaning and use of the term "system." We all know, for example, that one cannot "beat the system" (because it resists change). Many people have a "system" for filing, doing the laundry or even betting on horse races. How many times have we learned that our application, payment, or request for information cannot be processed because "the system is down?" These phrases illustrate the interrelatedness of parts, common purpose, and resistance to change which characterize a system.

The system cannot be beaten because it reacts and adapts to maintain normal functioning. In some way, over the long run, things will "even out." A system for filing papers or doing the laundry is a process composed of interrelated steps which, when taken in proper sequence, yield the desired result, i.e., being able to find papers quickly, laundry with "white whites and bright colors." Any breakdown in the system leads to undesired results: lost papers or discolored and shrunken laundry.

Systems theory is sensitive to the interdependency of the parts of the entire process. As Sutherland (1975:3) observed, systems theory requires the adoption of the "systems approach." This approach or perspective is more important than a theory that all the parts of a process are connected. The approach to study and problem-solving which comes from systems theory is very appropriate to the study of criminal justice. It compels the analyst to consider the interconnectedness of parts. It also sensitizes the analyst to the complexities inherent in the criminal justice system. In the next chapter, we will apply this perspective to the justice process and see how well suited it is to the study of crime control.

Types of Systems

There are a number of ways in which systems can be identified and classified (Sutherland, 1975). For our purposes, we need only differentiate between "closed" and "open" systems. These terms refer to the sensitivity of a system to its environment. Those systems which are relatively impervious and insensitive to the environment are "closed," while those which more freely interact with their environments are "open."

A closed system is often self-contained. One simplistic example of a closed system is an astronaut in a spacesuit. Whether on earth, conducting a spacewalk, or exploring another planet, the astronaut is insulated from the environment. To the degree that it functions regardless of surroundings, the life-support system of a spacesuit is a closed system.

An open system, on the other hand, is sensitive to its environment. An example can be seen in the operation of a business. Changes in tax laws, wage rates, markets, environmental protection regulations, shipping rates, costs of raw materials, or almost anything will affect the profits of the business. In order to remain profitable, the business must constantly adapt not only to internal pressures, but also to external or environmental changes. Most organizations are best understood as open systems.

It is most accurate and useful to classify the justice system as an open system. Clearly the justice process in American society must react to changes in the economy, population and political components of its environment. Less clearly, it must also adapt to changes in social values, ideology and information. We shall see in later chapters how influential the environment of the justice system is in explaining the operations of the justice process.

Before concluding this brief overview of systems theory, it is necessary to address one more aspect of this approach to the study of criminal justice. The systems analyst is faced with the task of defining system boundaries. In studying criminal justice, for example, must we include the economic system, the educational system, and the state of mass transportation? As Sutherland (1975:22-24) defined it, this is the level of abstraction.

Level of abstraction refers to how complex the system to be studied will be defined. General systems theory includes concepts of the *Whole System*, of the *Total System* and of *Subsystems*, as described in Box 1.4. The Whole System is comprised of everything. It would include the criminal justice system, the American social system, and larger sets of systems. In short, the Whole System is the entire universe of systems. Obviously, at this level, the analyst is dealing with issues far too complex to fully understand and explain.

In turn, each system is composed of various components. Depending upon the scope of the system in question, these components may themselves be full systems. A full system which is a component of a larger system is known as a subsystem. Thus, criminal justice is a subsystem of the American social system; it is itself comprised of subsystems of law enforcement, courts and corrections. These subsystems, in turn, are also comprised of subsystems. The delineation of components is nearly endless. It

is important for the analyst to define the level of abstraction (complexity) of the system to be analyzed. Sutherland
(1975:23) stated it thus, "The problem however, is in determining (for any given phenomenon or class of phenomena) just what the appropriate level of abstraction might
be."

Box 1.4
Criminal Justice in the Whole System

Three System Levels: The Subsystems (Agencies), the
Total System (Criminal Justice System), and the Whole
System.

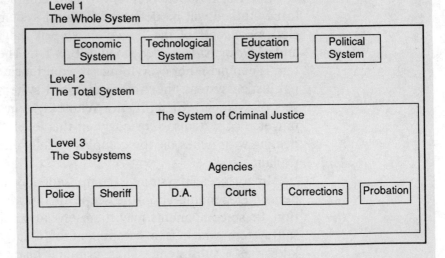

Three Systems Levels: The Subsystems (Agencies), the Total System (Criminal
Justice System) and the Whole System

Level 1
The Whole System

| Economic System | Technological System | Education System | Political System |

Level 2
The Total System

The System of Criminal Justice

Level 3
The Subsystems

Agencies

| Police | Sheriff | D.A. | Courts | Corrections | Probation |

SOURCE: John P. Van Gigch, *Applied General Systems
Theory*. (New York: Harper & Row, 1974): p. 25.

Fortunately, the systems approach serves to sensitize the analyst to the various degrees of complexity without requiring the selection of any particular level of abstraction. Thus, the analyst may decide to study the law enforcement subsystem of the justice process, examining decisions to investigate crime and arrest suspects. Yet, understanding different outcomes of decisions may require reference to community characteristics (e.g., small towns versus large cities) or prosecutorial policies (e.g., willingness to prosecute "victimless" crimes).

The analyst has the flexibility to expand or increase the level of abstraction as needed in order to understand some aspect of the particular system being studied. This feature of the systems perspective is what makes it most appropriate to the study of criminal justice. While the justice process would seem to have the properties of a system, and the systems approach appears to be well suited to the study of criminal justice, there are those who argue that such an approach is inappropriate.

The Nonsystem of Criminal Justice

The Omnibus Crime Control and Safe Streets Act of 1968 provided the impetus for the development of a systems perspective on criminal justice planning. This law established that states wishing to receive federal funds for crime control efforts would be required to create State Planning Agencies (SPAs). These SPAs were charged with administering federal funds *and* with the development of comprehensive, long-range plans for improvement of the total criminal justice system. It was not long before criticisms of the systems approach to criminal justice were raised.

In 1973, the National Advisory Commission on Criminal Justice Standards and Goals (NAC) reported, "'Fragmented,' 'divided,' 'splintered,' and 'decentralized' are the adjectives most commonly used to describe the American system of criminal justice (1973:59)." The early attempts to apply systems analysis to criminal justice planning ran afoul of the nature of the justice process. Criminal justice, in practice, is not the holistic entity envisioned in the systems approach (see Box 1.5).

Box 1.5
The Nonsystem of Criminal Justice

The effectiveness of the system of mission and priorities of the system are going to be viewed differently by the policeman, the trial judge, the prosecutor, the defense attorney, the corrections administrator, the appellate tribunal, the slum dweller and the residents of the suburbs. Isolated and antagonistic within their traditional responsibilities, each component analyzes its problems from its own point of view and each vies with the others for public funds. Each is jealous of its authority and each proceeds according to a different set of priorities. This attitude reflects a lack of guidance oriented toward a single criminal justice system.
– Richter Moore (1976:6)

Robin (1984:52-53) classified criticisms of criminal justice as a nonsystem into four categories according to what aspects of the justice system the critic examined to make the case. These categories are jurisdictional problems, differences in roles and goals, differences in personnel, and substantive issues. The federal government, the District of Columbia and the fifty states each have a subsystem of justice. Indeed, it can be argued that every municipality represents a "system" of justice. It is axiomatic that police, prosecutors, judges and correctional personnel differ among themselves about what strategies are best to control crime, and each group seeks to protect and enhance its position. Finally, the inefficiency of the system has been presented as evidence that it is, in reality, a nonsystem.

While these arguments are powerful and persuasive, they do not refute the systemic nature of the criminal justice process. It cannot be denied that criminal justice is complex, contradictory, inefficient and decentralized; criminal justice is not a "model" system. Yet, crime control is a manifest function or goal of each agency. The interrelatedness of the components of the justice process and the resistance of criminal justice to change also cannot be easily refuted. Whether or not we can establish that American criminal justice is a system is less important than recognizing that the operation of criminal justice in American society exhibits the characteristics of a system. For this reason, the systems approach seems well suited to the study of criminal justice.

The reliance upon the systems approach (which will characterize our treatment of criminal justice) is founded on its usefulness in understanding the operations of justice agencies. This perspective enables us to study decisions in areas such as arrest or sentencing within a broad context. It highlights the inconsistencies which exist in the justice system and directs our attention to explaining them. The systems approach provides us with a framework for the evaluation and comparison of various subsystems. It requires us to be open to viewing any number of factors as contributing to our understanding of the justice process. This openness in analysis is often lacking in other, nonsystems approaches (Van Gigch, 1974:21-31).

THE ENVIRONMENT
OF CRIMINAL JUSTICE

Having defined the criminal justice process as an open system, it is necessary now to examine briefly the environmental factors which affect the operations of criminal justice. These factors have, more or less, direct impact on all aspects of criminal justice. The environment of criminal justice is both material and ideological. The material environment includes concrete resources such as money, personnel, equipment and the like. The ideological environment is comprised chiefly of values and beliefs about how the justice process should operate. Box 1.6 illustrates the placement of criminal justice within this environment.

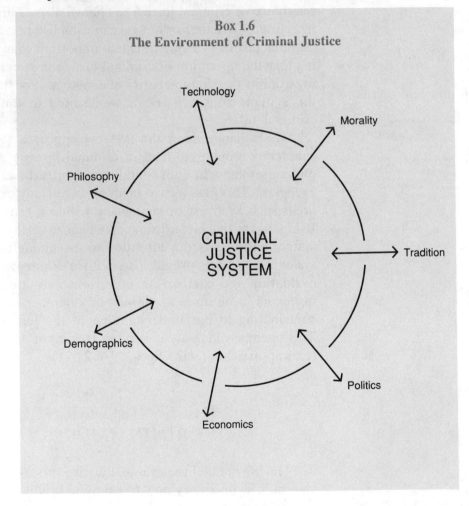

Box 1.6
The Environment of Criminal Justice

The Material Environment of Criminal Justice

In simplistic terms, each system has three stages: input, throughput and output. In manufacturing, for example, input is the reception of raw materials, throughput is the production process, and output is the final product. For the criminal justice system, criminal offenses are the input, throughput is the transformation of crime suspects into convicts, and ex-convicts are the output.

As with manufacturing, in reality the input stage of the criminal justice system also involves labor, machinery and capital. Therefore, law enforcement officers, prosecutors, judges, defense attorneys, correctional staff, police cars, courthouses, jails, and even paper clips for reports are parts of the justice system input. In addition, the output of the justice system is not always "ex-convicts." Some non-guilty suspects are released at various stages in the process, as well as some persons who are guilty but who are not convicted of crimes. Many ex-convicts do not retain that label long before they again commit a criminal offense. Yet, this illustration serves the purpose of identifying the principal material factors in the criminal justice system's environment: raw materials and the means of production.

Raw Materials

The raw material of the criminal justice system is criminal offenses. Thus, the system is affected by changes in the nature and distribution of crime. Suppose our petition pusher from the opening part of this chapter is successful and has a law passed requiring all drivers to wear seatbelts. Failure to wear seatbelts could become a rich new source of "raw material" for the criminal justice system. On the other hand, if all criminal laws were repealed, there would be no raw materials for criminal justice.

Unlike the manufacturing firm, the justice system has little control over the volume of raw material it receives. Imagine the effects on a manufacturing plant of materials deliveries which far exceed the plant's capacity to produce. For example, imagine the delivery of one million barrels of crude oil each day to a refinery which can only process 100,000 barrels every 24 hours. Similar situations have occurred in the justice process.

In cases of large crowds or demonstrations, police officers are often instructed to overlook minor violations and concentrate on the maintenance of order. In large measure, this is because large crowds are potentially dangerous, but it is also because there may be no capacity to handle mass arrests. Several years ago, a massive demonstration in Washington, D.C. resulted in thousands of arrests. Suspects were held in RFK Stadium until they could be processed.

While the Washington, D.C. example is perhaps the exception, we have long recognized the problem of an abundance of raw material for the justice system. One response to the heavy caseloads of criminal justice agencies seeks to alter this aspect of the environment. Proponents of *decriminalization* would remove certain categories of criminal behavior from the justice system. They suggest that the justice system devotes entirely too many resources to the control of essentially harmless or victimless crimes such as vagrancy, public intoxication and disorderly conduct (See Walker, 1985).

Means of Production

The "means of production" for the criminal justice system are the personnel, facilities and equipment of the various justice agencies. Changes in the capacity to process criminal cases will have an effect on the entire justice system. Increases or decreases in the numbers of police, prosecutors, judges, prisons or other components of the justice system will result in changes in the number of cases processed, or in the manner in which cases are handled.

Returning to our example of the manufacturing firm, a dramatic increase in the sales force, or vast improvement in efficiency in the sales force, will result in a tremendous increase in orders. The manufacturing plant will be required to expand production to keep pace with demand. So too, dramatic increases in the number of police officers or in the level of police efficiency may require enhanced capability in the courts and correctional aspects of the justice process. Several observers have argued, for example, that increasing the capacity of parts of the justice process will have the effect of increasing their use. Nagel (1973), as an illustration, suggested that prison cells will be filled and that building more prisons will result in imprisonment for more offenders. In contrast, the current problem of prison and jail crowding has meant that many offenders who would otherwise have been imprisoned have been released early or placed on probation instead of being sent to prison or jail.

For our purposes, the actual outcome of alterations in the criminal justice "means of production" are not as important as the fact that the alterations will lead to adaptations in the system. Thus, a person considering reform in one part of the justice system (more or better police, prosecutors, judges, prisons, or whatever) must be sensitive to the fact that such changes will have a "ripple effect" on the remainder of the justice process. Indeed, systems theory suggests that fluctuations in the environment will be met with changes in the system to limit the disruption of equilibrium. One of the most salient characteristics of the criminal justice system (and one strongly supporting the use of a systems perspective) is that it is resistant to change (Travis, 1982).

The Ideological Environment
of Criminal Justice

As a social institution, and particularly an institution of social control, perhaps the most important aspect of the environment in which the criminal justice system operates is ideological, and not material. The criminal justice system is rife with value conflicts, political and social controversy, and inefficient organization. These attributes of criminal justice reflect our deep ambivalence about social control.

Value Conflicts

Perhaps the most fundamental value conflict that is characteristic of American criminal justice is that between individual freedom and social regularity. In his discussion of policing, Richard Lundman (1980) determined that this conflict was one between liberty (freedom) and civility (order). Packer's two justice system models of "due process" and "crime control" reflect the same controversy. As Culbertson has observed (1984:vii):

> We demand that our police apprehend suspects, that our courts convict the accused, and that our correctional system, in some way, punish the convicted. We demand order. The tasks involved in insuring order would be relatively straightforward were it not for our simultaneous demand that the police, courts and correctional agencies operate within the constraints placed upon them by the law.

With some degree of irony, it could be stated that America is constitutionally unsuited for criminal justice.

Our emphasis on individual liberty and constrained governmental authority requires that a certain level of inefficiency in criminal justice be tolerated. We do not generally allow potentially effective crime control practices such as random wiretaps, warrantless searches, censorship of mail, or the use of "truth serum" during interrogation. We do provide defense counsel, pretrial release, and appellate review of trials and sentences in most cases. In an effort to preserve individual liberty, we not only constrain justice agencies from engaging in many activities, but we also actively impose barriers to the agencies' swift and simple operation. Dean Spader (1987) remarked that criminal justice practice represents a "golden zigzag" between social protection and individual rights.

As we shall see, the criminal justice system is designed for crime control, but the control of crime must be consistent with our social and political heritage. The justice system must achieve a balance or equilibrium (as do all systems) between competing values of federalism and uniformity, vengeance and assistance, and differing political persuasions as well as between individual actors and social regularity. It is the balance of these opposing forces which renders the justice system so complex.

Federalism and Uniformity

As we saw earlier, one of the major criticisms of the systems approach to criminal justice is based on the fact that the justice process is decentralized, disorganized, and lacks consistency. Yet, these limitations of the American criminal justice system are congruent with two of our social and political values: federalism, and the separation of powers.

The basic principle of governmental organization in the United States is that of federalism. Our nation is the result of a federation of sovereign states. The United States

Constitution enumerates the rights and obligations of the
federal government, and the Tenth Amendment includes
the "reservation clause." This amendment reads:

> The powers not delegated to the United States by the
> Constitution, nor prohibited by it to the states, are re-
> served to the states respectively, or to the people.

This amendment to the Constitution enables states to
pass and enforce criminal laws, and to create the offices
and agencies necessary to perform these tasks. Thus, a
federal justice system is created to deal with federal offenses (e.g., counterfeiting), and separate justice systems
are created to enable each state to deal with state crimes
(e.g., theft).

States, in turn, have constitutions under which they
charter municipalities. These counties, cities, towns and
villages are allowed (or required) to provide for their own
criminal offenses, and to create and maintain offices and
agencies to enforce local and state laws. This organizational structure of government insures local autonomy, so
that the citizens of each state and each community have a
fairly large degree of freedom from central control.

For the justice system, the result is thousands of police
agencies at federal, state and municipal levels, thousands of
jails, courts, probation agencies, prosecutors, and defense
offices, and scores of prison and parole agencies. It also
results in differences in the definitions of crimes and the
levels of punishments applicable to criminal behavior. Variety is central to American criminal justice.

The Constitution of the United States also creates and
maintains a separation of powers between the executive,
judicial and legislative branches of government. In simplistic terms, the legislature makes the law, the judiciary inter-
prets the law, and the executive enforces the law. Each

branch of government is *checked and balanced* by the other two branches. This tripartite governmental structure is found at the federal, state and municipal levels of government.

Obviously, this complex organization of the crime control function in America causes inefficiency. Yet, to preserve our interests in local autonomy and constrained governmental power, we must tolerate the inefficient organization of governmental service. As Martin Forst noted (1977:415-16):

> The strengths of the American system of criminal justice, especially for the courts, have rested in the separation of powers and the independence from outside interference. Systems analysis might be able to manage the criminal justice system more effectively, but it should not be allowed to alter the traditional structure and functions of governmental relations. These constitutional values must be reaffirmed in the face of potential erosion.

In short, a centralized, uniform system of criminal justice would be unconstitutional. Any efforts to understand the justice system and to promote consistency and simplicity in organization and in the processing of criminal cases must be sensitive to the values our society places on federalism. Effectiveness and efficiency of operation in the criminal justice system are not the only goals to be considered when analyzing its structure and operation.

The age-old dilemma of what to do for, with, and about criminal offenders plagues the justice system. The system is at one time required to penalize and stigmatize offenders while it is under an obligation to return law-abiding citizens to the streets. America is essentially a utilitarian society.

We are not generally content with punishment for punishment's sake (Finckenauer, 1988). Rather, we expect some ultimate "good" to arise from governmental action.

In this vein, John Griffiths (1970) suggested a third "model" of the justice system in opposition to those described by Packer. This third type is the "family model." At heart, this approach assumes that the interests of society and those of the offender are the same. The net effect of criminal justice processing of an offender should be beneficial to both the offender and the society.

"Family Model" is an apt description of the conflict between vengeance and assistance. While a parent may want or need to punish a child's misbehavior, the purpose of the punishment is to correct the child's error and to restore harmony in the family. Thus, actions taken by agents of the justice system are continually compared against two standards:

> *Has punishment been administered?*
> *Has the offender been "helped"?*

Samuel Walker (1985) examined these two approaches to crime control. Like others (Travis, 1982; Reckless & Allen, 1979), he used the crude classification of "liberals and conservatives." He wrote (1985:6):

> Conservative crime control proposals seek to strengthen the machinery of justice. We can reduce crime by catching more criminals, convicting more of them, and subjecting the convicted to more severe punishment. Deterrence and incapacitation are the two most important theoretical assumptions in conservative crime control policy. The machinery of justice is weakened by various "technicalities" of criminal procedure; the conservative agenda calls for removing them.
>
> Liberal crime control policy calls for reshaping individual offenders, the criminal justice system, or society as a

whole. Rehabilitation, the core theory in liberal policy, embraces a wide range of programs designed to alter the behavior of individual offenders and mold them into law-abiding citizens. Social reform, meanwhile, proceeds from the assumption that much criminal behavior is rooted in social injustice. Expanded educational and economic opportunities would allow people to choose constructive lives and reject the temptations of deviant and criminal activity.

Depending upon the political persuasion of criminal justice policy-makers, i.e., liberal or conservative, radically different strategies may be adopted to control crime. The attitudes, perceptions and tendencies of criminal justice agents and offenders are important factors in understanding the operations of the criminal justice system. The ability of individual actors to affect criminal justice decisions and processing is known as "discretion."

Individual Actors

In 1928, Sheldon Glueck observed that the criminal justice system was a "clumsy admixture of the oil of discretion and the water of rule" (1928:480). By this he meant that the rule or "law" serves to place constraints on the actions of agents of the criminal justice system, but that the system relies upon discretion to process cases smoothly. Regardless of the specificity of applicable law, there is always room for "judgment calls."

Kenneth Davis (1969) studied the pervasiveness of discretion in the justice process. He observed police, prosecutors, parole authorities and judges, and noted their wide-ranging discretionary powers. In any specific instance, a decision to arrest, charge a suspect, impose a sentence or grant release from prison is a "judgment call." For example, we all recognize the discretionary power of police officers, or we would not hope for a mere warning when we are caught exceeding the speed limit.

Box 1.7

A general view of The Criminal Justice System

This chart seeks to present a simple yet comprehensive view of the movement of cases through the criminal justice system. Procedures in individual jurisdictions may vary from the pattern shown here. The differing weights of line indicate the relative volumes of cases disposed of at various points in the system, but this is only suggestive since no nationwide data of this sort exists.

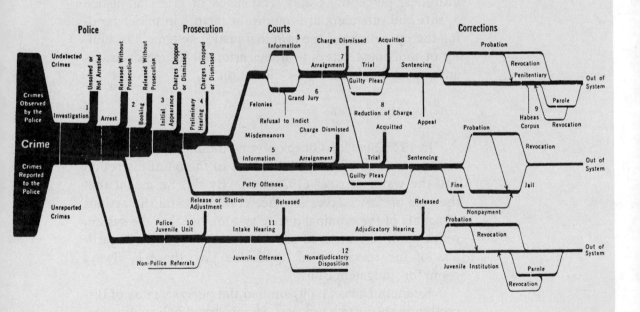

Refer to page 37 for further explanation.

Box 1.7 *(continued)*
The Criminal Justice System

1   May continue until trial.

2   Administrative record of arrest. First step at which temporary release on bail may be available.

3   Before magistrate, commissioner, or justice of peace. Formal notice of charge, advice of rights. Bail set. Summary trials for petty offenses usually conducted here without further processing.

4   Preliminary testing of evidence against defendant. Charge may be reduced. No separate preliminary hearing for misdemeanors in some systems.

5   Charge filed by prosecutor on basis of information submitted by police or citizens. Alternative to grand jury indictment; often used in felonies, almost always in misdemeanors.

6   Reviews whether Government evidence sufficient to justify trial. Some states have no grand jury system; others seldom use it.

7   Appearance for plea; defendant elects trial by judge or jury (if available); counsel for indigent usually appointed here in felonies. Often not at all in other cases.

8   Charge may be reduced at any time prior to trial in return for plea of guilty or for other reasons.

9   Challenge on constitutional grounds to legality of detention. May be sought at any point in process.

10   Police often hold informal hearings, dismiss or adjust many cases without further processing.

11   Probation officer decides desirability of further court action.

12   Welfare agency, social services, counseling, medical care, etc., for cases where adjudicatory handling not needed.

The fact of discretion in criminal justice decision-making renders the explanation of specific case decisions very complex. However, an understanding of the forces at work in any given decision will prove sufficient to explain it in most cases. This chapter has attempted to illustrate these forces.

It is important to realize that discretion is not totally unfettered. Every discretionary decision is made within a context of forces operating at all levels of the justice system previously described. Therefore, the day-to-day workings of the justice system are structured by these larger and more distant factors, which must be kept in balance.

PREVIEW

In the chapters to follow, we will examine the criminal justice system. Chapter 2 presents an overview of the operations and structure of the American criminal justice system. Chapter 3 includes a discussion of law and a description of some recent changes in criminal justice; the chapter illustrates how the system reflects changes in our thinking about crime and criminals. In Chapter 4, sources of data on the nature and extent of crime are reviewed, and an overview of the way in which cases are "selected" for justice processing is provided. The next section of the book addresses the subsystems of the criminal justice system from the detection of crime through investigation and arrest to initial appearance in court, through formal charging, trial and conviction, to sentencing and the goals of criminal penalties. The section concludes by describing the forms of penalties of incarceration or community-centered punishments. The third section of the book is devoted to a discussion of system-wide developments and issues, and to the future of criminal justice in America. In the final section, the juvenile justice system is described and discussed.

REVIEW QUESTIONS

1. What is the purpose of the criminal justice system?

2. What is a system?

3. Distinguish between "open" and "closed" systems.

4. How has criminal justice been characterized as a non-system?

5. Besides a system approach, what three other approaches to the study of criminal justice are common?

6. What components comprise the material and ideological environments of the criminal justice system?

REFERENCES

Culbertson, R.G., ed. (1984), *"Order Under Law": Readings in Criminal Justice, 2nd.* (Prospect Hts., IL: Waveland).

Davis, K.C. (1969), *Discretionary Justice.* (Baton Rouge, LA: Louisiana State University Press).

Dawson, R.O. (1969), *Sentencing.* (Boston: Little, Brown).

Finckenauer, J.O. (1988), "Public support for the death penalty: Retribution as just deserts or retribution as revenge," *Justice Quarterly* 5(1):81-100.

Forst, M.L. (1977), "To what extent should the criminal justice system be a system?" *Crime & Delinquency* 23(4):403.

Glueck, S. (1928), "Principles of a rational penal code," *Harvard University Law Review* 41:453.

Griffiths, J. (1970), "Ideology in criminal procedure or a third "model" of the criminal process," *Yale Law Journal* 79:359.

Kellogg, F.R. (1976), "Organizing the criminal justice system: A look at operative objectives," *Federal Probation* 40(2):9.

La Fave, W.R. (1965), *Arrest*. (Boston: Little, Brown).

Levin, M.A. (1972), "Urban politics and policy outcomes: The criminal courts," in George F. Cole (ed.) (1984), *Criminal Justice: Law & Politics, 4th*. (Belmont, CA: Brooks-Cole), p. 289.

Lundman, R.A. (1980), *Police and Policing: An Introduction*. (New York: Holt, Rinehart & Winston).

Miller, F.W. (1970), *Prosecution*. (Boston: Little, Brown).

Moore, R.H., Jr. (1976), The criminal justice nonsystem, in Moore, Marks and Barrow, (eds.) *Readings in Criminal Justice*. (Indianapolis, IN: Bobbs-Merrill), p. 5.

Nagel, W.G. (1973), *The New Red Barn: A Critical Look at the Modern American Prison*. (New York: Walker & Co).

National Advisory Commission on Criminal Justice Standards and Goals (1973), *A National Strategy to Reduce Crime*. (New York: Avon).

Newman, D.J. (1966), *Conviction*. (Boston: Little, Brown).

_____ (1978), *Introduction to Criminal Justice*. (Philadelphia: J.B. Lippincott).

O'Leary, V.I. and David D. (1971), "Correctional policy: A classification of goals designed for change," *Crime & Delinquency*. 18(3):379.

Orsagh, T. (1983), "Is there a place for economics in criminology and criminal justice?" *Journal of Criminal Justice* 11(5):391-402.

Packer, H.L. (1968), *The Limits of the Criminal Sanction*. (Stanford: Stanford University Press).

Parsons, T. (1966), *Societies: Evolutionary and Comparative Perspectives*. (Englewood Cliffs, NJ: Prentice-Hall).

Pound, R. (1929), *Criminal Justice in America*. (New York: Henry Holt and Company).

President's Commission on Law Enforcement and Administration of Justice (1967), *The Challenge of Crime in a Free Society*. (New York: Avon).

Reckless, W.C. and H.E. Allen (1979), "Developing a national crime policy: The impact of politics on crime in America," in *Criminology: New Concerns*. (Beverly Hills, CA: Sage).

Remington, F.J., D.J. Newman, E.L. Kimball, M. Melli and H. Goldstein (1969), *Criminal Justice Administration: Cases and Materials*. (Indianapolis: Bobbs-Merrill).

Robin, G.D. (1984), *Introduction to the Criminal Justice System, 2nd*. (New York: Harper & Row).

Spader, D.J. (1987), "Individual rights vs. social utility: The search for the golden zigzag between conflicting fundamental values," *Journal of Criminal Justice* 15(2):121-36.

Sutherland, J.W. (1975), *Systems: Analysis, Administration and Architecture*. (New York: Van Nostrand Reinhold Co.).

Tiffany, L.P., D.M. McIntyre and D. Rotenberg (1967), *Detection*. (Boston: Little, Brown).

Toder, H.A. (1987), "The necessity of taking an interdisciplinary perspective in criminal justice education," *The Justice Professional*, 2(2):92-99.

Travis, L.F., III (1982), "The politics of sentencing reform," in Martin L. Forst (ed.) *Sentencing Reform*. (Beverly Hills, CA: Sage), p. 59.

Van Gigch, J.P. (1974), *Applied Systems Theory*. (New York: Harper & Row).

Von Bertalanffy, L. (1950), "The theory of open systems in physics and biology," *Science* 3:23.

_____ (1968), *General Systems Theory*. (New York: Braziller).

Walker, S. (1985), *Sense and Nonsense About Crime: A Policy Guide*. (Belmont, CA: Brooks-Cole).

Williams, F. (1984) "The demise of the criminological imagination: A critique of recent criminology," Justice Quarterly 1(1):91-106.

Willis, C.L. (1983), "Criminal justice theory: A case of trained incapacity," Journal of Criminal Justice 11(5):447-458.

Wilson, J.Q. (1968), *Varieties of Police Behavior*. (Cambridge, MA: Harvard University Press).

2 The Justice Process

The cases processed in the justice system flow from the beginning stages of detection by law enforcement through subsequent stages to final discharge from the system. While there are some "feedback" mechanisms whereby a case can move back to an earlier decision point, on the whole, cases flow in one direction through the system.

In this chapter we will trace briefly the American criminal justice system. In doing so, we will skip many of the details and nuances of criminal justice processing in the interests of developing an understanding of the total justice system. In short, to some extent we will ignore the "trees" as we try to get a better look at the "forest."

It is important to remember that perhaps the greatest constant of criminal justice is *variety*. Even things as simple as titles differ among jurisdictions. For example, prosecutors are variously known as state's attorneys, district attorneys, U.S. attorneys, prosecutors, or by other titles. In most states, the highest court is called the state supreme court, in New York, the supreme court is a trial court and the highest court is the New York Court of Appeals. With an appreciation that what follows here is a sketch of the justice system, we are ready to proceed.

The President's Commission (1967) created the flow chart of the justice system presented as Box 1.7 in the previous chapter. While we follow the general model of the President's Commission, we will employ slightly different terminology. The criminal justice system begins with the detection of crime and then proceeds through investigation, arrest, initial appearance before the court, preliminary hearing, arraignment (charging), trial, sentencing, possible revocation and ends with discharge. We shall now briefly examine these decision points.

Detection

The criminal justice system is the formal social institution charged with the control of deviance identified as being criminal. As such, it does not become mobilized until a criminal offense is detected. Much crime goes undetected, and these undetected crimes do not influence the justice process directly. It is only when the justice system (usually through the police) notices a possible criminal offense that the process begins.

Perhaps more than half of all crime is never discovered by the justice system. Many crimes remain undetected; no one realizes that a crime was committed. Many others are detected but are not reported to the police, so the justice system is not aware that criminal offenses have occurred.

Have you ever reached into your pocket or wallet for a ten-dollar bill which you *knew* you had, only to discover that it was missing? Most of us at some time have experienced "missing money." We cannot be certain that we did not spend it, but we also cannot remember when it was spent. Have we been the victims of theft? Do we report the money as stolen?

If we assume that we spent or lost the money and do not believe it was stolen, a theft may go undetected. Similarly, if we are convinced the money was stolen, we may still not report it as the sum is so small and the chance of recovery so slim. In the latter case, a crime has gone unreported.

If a person has a fight with a friend or relative and assumes it is "personal," an assault will go undetected, or at least unreported. The first decision in the justice system is determining whether a crime may have occurred. This decision is made most frequently by a civilian, not a justice system official. A second decision is reporting a crime, and again is a decision made most often by someone other than a justice system official. If we witness a crime and decide not to report it to the police, for the purposes of the justice system, that offense has gone undetected. Box 2.1 presents the reasons typically given by people for not reporting crimes.

Box 2.1
Reasons Given for Not
Reporting Crimes to the Police

Reason	Percent Responding*
Offense was not serious	34%
Nothing could be done	27%
Reported to someone else	11%
Police wouldn't do anything	10%
Personal matter	9%
Don't want to take the time	2%
Fear of reprisal	1%
Other	7%

*Totals do not equal 100 due to rounding.
SOURCE: Bureau of Justice Statistics (1985), *Reporting Crimes to the Police*. (Washington, D.C.: U.S. Dept. of Justice): 8-9.

When a crime or suspected crime is reported to the police, the justice system is mobilized. The police respond to the report of a crime. It is then that case decision-making rests with official agents of the justice process. Once the police come to believe that a crime may have been committed, it is their decision whether and how to proceed.

Investigation

Upon deciding that a crime may have been committed, the next decision is whether to investigate, and if so, how thoroughly to investigate. Investigation is a process in which the results of initial inquiries often determine the intensity of the investigation. For example, someone may report a prowler. Responding officers may make a visual check of doors and windows, find nothing suspicious, and leave. They also may note footprints near a window, or find scratch marks on a door or window frame, and then intensify their investigation.

At the conclusion of the investigation, three outcomes are possible. First, no evidence of criminal activity is found and, thus, the possible crime is classified as "unfounded," or not real. Second, evidence of possible criminal activity supports the finding that a crime was committed or attempted, but there is not sufficient evidence for an arrest. In this case, the crime will be left "unsolved" (no offender known), and the investigation, at least theoretically, will continue. Finally, the investigation yields evidence of both criminal behavior and a probably guilty party. Under the last of the three possible outcomes, the next decision stage is reached: arrest.

Arrest

Despite our expectations, media portrayals or legal mandates, police officers do not *have to* arrest every violator of the criminal codes. As a result, the police officer must make a decision to arrest a suspected offender. Many factors affect the arrest decision.

Perhaps the two most important factors that determine whether an arrest will be made are the seriousness of the suspected offense and the quality of the evidence against the suspect. Yet, especially in less severe offenses, the officer can exercise tremendous discretion in this decision. For example, if a traffic officer stops you for speeding, a citation is not the only possible outcome, even if you actually were speeding. How often does a person give the officer excuses for his violation of the traffic laws? How does a person feel about the officer who issues a citation when he knows that the officer could have given a warning?

Discretionary decisions not to arrest are often the result of an officer's attempts to achieve "street justice." Street justice is the term used to describe attempts by police to deal with problems without formal processing. For example, an officer may counsel or warn loitering juveniles, rather than arresting them. In such a case, the officer tries to solve the problem in a way that avoids the negative consequences of formal processing. As we shall see in our discussion of the police, much police work is problem solving, and arrest is only one tool. Many times however, police officers do decide to arrest a suspect. If an arrest is made, the next decision stage is reached: initial appearance.

Initial Appearance

Arrested suspects are usually entitled to release before trial. With the exception of serious offenses (murder, terrorism, kidnaping, etc.) specified in some statutes, persons arrested for crimes may be released while awaiting trial. Traditionally, this release has been accomplished by the posting of bail.

The primary purpose of bail is to insure that the suspect will return to court for later hearings. The theory of bail is that a person will return to court if it would cost too much not to return. Thus, traditional bail involves the defendant "posting bond," or leaving money on deposit at the court. If the defendant returns, his bond is refunded. If the defendant does not return for the next hearing, the court keeps the bail money and issues a warrant for his or her arrest.

Recent criminal justice reforms have witnessed the rebirth of "release on recognizance" systems where suspects obtain pre-trial release without posting bond if they have a job, house, family and other ties to the community. If a person is expected to appear in court to avoid losing a few thousand dollars, it seems reasonable that he or she would also appear to keep his home, job and family ties.

In some jurisdictions, it is possible for the prosecutor to ask for "preventive detention." In these cases, the prosecutor believes that, if released on bail, the defendant will present a danger of continued crime in the community. Upon a hearing which establishes that the defendant is indeed dangerous, the magistrate is authorized to deny pre-trial release.

In many courts, "bail schedules" have been developed where different levels of bail amounts are tied to different types of crime. For instance, the going rate for burglary might be $2,500, but for robbery, $5,000. Yet, the bail decision is not automatic. If the magistrate believes that the suspect will flee or fail to appear for later hearings, a higher bail may be set. In other cases, a lower bail than usual may be set to allow the defendant to keep his or her job or to maintain family contacts. In either case, after the initial appearance the next decision relates to the specification of formal charges and arraignment.

Arraignment

Between the time of arrest and arraignment, the prosecutor reviews the evidence in the case and determines a formal criminal charge. The offense for which a person is arrested is not necessarily the offense with which they will be charged. For example, the police may arrest someone for armed robbery but be unable to prove that a weapon was used in the crime. The prosecutor may then formally charge the offender with unarmed robbery.

Charges are brought in two principal ways: indictment by grand jury or by information. With the indictment, the prosecutor presents the case in secret to a grand jury which decides if the evidence is strong enough to warrant the issuance of an indictment. With the information, the prosecutor presents the case in open court before a magistrate who determines if the evidence is sufficient to warrant a formal charge.

At the arraignment, the defendant is notified of the formal criminal charges against him or her and asked to plead to the charges. The arraignment is not a hearing on the facts of the case. The defendant may plead not guilty, guilty or *nolo contendere* (no contest), or he may stand silent. If the defendant pleads guilty or *nolo contendere*, a finding of guilt will be made. If the defendant remains silent, a plea of not guilty will be entered on his or her behalf and a trial date will be set. Most criminal defendants plead guilty at arraignment, often as part of an agreement negotiated with the prosecutor (Newman, 1966; Rosett & Cressey, 1976; McDonald, 1979). In the typical "plea bargain," the prosecutor and defendant compromise. The prosecutor drops charges or otherwise changes the seriousness of the formal charge in exchange for a certain conviction without trial by a guilty plea from the defendant.

Trial

While most cases result in a guilty plea at arraignment, those which receive the most media attention and publicity are those which involve a trial. The few cases that go to trial are what Samuel Walker (1985:17) termed "celebrated cases." In these cases, defendants receive full-blown trials, often jury trials. Because these are the cases which receive the most publicity, the public often believes that the jury trial is the normal operating procedure of the justice system.

At trial, the state (prosecutor) must prove, beyond a reasonable doubt, that the defendant committed the criminal offense for which he or she has been charged. The defense attorney seeks to discredit the state's case and, at a minimum, establish that there is some doubt as to whether the defendant committed the offense. Depending upon the nature of the case, one of two types of trials will be requested by the defense: a jury trial or a bench trial.

The jury trial is the "ideal" of the justice system. A panel of the defendant's peers hears all of the evidence and decides guilt or innocence. The bench trial is held before a judge alone, who hears all of the evidence and then decides guilt or innocence. If a case is particularly complex (for example, if a plea is entered of not guilty by reason of insanity), or if the jury is expected to be antagonistic to the defense, the defense attorney may opt for a bench trial in the belief that the judge alone will be more objective.

If the verdict is not guilty, the justice process ends with the acquittal of the defendant. On the other hand, if the verdict is guilty (or if the defendant pleads guilty), the defendant stands convicted of the crime and the next decision point in the justice system is reached: sentencing.

Sentencing

The sentencing decision has been described as bifurcated, or having two parts. First, the judge decides the type of sentence. This can range from a fine to incarceration and covers a wide variety of alternatives including probation, confinement in jail, and combinations such as probation with a fine. In capital cases such as murder, of course, the type of sentence may be death. The second part of the decision involves the conditions of sentence. These include the conditions of supervised release (probation), such as curfew, employment, etc., as well as the length of prison term for those incarcerated. In some states where offenders are convicted of capital offenses, this part of the decision may involve the method of execution, as illustrated in Box 2.2.

Box 2.2
Method of Execution, by State, 1985

Lethal Injection	Electrocution	Lethal gas	Hanging	Firing squad
Arkansas[a]	Alabama	Arizona	Delaware	Idaho[a]
Idaho[a]	Arkansas[a]	California	Montana[a]	Utah[a]
Illinois	Connecticut	Colorado	New Hampshire	
Mississippi[a,b]	Florida	Maryland	Washington[a]	
Montana[a]	Georgia	Mississippi[a,b]		
Nevada	Indiana	Missouri		
New Jersey	Kentucky	North Carolina[a]		
New Mexico	Louisiana	Wyoming[a]		
North Carolina[a]	Nebraska			
Oklahoma[c]	Ohio			
Oregon	Pennsylvania			
South Dakota	South Carolina			
Texas	Tennessee			
Utah[a]	Vermont			
Washington[a]	Virginia			
Wyoming[a]				

[a]Authorizes two methods of execution.
[b]Mississippi authorizes lethal injection for those convicted after 7/1/84; executions of those convicted prior to that date are to be carried out with lethal gas.
[c]Should lethal injection be found to be unconstitutional, Oklahoma authorizes use of electrocution or firing squad.

SOURCE: Bureau of Justice Statistics (1986), *Capital Punishment, 1985.* (Washington, D.C.: U.S. Department of Justice):4.

Box 2.3
Distribution of Sentencing Power
Among Branches of Government

States vary in the degree of judicial and parole board discretion in sentencing and release decisions provided by law. Currently, State sentencing systems involve:

Indeterminate sentencing. The judge has primary control over the type of sentence given such as prison, probation or fine, and the upper and lower bounds of the length of prison sentences within statutory limits, but the actual time served is determined by the parole board.

Determinate sentencing. The judge sets the type of sentence and the length of prison sentences within statutory limits, but the parole board may not release prisoners before their sentences (minus good time) have expired.

Mandatory prison terms. Legislation requires the imposition of a prison sentence, often of specified length, for certain crimes and/or certain categories of offenders.

Presumptive sentencing. The judge is required to impose a sentence whose length is set by law for each offense or class of offense. When there are mitigating or aggravating circumstances, however, the judge is allowed to shorten or lengthen the sentence within specified boundaries.

Some States employ other practices that affect sentencing and the actual time served:

Sentencing guidelines. The courts set sentences by using procedures designed to structure sentencing decisions usually based on offense severity and criminal history.

Parole guidelines. Parole boards use procedures designed to structure release decisions based on measurable offender criteria.

Good-time policies. In nearly all of the States, legislation allows for reduction of a prison term based on the offender's behavior in prison.

Emergency crowding provisions. Some States have statutes or policies that relieve prison crowding by systematically making certain inmates eligible for early release.

In recent years in many States, there has been a movement away from sentencing systems that give judges and parole boards great discretion in sentences and time served to more certain and fixed punishments for crimes through mandatory sentences, sentences of fixed length (determinate sentencing), and the abolition of parole boards.

Beginning with Maine in 1976, nine States had abolished parole as of 1983. In the five years from 1977 to 1982, the proportion of those released from State prisons by parole boards dropped from 72% to 52%.

By year end 1982, most of the States had also enacted mandatory sentences for certain types of offenses or offenders.

SOURCE: Bureau of Justice Statistics (1986), *Crime and Justice Facts, 1985.* (Washington, D.C.: U.S. Dept. of Justice): 20-21.

Sentencing power is shared among the three branches of the government. The legislative branch sets limits on penalties by establishing minimum and maximum prison terms and fine amounts, by declaring some offenses ineligible for probation and by other similar actions. The judicial branch is where the sentencing judge selects the actual type and conditions of sentence from alternatives allowed by the legislature. The executive branch has the power to pardon, to offer clemency and, often, to authorize parole. This shared power is indicated in Box 2.3.

Most convicted offenders are sentenced to probation or a fine, and not incarcerated. Those who are incarcerated most frequently gain release from prison through parole or mandatory release, where they are required to live in the community under supervision and to obey conditions of release similar to those placed on probation (Travis & Latessa, 1984). Failure to obey these conditions can lead to the next possible decision point in the justice process: revocation.

Revocation

The overwhelming majority of criminal offenders who are sentenced serve some portion of their sentence under community supervision on either probation or parole. Both of these forms of sentence are "conditional releases," whereby the offender is allowed to remain in the community if he or she abides by certain conditions, such as reporting regularly to a supervising officer, observing a curfew, or refraining from further criminal activity or from the consumption of alcohol.

Violation of the conditions of release constitutes grounds for the revocation of liberty. For example, a probationer who is ordered not to consume alcohol can lose his or her liberty if caught drinking. The revocation process is a miniature justice system where the probation or parole officer detects and investigates violations of conditions, arrests and prosecutes violators, who are "tried" by the sentencing judge (if on probation) or parole authority (if on parole). Upon "conviction" of violating the conditions of release, the violator may be "sentenced" to incarceration or continued supervision.

When the author was employed by the Oregon State Board of Parole, nearly half of all inmates admitted to that state's prisons each year were admitted as probation or parole violators. With the exception of the death penalty, incarceration in prison is our most severe penalty. Convicted offenders receive this sentence either directly from the court or, more circuitously, through the revocation of conditional liberty.

In comparison to the total number of convicted offenders, very few are sentenced to death or life imprisonment. Thus, for most offenders, a day comes when they are no longer under the control of the justice system. This last point in the justice process is discharge.

Discharge

Most criminal offenders will eventually be discharged from their sentences. For some, this discharge will occur at the expiration of their term. For someone sentenced to a ten-year prison term, discharge will take place ten years after the date of sentencing, whether the person was incarcerated for the full ten years or whether he obtains an earlier release by parole or reduction in term for good behavior.

Many states, however, have adopted procedures for "early" discharge. An offender serving a ten-year term may be paroled after serving three years, and then, after successfully completing three years (for example) under parole supervision, may receive an early discharge; the offender may be released from sentence after only six years. Other jurisdictions where no formal early discharge procedure exists may place similar offenders on "unsupervised parole status" after six years. In this case, the offender technically is still under sentence but is not being supervised in the community, and, for all practical purposes, the offender has been discharged.

Upon discharge from sentence, the convicted offender becomes a member of the free society again. In most cases, the record of conviction and collateral effects of conviction (limits on civil rights, employability, and the like) will haunt the ex-convict. Conviction of a crime, especially a felony, often disqualifies the offender from certain types of occupations, such as those requiring licensure or certification (teaching school, practicing law or medicine, and the like). In some states, felony conviction leads to "civil death," that is, the offender has no rights to enter contracts (including marriage), borrow money, vote, or hold public office (Burton, et al, 1987).

THE TOTAL CRIMINAL JUSTICE SYSTEM

As the brief description of the justice system presented above illustrates, cases move through the various decision points on a contingency basis. *If* a crime is detected, an investigation may begin. *If* the investigation yields sufficient evidence, an arrest may be made. *If* an arrest is made, formal charges may be brought. The operative word is *if*. Approaching this issue from the other direction, the sentence depends upon the conviction, which depends upon the charge, which depends upon the investigation, which depends upon the detection of crime. To paraphrase an old song about how bones are connected, we might say detection is connected to investigation; investigation is connected to arrest; arrest is connected to charging; charging is connected to arraignment; arraignment is connected to sentencing; sentencing is connected to correction; correction is connected to discharge.

Each decision in the justice process is, in large part, determined by previous decisions. To a certain degree too, earlier decisions depend upon past practices in later points of the justice process. For example, if a county prosecutor routinely dismisses cases involving possession of minor amounts of marijuana, law enforcement officers are more inclined to stop arresting persons for possession of small amounts of that drug.

As the concept of a system implies, the various components of the justice process (the decisions) are interdependent. As a result, the practices of all the justice agencies affect those of every other agency to some extent. Similarly, environmental pressures will affect the operations of each justice agency to some degree. Two examples from recent history illustrate the manner in which environmental pressures and agency changes have systemwide effects. These are the effort to control drunk driving, and New York state's attempt to control drug offenders.

Controlling the Drunk Driver

Drunk driving, while a serious safety problem on the nation's highways, traditionally has not been viewed as a particularly heinous offense. In the past few years, however, drunk driving has come to be seen as a serious crime. It is no longer fashionable to drink and drive, and sketches and jokes about drunk drivers in the entertainment media have been replaced with dramas depicting the devastating effects of drunk driving. Since 1981, the majority of states have taken steps to control drunk driving, most often by redefining the offense as a more serious misdemeanor or felony, and by requiring mandatory incarceration of those convicted of drunk driving (see Box 2.4).

This changing public attitude toward drunk drivers and the associated legislative changes have placed considerable strains on the criminal justice system. More persons are being arrested for driving under the influence of alcohol, more of those who are arrested are refusing to plead guilty, and many more of those who are found guilty are being incarcerated in jails than ever before. Further, many of those being sent to jail are first offenders with no prior record, and they are not typical jail inmates. In many ways, they require a different institutional setting than the jail, which is generally used for other types of criminal offenders.

Box 2.4
Provisions for Mandatory Incarceration
of Those Convicted of Driving While Intoxicated

State	Is imprison- ment man- datory?	After which of- fense does imprison- ment be- come man- datory?	Length of imprison- ment
Alabama	Yes	2nd offense	2 days
Alaska	Yes	1st	3
Arizona	Yes	1st	1
Arkansas	No		
California	Yes	2nd	2
Colorado	Yes	2nd	7
Connecticut	Yes	1st	2
Delaware	Yes	2nd	60
D.C.	No		
Florida	Yes	2nd	10
Georgia	Yes	2nd	2
Hawaii	Yes	1st	2
Idaho	Yes	2nd	10
Illinois	Yes	2nd	2
Indiana	Yes	2nd	5
Iowa	Yes	2nd	7
Kansas	Yes	1st	2
Kentucky	Yes	2nd	7
Louisiana	Yes	1st	2
Maine	Yes	1st	2
Maryland	Yes	2nd	2
Massachusetts	Yes	2nd	14
Michigan	No		
Minnesota	No		
Mississippi	No		
Missouri	Yes	2nd	2
Montana	Yes	1st	1
Nebraska	Yes	2nd	2
Nevada	Yes	1st	2
New Hampshire	Yes	2nd	7
New Jersey	Yes	2nd	2
New Mexico	Yes	2nd	2
New York	No		
North Carolina	Yes	2nd	7
North Dakota	Yes	2nd	4
Ohio	Yes	1st	3
Oklahoma	No		
Oregon	Yes	1st	2
Pennsylvania	Yes	2nd	30
Rhode Island	Yes	2nd	2
South Carolina	Yes	1st	2
South Dakota	No		
Tennessee	Yes	1st	2
Texas	Yes	2nd	3
Utah	Yes	1st	2
Vermont	Yes	2nd	2
Virginia	Yes	2nd	2
Washington	Yes	1st	1
West Virginia	Yes	1st	1
Wisconsin	No		
Wyoming	Yes	2nd	7

SOURCE: *A Digest of State Alcohol-Highway Safety Related Legislation, Fifth Edition.* National Highway Traffic Safety Administration. U.S. Department of Transportation.

With drunk driving defined and viewed as a more serious offense, police officers are more likely to investigate erratic drivers, to charge the offender with driving under the influence (DUI) rather than with reckless operation, to arrest rather than warn, and generally to "process" offenders. Prosecutors too are more likely to charge drunk drivers. With higher stakes (loss of driving privileges, stiff fines, mandatory incarceration), defendants are less likely to plead guilty and thus the courts must hold more trials. Mandatory sentences create overcrowding in the jails. All three components of the justice process must adapt to this new emphasis on DUI enforcement, as is seen in Box 2.5.

Interestingly, the National Institute of Justice evaluation of changes in drunk driving enforcement (1985) revealed how justice agency policies can affect the total system as well. In Memphis, with little publicity about drunk driving, law enforcement attitudes did not change, and thus arrest rates, court loads, and jail populations of drunk drivers also did not change. In Minnesota, no legislation was enacted, but judges adopted a policy of mandatory incarceration, successfully anticipated problems for police, courts and corrections, and took steps to minimize the problems.

Other analyses of drunk driving laws and enforcement practices show that organizational patterns of police agencies affect arrest decisions (Mastrofski, et al, 1987). Also, individual officer characteristics were found to be related to arrest decisions in drunk driving cases (Meyers, et al, 1987). These studies indicate that an understanding of the effect of justice reform is difficult. Knowledge of the changes in the law is only part of the answer. Organizational and individual characteristics of justice agencies and agents affect how a reform is implemented.

Box 2.5
Effects of Mandatory Jail Terms for Drunk Driving

To gauge the impact of tougher sanctions on the criminal justice system, National Institute of Justice researchers examined the effects of mandatory confinement for drunk driving in jurisdictions in Washington, Tennessee, Ohio, and Minnesota. The findings revealed:

* When mandatory confinement is introduced and well publicized, drunk driver arrests usually increase.

* The introduction of mandatory confinement imposes new and heavy demands on courts, incarceration facilities, and probation services.

* The adoption of mandatory confinement is frequently accompanied by increased public concern about drunk driving and is associated with a decline in traffic fatalities.

* Mandatory confinement can be imposed either through legislation or through judicial policy.

* The implementation of mandatory confinement often requires additional resources for the criminal justice system.

* Appropriate systemwide planning can minimize dysfunction and substantially reduce the impact of mandatory confinement on criminal justice operation.

SOURCE: National Institute of Justice (1985), "Jailing drunk drivers: Impact on the criminal justice system," *NIJ Reports*, SNI 192 (July): 2.

The New York State Drug Law

In 1973 New York State adopted legislation hailed as "The Nation's Toughest Drug Law" (U.S. Dept. of Justice, 1978). This law was intended to "crack down" on those who sold heroin and other dangerous drugs. It had provisions for very stiff sentences and controls on plea bargaining. Further, to cope with the anticipated increase in drug offense cases, it provided for the creation of forty-nine new judgeships. The intent of the legislation was clear: to apprehend, convict and punish those who sold heroin.

The effect of the law, however, is less clear. The officers and agencies of the justice system appear to have adapted to the changes in order to reduce the potentially disruptive effects on normal court operations resulting from the new law. While there were no dramatic increases in arrests for sale of heroin, fewer of those arrested were indicted, with fewer of those indicted pleading guilty and fewer being convicted. For those convicted, both the rate of incarceration and the length of prison terms did increase after the law took effect. However, in the final analysis, three years after the law was passed, the percentage of those arrested for heroin sale or possession who went to prison remained stable at 11 percent, which is identical to what the percentage had been before the law was passed in 1973.

There are several possible explanations. First, the number of arrests probably did not increase because the sale and possession of large quantities of heroin were already considered serious offenses (even before the new law was enacted). Neither law enforcement nor public attitudes were changed by the new legislation. The fact that fewer defendants pleaded guilty meant that prosecutors needed to be more sure of getting the guilty verdict before taking a case to trial. Thus, indictments decreased as "marginal" cases were dismissed or downplayed. The increased number of trials created a backlog for the courts, so that fewer cases were processed, and further, acquittals were handed down in some cases where previously a plea of guilty had insured conviction.

The mandatory sentencing provisions of the legislation may account for the higher incarceration rate and more severe prison terms imposed after the legislation was enacted. What is suggested is that there was no conscious effort to undermine the intent of the tough anti-drug law, but rather, the court component of the justice process adapted to new pressures reflexively. As part of a system, the courts sought to maintain an equilibrium and adapted to stresses and strains so as to minimize their impact.

In this example, the effect of the legislation was initially and most specifically directed at the criminal courts. Also, an effort was made to alleviate the strains through the creation of new courts. Had these new courts not been provided, it is likely that even more cases would have been dismissed and/or the backlog of cases would have been even greater. The law did not directly affect law enforcement. The effect of changes in prison sentences on corrections would not be dramatic for two reasons. First, heroin dealers are only a very small proportion of all those sentenced to prison, so that even large increases in their terms or rate of incarceration would not dramatically affect prisons. Second, the percentage of those arrested who were actually sentenced to prison did not change, and the effects of longer terms would not be felt until several years after those who received longer sentences had been imprisoned.

The examples of the effort to control drunk driving and the attempt to crack down on drug offenders illustrate how the justice system interacts with its environment. In the case of controlling drunk driving, changes in all aspects of the justice process resulted. In the case of the drug law, the justice process was able to adapt to the pressures and generally to maintain the pre-existing *status quo*. The purpose of these illustrations is to show how the justice process operates as a system, and to provide a beginning indication of the complexity of evaluating the operations of the criminal justice process. This complexity becomes more clear when one examines the structure and organization of the agencies which comprise the American criminal justice system.

THE COMPONENTS
OF CRIMINAL JUSTICE

As was done in Chapter 1, it is common to divide the criminal justice system into three parts: law enforcement, courts and corrections. Each of these three parts of the justice system is itself comprised of a multitude of separate agencies and actors. The organizations which are part of the total criminal justice system are differentially structured and funded, and draw from different personnel pools.

One of the most important distinctions among similar agencies is *jurisdiction*. Police departments, courts, and correctional agencies may be municipal (village, township, city or county), state, or federal. They may be specialized, as are the U.S. postal inspectors, or they may have general duties, as does a typical police department. And, increasingly, they may be public or private (such as security guards, many halfway houses and others that provide crime control services). In this section, we will examine the nature of criminal justice agencies in law enforcement, courts and corrections.

Law Enforcement

There are so many agencies with law enforcement mandates that it is not possible to state their true number with confidence. In 1967, the President's Commission on Law Enforcement and Administration of Justice estimated (in its task force report on police) that over 40,000 police agencies were in existence. Later, the Department of Justice reported that there were close to 20,000 state and local law enforcement agencies. This report, however, did not include townships with populations of less than 1,000 (1980:24), nor did it include federal law enforcement agencies. Most recently, the Bureau of Justice Statistics (1989) identified about 15,000 state and local police agencies.

Federal Law Enforcement

A number of federal law enforcement agencies exist. These agencies tend to be small with specific mandates, yet in total, federal law enforcement is very complex. We are all aware of the Federal Bureau of Investigation, and most of us have heard of U.S. Marshals, Postal Inspectors, the Drug Enforcement Agency, the Bureau of Alcohol, Tobacco and Firearms, Immigration and Naturalization, Customs, Internal Revenue, and the Secret Service. Yet, many are unaware of the law enforcement duties of the National Park Service, U.S. Supreme Court Police Department, National Gallery of Art Protection Staff, and other federal "police" agencies. We seldom consider the military police, tribal police departments on Indian reservations, or the investigative duties of auditors and staff of such organizations as the Federal Trade Commission (Walker, 1983:43-45).

Because they serve the entire nation, these agencies recruit nationally and tend to have more stringent entry requirements than do most police departments. The FBI, for example, requires a bachelor's degree in combination with investigatory experience or postgraduate training. Because federal law enforcement is funded at the federal level, salary and benefits for federal law enforcement officers are often higher than those paid to municipal police.

State Law Enforcement

The most common form of state police agency is the highway patrol. These agencies are charged with enforcing traffic laws on state and federal highways. Many states, however, also charge their state police with general law enforcement duties (IACP, 1975). The New York State Police, for example, not only serve as traffic officers on that state's highways, but also provide general law enforcement service to residents in rural and unincorporated areas as a primary duty. In addition, several states have specialized state units to combat drug offenses, organized crime, liquor and cigarette tax violations, and the like. Finally, many states also charge their park services with law enforcement obligations.

Like federal agencies, state agencies recruit from a pool of candidates which is considerably larger than that tapped by most local police departments. Further, in many states the salary and benefits paid to state police officers are higher than those paid in most local departments. (Bureau of Justice Statistics, 1989).

Municipal Law Enforcement

The bulk of law enforcement services are provided through municipal or local police departments, as shown in Box 2.6. These include the traditional city or township police department, as well as the county sheriff. The majority of police departments in the United States are local ones, and most police agencies are small, employing fewer than ten officers (Bureau of Justice Statistics, 1989). Yet, most police officers work for large departments because the relatively few large departments employ many officers.

Box 2.6
**Distribution of Police Personnel
and Costs by Level of Government**

Level of Government	% Police Personnel	% Police Costs
Federal	8.3%	10.4%
State	14.6%	13.7%
County	17.7%	16.8%
Local	59.4%	59.1%

SOURCE: Bureau of Justice Statistics (1987), *Justice Expenditure and Employment, 1985.* (Washington, D.C.: U.S. Department of Justice): 3.

Municipal police departments rarely conduct national searches or recruitment drives, with the exception of a few, usually larger, police departments such as those in Atlanta, Houston and Dallas. Thus, most local police departments recruit locally and employ civil service testing to enlist new officers. Sheriffs are generally elected, but many sheriff's deputies are recruited through civil service. It is common for police protection to comprise a major portion of a municipality's budget. In over forty states, law enforcement officers must first pass a required training curriculum before being sworn-in.

Private and Other Public Law Enforcement

In addition to the agencies described above, there are hundreds of special purpose law enforcement agencies in cities and counties, ranging from parkway police and transit authority police to housing authority police. Further, there are thousands of private and semi-public law enforcement agencies in the United States. For example, most factories, amusement parks, and hospitals have security staff, as do most retail chain stores. Many residential buildings and developments also have private security. Finally, the coroner or medical examiner is often considered to be a law enforcement official because of the investigative duties of that position.

As we have seen, it may not be possible to speak accurately of American law enforcement, or even of the American police. The diversity of agencies, standards and duties is nearly mind-boggling. Because law enforcement is the largest (numerically) component of the justice process, a review of justice agencies in courts and corrections is less complicated, but only marginally so.

Courts

In 1977, the U.S. Department of Justice reported that there were over 3,600 courts of general or appellate jurisdiction in the United States, exclusive of tribal courts and the federal judiciary. In addition, there were thousands of courts of limited jurisdiction also in operation at that time. Like law enforcement, the court system is fragmented and complicated (National Survey of Court Organization, 1977). There are federal, state, and municipal courts. These courts are divided further in terms of the types of cases they may hear, and the types of decisions they may reach.

Federal Courts

In 1982, there were 1,320 federal justices, judges and magistrates, with a total judiciary staff exceeding 15,000 (Administrative Office of the U.S. Courts, 1982). Federal judges and justices of the United States Supreme Court are nominated by the President and appointed with the advice and consent of the U.S. Senate. These judges have lifetime tenure. Federal magistrates are appointed to eight-year terms by federal district judges.

The federal courts are organized by "circuits," with eleven circuits covering the entire nation. Within these circuits, 89 district courts are trial courts. Further, more than 400 federal magistrates within these districts may hear minor offenses and conduct the early stages of felony trials, and more serious civil trials. Pay for federal judicial officers ranges from over $63,000 per year for magistrates to over $100,000 per year for the Chief Justice of the United States Supreme Court (Neubauer, 1984).

Federal courts decide cases of federal interest; for example, charges of federal law violation. Federal appeals courts also decide federal constitutional issues, even if those issues were raised during state trials or proceedings.

State Courts

State judicial systems are similar to the federal judiciary in structure. They are generally comprised of trial courts, intermediate appellate courts and a state supreme court. State judges and justices are either appointed (as is the federal judiciary) or elected. Members of state judiciaries are in office for specified terms of office, unlike federal judges, who have lifetime tenure.

While federal judges are recruited nationally (although district court judges and circuit court judges are generally selected from among candidates residing in the particular district or circuit), state court judges are elected statewide (or appointed) for statewide posts (for example, the office of justice of the state supreme court), or from the jurisdiction of the lower court (for example, the county of a specific county court). While there may be no constitutional provision (as with U.S. judges) or statutory requirements that judges be members of the bar, most judges are attorneys.

Local Courts

There are a plethora of local courts in the United States. These are courts of limited jurisdiction because they are not allowed to decide felony cases, serious misdemeanors, or civil suits seeking damages above fairly low dollar amounts. Typically these are known as "justice of the peace" courts. In many places, these limited jurisdiction courts are known as police courts or mayor's courts. These courts usually decide traffic offense cases, hear violations of local ordinances and petty offenses, and make bail determinations.

Many of these judgeships are "ex officio" so that, upon being elected mayor in Ohio, for example, the new mayor becomes the "judge" of mayor's court. In many states which still retain the office of justice of the peace, there is no formal legal training required for this position. These limited jurisdiction courts are not authorized to conduct jury trials and their decisions may be appealed to courts of general jurisdiction, which are also known as "trial courts."

Salaries for these local courts are usually not commensurate with what an attorney could earn in the private practice of law. However, many of these courts operate on a part-time basis, and members of the bar may serve as justices of the peace.

Other Courts

Every court system has a number of special jurisdiction courts. For example, the federal judiciary has a "tax court,"

and a state usually has family court, courts of domestic relations, and/or a juvenile court. Several jurisdictions have
bankruptcy courts and other special jurisdiction courts.
Another relatively recent innovation is what may be called
a "private court." In some places, offices or commissions
for dispute resolution have been developed to divert cases
away from the formal courts (Aaronson, et al, 1977). Here
the parties to a dispute sit with a lay negotiator (or team of
negotiators) and attempt to resolve their problem without
resorting to the courts. Most of these "private courts" are
staffed by volunteers or by paid staff whose salaries are
lower than that of a judge. An example of this type of
"private court" is seen on television as "The People's
Court."

Prosecution

At all levels of courts from local to federal, the interests of the state (not the victim) are represented by the
prosecutor. In the federal system, the prosecutor is the
U.S. Attorney or the Deputy U.S. Attorney. These are
lawyers appointed by the nomination of the President with
the consent of the Senate. Local prosecutors are common
in most states and, for the most part, are lawyers elected at
the county level. In some states, the prosecutor is known as
a State's Attorney (Neubauer, 1984:105-6).

The salary of a prosecutor generally is not very high in
comparison to potential private practice earnings or judicial salaries. Many assistant prosecutors (also known as assistant district attorneys) seek these positions at the start of
their careers in order to gain trial experience prior to
starting their own practices (Rubin, 1984).

Defense

There are three basic structures for the provision of defense counsel: private retention, public defenders, and assigned counsel. Private retention refers to the possibility of the defendant retaining his or her own attorney. Private retention is unusual because most criminal defendants cannot afford attorney fees, but in cases involving wealthy or notorious defendants, celebrated defense attorneys are often retained. Public defenders are organized like prosecutors, that is, they usually work with an appointed director or administrator who hires a sufficient staff of attorneys to represent indigent clients in court (Guide to Establishing a Defender System, 1978). Finally, the most common form of criminal defense system is assigned counsel.

In the provision of assigned counsel, judges are presented either with a list of all attorneys practicing in their jurisdiction, or with a list of those attorneys willing to take on criminal defense cases. The judge then appoints an attorney for each indigent defendant from this list; he usually moves down the list from the first name to the last. The attorneys thus selected and assigned are then paid a set fee, which is usually on an hourly rate not to exceed some upper limitation per case.

Like prosecutors, defense attorneys employed in public defender offices (and most assigned counsel schemes) are not paid as well as judges, nor are they paid as much as they could earn in private practice as retained defense attorneys. Again, like prosecutors, young attorneys often seek this kind of work to gain trial experience.

In the cases of both prosecutors and defense attorneys, staff are recruited from local bar associations. While the local nature of the recruitment is comparable to recruiting for most police officers and judges, the requirement of membership in the bar limits the pool of possible applicants.

Witnesses and Jurors

Many other persons are involved in the court process in addition to prosecutors, defense counsel and judges. There are court support staff members, such as court clerks, stenographers, bailiffs and administrators; however, we will focus here on witnesses and jurors.

A variety of persons may serve as witnesses in a criminal case (Victim/Witness Legislation, 1984). Generally the arresting officers and any investigators are called as witnesses in a criminal case. If any passersby saw the offense, they too may be called to testify. Sometimes the defendant (or a codefendant) is called to testify in criminal cases, but the defendant may not be required to be a witness. Depending on the nature of the case, or of the defense, expert witnesses may be called. These individuals are first established as having special knowledge not commonly available to the average citizen. Experts in areas such as ballistics, forensic medicine, and psychology or psychiatry (when an insanity defense is raised) are asked to bring special knowledge to bear on issues at trial. The victim of a crime is "useful" only as a witness. Crimes are public wrongs and individual suffering is not at issue in criminal trials.

Citizens participate directly and most strongly in the criminal justice process in the courts. Citizens make up the two types of juries used in the courts. For decisions at arraignment, grand juries of citizens sit and listen to the prosecutor's case before deciding if an indictment should be issued. Trial juries sit and listen to the criminal trial before deciding if the defendant should be convicted. In several states, and in death penalty cases, the jury also recommends a sentence to the judge after deciding to convict the defendant. Box 2.7 describes the use of jurors in the federal courts.

Jurors are selected from lists of residents in the court's jurisdiction. Often these lists are voter registration rolls, telephone books or the billing records of utility companies. Trial jurors are then subjected to *voir dire*, a process by which the prosecutor and defense attorney seek to discover whether the jurors have any prejudices which will affect their decision in the trial. A juror suspected of being unable to make an objective decision may be challenged by the attorneys and dismissed by the judge.

Box 2.7
Juror Usage in the Federal Courts, 1984

<u>Grand Juries</u>

Total number of:

sessions	11,804
jurors in session	232,844
hours in session	61,425

Average number of:

jurors per session	19.7
hours per session	5.2

<u>Petit Juries</u>

Jury trial days

criminal	39,580
civil	22,798

Total jurors selected	431,052

SOURCE: Flanagan, T.J. & E.F. McGarrell (1986), *Sourcebook of criminal justice statistics, 1985.* (Washington, D.C.: U.S. Government Printing Office): 85.

Corrections

Corrections can be divided into the general categories of incarceration and community supervision. This general classification simplifies a description of American corrections, but grossly oversimplifies this complex component of the justice system. In the area of incarceration are found both prisons and jails, while both probation and parole comprise the non-incarceration parts of corrections. It is not clear, with this dichotomy, where such sanctions as halfway houses or "split-sentences" fall.

Incarceration

The most frequent place of incarceration for criminal offenders and those suspected of criminal acts is the jail. There are over 3,300 jails in the United States (U.S. Department of Justice, 1985), most of which are municipal (either city or, more frequently, county jails). Most jails do not have treatment staffs of counselors, psychologists and therapists. The major occupational group in jails is correctional officers. Most jail correctional officers are poorly trained and low-paid. Often, jail officers are members of the police department or the sheriff's department that is responsible for jail operation. Starting salaries for jail officers in 1982 were reported to be at an average of less than $11,000 per year (Kerle & Ford, 1982), which was $1,700 per year lower than the average starting salary of a patrol officer in the same jurisdiction. Jail officers often are recruited in the same way as police officers, which is through local searches and civil service testing.

The nation's jails hold about 220,000 inmates on any given day, but because of the relatively short time most persons stay in jail, as many as five million (or more) people may "do time" in jail each year. The Department of

Justice reported more than eight million admissions to jails in 1983. It is not possible to determine how many of these were repeat offenders. More than half of those held in jail are not yet convicted and are awaiting trial.

The nation's 637 prisons house more inmates than do jails on any given day (over 500,000), but because of the longer terms, fewer people serve prison time each year than serve jail time. While jails usually are municipal, prisons are operated by the state or federal governments. Prisons are more apt to have counselors, therapists, industries and educational programs than are jails, partly because prisons are larger and hold inmates longer, and partly because they have a larger resource base (state taxes) than do city and county jails. Still, the most common occupational category in prisons is that of correctional officers. Like jail officers, correctional officers in prisons are typically selected through civil service and are not particularly well paid (Camp & Camp, 1984).

Non-Incarceration

The most common form of non-incarcerative sanction (after fines, perhaps) is probation. On any day there are approximately 1.5 million persons under probation supervision. Probation officers supervise these persons in the community and are also responsible for the compilation of presentence investigation reports and other programs, depending upon the jurisdiction.

Probation officers are typically assigned to courts, although over half of the probation departments in the country are run by states. Unlike police or correctional officers, it is common for a probation officer to be required to have a college degree. Searches for probation officers tend to be local, on the basis of the court's jurisdiction. The average salary for probation officers reported by Camp & Camp (1984:55) was $16,533 per year.

Box 2.8
Government Contracts with Private Firms
for Management of Correctional Facilities,
by Level of Government

Federal contracts	State corrections contracts	Local jail contracts
Immigration and Naturalization Service • Four facility contracts for aliens awaiting deportation were operating in San Diego, Los Angeles, Houston, and Denver. Capacity: 625 beds. • Three facility contracts were nearing award in Las Vegas, Phoenix, and San Francisco. Capacity: 225 beds. • Two facility contracts were planned in the near term in Laredo and El Paso, Texas. Capacity: 270 beds. U.S. Marshals Service • Two small facilities were operating under contract in California. Capacity: 30 beds. • One contracted facility for alien material witnesses was planned in Los Angeles. Capacity: 100-150 beds. Federal Bureau of Prisons • One contracted facility for sentenced aliens was planned in the Southwest region. (Project delayed due to siting difficulties.) Capacity: 400-600 beds. • One contracted facility for offenders under the Federal Youth Corrections Act was operating in La Honda, California. Capacity: 60 beds.	Secondary adult facilities • A total of 28 States reported use of privately operated prerelease, work-release, or halfway house facilities. Largest private facility networks found in California, Massachusetts, Michigan, New York, Ohio, Texas, and Washington. Primary adult facilities • Kentucky Corrections Cabinet issued an RFP in late 1984 to contract for minimum security housing for 200 sentenced felons. However, no contracts for the confinement of mainstream adult populations were reported in operation. • Two interstate facilities for protective custody prisoners were planned by private contractor. Juvenile facilities • A 1982-83 survey of private juvenile facilities found 1,877 privately operated residential programs holding a total of 31,390 juveniles, of whom 10,712 were held for delinquency. Only 47 institutions were classified as strict security and 426 as medium security. The rest were primarily small, less secure facilities.[b] • An exception was Florida's Okeechobee Training School for 400 to 500 serious juvenile offenders, operated by a private contractor.	• Legislation enabling private jail operations was pending in Colorado and had passed in New Mexico and Texas. • Corporate providers reported significant interest, and there were a number of pending proposals for jail operations in the South and West, in spite of the formal opposition of the National Sheriffs' Association. • In Hamilton County, Tennessee, a private contractor took over operation of a local workhouse for 300 men and women awaiting trial or serving sentences of up to 6 years. Shared facilities • One private organization in Texas was planning to construct and operate a facility to serve both local detention needs and the needs of Federal agencies responsible for confining illegal aliens. • Other proposals called for the development of regional jail facilities to serve multicounty detention needs.

SOURCE: National Institute of Justice (1985),
"Corrections and the private sector," *NIJ Reports* SNI 191
(May): 4.

Parole is similar to probation, except that parole is a state agency and parole officers are therefore state employees. At any given time, approximately 400,000 persons are under parole supervision. These persons have been granted an early release from incarceration (mostly from prison) and are supervised by parole officers. Thirty-eight states have parole boards in the executive branch of government which are responsible for deciding which inmates to grant early release to and what will be the conduct of the prisoners' parole periods.

A parole officer is often required to have a college education and to perform duties similar to those of a probation officer, except that a parole officer typically has a lighter caseload comprised of ex-inmates. Parole officers, on the average, receive slightly higher wages than do probation officers, and are selected from statewide pools through civil service procedures.

Private Sector Corrections

As with law enforcement and the courts, there is a private involvement in corrections as well. Traditionally, many correctional practices were the province of voluntary or private initiatives. Today, there is a growing movement to "privatize" corrections with proposals offered that would have private companies construct and operate prisons and jails in addition to providing other services on a contract basis (Travis, et al, 1985). Box 2.8 gives an indication of private involvement in corrections through contracts with public agencies.

In addition to these for-profit private correctional enterprises, volunteer service is relatively high in corrections. Volunteers write to and visit prison inmates, provide services to probation and parole offices and clients, and serve on a variety of boards and commissions. The boards and commissions range from those that govern halfway houses to citizen court-watching groups. Recent development of "Neighborhood Watch" programs and other citizen crime-prevention projects also has increased the citizens' role in law enforcement. One of the most important trends in criminal justice over the past decade has been the resurgence of private initiative in the criminal justice system. Corrections, too, is being affected by this development.

SYSTEMS AND
CRIMINAL JUSTICE STRUCTURE

What this chapter has demonstrated thus far is that the criminal justice system in the United States is extremely complex. The many various agencies which comprise the system are organized at different levels of government, utilize different resource bases and select differentially qualified personnel in different ways. In short, the justice system would appear to be anything but a system, as is shown in the different roles and salaries for justice personnel (presented in Box 2.9).

There are at least 52 criminal justice systems in America. One for each state, the federal government and the District of Columbia may, in fact, be an underestimate of their numbers. For example, if city police can arrest someone for violating a city ordinance, and that person can be convicted and fined in mayor's court, do we have a city justice system? Even though it appears that there are many criminal justice systems in America, we will continue to examine and discuss *the* criminal justice system.

Box 2.9
Criminal Justice Positions and Salaries

Justice dollars pay personnel costs

(Average annual salary. There are jurisdictions where the salaries
are higher or lower than these averages.)

Law enforcement officers (1985 and 1986)

City police officer (entry level)	$18,913
City police officer (maximum)	$24,243
City police chief	$33,158
County sheriff patrol officer	Not available
State trooper (entry level)	$18,170
State trooper (maximum)	$28,033
Deputy U.S. marshal	$19,585
U.S. border patrol agent	$23,058
U.S. immigration inspector	$24,719
U.S. immigration agent	$34,259
Federal drug agent	$36,973
FBI agent	$40,321

Prosecutors (1986)

State and local prosecution personnel	Not available
Federal prosecutor	$53,027

Defenders (1986)

State and local defense personnel	Not available
Federal defender	$43,582

Court personnel (1986 and 1987)

State court administrator	$59,257
State general jurisdiction trial court judge	$60,697
State intermediate appellate court justice	$67,172
State associate supreme court justice	$67,434
State supreme court justice	$70,161
U.S. Magistrate	$72,500
U.S. Bankruptcy Court Judge	$72,500
U.S. Court of Claims Judge	$82,500
U.S. Court of International Trade Judge	$89,500
U.S. District (trial) Court Judge	$89,500
U.S. Circuit (appellate) Court Judge	$95,000
U.S. Supreme Court Associate Justice	$110,000
U.S. Supreme Court Chief Justice	$115,000

Correctional officers (adult facilities, 1986)

Local jail officer (entry level)	$16,939
State correctional officer (entry level)	$14,985
State correctional officer (maximum)	$16,427
State director of corrections	$59,947
Federal correctional officer	$22,857

Probation and parole officers (adult clientele, 1986 and 1987)

Local probation officer	Not available
State probation officer (entry level)	$19,402
State parole officer (entry level)	$19,986
State chief probation officer	$28,600
State chief parole officer	$31,233
State parole board member	$43,429
State parole board chairman	$46,100
Federal probation officer (entry level)	$22,458
Federal parole case analyst	$22,458–42,341
Federal parole hearing examiner	$38,727–59,488
Federal regional probation/parole administrator	$53,830–69,976
U.S. Parole Commissioner	$72,500

Note: Multiple sources supplied the data in this table. Ranges are presented when the source did not provide enough information to compute an average. The list of sources for this table is available from BJS either in the technical appendix or separately upon request.

SOURCE: *Report to the Nation on Crime and Justice, Second Edition*. (Washington, D.C.: U.S. Department of Justice, 1988): 126.

This systems approach to the study of criminal justice seems especially appropriate. Without a prevailing approach, we might be forced to throw up our hands in despair, unable to make sense of the confusion. Why do we have so many agencies? Why do these different agencies have conflicting and sometimes competing jurisdictions and goals? The answer is because they are part of an open system. The large number of agencies, and the various levels and branches of government involved can be understood as a manifestation of the environmental impact on American criminal justice. Given our political and cultural values of federalism, local autonomy and the separation of powers, we should not be surprised at the confusion in the justice system; it would be more surprising if there was no confusion. A single, well organized, monolithic criminal justice system for the entire nation may well be "un-American".

REVIEW QUESTIONS

1. Identify the ten decision points of the criminal justice process discussed in this chapter.

2. How does the justice process work as a *directional* flow of cases in the total system?

3. Give two examples of how the environment of the justice process affects the operations of all justice agencies.

4. What are the basic components of the justice process?

5. Describe the different types, levels and staffing patterns of the components of the justice process.

6. Why is the "systems" approach especially appropriate to the study of American criminal justice?

REFERENCES

Aaronson, D.E., N.N. Kittrie, D.J. Saari, and C.S. Cooper (1977), *Alternatives to Conventional Criminal Adjudication.* (Washington, DC: Government Printing Office).

Administrative Office of the U.S. Courts (1982), *Annual Report of the Director.* (Washington, DC: Administrative Office of the U.S. Courts).

Bureau of Justice Statistics (1985), *Prisoners in 1984.* (Washington, DC: U.S. Department of Justice).

Bureau of Justice Statistics (1985), *The 1983 Jail Census.* (Washington, DC: U.S. Department of Justice).

Bureau of Justice Statistics (1989), *Profile of State and Local Law Enforcement Agencies, 1987*. (Washington, DC: U.S. Department of Justice).

Burton, V.S., F.T. Cullen & L.F. Travis, III (1987), "The collateral consequences of a felony conviction: A national study of state statutes." *Federal Probation* 51(3):52-60.

Camp, G. and C. Camp (1984), *The Corrections Yearbook*. (South Salem, NY: Criminal Justice Institute).

_____ (1978), *Guide to Establishing a Defender System*. (Washington, DC: Government Printing Office).

International Association of Chiefs of Police, Division of State and Provincial Police (1975), *Comparative Data Report*. (Gaithersburg, MD: IACP).

Jailing Drunk Drivers (1985), (Washington, DC: U.S. Department of Justice).

Kerle, K.E. & F.R. Ford (1982), *The State of Our Nation's Jails, 1982*. (Washington, DC: National Sheriffs' Association.)

Mastrofski, S., R. Ritti & D. Hoffmaster (1987), "Organizational determinants of police discretion: The case of drinking-driving," *Journal of Criminal Justice* 15(5):387-402.

McDonald, W. (ed.) (1979), *The Prosecutor*. (Beverly Hills: Sage).

Meyers, A., T. Heeren, R. Hingson & D. Kovenock (1987) "Cops and drivers: Police discretion and the enforcement of Maine's 1981 DUI law," *Journal of Criminal Justice* 15(5):361-68.

National Survey of Court Organization (1977), (Washington, DC: U.S. Department of Justice).

Neubauer, D.W. (1984) *America's Courts and the Criminal Justice System*. (Monterey, CA: Brooks-Cole).

Newman, D.J. (1966). *Conviction: The Determination of Guilt or Innocence without Trial.* (Boston: Little, Brown).

_____ (1986), *Introduction to Criminal Justice, 3rd edition.* (New York: Random House).

President's Commission on Law Enforcement and Administration of Justice (1967), *The Challenge of Crime in a Free Society.* (Washington, DC: Government Printing Office).

President's Commission on Law Enforcement and Administration of Justice (1967), *Task Force Report: The Police.* (Washington, DC: Government Printing Office).

Rosett, A. and D. Cressey (1976), *Justice by Consent.* (Philadelphia: J.B. Lippincott).

Rubin, H.T. (1984), *The Courts: Fulcrum of the Justice System, 2nd Edition.* (New York: Random House).

Travis, L.F. and E.J. Latessa (1984), "A summary of parole rules--thirteen years later: Revisited thirteen years later," *Journal of Criminal Justice* 12(6):591-600.

Travis, L.F., E.J. Latessa, and G.F. Vito (1985), "Private enterprise in institutional corrections: A call for caution," *Federal Probation* 49(4):11-16.

U.S. Department of Justice (1980), *Justice agencies in the united states.* (Washington, DC: Government Printing Office).

U.S. Department of Justice (1978), *The Nation's Toughest Drug Law.* (Washington, DC: Government Printing Office).

Victim/Witness Legislation: An Overview (1984). (Washington, DC: U.S. Department of Justice).

Walker, S. (1983), *The Police in America.* (New York: McGraw-Hill).

3 Crime and Crime Control

The business of the American criminal justice process is "crime." Yet, this easy answer is not really an answer at all. One obstacle to the study of the system of criminal justice is our lack of precision in discussing the issue of crime. What is crime?

It is relatively easy to provide examples of crime, but that is not the same as *defining* crime. There is a tendency to assume a common meaning for the word "crime." The variety of actions and nuances of behavior which are crimes is nearly infinite. If asked to name a crime, how many of us would say shoplifting, drunken driving, price fixing or failure to register for the selective service? We are far more likely to mention murder, bank robbery, rape or burglary. In that sense, we have a fairly clear common definition of crime, but one which is inadequate for the study of criminal justice.

These mental images of crime reflect those offenses which cause the most concern. Of the many different types of behaviors which we have defined as criminal, some types are more commonly agreed upon to be criminal than others. There tends to be consensus among us about the criminality of the more serious offenses which involve actual physical harm or direct economic harm to individuals (Cullen, Link, and Polanzi, 1982). There is considerably less agreement about those offenses which do not cause such direct and potentially personal harm (Newman & Trilling, 1975; Miethe, 1982).

Similarly, we carry mental images of criminals about which there is general agreement. The average criminal probably appears as a relatively young, mean, menacing male. Most people seem to believe that the criminal knows that his or her behavior is wrong and harmful, but that the criminal does not care. The criminal is simply bad or lazy, preferring crime to some other more appropriate mode of earning a living. Yet, as with crimes, there is a wide variety of criminals. The hulking street offender, bullying rapist, calculating white-collar offender, college student selling or using drugs, and the political terrorist are all criminals.

Faced with this wide array of crimes and criminals, we need to organize our understanding of each in order to appreciate the demands placed upon the justice system. Both crimes and criminals have been sorted into classes for ease of understanding. Before turning to these, however, we should try to answer the question: what is crime?

DEFINING CRIME

"Crime" refers in part to a set of behaviors which we feel are wrong and in need of control. Most often, classifying a behavior as a crime includes a reference to the "intent" of the actor. The specification and definition of crimes is a legislative function in our society. It is the legislature that declares certain behaviors to be "criminal" and describes the conditions under which a person may be said to have committed a crime. (Box 3.1 provides an example of a criminal statute). Therefore, from a legalistic perspective, we can conclude the "cause" of crime in America is the legislature. Without legislative action, there would be no conduct designated as "crime".

Box 3.1

Legislative Definition of Crime: Burglary as Defined in the Oregon Revised Statutes

164.215 Burglary in the Second Degree

(1) A person commits the crime of burglary in the second degree if he enters or remains unlawfully in a building with intent to commit a crime therein.

164.225 Burglary in the First Degree

(1) A person commits the crime of burglary in the first degree if he violates ORS 164.215 and the building is a dwelling, or if in effecting entry or while in a building or in immediate flight therefrom he:

    (a) Is armed with a burglar's tool as defined in ORS 164.235 or a deadly weapon; or

    (b) Causes or attempts to cause a physical injury to any person; or

    (c) Uses or threatens to use a dangerous weapon.

(2) Burglary in the first degree is a Class A felony.

Of course, without the designation of certain conduct as "crime," we would still have troublesome behavior, such as the taking of property or the infliction of injury. These actions would not be crimes, however, unless they were first so defined by the legislature. A crime is "an act or omission in violation of the law and punishable by the state."

While most of us do not think of legislative action as a necessary "cause" of crime, we understand the legislative role. Indeed, if asked what is the cause of crime, most people will contend that bad companions, ignorance, poverty, psychological disturbance or some other factor is what makes people break the law. Yet, when we see someone doing something which we believe is wrong, we are also apt to say, "There oughta be a law." This statement reflects an understanding of the role of the legislature. No matter how wrong is the behavior in question, we really cannot do anything about it unless there is a law against it.

This is an important concept for understanding the criminal justice system. The justice system is constrained by the law. We generally cannot use the justice process to control behavior which is unpleasant but not criminal. There are limits, then, to what level of control can be asserted by agents of the criminal process.

Criminologists have debated the definition of crime for many years (Schwendinger & Schwendinger, 1975). Some argue that only those behaviors identified in criminal laws are crimes. Others seek a broader definition that includes actions which are socially harmful or immoral. The issue of defining crime is somewhat different for these criminologists than it is for our purposes.

We require a definition of crime which identifies those behaviors on which the criminal justice system focuses. Criminologists, on the other hand, are seeking to identify a set of behaviors which can then be explained by theory. Criminologists seek to explain the behavior of individuals, while we wish to understand the criminal justice system as a social institution.

The definitions of most crimes contain two components. First, there is an action (or lack of action) known as *actus reus*. Second, there is the intent or mental condition of the offender, known as the *mens rea*. It is usually not enough to do something illegal if one is to be considered a criminal. One must also intend to do what is illegal to be convicted of a crime.

Most jurisdictions define the crime of burglary as the unlawful entry of a place for the purpose of committing a crime therein. To be convicted of burglary, one must unlawfully enter a place (a home, business, storage building, etc.) Simply entering, however, does not make one a burglar. The entry is the *actus reus*. To be a burglar, it is also necessary that one enter with the intent to commit a crime inside. The intent to commit a crime once inside is the mental state of the offender, or *mens rea*.

Neither of the two hypothetical persons below is a burglar.

P. was invited to a party at a neighbor's home. P. did not care much for these neighbors, but cared greatly for several of their possessions. P. accepted the invitation and attended the party for the express purpose of obtaining the property of the neighbors. P. is not a burglar, for the entry was achieved lawfully. In this case, P. is a thief (and a boor whose social life will suffer if word gets around).

Q. was walking home from a party at which large quantities of alcoholic refreshments were consumed (the largest quantity by Q). Passing a furrier's, Q. blacks out from the combined effects of too many beverages and a long and tedious conversation with someone named P., a neighbor of the host. Q. falls over and crashes through the display window of the furrier's shop, landing in a huge pile of fur coats, on which Q. falls fast asleep. The police arrive within minutes, responding to the alarm at the furrier's, to discover the quietly resting Q. Q. is not a burglar, for there was no intent to commit a crime in the furrier shop. (Indeed, there was not even an intent to enter.)

In order to obtain a criminal conviction, the state must prove all elements (both *actus reus* and *mens rea*) of an offense beyond a reasonable doubt. Television murder-mystery plots often include a missing victim where there is reason to believe that someone has been murdered, but the body cannot be found. The characters remark that it will be difficult to bring charges without the *corpus delicti*. Because of the plot, and the similarity between the words corpus and corpse, audiences often think that *corpus delicti* refers to the dead body. In fact, it refers to the body of the crime. The lack of a motive (also a frequent plot line) also hinders the filing of charges because, without a motive, it is difficult to establish intent, another part of the *corpus delicti*.

For some crimes the job of the state in proving the guilt of an offender is somewhat easier. Some crimes, known as "strict liability" offenses, presume *mens rea* (Lilly & Ball, 1982). In these cases, if it can be proved that the defendant engaged in the prohibited behavior, a conviction will occur. Regardless of the intent of the offender, she or he is strictly liable for the consequences of the behavior.

Strict liability commonly applies to white collar crimes. For example, the law may presume the head of a company is responsible for the wrongdoing of his or her employees, even if the company head is unaware of the activity. Especially with strict liability offenses the old adage is true, "Ignorance of the law is no excuse."

This brief explanation of the definition of crimes and of the elements of an offense is needed to understand the nature of crime. However, this explanation alone does not help us to obtain a perspective on crime which will be useful to our examination of the criminal justice process. The legislatures in the various American criminal jurisdictions have managed to adequately define a very large number of widely divergent behaviors and mental states as crimes. The justice system must respond to all of them with limited resources and ability. To better organize and deploy limited resources for the control of crime, this plethora of offenses must be sorted and ranked.

CLASSIFICATION
OF CRIMES AND CRIMINALS

One simple classification of crimes has already been alluded to as the dichotomy between "serious" and "less serious" offenses. This same simplistic distinction is frequently drawn between "dangerous" and "normal" crimes. Those offenses which are most threatening to individuals are usually defined as serious or dangerous, while those which are less directly threatening are classed as less serious, or normal.

Sometimes this distinction between dangerous and normal crimes is explained as the difference between offenses that are wrong in themselves (*mala in se*) and those which are wrong because they are prohibited (*mala prohibita*). That is, certain crimes appear to be obviously criminal, while others are apparently criminal only because we say they are wrong.

Mala in se offenses encompass traditional or street crimes which seem wrong regardless of their legality. Purposely or carelessly causing physical harm or suffering for someone, or taking the property of others are acts that most believe are simply wrong. One does not need a criminal law to realize that killing a person without cause (and often with cause) is "wrong." These are the very offenses about which we have the most agreement and around which most of our mental images of crime focus.

Mala prohibita offenses are those acts which are wrong because they are defined as wrong. The use of narcotics by adults within the confines of their own homes and refusal to pay income taxes (especially if the money could be better spent on something else) are not behaviors which are necessarily wrong, at least in a secular perspective. What makes these behaviors criminal, and therefore wrong, is that we have prohibited them and defined them as crimes. These are the offenses about which we have the least agreement and which raise the most serious issues of individual liberty and the needs of the state.

A second major way in which criminal offenses have been classified is into categories of *felony, misdemeanor,* or *violation*. These three levels of crime reflect the different seriousness of behaviors, in large part, on the basis of the extent of punishment authorized. Before explaining this difference, it is important to remember that there are exceptions to every rule, and thus what follow are merely rules of thumb.

Felonies are the most serious offenses and generally are punishable by a term of more than one year in a state prison. *Misdemeanors* are less serious offenses, which are generally punishable by terms of no more than one year in a local jail. *Violations* are the least severe offenses and typically do not carry an incarcerative penalty; the penalty is limited to a fine. For example, in most states, theft of $1,000 or more is a felony and can be punished by imprisonment for a number of years, while theft of $50 is a misdemeanor and can be punished by a jail term of up to several months. Exceeding the speed limit is a violation and is punished by a fine of less than $100 (except for repeated offenses). As these examples illustrate, the classes of crimes reflect the amount of harm caused by the criminal behavior.

Yet another distinction drawn between crimes is to label them as being either *ordinary* (normal) or *aggravated* (dangerous) (Newman, 1987:28-30). As unbelievable as it may seem, with enough experience it is possible to rate crimes as being "better" or "worse" than each other, within the same crime type. A burglar may take pains not to do any more damage to a home than that required for entry and theft; this is an ordinary burglary. On the other hand, the burglar may vandalize the home in addition to breaking-in and stealing; this might be an aggravated burglary. (We will return to this type of classification system later when we discuss sentencing).

The *ordinary/aggravated* distinction is generally used within some less precise classification (such as "felony") to differentiate between the seriousness of several instances of the "same" behavior. As with the other classifications of crimes, the purpose of this distinction is to clarify the response which should be taken by the justice system. Typically, the agents and agencies of the justice system are more willing to expend resources in response to aggravated felonies than in response to ordinary violations. Indeed, many of us express this rational choice upon being stopped for a traffic violation by wondering why the officer is not out "fighting crime" rather than harassing us for a trivial matter.

DEFINING CRIMINALS

Like crimes themselves, the people who engage in criminal behavior are of an almost infinite variety. Assuming that there is a preventive component to the justice system's overall mission to control crime, knowledge of the type of offender is as important as knowledge about the type of crime. Certain types of offenders have been identified as deserving specific types of justice system responses. A Bureau of Justice Statistics Report stated:

> Programs aimed at the serious, recidivistic offender require the capability to identify dangerous offenders at key decision points in the criminal justice system, such as pre-trial release and sentencing...

> These programs are designed primarily to increase the effectiveness of criminal justice by targeting resources on offenders considered most likely to recidivate and on of-

fenders whose detention is most likely to have an incapacitative or deterrent effect. (1985:1)

One common method of classifying offenders is by the crime they committed, so that one guilty of murder is a murderer, one guilty of robbery is a robber, one guilty of burglary is a burglar, and so on. This is often how the media and correctional authorities identify offenders. Police frequently improve on this simple scheme by adding details of crimes such as the time of the crime, type of weapon used, and characteristics of the victim. These added details comprise a *modus operandi*, or M.O., file. This type of classification is limited because it does not tell much about the offender. A study conducted by the RAND corporation (Chaiken & Chaiken, 1982) showed that offenders often engage in a variety of criminal behavior. Today's robber may have been yesterday's thief and may be tomorrow's burglar.

Another typical classification of offenders is similar to the ordinary/aggravated distinction applied to crimes. Here, offenders are identified as either "first-time" (ordinary) or "repeat" (more dangerous). Several jurisdictions have special procedures for the handling of repeat offenders known as *career criminals*. The distinction drawn is one between periodic or occasional criminality and a criminal lifestyle. Those who lead a criminal life, that is, who routinely engage in criminal behavior, are responsible for a disproportionate share of crime committed (Greenwood, 1982).

Criminal Careers vs. Career Criminals

Criminologists have begun to study criminal behavior through examining the "criminal careers" of offenders (Nettler, 1982; Gibbons, 1973). In their efforts, these researchers seek to identify the paths followed by offenders throughout their lives that lead them into and out of crime. They recognize that criminality is not always central to the personality of an offender. The average person probably has committed (or will someday commit) a crime. Yet, few of us are (or will be) criminals.

The "career criminal" is someone for whom crime is a normal activity and for whom being a criminal is part of self-identification. This person is often called a "hardened criminal" or persistent offender. It has been suggested that these persistent offenders commit the majority of crimes. Justice officials attempt to focus their attention on these individuals. In this way, the officials hope to have the greatest impact on the crime rate.

For decades, some criminologists argued that the most useful classification of offenders would be one based on behavioral characteristics. They advanced several means of distinguishing among criminals based on the psychological or sociological traits of the offender. These have been used for prison classification (Fox, 1983:59-62), probation and parole classification (Warren, 1973), and prevention programs. Perhaps the most wide-ranging classification system which retained links to type of crime was suggested by Clinard and Quinney (1983).

The principal goal of these criminologists is the explanation of criminal conduct, that is, to understand why persons commit crimes or why certain persons commit certain crimes (Cullen, 1983). For criminal justice agencies, this knowledge is useful only in so far as it can guide reactions to crime and criminals. Clinard and Quinney classified offenders by the major forms of crime committed. They identified nine categories ranging from violent personal offenders through opportunistic property offenders. (See Box 3.2.) Agents of the criminal justice system appear to use a similar classification scheme in their handling of offenders.

Box 3.2
Criminal Behavior Systems

	Violent Personal Criminal Behavior	Occasional Property Criminal Behavior	Public Order Criminal Behavior
Legal Aspects of Selected Offenses	The criminal laws of homicide, assault, and forcible rape are of ancient origin. Yet the legal categories are qualified and interpreted in their respective social and historical contexts. Likewise, the ruling class is able to exclude the forms of violence that enhance its own position.	Criminal laws protect the material interests of the propertied classes. Specific laws prohibit forgery, shoplifting, vandalism, and auto theft.	Specific criminal laws embody the moral sense of particular segments of the community. Such offenses as prostitution, homosexuality, drunkenness, and drug use are disturbing to some community members. Many of the crimes are "victimless" in that only willing participants are involved. Yet it is easier for the power elite to outlaw these behaviors than to either accept them or to change the social arrangements that produced the behaviors.
Criminal Career of the Offender	Crime is not part of the offender's career. He usually does not conceive of self as criminal.	Little or no criminal self-conception. The offender does not identify with crime. He is able to rationalize his behavior.	Most offenders do no regard their behavior as criminal. They do not have a clearly defined criminal career. Ambiguity in self-concept produced in continued contact with legal agents.
Group Support of Criminal Behavior	Little or no group support. Offenses committed for personal reasons. Some support in subcultural norms.	Little group support. Generally individual offenses. Associations tend to be recreational.	Offenses such as prostitution, homosexual behavior, and drug use grow out of, and are supported by, rather clearly defined subcultures. Considerable association with other offenders.
Correspondence between Criminal and Legitimate Behavior	Violations of values on life and personal safety.	Violation of value on private property. Offenders tend to be committed to the general goals of the society.	Some of the offenses are required by legitimate society. Much of the behavior is consistent with legitimate behavior patterns.
Societal Reaction and Legal Processing	Strong social reaction. Harsh punishments. Long imprisonment.	Social reaction is not severe when the offender does not have a previous record. Leniency in legal processing. Probation.	Strong reaction by some segments of society, weak reaction by others. Only a small portion of the offenses result in arrest. Sentences are strong for some offenses, such as the possession of narcotic drugs.

SOURCE: M. Clinard & R. Quinney (1983), *Criminal Behavior Systems*. (Cincinnati, OH: Anderson): 18-20.

Conventional Criminal Behavior	Political Criminal Behavior	Occupational Criminal Behavior
The laws that protect private property include such crimes as larceny, burglary, and robbery. Since the primary interest is in protecting property, general laws regarding property do not need to distinguish the career nature of many property offenders.	Criminal laws are created by governments to protect their own existence. Specific criminal laws, such as conspiracy laws, as well as traditional laws, are made to control and punish those who threaten the state. Yet the government and its officials often violate criminal laws. Political criminal behavior thus includes crimes against government and crimes by government.	Legal regulation of occupations has served to protect the interests of occupational groups, and in some cases to regulate harmful occupational activities. The legal codes that control occupations and professions tend to be made by the occupations and the professions themselves, representing their own material interests.
Offenders begin their careers early in life, often in gang associations. Crimes committed for economic gain. Vacillation in self-conception. Partial commitment to a criminal subculture.	Political offenders do not usually conceive of themselves as criminals and do not identify with crime. They are defined as criminal because they are perceived as threatening the status quo (as in crime against government), or they are criminal when they violate the laws that regulate the government itself (crime by government).	Little or no criminal self-conception. Occasional violation of the law, accompanied by appropriate rationalizations. Violation tends to be a part of one's work. Offenders accept the conventional values in the society.
Behavior supported by group norms. Early association with other offenders in slum areas. Status achieved in groups. Some persons continue primary association with other offenders, while others pursue different careers.	Support is received by particular groups or by segments of society. They identify or associate with persons who share similar values. Behavior is reinforced by specific norms.	Some occupations, or groups within occupations, tolerate or even support offenses. The offender is integrated into social groups and societal norms.
Consistent with goals of economic success, but inconsistent with sanctity of private property. Gang delinquency violates norms of proper adolescent behavior.	Crimes against government usually correspond to basic human rights. The actions and beliefs, however, are opposed by those who are threatened by these freedoms. Crimes by government correspond to contrary behavior patterns that promote the sovereignty of government rulers.	Behavior corresponds to the pursual of business activity. "Sharp" practices and "buyer beware" philosophy have guided work and consumption patterns.
A series of arrests and convictions. Institutionalization and rehabilitation of the offender. Agency programs that preserve the status quo without changing social conditions.	Official reactions tend to be severe in the case of crimes against government. Considerable harassment may be experienced and heavy sentences may be imposed. Public acceptance of political offenses depends on the extent to which the policies and actions of the government are accepted. Reactions to governmental crime depends on the consciousness of the public regarding the activities of the government.	Reactions have traditionally been mild and indifferent. Official penalties have been lenient, often restricted to the sanctions administered by the professional association. Public reaction is becoming less tolerant.

Typology of Criminal Behavior Systems (Continued)

	Corporate Criminal Behavior	*Organized Criminal Behavior*	*Professional Criminal Behavior*
Legal Aspects of Selected Offenses	With the growth of corporations, criminal laws have been created to regulate such activities as restraint of trade, false advertising, fraudulent sales, misuse of trademarks, and manufacture of unsafe foods and drugs. Criminal laws —especially administrative regulations—have been established by the corporations themselves to secure a capitalist economy.	Many traditional laws have been used in the attempt to control organized crime, especially those regarding gambling, prostitution, and drug traffic. The government has more recently enacted special criminal laws in order to infiltrate organized criminal activity in legitimate business and racketeering. But since organized crime is closely tied to the general business economy, these laws tend to invade the privacy of all citizens rather than to control organized crime.	Professional crimes are distinguished by the nature of the criminal behavior rather than by specific criminal laws. Such professional activities as confidence games, pickpocketing, shoplifting, forgery, and counterfeiting are regulated by the traditional laws that protect private property.
Criminal Career of the Offender	The violating corporate official and his corporation have high social status in society. Offenses are an integral part of corporate business operations. Violations are rationalized as being basic to business enterprise.	Crime is pursued as a livelihood. There is a progression in crime and an increasing isolation from the larger society. A criminal self-conception develops.	A highly developed criminal career. Professional offenders engage in specialized offenses, all of which are directed toward economic gain. They enjoy high status in the world of crime. They are committed to other professional criminals.
Group Support of Criminal Behavior	Crime by corporations and corporate officials receives support from similar, even competing, businesses and officials. Lawbreaking is a normative pattern within many corporations. Corporate crime involves a great amount of organization among the participants.	Support for organized criminal behavior is achieved through an organizational structure, a code of conduct, prescribed methods of operation, and a system of protection. The offender is integrated into organized crime.	Professional offenders associate primarily with other offenders. Behavior is prescribed by the norms of professional criminals. The extent of organization among professional criminals varies with the kind of offense.
Correspondence between Criminal and Legitimate Behavior	Corporate crime is consistent with the prevailing ideology that encourages unlimited production and consumption. Only recently has an alternative ethic developed that questions practices that support corporate crime.	While organized crime may be generally condemned, characteristics of American society give support to organized crime. The values underlying organized crime are consistent with those valued in the free enterprise system.	Professional criminal activity corresponds to societal values that stress skill and employment. Some of the offenses depend upon the cooperation of accomplices. The operations of professional crime change with alterations in the larger society.
Societal Reaction and Legal Processing	Strong legal actions have not usually been taken against corporations or their officials. Legal actions have been in the form of warnings and injunctions, rather than in terms of criminal penalties. Public reactions and legal actions, however, are increasing in respect to corporate crime.	Considerable public toleration of organized crime. Offenses are not usually visible to the public. Immunity of offenders, as provided by effective organization, prevents detection and arrest. Convictions are usually for minor offenses.	Considerable public toleration because of the low visibility of professional crime. Offenders are able to escape conviction by "fixing" cases.

Typologies of crimes and criminals are used to plan and evaluate the uses to which criminal justice resources are put. Without such "short-hand" categorization of its basic types of business, the justice system would be overwhelmed by idiosyncracies. While by no means perfect, these classification schemes allow an organization of the justice system which is necessary to making the system's operation more efficient.

For example, police officers frequently distinguish burglars as either juvenile burglars, average burglars or cat burglars. The juvenile burglar, as the name implies, is a youth who commits an opportunistic burglary with little forethought and perhaps less care in the commission of the offense. The average burglar plans his or her crime and is careful to avoid detection. The "cat burglar" is someone who burglarizes a dwelling while the occupants are on the premises (Gibbons, 1973:14).

While all of these are correctly labeled or categorized as "burglars," it is clear that they pose different levels of risk to citizens and that they require different responses by the police. The juvenile burglar is likely to grab whatever valuables can be quickly obtained and easily carried. The average burglar is unlikely to be discovered during the crime and will generally take more property. The cat burglar, while also unlikely to be detected, usually restricts his or her thefts to cash, jewels or specific high-value items.

Increasingly, agents and agencies of the justice system are organizing to better combat the more serious offenses and offenders. The career criminal is the target of special crime control efforts and programs. "The concept of the career criminal has led to police and prosecutor programs that target resources on those offenders identified as the most persistent and frequent in their commission of serious crimes." (National Institute of Justice, 1986).

CONTROLLING CRIME AND CRIMINALS

Francis A. Allen, Professor of Law and Dean of the University of Michigan Law School, was one of the first observers of American criminal justice to identify the increasing burden placed on the justice system by expansions of the criminal sanction. Allen described the tremendous growth of criminal laws and increasing use of the justice system to deal with social problems ranging from substance abuse through health care. He clearly stated the most important task as being the definition of what could reasonably be expected from the criminal justice system. In 1964, he wrote:

> The time has long been ripe for some sober questions to be asked. More and more it seems that the central issue may be this: What may we properly demand of a system of criminal justice? What functions may it properly serve? There is a related question: What are the obstacles and problems that must be confronted and overcome if a system of criminal justice is to be permitted to serve its own proper ends? These are broad and difficult questions, and the way in which they are answered will affect much that is important to the community at large (Allen, 1964:4).

At base, Allen was attempting to set priorities for the use of the criminal law. His position was that the criminal law was increasingly being applied to social welfare problems (such as public intoxication) and regulatory needs. He decried our growing reliance on the criminal law to solve our social problems. Instead, he urged that we decide upon those behaviors which would best be the objects of criminal law and that we limit the activities of the justice system to the control of these behaviors.

Other observers of American criminal justice shared this sentiment (American Friends Service Committee, 1971; National Advisory Commission, 1973). During the 1970s, a growing number of scholars and practitioners came to agree that the most sensible approach to crime control required the identification of "serious" crimes and the focusing of enforcement resources on those crimes. As the National Advisory Commission on Criminal Justice Standards and Goals (1973:84) put it, "The empire of crime is too large and diverse to be attacked on all fronts simultaneously."

Observers and agents of the justice system have long recognized the fundamental truth of this comment. Traditionally, police officers, prosecutors, judges, correctional personnel and parole boards have adopted *ad hoc* strategies to maximize the effectiveness of criminal justice processing in controlling crime. In this vein, Kenneth C. Davis (1975:1) noted:

> The police make policy about what law to enforce, how much to enforce it, against whom, and on what occasions. Some law is always or almost always enforced, some is never or almost never enforced, and some is sometimes enforced and sometimes not.

With a large number of criminal laws applied to a broad variety of behavior, agents of the justice system must often choose which laws to enforce and when to enforce them. Further, with the wide variety of offenders, it is similarly common for laws to be enforced differently against different types of individuals. The dangerous, repeat offender is not likely to be ignored, regardless of the violation. In a sense, this approach to the "rationing" of justice resources seeks to maximize effectiveness. Officials use the criminal law to control the most serious offenses and offenders.

Criminal justice officials historically have devoted most of their resources to the control of more dangerous crimes and criminals. For the most part, this focus of attention on serious crimes (such as felonies and violent acts) has not been a conscious policy decision. For example, police more thoroughly investigate suspected felonies than misdemeanors, and prosecutors are less willing to negotiate for guilty pleas from repeat felons.

Recently, this unconscious rationing of resources (by justice officials choosing cases on which to concentrate) has been exposed and adopted as formal policy in many jurisdictions. As Walker (1985:117) observed, "Career-criminal programs are the hottest fad in criminal justice these days." A brief review of the programs which flow from these policies serves to illustrate the point and to identify priorities in the justice system. Policies and programs directed at the control of serious offenses and offenders exist in law enforcement, courts and corrections.

Law Enforcement Programs

Police activities aimed at the control of serious crime and criminals are of two basic types. In the first, the police focus attention on identified serious offenders and carefully watch them for evidence of criminal conduct. In the second, the police identify high-risk areas where serious crimes appear likely to occur, and they devote increased patrol resources to those areas. In both cases, a decision is made that the best investment of police resources involves targeting specific locations or individuals.

Traditionally, police departments have responded to "crime waves" by increasing police presence in a given area. If there were an increase in the number of burglaries in a particular neighborhood, the historical response would be to increase the number of officers assigned to that neighborhood, or to increase the number of times the officers passed through that area on their patrols. In recent years, this traditional response has been formalized.

In 1975, the New Haven, Connecticut police began what were called "D Runs" or directed deterrent patrol. Police administrators selected target crimes and pinpointed their occurrence by time and location. Next, they wrote a specific set of instructions for the patrol officer. For example, the instructions typically told the officer to "cruise around a certain block slowly, park the car and walk down the street, get back in the car, cruise down another street." (Krajick, 1978)

Minneapolis, Minnesota instituted a "Target 8" program, in which eight suspects are identified as career criminals and all officers are expected to be alert for these suspects. Any officer may nominate a candidate for the list, provided that the suspect has had at least two felony convictions and one prison term within the past ten years, and the officer believes that the suspect is engaged in criminal enterprise (Walker, 1985).

Earlier, Kansas City, Missouri experimented with three methods of crime control: traditional patrol, location-oriented patrol and perpetrator-oriented patrol (Pate & Bowers, 1976). Location-oriented patrol, or LOP, worked much the same as New Haven's D Runs, with police patrol targeted to certain high crime areas or locations. Perpetrator-oriented patrol was similar to Minneapolis' Target 8, as patrol was focused on likely criminal offenders.

More recently, the police in Washington, D.C. have attracted attention with a program called "Repeat Offender Project," or ROP (pronounced "rope"), described in Box 3.3. This program assigns a special team of over sixty officers to focus their attention on persons thought to be committing at least five major offenses each week. A team of officers is given forty-eight hours to make an arrest. If, after that time, there is no arrest, the team is reassigned to another suspected repeat offender (Walker, 1985).

Box 3.3
Career Criminals and the Police

The jury is still out on the effectiveness of the Washington, D.C. Repeat Offenders Project (ROP). But the new program has attracted the attention of other metropolitan police departments who eagerly await the results of a study on the program by the Police Foundation, under a $100,000 grant from the U.S. Justice Department's National Institute of Justice.

It was the boss' idea. Captain Edward J. (Caesar) Spurlock, 49, blond-haired and thick-necked with a deep, toothy laugh, remembers that during his years in uniform "I knew the names of a small number of crooks who were all the time hittin' us, constantly committin' crimes, constantly comin' in to my station. It became obvious to me that if you could knock out those guys, you could make an impact on crime and make maximum use of your resources."

...Often the ROP officers arrest felons on relatively minor charges, a practice that cops in other parts of the city and prosecutors in the U.S. attorney's office say isn't cost-effective.

The ROP officers vehemently disagree. To them, if a few days of waiting and watching for a bigger crime doesn't materialize, it's better to take the smaller offense and move on to another target. If that results in a light sentence, as often happens, that's not the end of it.

"We're not too concerned with what they do in court...All we know is that if they let him out again, we'll target him again."

SOURCE: Epstein, A. (1983), "On the hunt for career criminals," *Centurion* 1(6): 23-4; 26.

In each of these programs, police administrators decide to devote resources to the control of specific crimes and criminals, or to the control of crime in areas where they have reason to believe that serious crime is most likely to occur. At the same time, regular police patrol and response to calls for service in the jurisdiction continues. In the departments mentioned, and in others with similar programs, police administrators have at least tacitly decided that some crimes or criminals are more deserving of police attention than others.

Court Programs

The repeat or career criminal is the subject of special treatment in at least two points of the court process: prosecution and sentencing. The goal of these special procedures is to insure the conviction and punishment of offenders posing the greatest threat of future criminality.

Today, many trial jurisdictions have "career-criminal programs." In these programs, the prosecutor's office develops criteria to select cases involving repeat or career criminals. These cases become a priority in the system. Officials try to secure convictions in these cases even when, under normal circumstances, the case might have been dropped. Brosi (1979) explained the justification for these programs:

> Given the disproportionately large share of crime committed by repeat offenders, prosecutors seem justified in structuring their discretion so that an appropriate percentage of time and staff is focused on recidivists, even though this might mean that other cases with as much or more evidence and involving less frequent offenders would have to be rejected or pursued with less than normal intensity.

Box 3.4
Proposed Scoring Criteria for the Selection
of Career Criminals for Special Attention
by Federal Prosecutor

Variable	Points	
Heavy use of alcohol	+ 5	
Heroin use	+10	
Age at time of instant arrest		
Less than 22	+21	
23 – 27	+14	
28 – 32	+ 7	
33 – 37	0	
38 – 42	− 7	
43+	−14	
Length of criminal career		
0-5 years	0	
6-10	1	
11-15	2	
16-20	3	
21+	4	
Arrests during last 5 years		
Crimes of violence	4	per arrest
Crimes against property	3	per arrest
Sale of drugs	4	per arrest
Other offenses	2	per arrest
Longest time served, single term		
1-5 months	4	
6-12	9	
13-24	18	
25-36	27	
37-48	36	
49+	45	
Number probation sentences	1.5	per sentence
Instant offense was crime of violence*	7	
Instant offense was crime labeled "other"**	−18	

Critical Value to Label of Offender
As a Career Criminal:
47 points

*Violent crimes consist mostly of bank robberies, but also include homicide, assault, sexual assault, and kidnapping.

**Other crimes include military violations, probation, parole, weapons and all others except arson, burglary, larceny, auto theft, fraud, forgery, drug sale or possession, and violent crimes.

SOURCE: Forst, B., W. Rhodes, J. Dimm, A. Gelman, & B. Mullin (1983), "Targeting federal resources on recidivists: An empirical view," *Federal Probation* 46(2): 18.

The organization of career criminal prosecution programs differs by jurisdiction. The theory behind the use of these programs is the same as that underlying the law enforcement programs described earlier. If identifiable individuals exist who will be continuing targets of prosecution, it is a wise investment of resources to devote attention to them in the present (INSLAW, 1977:8). That is, it makes sense to devote crime control resources to those cases where the greatest pay-off in crime control can be expected.

Brosi (1979) described career criminal prosecution programs operating in the United States. All but the District of Columbia program used a procedure that assigned one prosecutor to each career criminal case. That prosecutor stayed with that case from arrest through final disposition. The District of Columbia program used one prosecutor to stay with the case from arrest through indictment, and then the case became the responsibility of another prosecutor in the trial division.

Each program established criteria for selecting cases for treatment in the career criminal program. In the District of Columbia, the program, known as "Operation Doorstop," took cases involving those arrested for a crime of violence or a felony while on probation or parole. Those arrested for a crime of violence and possibly subject to pretrial detention also received special attention. The Prosecutor's Repeat Offender Bureau (PROB) in Detroit took cases involving arrests for burglary or violent felonies by those having three prior felony convictions, and arrests of those having a combination of three prior convictions or pending charges. Other jurisdictions developed different methods of selecting cases.

Career criminal prosecution programs in other jurisdictions used a "point" system for selecting cases. Box 3.4 gives an example of one such scoring system. The Indianapolis program assigned points for previous violent and burglary convictions, any felony convictions or arrests, and pending cases. Milwaukee County employed a similar point system, assigning points for prior convictions, current status on bail, probation or parole, and current charges involving injury or weapons. Other jurisdictions target specific crimes, such as burglary or robbery.

In general, these career-criminal prosecution programs have the effect of "flagging" specified cases for special treatment. This results in slightly higher rates of conviction and greatly increased rates of incarceration for those identified as career criminals. In most programs, career-criminal cases are also disposed of more quickly than cases in the regular caseload. Again, prosecutors decide which cases deserve increased attention and investment of limited prosecutorial resources.

Differential handling of career criminals at sentencing has long been a tradition in America. Most states have had habitual offender or recidivist sentencing statutes for decades. These statutes essentially make it criminal and thereby separately punishable for someone to have prior felony convictions. For example, in many states, upon conviction of a third felony offense, one can be tried as an "habitual offender" and receive an extended prison term, even life imprisonment.

More recently, two sentencing "programs" have been receiving increasing attention and support: selective incapacitation and mandatory sentencing. In each, the goal is to control the incidence of either specific crimes, or to lessen the opportunity of specific criminals to commit crime in the future through incarcerating offenders.

Selective incapacitation seeks to identify those offenders who are most likely to commit future crimes. This program reserves incarceration for these habitual offenders (Greenwood, 1982). Research showing that the majority of crimes are committed by a minority of offenders supports the idea that imprisoning those few would result in less crime. Selective incapacitation argues that prison space is

a scarce resource. Thus, reserving space for the most pro-
lific offenders is a wise investment of prison.

Mandatory sentencing is another strategy to control
crime. In practice, mandatory sentencing really means
mandatory incarceration. This approach relies on deterrence and does not target specific criminals, focusing rather
on specific crimes. The examples discussed earlier dealing
with drunk driving and the New York State drug law illustrate the strategy of mandatory sentencing. By "insuring"
that those convicted of specific crimes, which we believe to
be dangerous, will be imprisoned, the hope is that the program will deter those who might consider committing the
offense.

As with several of the career-criminal prosecution programs, sentencing programs either target criminals
(selective incapacitation) or crimes (mandatory sentencing). In both cases, a decision has been made that resources (for example, prison) should be targeted to specific
cases of criminality.

Corrections Programs

Efforts to identify and provide special services and
controls for repeat offenders in correctional settings are
traditional. Recently, however, officials have increased attention to classification of offenders, and have begun development of special "intensive supervision" programs for
probationers and parolees. These efforts try to focus correctional resources on those offenders most in need of such
attention.

Van Voorhis (1986) indicated the importance of classification for the organization and delivery of correctional
services. She suggested that the greatest return on the correctional investment would be obtained through matching
the available services and programs with the needs of individual offenders. The implications of classification deci-

sions for the effectiveness of correctional treatments is only one spur to the increasing emphasis on this process.

In an age of prison crowding, classification has become important as a check on the efficient use of correctional resources. As Clear and Cole (1986:320) noted:

> The prison crowding crisis and litigation challenging existing procedures have forced many correctional systems to reexamine their classification procedures. As space becomes a scarcer and more valuable resource, administrators feel pressured to ensure that it is used as efficiently as possible: that levels of custody are appropriate and that inmates are not held in "oversecure" facilities.

The other side of this, of course, is that certain dangerous prisoners should not be held in "undersecure" facilities. Among other things (such as amenability to certain types of treatment or aptitude for certain job assignments) classification also reflects risk of future criminality. A large part of the classification decision in prisons, or within probation or parole caseloads, reflects a desire to identify and control the repeat offender.

A related development in corrections involves the use of "intensive supervision" with probationers and parolees. In these programs, offenders under community supervision are classified by risk and need. Those posing the greatest risk of future crime and those presenting the greatest needs for service are assigned to special "intensive supervision" caseloads. Box 3.5 shows the major components of intensive probation supervision programs. These caseloads are smaller than the average probation or parole caseload, and the supervising officer is expected to make more contacts with his/her clients each month. Thus, the title "intensive supervision" reflects a greater concentration of traditional probation and parole resources on offenders, who are selected because this greater investment is expected to produce higher returns in the control of future criminality (Travis, 1984; Latessa, 1985).

Box 3.5
Key Features of Intensive Probation Supervision Programs in the United States [1,2]

Program Components	AZ	CA	CO	CT	FL	GA	ID	IL	IN	IO	KS	KY	LO•	MA	MD•	MO	NJ	NV	NY	NC	OH	OK	OR	PA	SC	TE	TX	UT	VA	VT	WI
Objective Risk Assessment	X	X	X	X	X	X	X	X	X	X	X	X	X	X	X	X	X	X	X	X	—	X	X	X	X	X	X	X	X	X	X
Objective Needs Assessment	X	X	X	X	X	X	X	X	X	X	X	X	X	X	X	X	—	X	X	X	—	X	X	X	X	X	X	X	X	X	X
Periodic Record Checks	X	—	X	—	X	X	X	X	X	O	X	X	X	X	—	—	X	—	X	X	—	X	X	—	X	X	—	—	X	X	X
Mandatory Referrals	—	X	X	X	X	X	—	X	X	X	X	X	X	—	—	X	X	X	—	X	—	—	X	U	X	X	—	—	X	X	X
Probation Fees	X	—	—	—	X	X	X	X	—	—	X	—	—	—	—	—	—	X	—	X	—	—	X	—	X	X	X	—	X	—	—
Restitution	X	—	—	—	X	X	X	X	X	O	X	X	X	O	O	O	X	O	—	—	—	—	X	—	O	—	X	X	O	O	—
Community Service	X	X	X	—	X	X	X	X	X	O	O	O	X	O	O	—	X	O	—	X	—	—	X	—	—	X	X	X	—	O	—
Curfew/House Arrest	X	—	X	O	X	X	X	X	X	X	X	X	X	X	X	X	X	—	O	X	—	X	X	—	O	—	—	X	O	O	O
Test Substance Abuse	X	X	X	X	X	X	X	X	X	X	X	X	—	X	X	X	X	X	X	—	X	O	X	X	—	X	X	—	X	O	X
Test Alcohol Abuse	X	X	X	X	X	X	X	X	X	X	X	X	—	X	X	X	X	X	X	—	X	O	X	X	—	X	X	—	X	X	X
Training for PO's	X	X	X	—	X	X	X	—	X	X	—	X	X	X	—	X	—	—	X	X	X	—	—	—	—	X	—	X	X	—	—
Community Sponsors	—	—	—	—	—	—	—	X	—	—	X	X	—	—	—	—	X	—	—	—	—	—	—	—	—	—	—	—	—	—	—
Team Supervision	O	X	X	—	O	X	X	X	X	—	—	—	X	—	X	—	X	X	—	X	X	X	X	—	—	—	—	—	X	—	X
Shock Incarceration	X	O	X	X	—	X	X	—	—	X	X	X	X	—	X	O	X	—	X	X	X	X	X	—	—	—	X	—	—	—	—
Split Sentence	—	—	—	—	—	—	—	—	X	—	X	X	—	—	—	O	X	—	X	X	X	—	—	—	X	—	—	—	—	X	—
Electronic Surveillance	X	—	—	—	X	—	—	—	—	—	—	—	—	—	X	—	X	—	—	—	—	O	—	—	—	—	—	X	—	—	—

Note:

- — = not a program component
- O = optional program component
- U = unclear from program description
- X = component of program model
- • = program in developmental stages, subject to change
- 1 = In the following states there was intercounty variation either in the use of IPS or in the specific program components adopted: Arizona, New York, Ohio, Pennsylvania, and Virginia.
- 2 = We have excluded states in which legislative approval and/or funding was still pending as of 5/15/86. (This includes Delaware, Washington, D.C., Maine, and New Hampshire.)

SOURCE: Byrne, J.M. (1986), "The control controversy: A preliminary examination of intensive probation supervision programs in the United States," *Federal Probation* 50(2): 15.

SUMMARY AND CONCLUSION

This chapter began with a definition of crime and an explanation of the elements of criminal offenses. It then moved to a discussion of criminals and criminal types. Throughout these topics, it was suggested that the variety of behaviors and individuals included in the concepts of crime and criminal, respectively, are exceedingly diverse. The justice system must respond to a large number of widely divergent instances and individuals.

To organize this otherwise cumbersome task, the use of classes of crime or classes of offenders to allocate justice system resources was discussed. The current efforts of police, court and correctional agencies to focus attention and resources on the most serious crimes and criminals were described. Given the broad crime control mandate of the criminal justice system, priorities must be established.

In practice, agents and agencies of criminal justice will respond to more serious crimes and more dangerous offenders before the less serious incidents. For the most part, felonies and repeat offenders are more likely to attract the attention of the justice system and to receive full-scale justice processing than are misdemeanants and first offenders.

REVIEW QUESTIONS

1. Define "crime."

2. What are the elements of a criminal offense?

3. Identify at least two ways in which crimes can be classified according to the level of their severity.

4. Define what is meant by the term "career criminal."

5. Give an example of career-criminal programs in each segment of the criminal justice system (law enforcement, courts and corrections).

REFERENCES

Allen, F.A. (1964), *The Borderland of Criminal Justice.* (Chicago: University of Chicago Press).

American Friends Service Committee (1971), *Struggle for Justice.* (New York: Hill & Wang).

Brosi, K.B. (1979), *A Cross-City Comparison of Felony Case Processing.* (Washington, DC: Institute for Law and Social Research).

Bureau of Justice Statistics (1985), *Special Report: Crime Control and Criminal Records.* (Washington, DC: U.S. Department of Justice).

Chaiken, J.M. & M.R. Chaiken (1982), *Varieties of Criminal Behavior.* (Santa Monica, CA: RAND).

Clear, T.R. & G.F. Cole (1986), *American Corrections.* (Monterey, CA: Brooks-Cole).

Clinard, M.B. & R. Quinney (1983), *Criminal Behavior Systems: A Typology.* (Cincinnati, OH: Anderson).

Cullen, F.T. (1983), *Rethinking Crime and Deviance Theory: The Emergence of a Structuring Tradition.* (Totowa, NJ: Rowman & Allenheld).

Cullen, F.T., B.G. Link & C.W. Polanzi (1982), "The seriousness of crime revisited," *Criminology* 20(1):83-102.

Davis, K.C. (1975), *Police Discretion.* (St. Paul, MN: West).

Fox, V. (1983), *Correctional Institutions.* (Englewood Cliffs, NJ: Prentice-Hall).

Gibbons, D.C. (1973), *Society, Crime, and Criminal Careers, 2nd.* (New York: Prentice Hall).

Greenwood, P.W. (1982), *Selective Incapacitation.* (Santa Monica, CA: RAND).

INSLAW (1977), *Curbing the Repeat Offender: A Strategy for Prosecutors.* (Washington, DC: U.S. Department of Justice).

Krajick, K. (1978), "Does patrol prevent crime?" *Police Magazine* 1(5):1.

Latessa, E.J. (1985), "Community supervision: Research, trends, and innovations," in L.F. Travis, M.D. Schwartz, & T.R. Clear (eds.) *Corrections: An Issues Approach.* (Cincinnati, OH: Anderson):159-67.

Lilly, J.R. & R.A. Ball (1982), "A critical analysis of the changing concept of criminal responsibility," *Criminology* 20(2):169-84.

Miethe, T.D. (1982), "Public concensus on crime seriousness," *Criminology* 20(3-4):515-26.

National Advisory Commission on Criminal Justice Standards and Goals (1973), *A National Strategy to Reduce Crime.* (Washington, DC: U.S. Government Printing Office).

National Institute of Justice (1986), *Research Program Plan: Fiscal Year 1987.* (Washington, DC: U.S. Department of Justice).

Nettler, G. (1982), *Explaining Criminals.* (Cincinnati, OH: Anderson).

Newman, D.J. (1987), *Introduction to Criminal Justice, 3rd.* (New York: Random House).

Newman, G.R. & C. Trilling (1975), "Public perceptions of criminal behavior," *Criminal Justice & Behavior* 2(2):217.

Pate, T. & R.A. Bowers (1976), *Three Approaches to Criminal Apprehension in Kansas City: An Evaluation Report.* (Washington, DC: The Police Foundation).

Schwendinger, H. & J. Schwendinger (1975), "Defenders of order or guardians of human rights?", in I. Taylor, P. Walton, & J. Young (eds.), *Critical Criminology.* (London: Routledge & Kegan Paul): 113-46.

Travis, L.F. (1984), "Intensive supervision in probation and parole" *Corrections Today* 46(4):36-38.

Van Voorhis, P. (1986), "The promise of confronting important gaps between knowledge and applications," First International Conference on Reaffirming Rehabilitation, Alexandria, VA, June, 1986.

Walker, S. (1985), *Sense and Nonsense About Crime: A Policy Guide.* (Monterey, CA: Brooks-Cole).

Warren, M.Q. (1973), "All things being equal..." *Criminal Law Bulletin* 9:482.

4 Counting Crimes and Criminals

If the criminal justice system can be likened to a business, it is a business run by individuals who have no clear understanding of the market, production and distribution process, and customer satisfaction. Not many commercial enterprises could succeed in such a state of ignorance. Yet, the criminal justice system does operate in ignorance. It seems difficult, perhaps impossible, to even keep track of crimes, much less understand their causes and cures.

Lack of knowledge about the types of crimes and criminals is not the only form of ignorance which hinders the criminal justice system in the United States. Not only do we not know very much about the nature of crimes and offenders, we also find difficulty in figuring the numbers of them. For years critics have written about the "dark figure" of crime, that is, the unknown amount of crime which occurs.

The "dark figure" represents crime of which we are ignorant. Like a half-moon where part of the moon is in shadow and we can see only half of the lunar surface, current crime statistics may reveal only half (more or less) of

the actual amount of crime; the remainder is hidden in the
"shadows." It is this crime in the shadow which is the "dark
figure."

The Need for Numbers

At first reaction, we may be tempted to ask, so what?
How important can it be that we do not know how much
crime there really is? Even when we cannot see the full
moon, we know that it is there. Paradoxically, the problem
is that without knowing what is in the shadows, we cannot
know how important is that of which we are ignorant. Old
sayings, such as "Ignorance is bliss," and "What you don't
know can't hurt you," do not always apply. This problem
becomes clearer when we examine the uses to which we put
criminal statistics.

Nettler (1984) listed four reasons for counting crime:

1. description
2. risk assessment
3. program evaluation
4. explanation

Description is exactly what the term implies: painting
an accurate picture of the number and distribution of
criminal offenses. Such information is useful for the allocation of resources. It is used to determine where to concentrate police patrol, or to estimate the number of prosecutors or judges needed. Descriptive measures of crime allow
planners to detect changes in crime patterns over time and
to adjust criminal justice operations.

Risk assessment was discussed earlier, when we examined the differences between ordinary and dangerous
criminals. Accurate data about crime allows us to make estimates about the risks of people becoming offenders, and
of people becoming victims of crime. Not knowing how

much crime actually occurs makes it impossible to predict how much crime is likely to occur. To the degree that the justice process attempts to reduce criminality, lack of knowledge about the actual level of crime hinders our ability to affect future levels.

Program evaluation is an effort that often relies on estimates of a program's effect on crime. In the previous chapter, we discussed several programs aimed at controlling career criminals. Evaluations of these programs each attempted to compare the program's effects on the criminality of offenders with the effects of "normal" criminal justice processing. Should we continue or expand these programs? An informed and cautious response to this question is that we do not know. Assuming a dark figure of crime, there is no way to tell what effect these programs have had on that figure.

Explanation is the most troublesome of all the reasons for accurate numbers about crime and criminals. Why do some people break the law? If we are unaware of many criminal offenses, we only can offer partial explanations. Many people believe that poverty causes crime, and most persons whom we know to have committed crimes can be classified as "poor." A problem arises in that we do not know whether those who commit the dark figure of crime offenses are poor or wealthy. If these unknown offenders are not poor, then poverty only offers an explanation as to the criminality of those whom we can identify (if it is an explanation at all).

We have long recognized the inadequacies of our data about crimes and criminals. Yet, with repeated calls for improvement in the collection and use of statistics on crime, how is it that we have made so little progress? The answer lies within the complex nature of criminal justice in the United States.

Information is gathered by thousands of agencies in thousands of separate jurisdictions. These agencies often use their own definitions of crimes and criminals, and report their data to national centers on a voluntary basis. To further complicate an already complex problem, each agency needs different types of information for its own planning and operation. It is very difficult then to follow cases through the justice process as the police, prosecutor, criminal court and correctional agencies use their own forms to collect that information which is useful to them, with little regard to a system-wide need for information.

A great deal of data is available concerning the number of crimes and criminals, justice agencies and operations of the justice system. Yet, we do not know exactly how much crime exists and where it occurs. The crime problem is one without clearly marked boundaries. The sources of information about crime and criminal justice are of two basic types: *official statistics* and *unofficial statistics*.

OFFICIAL STATISTICS

Official statistics are those that are provided by criminal justice agencies as official records of their activities. The most familiar of all official crime statistics is the Uniform Crime Reports (UCR), published annually by the Federal Bureau of Investigation (FBI) from reports received by the nation's police departments. These data describe the volume of business handled by the law enforcement agencies of the country. The basic statistic of the UCR is "crime known to the police."

Only those offenses detected by the police are crimes known to the police. Should someone steal your wallet and you do not report the theft to the police, the crime is not known to the police and is not counted in the UCR. If you report the theft, or a police officer witnesses the crime, then the offense will be "known to the police." In addition, the police officer decides whether a crime has occurred, and, if so, what crime it was.

In the example above, suppose you report the theft to a police officer, but the officer decides that you are not telling the truth? The officer may decide that your criminal complaint is "unfounded," that is, the officer believes that the crime you reported is not supported by available evidence and, therefore, there is reason to believe that no crime occurred. In this instance, the theft will remain "unknown" to the police because the officer considers your report untrustworthy.

A similar decision is "defounding." In defounding a crime, the officer decides that the offense was less serious than reported. If the criminal stole your wallet by threatening to harm you with a knife, an armed robbery occurred. If the police officer does not believe that you were actually threatened, he or she may simply record a theft of your wallet. In this instance, a crime is known to the police, but it is a crime less serious than that which actually happened.

An English economist, Sir Josiah Stamp, warned of the dangers of official statistics. He stated that, "the government are very keen on amassing statistics. They collect them, raise them to the nth power, take the cube root and prepare wonderful diagrams. But you must never forget that every one of these figures comes in the first instance from the village watchman, who just puts down what he damn pleases."

The UCR

The UCR covers twenty-nine different crimes, including eight crimes known as the "Crime Index." The total number of these eight crimes (which are known to the police) represent the Index of Crime. This total is used to compare levels of crime over time. The eight index offenses are: homicide, forcible rape, robbery, aggravated assault, burglary, larceny-theft, auto theft and arson. Box 4.1 illustrates the crime index for 1987.

Box 4.1
United States Crime Index, 1987

Area	Population¹	Crime Index total	Modified Crime Index total²	Violent crime¹	Property crime¹	Murder and non-negligent man-slaughter	Forcible rape	Robbery	Aggra-vated assault	Burglary	Larceny-theft	Motor vehicle theft	Arson¹
United States Total	243,400,000	13,508,708		1,483,999	12,024,709	20,096	91,111	517,704	855,088	3,236,184	7,499,851	1,288,674	
Rate per 100,000 inhabitants		5,550.0		609.7	4,940.3	8.3	37.4	212.7	351.3	1,329.6	3,081.3	529.4	
Metropolitan Statistical Area	186,637,562												
Area actually reporting⁴	98.1%	11,613,326		1,333,808	10,279,518	17,028	78,454	499,116	739,210	2,738,932	6,346,964	1,193,622	
Estimated totals	100.0%	11,747,875		1,343,765	10,404,110	17,132	79,264	501,347	746,022	2,771,222	6,427,814	1,205,074	
Rate per 100,000 inhabitants		6,294.5		720.0	5,574.5	9.2	42.5	268.6	399.7	1,484.8	3,444.0	645.7	
Other Cities	22,752,410												
Area actually reporting⁴	93.3%	1,039,689		74,045	965,644	960	5,161	10,499	57,425	220,550	702,052	43,042	
Estimated totals	100.0%	1,114,517		79,814	1,034,703	1,032	5,541	11,357	61,884	237,082	751,440	46,181	
Rate per 100,000 inhabitants		4,898.5		350.8	4,547.7	4.5	24.4	49.9	272.0	1,042.0	3,302.7	203.0	
Rural Counties	34,009,028												
Area actually reporting⁴	89.3%	592,456		54,930	537,526	1,720	5,846	4,572	42,792	208,390	294,997	34,139	
Estimated totals	100.0%	646,316		60,420	585,896	1,932	6,306	5,000	47,182	227,880	320,597	37,419	
Rate per 100,000 inhabitants		1,900.4		177.7	1,722.8	5.7	18.5	14.7	138.7	670.1	942.7	110.0	

¹Populations are Bureau of the Census provisional estimates as of July 1, 1987, and are subject to change.
²Although arson data are included in the trend and clearance tables, sufficient data are not available to estimate totals for this offense.
³Violent crimes are offenses of murder, forcible rape, robbery, and aggravated assault. Property crimes are offenses of burglary, larceny-theft, and motor vehicle theft. Data are not included for the property crime of arson.
⁴The percentage representing area actually reporting will not coincide with the ratio between reported and estimated crime totals, since these data represent the sum of the calculations for individual states which have varying populations, portions reporting, and crime rates.

SOURCE: Federal Bureau of Investigation (1988), *Crime in the United States, 1987*. (Washington, DC: U.S. Department of Justice):42.

Participating police agencies voluntarily report data to the FBI. Most police departments (but not all) report to the FBI. The UCR has been published since 1930 (Cole, 1983:10), and thus has provided information on the rate and level of crime in the United States for more than fifty years. Nonetheless, criminologists question the value of the UCR on several grounds (Kleinman & Lukoff, 1981; Menard, 1987).

Criminologists warn that UCR data must be used cautiously. The data are voluntarily reported and reflect different definitions of offenses employed by the multitude of police departments participating. Further, the UCR excludes many types of crimes (such as white-collar crimes), and it is open to police manipulation. The data also mask the actual numbers of offenses and offenders through reporting procedures. For example, if a number of crimes are committed during a single criminal episode (say a bank robber kills a teller, kidnaps a hostage, steals a car for the escape and flees across state lines), only the most serious is counted (in this case, the homicide). Gilbert Geis (1986) also noted that changes in UCR data may reflect police efficiency more than changes in crime.

Other criticisms have been leveled about the reporting of crimes as the "*crime rate*," that is, the number of crimes is reported as a function of population such that:

$$\frac{\text{Crime}}{\text{Total Population}} \quad X \quad 100{,}000 = \text{CRIME RATE}$$

In this way, the index treats crimes such as homicide and theft as equal. Also, until recently, the FBI used the decennial (ten-year) census for the population total. Thus the UCR based the 1969 crime rate on the same population as it did the 1960 rate. This caused an artificial inflation of the crime rate because the actual increase in the population was not reflected in the formula (Eck & Riccio, 1979).

The purpose of the crime rate is to make fairer comparisons between jurisdictions. If we have a city of 100,000 people where 20 murders occurred last year, and a town of 5,000 people where one murder occurred last year, which is safest? The raw numbers indicate that murder is 20 times as likely to occur in the city as in the town. In fact, if you reside in either community, your chances of being a homicide victim are equal. The city has a *homicide rate* of 20 per 100,000 population. The town has a homicide rate of 1 per 5,000 or 20 per 100,000, which is exactly equal to the homicide rate in the city, as the city is twenty times larger than the town in population.

Despite the problems with UCR data, the UCR is still considered an important indicator of the nature and extent of crime in the nation (Hindelang, 1974; Lab & Allen, 1984). The UCR also includes data on the characteristics of persons arrested for crimes and on the numbers of police officers killed and assaulted in the line of duty. As long as the user is aware of the limitations of the UCR and is cautious in its interpretation, it is an important source of information.

Other Official Statistics

Other criminal justice and governmental agencies also collect and publish data that are relevant to measuring crime and criminals in America. A partial listing of such sources includes the Uniform Parole Reports, which gives data on the characteristics and numbers of persons released on parole or returned to prison as parole violators. The Uniform Probation Reports gives similar data for probation. Other sources are the National Prisoner Statistics, which provide the numbers of persons incarcerated in the nation's prisons, and demographic and legal characteristics of those incarcerated. Periodic censuses of the nation's jails also are conducted and reported, as are data on case filings in the courts of America. Still more official data are available regarding the numbers and distribution of juvenile offenders, operations of pre-trial release programs and other aspects of justice processing.

UNOFFICIAL STATISTICS

Recognizing that official statistics tell only part of the story of crime in the United States, criminologists have developed other ways of estimating how much crime occurs and who commits criminal offenses. Two basic sources of crime data (collected without relying upon the official reports of justice agencies) are victim surveys and self-reports. These data reveal that official statistics cover only about half of all crime. They also show that persons arrested for criminal offenses are not representative of all those who commit crimes. To avoid the problems and limitations of official statistics, especially the UCR, researchers developed these other methods of counting crimes and criminals (Salas & Surette, 1984). Each gives a slightly different view of the overall crime picture and thus serves as an aid to understanding the true nature and extent of crime in the United States.

Victim Surveys

In 1965, the National Opinion Research Center of the University of Chicago (NORC) conducted the first survey of crime victims. The researchers used the results to estimate the nature and extent of crime. The President's

Commission on Law Enforcement and Administration of Justice instructed the NORC to conduct a survey of 10,000 households (President's Commission, 1967:96). The survey results indicated that crimes known to the police were only a fraction of all crimes committed.

The NORC survey contacted a spokesperson for each household surveyed and asked if that person, or anyone else residing in the household, had been the victim of certain crimes in the past year. Respondents also were asked whether the crime had been reported to the police and, if not, why it had not been reported. Since the original 1965 survey, similar data have been collected annually by the U.S. Bureau of the Census through the National Crime Survey.

Results of the survey over the years continue to indicate that the UCR data are incomplete. Respondents to victim surveys report that many crimes, especially less serious property crimes and violent crimes among friends and acquaintances, remain unreported to the police. Box 4.2 compares the victim surveys of the National Crime Survey (NCS) with the UCR.

The National Crime Survey asks about the number of times that members of the responding household have been the victims of assault, personal larceny, robbery and forcible rape. It also counts automobile theft, burglary, and household larceny as crimes against households. Similar data are collected from a survey of businesses and counted as burglaries, robberies and thefts against businesses. The data are not directly comparable to the UCR. Nonetheless, the wide gap between the number of victimizations reported in the surveys and the number of crimes reported in the UCR indicates that much more crime occurs than is brought to the attention of the justice system. However, victim survey reports reveal that the types of crimes and their relative numbers are accurately portrayed in the UCR (Hindelang, 1978; Cohen & Lichbach, 1982; Booth et al, 1977).

Box 4.2

**Comparison of the Uniform Crime Reports
with the National Crime Survey**

How do UCR and NCS compare?

	Uniform Crime Reports	National Crime Survey
Offenses measured:	Homicide Rape Robbery (personal and commercial) Assault (aggravated) Burglary (commercial and household) Larceny (commercial and household) Motor vehicle theft Arson	Rape Robbery (personal) Assault (aggravated and simple) Household burglary Larceny (personal and household) Motor vehicle theft
Scope:	Crimes reported to the police in most jurisdictions; considerable flexibility in developing small-area data	Crimes both reported and not reported to police; all data are available for a few large geographic areas
Collection method:	Police department reports to FBI or to centralized State agencies that then report to FBI	Survey interviews; periodically measures the total number of crimes committed by asking a national sample of 49,000 households encompassing 101,000 persons age 12 and over about their experiences as victims of crime during a specified period
Kinds of information:	In addition to offense counts, provides information on crime clearances, persons arrested, persons charged, law enforcement officers killed and assaulted, and characteristics of homicide victims	Provides details about victims (such as age, race, sex, education, income, and whether the victim and offender were related to each other) and about crimes (such as time and place of occurrence, whether or not reported to police, use of weapons, occurrence of injury, and economic consequences)
Sponsor:	Department of Justice Federal Bureau of Investigation	Department of Justice Bureau of Justice Statistics

The portraits of crime from NCS and UCR differ because they serve different purposes and are based on different sources.

These are some of the more important differences in the programs, thought to account for much of the difference in resulting statistics:

- The UCR counts only crimes coming to the attention of the police. The NCS obtains information on both reported and unreported crime, though not necessarily all unreported crime.

- The UCR counts crimes committed against all people and all businesses, organizations, government agencies, and other victims. NCS counts only crimes against persons age 12 or older and against their households.

- The two programs, because they serve different purposes, count crimes differently in some instances. For example, if a criminal robs a victim and steals someone else's car to escape, UCR counts only the robbery, the more serious crime. NCS could count both, one as a personal crime and one as a household crime.

- Each program is subject to a variety of limitations that affect its estimate of crime. For example, an increased willingness by victims to report crimes to police could produce an apparent increase in UCR estimates, even if the "true" amount of crime remained stable. Similarly, the NCS is known to undercount crimes committed by persons related to the victim, specifically domestic violence. The result of these limitations, some of which result in overcounting crime while others result in undercounting it, serve to create differences in the estimates that the two programs produce.

SOURCE: *Report to the Nation on Crime and Justice, Second Edition.* (Washington, DC: U.S. Department of Justice, 1988):11.

That is, while victim surveys and the UCR differ over the absolute number of crimes committed, their respective findings are similar in other regards. Both show similar relative proportions of crime which consist of burglaries, or robberies, and both have similar findings as to the location of crimes (urban, lower classes, etc.). Thus, UCR data may underestimate the amount of crime, but it may accurately reflect the types of crimes committed and where and when criminal offenses are likely to occur.

In addition to the National Crime Survey, researchers have adopted the victim survey to measure the level and extent of crime for other purposes. While the NCS allows us to compare national victim survey results with the UCR, the technique of surveying crime victims is useful for any measure of changes in crime. In addition to official police reports, researchers have conducted victim surveys in evaluations of several programs. The victim survey has become an important tool in studying crime.

Victim surveys, too, have their limitations (O'Brien, 1986). It has been suggested that the major problems may revolve around what are known as "telescoping" and "forgetting." The interviewer asks the respondent if anyone in the household has been the victim of a particular crime in the past six months. In telescoping, the respondent errs by including an offense which may have occurred seven months ago, thereby "telescoping" it into the covered time period. "Forgetting," as the name suggests, is when the respondent forgets about a crime that occurred in the period (Schneider & Sumi, 1981). In addition, it is always possible when interviewing a person that, for whatever reason, the person is not telling the truth in answering the questions.

Another limitation on victim surveys is that many crimes may have gone unnoticed by the respondent or unreported to him. The NCS interviewer relies on that one individual to have knowledge of the criminal victimizations experienced by the entire household. Finally, certain offenses are not covered in the victim surveys. For example, the National Crime Survey only asks about a small number of offenses, and it is not possible to gather data about homicide, for example, from the victims of the crime.

Self-Reports

Both the UCR and victim surveys attempt to describe criminal offenders. The FBI reports the characteristics of persons arrested for crimes, and thereby provides descriptions of those persons who have been officially recognized as probably having committed crimes. The respondents to victim surveys are asked to describe the offenders involved, if possible. These data provide a description of criminal offenders as seen by the victims of crime. Both efforts at describing criminal offenders are severely limited. Additionally, although there is a fair degree of agreement between victim survey and UCR data, it is possible that both measures do not accurately reflect all crime. Thus a third method of counting crimes has been employed: surveys of criminal offenders.

Self-report studies attempt to measure the amount of crime committed and to describe the characteristics of criminal offenders by asking people if they have committed offenses. In these studies, researchers ask a sample of the public if they have committed any crimes. This type of crime measure yields information on the types of persons likely to commit crimes as well as another estimate of the amount of crime which is committed each year.

Traditionally, self-report studies have been conducted with juvenile populations. As such, the studies frequently include questions about behaviors which would not necessarily be crimes if committed by adults. For example, disobeying teachers or parents, and skipping classes are "delinquent" acts for those with the status of juvenile, but such acts are not crimes for adults. Such "status offenses" included in self-report surveys cloud the issue of how much crime is committed, and by whom (Hood & Sparks, 1970).

These studies have other limitations. They share the problems of telescoping and forgetting, which afflict victim surveys. It is also difficult to tell whether respondents are telling the truth. There is common-sense reason to believe that some may exaggerate to make themselves appear to be notorious, and that some will be reticent, fearing that disclosure of their criminality will lead to punishment. When researchers have compared reported crimes and arrests with official records, however, respondents were generally found to be telling the truth (Cantner, 1982; Lab & Allen, 1984; but also see Nettler, 1984).

Self-report studies indicate that almost everyone will admit to having violated some criminal law. The most important finding of self-report studies is not who does or does not break the law, but rather how often crimes are committed and how serious are those violations. Institutionalized populations of delinquents or adult criminals report more frequent and more serious law violations than do "free citizens." Males report more criminal activity than females; blacks report more often and more serious offenses than whites. In general, with the exception that self-reports indicate that everyone probably breaks some law, the findings of these studies echo those of victim surveys and official reports.

Summary of Crime Statistics

While each of these ways of counting crimes and criminals uses different means of gathering data and collects information from different sources, in total, the "picture" each paints of crime is generally consistent (Nettler, 1984:98-156). Absolute numbers may vary (for instance, victim surveys may show much more crime than police reports), but the relative frequency of crimes (more thefts than robberies, more robberies than assaults, more assaults than rapes) reported by all three procedures is similar.

Where these three research methods differ is in the picture they paint of offenders. In a comparison of self-report, victim survey and arrest data, Hindelang (1978) noted that self-report studies show little difference between race and offense behavior while the other two measures are in general agreement that blacks are more likely to be offenders. Self-report studies also show little difference between social classes in likelihood of engaging in crime. Both upper and lower class respondents admit to committing criminal offenses. However, lower-class youths are more likely to commit crimes more frequently and to commit more serious crimes than middle- or upper-class youths (Williams & Gold, 1972).

One point, which is apparent (assuming that victim and self-report measures are accurate), is that persons arrested and therefore subjected to justice system processing are not representative of the general population (O'Brien, 1985). The poor, urban dwellers and minority-group members are far more likely to be arrested and processed than their numbers in the population suggest. Also, females are less likely to become involved in the justice process than the number of females engaged in crime would indicate (Wolfe, Cullen & Cullen, 1984).

One of the questions which has been raised in response to these findings concerns the fairness of the justice process. If nearly everyone admits to committing some crimes, why is it that blacks and the poor are most often arrested, convicted and incarcerated? Why are women less likely to be arrested and convicted for crimes than are men? Is the justice system racist, sexist, and prejudiced against the poor? In short, the evidence of differential treatment of certain classes of the population has led some observers to suggest that the justice system is discriminatory.

DISCRIMINATION
IN THE JUSTICE SYSTEM

The data suggest that the justice process appears to identify and select certain offenders for processing in a manner that yields a reflection of their relative involvement in crime. Indeed, some have argued that the justice process is discriminatory and repressive because it differentially selects and processes members of disadvantaged groups, such as youth, blacks and other minorities, and the poor and urban residents (Petersilia, 1983). Others suggest that the justice system is sexist because it does not subject females to equal treatment as offenders (Visher, 1983). On the basis of the data presented in Box 4.3, these criticisms seem well-founded. Yet, there are some other possible explanations.

Recall that the justice system exists in an ideological environment which contains our society's values and biases. Differences are more understandable between victim and self-report surveys' conclusions as to who are criminals and who actually is apprehended and processed through the justice system. Females are less likely to engage in most crimes than are males, partly because of socially defined opportunities for women (both criminal and non-criminal). Additionally, the types of offenses for which most women are apprehended, and in which most women appear to engage, are less serious and less threatening than are those dominated by males. We are far more likely to fully process robbers, rapists and assaulters than we are prostitutes, thieves and drug offenders. Even if they are aware of the relatively large number of female offenders, agents of the justice system are likely to concentrate their resources on the more serious offenses. Until there are greater numbers of female offenders engaged in homicide, rape and robbery, it is not possible accurately to assess the extent of the sexism and paternalism in operation in the justice system.

Box 4.3
Evidence of Possible Discrimination
in Criminal Justice Processing of
Arrestees by Sex, Race, Ethnic Origin, and Age

| | U.S. population 1980 | Index crime arrestees | | 1981 Convicted jail inmates | State prison inmates | Federal prison inmates |
		Violent	Property			
	226,545,805	464,826	1,828,928	91,411	340,639	28,133
Sex						
Male	49%	90%	79%	94%	96%	94%
Female	51	10	21	6	4	6
Race						
White	86	53	67	58	52	63
Black	12	46	31	40	47	35
Other	2	1	2	2	1	2
Ethnic origin						
Hispanic	6	12	10	10	9	16
Non-Hispanic	94	88	90	90	91	84
Age						
Under 15	23	5	14	*	0	0
15–19	9	25	36	14	7	0
20–29	18	42	31	53	56	34
30–39	14	17	11	19	25	40
40–49	10	7	4	9	8	17
50–59	10	3	2	4	3	7
60+	16	1	2	1	1	2

*Less than 0.5%.

SOURCE: Bureau of Justice Statistics (1983) *Report to the Nation on Crime and Justice: The Data.* (Washington, DC: Bureau of Justice Statistics):31.

As for the disparities between those arrested for crime and those who report having committed crimes (or whom victims report having seen commit crimes), the explanation is equally plausible. Research has documented that minority-group members are likely to engage in more serious crimes over a longer period of time than are white offenders. Thus, the arrest statistics will reflect the increased probability of being caught, which is a result of the greater frequency of criminal conduct. The concentration of justice system resources on the more serious offenses also produces disproportionate numbers of arrests of minority-group members as compared to the numbers of whites arrested.

Further, the greater numbers of youths in arrest statistics reflects the fact that crime is a young person's game. The idleness, good physical condition and lack of responsibilities which many youths enjoy may create special opportunities for them to commit crime. As one who engages in crime grows older, she or he generally risks longer prison terms as an habitual offender. Giving longer terms to older offenders means they are less likely to have the opportunities to commit crimes which are available to the young. Finally, in a "Catch-22" fashion, the police actually are more likely to look for crimes among the young precisely because so many of the young have been found to be engaged in crime.

Similar reasoning applies to members of minority groups. Idleness (even if forced by unemployment) allows more time for crime and subjects people to greater police scrutiny. However, the greatest factor would appear to be urbanism. Most arrests are of young, urban offenders. Minority groups tend to be concentrated most greatly in the cities of America. Simply put, both the police and young, minority males are overrepresented in the cities (Swanson, 1981). The justice system statistics reflect the organization, both social and geographical, of our society.

In rural and suburban areas, the population is more dispersed and there are fewer police officers. It is more difficult for police to observe crimes and to respond quickly to reports of crime. Also, in smaller communities, more informal mechanisms of social control are available. People

are less frequently strangers to one another and can, therefore, resolve differences more easily without involving the
police. It is more likely that disputes will be defined as
"personal" and not requiring police intervention.

OTHER MEASURES OF CRIME
AND CRIMINAL JUSTICE

Researchers have used several other methods to measure crime and study the criminal justice process. Information gathered from *cohort studies* and *observations* help to
better describe and explain the operations of the criminal
justice process and the nature and extent of crime.

Cohort studies begin with an identifiable group (or
"cohort") and trace the group's interaction with the justice
system over a period of time. Individuals studied in such
research are members of a cohort. The cohort is a collection of all persons sharing a common selection characteristic. Thus, a cohort might be all entering freshmen at a university, or all of those persons married in a given year. For
criminal justice research, the selection criterion normally
relates to a justice system decision, such as all those arrested in a given time period, or to an age limit, such as all
those born in a specified year.

The most famous cohort study selected cases by speci-
fying all males born in Philadelphia in the year 1948.
Delinquency in a Birth Cohort (Wolfgang, et al, 1978) was
the report of a study designed to examine the criminal careers of youth. All males born in 1948 were tracked for a
twenty-year period to determine which of them were arrested, tried and sentenced for delinquent behavior. Additionally, the distribution of delinquent offenses among the
cohort was studied, as were characteristics of individuals
most often involved in delinquent behavior.

This study allowed the researchers to estimate the proportion of youths that would become entangled in the juvenile justice process, how serious the youths' misbehavior would be, and who among them were most likely to be delinquent. Similar cohort analyses of persons arrested for crime could be used to estimate how the justice system processes cases from arrest to final disposition. Such data would be invaluable to an understanding of the justice process.

The problem with cohort studies is one of expense. By definition, most cohort studies must be extensive, that is, they involve large numbers of cases followed over a period of several years.

For *Delinquency in a Birth Cohort*, the researchers actually identified their cohort in 1976, and backtracked through official records to estimate the subjects' involvement in juvenile delinquency. A similar study for those born in 1988 could not be completed until 2008. Despite this limitation, cohort studies allow us to examine the operations of criminal justice agencies in a broader context than is normally possible. Cohort studies provide an estimate of the distribution of crime across an entire population.

Observations, as the term implies, involve researchers watching the behavior of criminals, agents of the justice system, or other samples of people. The American Bar Foundation series, mentioned in Chapter 1, which reported observations of police, prosecutors, judges and correctional personnel at the investigation, arrest, conviction, and sentencing decisions is one example of such studies. Other observation studies have been conducted which seek to determine when people break the law, when they report lawbreaking, what factors justice system agents consider in their decision-making, and how cases move from one stage of the justice process to the next.

Like cohort studies, observational methods are fairly expensive to use and, thus, often result in limited data confined to one location, or in a few decisions rather than national, systemwide descriptions. These data, however, provide a different perspective from which to view crime and criminal justice, giving us a better feel for the reasons behind decisions and behaviors.

DESCRIBING THE JUSTICE SYSTEM

Counting the number of crimes and criminals yields an estimate of the volume of business conducted by the criminal justice system. Other data are available which lend insight into the complex operations of criminal justice in the United States. Statistics which detail the numbers of persons arrested, prosecuted, tried, convicted, sentenced, incarcerated or placed under community supervision, released and discharged describe the workings of the system.

Ideally, data obtained from all of the methods discussed above would be available for answering whatever questions we might have about crime and criminal justice. Unfortunately, such data (at least on a national level) are not always available, and the student of criminal justice is forced to rely upon limited information, or to make inferences from what information can be obtained.

One fact readily apparent in an overview of these data is that the criminal justice system operates like a giant sieve. It continuously filters the huge volume of crimes and criminals to the relatively small number of offenders who are incarcerated in the nation's prisons. By beginning with crimes known to the police and then using different data sources to track arrests, prosecutions, convictions and sentences, it is possible (as is illustrated in Box 4.4) to observe this "funneling" effect.

The flow-chart of the justice system presented in Chapter 1 (Box 1.7) is drawn in scale to the volume of cases involved. It is clear that the starting point, Crime & Law, is much wider (containing many more cases) than any of the later points. As one reads along the diagram from crime through police, courts and correctional processing to discharge, the volume of cases becomes progressively smaller.

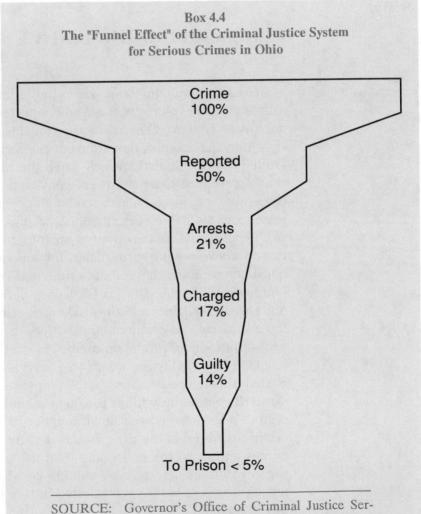

Box 4.4
The "Funnel Effect" of the Criminal Justice System
for Serious Crimes in Ohio

Crime
100%

Reported
50%

Arrests
21%

Charged
17%

Guilty
14%

To Prison < 5%

SOURCE: Governor's Office of Criminal Justice Services (1987), *The State of Crime and Criminal Justice in Ohio*. (Columbus, OH: Governor's Office of Criminal Justice Services). Figure is derived from data and text presented on pages 30-36.

At each successive stage, the less serious offenses and less dangerous offenders are diverted from the justice system. "Weak cases," those in which the evidence against the offender is less complete or less compelling, are also dropped. Some accused offenders who are innocent are removed from the process. In the end, it is a very select group which is subjected to the full force of the criminal law.

From this perspective, it is clear that crime does indeed pay, at least in practice. The chances of going to prison for a criminal act are slim (except regarding certain criminal acts, such as homicide, which have higher risks of imprisonment). It may be that we have too many criminals for the justice system to accommodate, and that this selection process is required so that the entire justice system does not collapse under the number of cases. This is the argument most commonly raised in support of such practices as plea bargaining: that the courts could not handle the volume of criminal trials if bargaining were abolished. It is in the close observation of the filtering process that we begin to understand our society's crime control priorities. It is here, too, that we see most clearly the systemic nature of the criminal justice process.

The next section of the book is dedicated to a more in-depth examination of the practices of the agents and agencies of the justice system. In this examination, we will identify which factors seem to be most important in determining which cases will be retained in the system and which ones will be diverted.

REVIEW QUESTIONS

1. What is meant by the "dark figure" of crime?

2. Give four reasons for counting crime.

3. What are "official statistics"? Give an example of one.

4. Define the terms "unfounding" and "defounding."

5. Explain how to calculate a "crime rate." What does the term mean?

6. Describe two types of "unofficial" crime statistics.

7. What do the data reveal about discrimination in the criminal justice system?

8. Describe "cohort" and "observation" studies of crime and criminal justice.

9. Explain how it can be said that the criminal justice system operates like a "funnel."

REFERENCES

Booth, A., D.R. Johnson, & H.M. Choldin (1977), "Correlates of city crime rates: Victimization surveys versus official statistics," *Social Problems* 25:187-97.

Cantner, R.J. (1982), "Sex differences in self-report delinquency," *Criminology* 20(3-4):373-93.

Cohen, L.J. & M. Lichbach (1982), "Alternative measures of crime: A statistical evaluation," *Sociological Quarterly* 23:253-66.

Cole, G. (1983), *The American System of Criminal Justice, 3rd.* (Monterey, CA: Brooks-Cole).

Eck, J.E. & L.J. Riccio (1979), "Relationship between reported crime rates and victimization survey results: An empirical and analytical study," *Journal of Criminal Justice* 7(4):293-308.

Geis, G. (1986) "On the declining crime rate: An exegetic conference report," *Criminal Justice Policy Review* 1(1):16-36.

Hindelang, M.J. (1978), "Race and involvement in crimes," *American Sociological Review* 43(1):93-109.

Hindelang, M.J. (1974), "The Uniform Crime Reports revisited," *Journal of Criminal Justice* 2(1):1-17.

Hood, R. & R. Sparks (1970), *Key issues in criminology.* (London: World University Library).

Kleinman, P.H. & I.F. Lukoff (1981) "Official crime data: Lag in recording time as a threat to validity," *Criminology* 20(2):169-84.

Lab, S.P. & R.B. Allen (1984), "Self report and official measures: A further examination of the validity issue," *Journal of Criminal Justice* 12(5):445-56.

Menard, S. (1987), "Short-term trends in crime and delinquency: A comparison of UCR, NCS and self-report data," *Justice Quarterly* 4(3):455-74.

Nettler, G. (1984), *Explaining Crime, 3rd.* (New York: McGraw-Hill).

O'Brien, R. (1985), *Crime and Victimization Data.* (Beverly Hills, CA: Sage).

O'Brien, R. (1986), "Rare events, sample size, and statistical problems in the analysis of NCS city surveys," *Journal of Criminal Justice* 14(5):441-48.

Petersilia, J. (1983), *Racial Disparities in the Criminal Justice System.* (Santa Monica, CA: RAND).

President's Commission on Law Enforcement and Administration of Justice (1967), *The Challenge of Crime in a Free Society.* (Washington, DC: U.S. Government Printing Office).

Salas, L. & R. Surette (1984), "The historical roots and development of criminological statistics," *Journal of Criminal Justice* 12(5):457-66.

Schneider, A.L. & D. Sumi (1981), "Patterns of forgetting and telescoping: An analysis of LEAA survey victimization data," *Criminology* 23(1):41-50.

Swanson, C.R. (1981), "Rural and agricultural crime," *Journal of Criminal Justice* 9(1):19-28.

Visher, C.A. (1983), "Gender, police arrest decisions and notions of chivalry," *Criminology* 21(1):5-28.

Williams, J. & M. Gold (1972), "From delinquent behavior to official delinquency," *Social Problems* 20:209-28.

Wolfe, N.T., F.T. Cullen, & J.B. Cullen (1984), "Describing the female offender: A note on the demographics of arrest," *Journal of Criminal Justice* 12(5):483-92.

Wolfgang, M.E., R.M. Figlio, & T. Sellin (1978), *Delinquency in a Birth Cohort.* (Chicago: University of Chicago Press).

Command inspection of the Berkeley Police Department circa 1929. Chief August Vollmer is shown second from left.

5   Police and Policing

There are nearly 20,000 police agencies in the United States, according to the available data (Walker, 1983:31), but even this number is not certain. A variety of federal, state, municipal, special jurisdiction (housing authority, transit authority, etc.) and private agencies provides law enforcement services. The Bureau of Justice Statistics (1989) identified nearly 12,000 local agencies alone. The President's Commission on Law Enforcement and Administration of Justice estimated more than 40,000 police agencies existed in 1967 (Task Force Report: *Police*, 1967).

Law enforcement agencies provide a variety of services to the communities they serve, ranging from traveler's aid through ambulance service. Yet, we continue to think of them as "law enforcement." Indeed, enforcing criminal laws is, at best, a part-time activity for most police departments and police officers. The police are what James Q. Wilson (1968) called the "agency of last resort." While we must focus upon the law enforcing duties of police agencies because of our interest in criminal justice, it is also important to note the non-enforcement demands placed on police.

Because police are available twenty-four hours each day, are mobile, and carry authority, we call upon them to resolve many issues and problems. Most of these are not, strictly speaking, law enforcement in nature (Kennedy, 1983). The principal task of a police agency is best described as "order maintenance." The peace-keeping function of police is far more important than the law enforcement function. Law enforcement is only a small part of "order maintenance" (Eck & Spelman, 1987).

The criminal law is only one of many tools available to police officers and police agencies in their efforts to keep peace in our communities. The police are responsible for dealing with stray children and dogs, lost travelers, injured persons, stranded motorists, traffic accidents, parades, domestic disputes, and crime. It seems that almost any disruptive event can be resolved by "calling the cops" (Bittner, 1970). In many cases, people have reported fires to the police first, rather than to the fire department. The police are often called to deal with abandoned cars, but the reason they are called is not because the car may have been involved in a crime. People call the police because the police are the first agency which comes to mind.

Given the scope of police responsibilities (some assigned, some assumed, and some simply evolved), it is clear that law enforcement is only a small part of police duties. Studies of police tasks have revealed that actual crimes consume a small portion of police resources and comprise a small percentage of police tasks (Wilson, 1968; Webster, 1970). Depending upon the definitions used by the researchers, the majority of police time is devoted to service calls and paperwork. Nonetheless, the public, the media and the police themselves continue to define policing as principally crime fighting (Manning, 1978). This definition of the police as "crime fighters" developed historically as a response to difficulties encountered in the police role.

THE DEVELOPMENT
OF AMERICAN POLICING

The idea of police controlling the behavior of individuals is a relatively recent addition to society. The American colonists did not employ police and no police forces were created in the United States until the 1840s. In colonial times, law enforcement was the duty of every citizen, and no specialized occupational group was given a mandate to insure public order. As with so much of our justice system, the origins of public police can be traced to our English tradition.

Law Enforcement in England

The English had no specialized police force or public office charged with maintaining public order until after the Norman conquest in 1066. At that time, the Normans, having gained control over England and occupying a hostile population, created a centralized governmental structure based on feudalism. High-ranking officers and noblemen of William the Conqueror's army were given control of large parcels of England. These noblemen were expected to provide a percentage of the production from these lands to the king, as taxes, and to supply soldiers in time of war. They also were required to obey the commands of the king, and to ensure the King's Peace in their lands.

To accomplish this administrative task, these nobles further subdivided their lands to lesser officers and noblemen and required them to remit a portion of their profits and to supply a number of soldiers when necessary. The subdivision continued, with each successive rank being required to pay a larger portion of taxes, but supply a smaller number of soldiers. The increased taxes represented the need to meet the demands of the king and the higher nobility for income. The lower number of soldiers reflected the increased number of "officers" who were granted lands. If a Duke promised to provide 10,000 soldiers and five percent of profits to the king, this could be accomplished by dividing the land among ten barons. Each Baron might be required to provide 1,000 soldiers (10,000 total) and eight percent of profits (5% for the king, and 3% for the Duke). Feudalism provided a structure for government in medieval times.

Essentially rural and agrarian, England was divided into ten family units called "tythings." Each tything was responsible for its own tax collection and order maintenance. With the advent of Norman control, new units of 100 families, called "Shires," were created. Being an occupied country, maintenance of the Norman king's law was problematic, and tax collection difficult. The office of "Shire Reeve" was created.

The Shire Reeve was responsible for the collection of taxes and the maintenance of the King's Peace. The Reeve was elected from a list of candidates approved by the Lord of the Manor. Over time, the Shire Reeve became known as the "Sheriff." The resistance of the English to this new structure can be seen in the tales of Robin Hood, whose nemesis was the "Sheriff of Nottingham."

Each manor also operated a manorial court. To assist in the day-to-day operation of the court functions, the office of constable was created. The Lord of the Manor selected the constable from qualified property holders. The constable performed the clerical duties of the court, and housed prisoners awaiting trial. Over time, these functions were expanded to include general "peacekeeping."

As villages and towns developed, this rural order-maintenance apparatus proved to be inadequate to the task of law enforcement in congested areas. Traditionally, every citizen was responsible for order maintenance. Drawing on this tradition, town constables were empowered to draft citizens for a "watch" system. In this system, citizens were required to provide unpaid watchman service (typically at night) to patrol for fires and breaches of the peace. As towns grew larger and cities developed, it became increasingly difficult to find either adequate watchmen or persons willing to take the role of constable.

By the early 1800s, English towns and cities were crowded and unruly. The nobility and wealthy citizens traveled with hired guards (footmen) and avoided the more dangerous sections of town. Several experiments with paid watches, "private" law enforcement, and rejuvenated constabulary offices all failed to adequately provide for order maintenance. There was clearly a need to create a specialized body charged with maintaining the peace.

During the 1820s, Sir Robert Peel, British Home Secretary, proposed to create a police force for England. This force would be comprised of paid, uniformed, armed, disciplined officers whose job would be the enforcement of the law and the maintenance of order. Parliament, fearing the effects of such an armed force on the "rights of Englishmen," resisted Peel's idea. Peel revised his proposal and, in 1829, Parliament agreed to "experiment" with a Metropolitan Police Force in London. This force would not be armed, but in every other respect, it would mirror Peel's original plan. If it worked in London, the idea might be expanded. The Metropolitan Police Force of London, created in 1829, was the first modern police force.

The Colonial and Early American Experience

As in many other areas of social life, the colonists relied upon their traditions and experience. As in England, colonial villages and towns normally had the offices of Constable and/or Sheriff. The duties of each were similar to those of its English counterpart (Johnson, 1988). As towns and cities grew, the Americans experimented with watch systems. In time it became clear that these less formal systems for order maintenance were inadequate to the task.

Unlike England, however, there was no strong central government in America, and weapons and violence were more commonplace in the New World. While the same general pattern of development was followed in America, these differences would result in a modification of the English police structure.

By the 1840s, waves of immigrants began arriving on the shores of America, and industrialization was beginning. The population of American cities swelled, and the cities became unruly and dangerous places. The urban poor, and especially the immigrants, came to be defined as pre-revolutionary by the upper and middle classes. It became common to speak of the immigrant poor in America's congested cities as the "dangerous classes."

To control these "dangerous" people, and to bring order and stability to the cities, Americans began to consider the creation of police forces. On many occasions, the militia, or the army, was used to quell riots or to break strikes (and would still be used for these purposes in the future), but these were extraordinary circumstances. Many people believed a more permanent solution to the problems of day-to-day disorder was required.

Knowing about the English experiments and developments, many reformers began to advocate the creation of police forces for the cities. In 1844, New York City created a police force modeled after the Metropolitan Police of London, but with several significant differences (Johnson, 1988:178-81). The New York City Police were appointed by the mayor from candidates recommended by political ward leaders. The police force was to be administered by a Board of Police Commissioners. Each officer was to be a resident of the ward in which he would work; these officers objected to wearing uniforms and being unarmed.

The New York City Police were locally created and funded. This new American police department was characterized by a weak central administration, municipal organization and direct political involvement. Over the years, the issues of uniforms and arms were resolved, so that municipal police were both armed and uniformed. Each city created its own police force and organizational structure. In the next ten years, the New York City police were followed by the creation of police in most major American cities (See Box 5.1).

Box 5.1
Early Milestones in American Law Enforcement

1829   Metropolitan Police created in London, England.
1838   Boston Police created with 9 officers.
1844   New York City Police created with 800 officers.
1852   Cincinnati & New Orleans Police created.
1854   Philadelphia & Boston Police created.
1855   Chicago Police created.
1857   Baltimore Police created.
1908   Bureau of Investigation (later FBI) created.
1924   J. Edgar Hoover named Director of FBI.
1930   Uniform Crime Reports first published.
1931   Police Science Program started at San Jose State University
1935   FBI National Police Academy opened.

The American Police

As in New York, early police departments in America were not centrally organized and did not have strong leadership. This was in response to a fear of the effect of police on the exercise of rights by individuals, similar to the English Parliament's fears regarding the Metropolitan Police. Rather, it was more common to employ a "police commission" to govern the department so that no single individual would gain too much power. With the growth of political machines in the cities, however, this weak administrative structure left city police forces open to manipulation and corruption.

The principal duty of the police initially was to maintain order. The success of a police officer was most easily established by the absence of disorder on his patrol beat. That officers were recruited from the neighborhoods they were to patrol meant that officers tolerated much "deviance," which was found frightening by the upper and middle classes who created the departments. Drinking, for example, was viewed with suspicion by many city leaders, yet tolerated (even shared) by many officers. The failure of the police to remain free of political influence and corruption, coupled with neighborhood enforcement styles, led to an early call to reform the police.

In the latter part of the nineteenth century, a reform effort was mounted to enhance police accountability and to professionalize the police. August Vollmer, perhaps the foremost proponent of police professionalism, led the reform. Vollmer sought higher personnel standards and stronger police leadership. The push for police professionalism continued well into the twentieth century and is still felt (Vogel & Adams, 1983). The police were given strong central administration and a clear "crime control" mandate. The focus on law enforcement was believed to avoid the difficulties which accompanied the more general role of maintaining order (Johnson, 1981).

With the crime control mandate came an equally important definition of the police as serving a crime prevention function. The police were not only expected to detect and apprehend offenders, but the police presence on the streets of a city was expected to deter others from committing crimes. From this came the tradition of preventive patrol. The uniformed officer on patrol would not only be better able to detect crime, but his presence would prevent crime as well. While the technology may have changed from foot patrol to motorized patrol (and perhaps back again), the idea is essentially the same.

The tradition of police as peacekeepers (order maintenance), however, has remained. While the definition of the police became (and remains) one of a crime control force, the functions of a modern police department are far broader. The police are the most visible representatives of government in a community, and they represent the legitimate authority of the law. As they are always (theoretically) present and available, the police have become ombudsman for all social and legal problems.

THE FUNCTIONS OF POLICE

The role of the police has been broadly classified into three categories. Wilson (1968) suggested that the police are responsible for three types of activities: law enforcement, order maintenance and service. Further, he argued that, of the three, order maintenance is at once both the most important and the most troublesome. Order maintenance is the main purpose of police. If they do nothing else, the police must insure that the citizens can go about their daily business safely and efficiently.

Order maintenance activities include settling disputes, dispersing crowds, keeping sidewalks and streets clear and traffic flowing smoothly, and other important, but often noncriminal activities. These are troublesome responsibilities because the officer often must operate in the gray areas of the law and must choose whether to intervene, and, if so, how and with whom (Eck & Spelman, 1987).

The service functions of police have evolved over time out of necessity. In part because they are available, police are called upon to provide a variety of services from giving directions to travelers to finding missing children. In part because of a potential link to criminal behavior, police also investigate traffic accidents, provide first aid to victims and, often, transport the injured to medical facilities. Whatever

the reasons, modern police provide a wide variety of services to the community which do not strictly conform to the
role of crime control (Bittner, 1970; Das, 1987).

Law enforcement activities are those which relate directly to the detection and apprehension of criminal offenders. Responding to alarms and citizen complaints of
crime, investigating suspicious persons and circumstances,
and arresting suspected offenders are all law enforcement
activities. While these duties do not comprise the bulk of
police tasks, it is the crime control function of the police
which will be our focus. Before turning our attention to the
crime control activities of the police, however, we must
more fully explore the diverse obligations of contemporary
police.

The Police as a Human Services Agency

To understand the role of the police, it is helpful to describe what it is that the police do. Ideally perhaps, it
would be possible to determine what it is that police are
supposed to do and, from that, develop a definition of the
police role. The problem is that it is not clear what it is
that we want the police to do. Walker (1983:57) observed
that "the police role has evolved without any rational planning. Historically, the police acquired responsibilities because no other agency existed to perform particular tasks.
Today, the police role is shaped by a variety of social, political, legal and administrative factors."

Whatever it is that the police do, research shows that
most of what they do is *not* criminal law enforcement. Box
5.2 displays the results of several analyses of police work.
While the exact percentages for each category differ, in all
cases, the majority of police resources were not spent on
enforcing the criminal laws. Rather, administrative tasks
and service provision are important components of the police task, and thus, the police role.

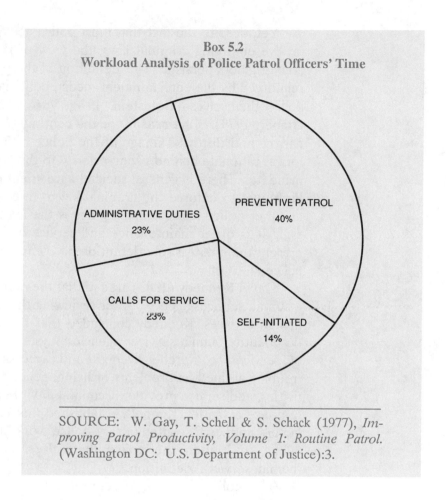

Box 5.2
Workload Analysis of Police Patrol Officers' Time

PREVENTIVE PATROL
40%

ADMINISTRATIVE DUTIES
23%

CALLS FOR SERVICE
23%

SELF-INITIATED
14%

SOURCE: W. Gay, T. Schell & S. Schack (1977), *Improving Patrol Productivity, Volume 1: Routine Patrol.* (Washington DC: U.S. Department of Justice):3.

Many of the services provided by police departments to citizens have already been identified. If you think of your own interactions with the police over the course of your lifetime, how often have you dealt with police officers in non-law enforcement situations? The investigation of traffic accidents and crowd control at parades, demonstrations, sporting events, and the like, are important, non-law enforcement services provided by the police.

Yet, despite the fact that most police activities do not involve enforcing criminal laws, the view of the police as crime fighters persists. This definition of the police role is reinforced by the entertainment media, politicians, and the police themselves (Goldstein, 1978; Van Maanen, 1978; Graber, 1979). One reason for the continuation of such a narrow and distorted image of the police reflects the historical rationale behind giving priority to the crime control mandate. There is general societal agreement that the police ought to enforce the criminal laws. In comparison to all other police tasks, crime control is the least controversial. It is order maintenance and service activities which present the greatest role definition problems for American police.

David Kennedy (1983) argued that the police qualify as a human services agency. After reviewing the literature on human services, Kennedy concluded that five characteristics identify human services agencies: systemic integration of services, comprehensiveness and accessibility, client troubles defined as problems in living, generic helping activities, and service provider accountability. In an overview of police activities, Kennedy established that each of these factors applies to contemporary police work, although the public, and often the police themselves, object to the "human services" definition.

The police serve as a referral center for people in trouble, linking victims, the ill, and others in need of service with available community resources (hospitals, mental health clinics, travelers' aid societies, etc.). The police are available all day and every day throughout their jurisdiction. Whether crime, injury, illness, or disputes cause the police to intervene, police problems can generally be reduced to problems in living. The sheer scope and variety of situations in which the police are called to intervene are evidence of their generic helping activities. Finally, the police, like all governmental agencies, are ultimately responsible to the public, their clients, and the courts.

As a human services agency, the most important role of the police is that of "first aid." Whether, the problem is a lost child, domestic disturbance, landlord/tenant dispute, public intoxication, or traffic accident, the police are normally first on the scene. In this role the police provide "first aid" by taking charge of the situation, by providing immediate help and counseling, and by giving referrals to later care. It is common, especially in larger police departments, to give officers a directory of social service agencies to which the officers can refer citizens. That the police do not always provide complete human services to resolve living problems of those with whom they come into contact does not negate the important role of the police in the first stages of human service (Das, 1987).

The Police as a Crime Control Agency

The police control crime in one of two basic ways: reactively or proactively (Black, 1972). These types of policing represent ideal types. A reactive police department would only respond (or react) to crime. A proactive police department would use its own initiative in aggressively seeking out crimes and criminals. The most strict type of reactive police department would remain at the police station, watching television, cleaning cruisers, etc. When a complaint of a crime was received or when an alarm sounded, the officers would rush to their cruisers and speed to the scene of the crime. Having investigated or made an arrest, the officers then would return to the station to await their next call.

In contrast, a typical example of a proactive police department would resemble the vice squad. All officers would be in the field seeking out crime. Much of the work of the police would be accomplished by undercover officers, as marked cars and uniforms would forewarn offenders. Traffic officers would establish "speed traps" rather than patrol stretches of highway. Decoy teams and "sting operations" would be prevalent.

In reality, of course, one does not find the ideal type. Rather, it is possible to classify police departments as being more or less proactive or reactive. As a result of the democratic nature of our society, and of the municipal organization of the majority of our police forces, American police are more reactive than proactive. That is, as a society, we prefer to set policing priorities through our complaints and calls. The alternative is for the police to set priorities through deciding how and when to combat crime.

The Police as a Peacekeeping Agency

In television and motion picture westerns, the sheriff is charged with "keeping the peace." At base, peacekeeping means the maintenance of order. The police control disruption such as fights and riots. They maintain traffic flow and insure a general level of satisfaction with living in the community. Police protect and enhance orderly social interactions. James Q. Wilson (1968:16) argued that order maintenance is at the core of the police task. He wrote:

> The patrolman's role is defined more by his responsibility for *maintaining order* than by his responsibility for enforcing the law. By 'order' is meant the absence of disorder, and by disorder is meant behavior that either disturbs or threatens to disturb the public peace or that involves face-to-face conflict among two or more persons. Disorder, in short, involves a dispute over what is "right" or "seemly" conduct or over who is to blame for conduct that is agreed to be wrong or unseemly.

As Wilson's explanation implies, disorder is often noncriminal. Rather than questions of legality, order-maintenance problems often involve questions of propriety. Youths loitering on a street corner, a neighbor who plays her stereo too loudly, homeless persons congregating in a park, and other non-criminal events are frequently the basis for order-maintenance calls to the police. In these situations, the responding officer is expected to resolve the conflict and thereby restore order.

Most order-maintenance problems fall into a gray area of the law where frequently the officer is not authorized to act. As a matter of practicality, the officer is compelled to do something. Order maintenance is the most common activity of police officers. These tasks often expose officers to physical danger, and involve the exercise of discretion by the officer. Order maintenance is the least "consensual" part of the police task (Wilson, 1968). For these reasons, order maintenance is perhaps the most difficult aspect of policing.

While there may be a consensus that robbery will not be tolerated, police should arrest robbers, and that accident victims should be helped and that the police should help them, there often is no such consensus for order-maintenance questions. In the case of the neighbor with the loud stereo, it is clear that dissension or disagreement exists; one party feels that the stereo is too loud, and the other feels that it is set at an acceptable level. Into this conflict steps the officer. Regardless of the outcome, at least one (if not all) of the parties will be dissatisfied.

As difficult as order maintenance is, it is a critical component of policing. Left unattended, minor disputes can escalate into criminal acts (such as assault or vandalism if the complaining neighbor takes the matter of the loud stereo into his or her own hands). Further, the police and the entire justice system must serve the major function of *social control*. We must be able to go about our daily lives in a relatively smooth and predictable fashion. It is order maintenance, more than any other police function, that insures the routine functioning of society.

THE STRUCTURE
OF AMERICAN POLICING

The structure and organization of law enforcement agencies in America reflect the influences of historical development and the conflicting tasks. Unlike the police of other countries, most American police agencies exist at a local level. This fragmentation of police service supports the value we place on federalism and local autonomy. Americans do not want national police, and we insist on maintaining a civilian police force, distinct from the military (Moore, 1987).

Geoffrey Alpert and Roger Dunham (1988) stated that police organization and administration focus on standardizing the use of civil force. The police must balance the mandate to control behavior against the requirement that they respect individual rights. This double responsibility places a premium on controlling and directing the actions of individual police officers.

Organizational options were limited at the time police departments came into being in the middle 1800s. The only organizational model available that allowed control of large groups of personnel was the military model. For this reason above any other, the police adopted a "paramilitary" structure. This structure included ranks and a chain of command. The trappings of a military organization are still a part of American policing.

In the military model, information flows up the chain of command from the street officers to the police administrator. Orders and commands flow down the chain to the street officers. In this fashion, the police administrator controls the actions of officers on the street. Organizationally, this structure enables the police to meet their conflicting functions in a routine manner.

In practice, the structure of policing is different from the military model. James Wilson (1968) noted that, unlike in other organizations, street officers have more discretion than police administrators. The reality of police work is that officers on the street must react to a variety of situations. It is not practical for police officers to report every call and to await instructions from above.

The original fear of a strong, centralized police force was one cause of decentralization. The variety of calls for service received by the police further supported allowing individual initiative among officers. Most police departments did not closely supervise street officers (Kelling, 1988). Rather, patrol officers were generalists, who were expected to deal appropriately with the majority of calls for assistance without guidance from higher ranks.

As policing entered the twentieth century, the automobile and changes in American cities affected the structure of the police department. While the paramilitary model was retained, policing became increasingly bureaucratic. The radio and telephone allowed more communication between officers and supervisors. The new communication tools also increased demand for police service because a citizen only had to pick up a telephone to request help. However, these changes also alienated the officer from the community (Sherman, 1988).

The separation of the police from the community led to increased concern over controlling police behavior. The bureaucratic response to this concern was the creation of rules and procedures for officers to follow. These departmental policies, or "standard operating procedures," became a factor determining the actions of individual officers. While not perfect, the rules affect how officers decide to handle cases (Fyfe, 1979; Mastrofski, Ritti & Hoffmaster, 1987).

Early police officers were sworn into office, issued uniforms and weapons, and sent to the streets. Most states now require training and certification of recruits prior to the assignment to patrol. Beginning in 1972, many police agencies developed field training programs to evaluate how well new officers apply laws and departmental policies to field situations (McCampbell, 1986). These programs help insure that police officers know and follow the rules of the police bureaucracy.

Another development in policing during the twentieth century is specialization. Large police departments, especially those in our biggest cities, use task specialization to assign officers. These departments divide tasks into special units or divisions. While departments differ among themselves in how tasks are divided and named, Alpert and Dunham (1988:59) identified four basic elements: administration, communication, patrol and internal review. They observed that many police agencies use more precise divisions. Patrol and investigation are two units which include the crime control function of the police. A traffic division and community relations unit may combine with the patrol unit to provide service and order maintenance. Administrative services and internal affairs units assist police administrators in running and controlling the department.

A typical large police department may have several divisions. The investigation unit, for example, may be further divided into homicide, robbery, fraud, vice and other squads. Similarly, the patrol unit may be organized by geography into precincts or districts. Regardless of the complexity of the police bureaucracy, the military ranks and chain of command are retained. Box 5.3 presents a model organizational chart for a specialized police department.

We must remember that even in the most specialized city police department, patrol officers are generalists. Patrol has been called the "backbone of policing." The majority of police services are still performed by patrol officers. It is unlikely that the decentralized performance of police service by patrol officers will change in the future.

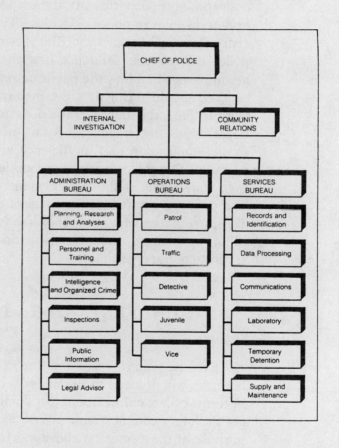

Box 5.3
Organizational Chart for a Police Department

SOURCE: President's Commission on Law Enforcement and Administration of Justice (1967), *Task Force Report: The Police.* (Washington, DC: U.S. Government Printing Office):47.

The degree of specialization in any police department is, at least partly, the result of the size of the department (Langworthy, 1985). Larger departments are more likely to be specialized than are smaller ones. Additionally, the police in larger departments are less likely to reflect neighborhood values in police activities. This is a result of specialization and bureaucracy. The varying sizes of American police departments influence how the tasks of police are accomplished and how the public perceives the police.

We should recall that the majority of police officers work in the large, bureaucratic departments, but that most departments are small. This fact of police organization means duplication and inefficiency are part of American policing. Our police serve communities as much, or more, than they serve in the enforcement of the criminal law. The price we pay for local control of police is inefficiency. To insure police who are responsive to local needs, we are willing to tolerate multiple jurisdictions and thousands of separate police agencies.

UNDERSTANDING POLICE

Because we are examining the criminal justice system here, we will proceed to discuss policing almost exclusively in terms of law enforcement. In doing so, it is easy to forget the other complex demands placed on the police. The purpose of the discussion above was to recognize and highlight the fact that enforcing the criminal law is only one part of the police function. Requiring our police to provide services, to maintain order *and* to serve crime control ends means that police resources cannot be totally devoted to law enforcement.

It also means that law enforcement is not entirely comprised of detecting and apprehending serious criminal offenders. On occasion, the criminal law is used by police officers to achieve order-maintenance or service ends. It is not uncommon, for example, for the police in some large cities to employ "mercy bookings" to provide shelter and medical care for the poor (Newsweek, 1987:48; Finn & Sullivan, 1988). Thus, the multiple goals of policing complicate an analysis of the crime control actions of police departments. Nonetheless, we shall endeavor to focus on the role of the police in the criminal justice system, and that role includes crime control.

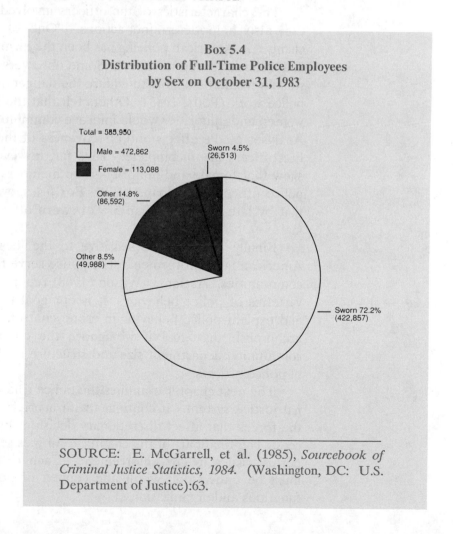

Box 5.4
Distribution of Full-Time Police Employees
by Sex on October 31, 1983

Total = 585,950

☐ Male = 472,862

■ Female = 113,088

Sworn 4.5%
(26,513)

Other 14.8%
(86,592)

Other 8.5%
(49,988)

Sworn 72.2%
(422,857)

SOURCE: E. McGarrell, et al. (1985), *Sourcebook of Criminal Justice Statistics, 1984.* (Washington, DC: U.S. Department of Justice):63.

Beyond recognizing the multiple functions served by police, we also must remain aware of the structure and organization of policing. The actions of police officers and of police departments reflect different patterns of organization. Departmental policies and procedures, as well as recruit training, serve as boundaries on police behavior. The diversity of organizational sizes, structures and policies insures variety in the practice of policing.

The characteristics of the officers involved in a situation also help determine actions. One of the recent changes in American policing has been the hiring of women and minority group members. Some observers feared that women would be unable to endure the danger and rigors of police work (Potts, 1983). Others felt that the inclusion of women and minorities would improve community relations. Analyses of the effects and effectiveness of these new police officers are incomplete. Thus far, however, the data show that female and minority-group members make good police officers (Grennan, 1987). Box 5.4 shows, however, that by late 1983, less than 5% of sworn officers were female.

Finally, we must be sensitive to the local nature of American law enforcement. The police serve their various communities. As James Wilson (1968) reported, there are varieties of police behavior. It is our goal to understand and explain police behavior in crime control. We cannot accomplish that goal if we ignore the contributions of community, department size and structure in the decisions of police officers.

The next chapter examines the police role in the criminal justice system. It continues with a brief discussion of the forces that affect discretionary decisions by police officers. The final part of the chapter examines some contemporary issues in law enforcement. Each of these topics must be understood within the context of police history, functions and organization.

REVIEW QUESTIONS

1. What is meant by calling the police the "agency of last resort"?

2. Explain the tension that exists between "liberty" and "civility" as it applies to contemporary policing.

3. Briefly trace the development of policing in the United States.

4. Describe how the police can be considered to be a human services agency.

5. Differentiate between reactive and proactive policing.

6. How do the multiple tasks expected of the police affect them as part of the justice system?

REFERENCES

Alpert, G. & R. Dunham (1988), *Policing Urban America.* (Prospect Heights, IL: Waveland)

Bittner, E. (1970), *The Functions of Police in Modern Society.* (Rockville, MD: National Institute of Mental Health).

Black, D.J. (1972), "The mobilization of law," *Journal of Legal Studies* 2(1):125-49.

Bureau of Justice Statistics (1989), *Profile of State and Local Law Enforcement Agencies, 1987.* (Washington, DC: U.S. Department of Justice).

Das, D. (1987), *Understanding Police Human Relations.* (Metuchen, NJ: Scarecrow Press).

Eck, J. & W. Spelman (1987), "Who you gonna call? The police as problem busters," *Crime & Delinquency* 33(1):31-52.

Finn, P.E. & M. Sullivan (1988), "Police respond to special populations," *NIJ Reports* (May/June):2-8.

Fyfe, J.J. (1979), "Administrative intervention on police shooting discretion: An empirical examination," *Journal of Criminal Justice* 7(4):309-24.

Goldstein, H. (1978), *Policing a Free Society.* (Cambridge, MA: Ballinger).

Graber, D. (1979), "Evaluating crime-fighting policies: Media images and public perspective," in R. Baker & F. Meyer, Jr. (eds.), *Evaluating Alternative Law-Enforcement Polices.* (Lexington, MA: Lexington Books):179-99.

Grennan, S. (1987), "Findings on the role of officer gender in violent encounters with citizens," *Journal of Police Science and Administration* 15(1):78-85.

Johnson, D.R. (1981), *American Law Enforcement: A History.* (St. Louis, MO: Forum Press).

Johnson, H. (1988), *History of Criminal Justice.* (Cincinnati, OH: Pilgrimage).

Kelling, G. (1988), *Foot Patrol.* Crime File Study Guide. (Washington, DC: National Institute of Justice).

Kennedy, D.B. (1983), "Toward a clarification of the police role as a human services agency," *Criminal Justice Review* 8(2):41-45.

Langworthy, R.H. (1985), "Police department size and agency structure," *Journal of Criminal Justice* 13(1):15-28.

Manning, P.K. (1978), "The police: Mandate, strategies and appearances," in P.K. Manning & J. Van Maanen (eds.) *Police & Policing: A View from the Street.* (Santa Monica: Goodyear):7-31.

Mastrofski, S.D., R.R. Ritti & D. Hoffmaster (1987), "Organizational determinants of police discretion: The case of drinking-driving," *Journal of Criminal Justice* 15(5):387-402.

McCampbell, M.S. (1986), *Field Training for Police: State of the Art.* (Washington, D.C.: National Institute of Justice).

Moore, R. (1987), "*Posse comitatus* revisited: The use of the military in civil law enforcement," *Journal of Criminal Justice* 15(5):375-86.

Newsweek, (1987), "Forcing the mentally ill to get help," *Newsweek* (November 9, 1987):47-8.

Potts, L. (1983), "Equal employment opportunity and female employment in police agencies," *Journal of Criminal Justice* 11(6):505-524.

President's Commission on Law Enforcement and Administration of Justice (1967), *Task Force Report: Police.* (Washington, D.C.: U.S. Government Printing Office).

Sherman, L. (1988), *Neighborhood Safety.* Crime File Study Guide. (Washington, DC: National Institute of Justice).

Van Maanen, J. (1978) "Observations on the making of policemen," in P.K. Manning & J. Van Maanen (eds.) *Policing: A View from the Street.* (Santa Monica, CA: Goodyear):292-308.

Vogel, R. & R. Adams (1983), "Police professionalism: A longitudinal cohort study," *Journal of Police Science and Administration* 11(4):474-84.

Walker, S. (1983), *American Policing: An Introduction.* (New York: McGraw-Hill).

Webster, J.A. (1970), "Police task and time study," *Journal of Criminal Law, Criminology & Police Science* 60(1):94-100.

Wilson, J.Q. (1968), *Varieties of Police Behavior.* (Cambridge, MA: Harvard University Press).

6 Law Enforcement in the Criminal Justice System

Three principal decision points or processes of the criminal justice system occur in the law enforcement segment of the process: detection of crime, investigation and arrest. These activities comprise the scope of police crime control, with the exception of preventive practices such as uniformed patrol, and it is these three decision points to which we will turn our attention in this chapter.

DETECTION

The police detect crime in the two major ways described in the previous chapter, that is, reactively or proactively. The most common way in which police come to learn about crime is reactively, through the receipt of citizen complaints. Most crimes are brought to the attention of the police rather than discovered by them (Tiffany, McIntyre & Rotenberg, 1967). Some, however, are detected proactively, through undercover operations or through the observations of officers on patrol. Still other crimes are discovered through the actions of related agents such as investigative grand juries, legislative committees, and the like. These latter means of detection can best be subsumed under the heading of reactive detection, as police gain knowledge of the existence of crimes from complaints.

The detection decision is simply whether it is likely that a crime has been committed. Once the police come to believe that a crime has been committed, the justice process begins. Detection hinges on many factors, ranging from the seriousness of the alleged crime and the observation powers of the officer, to the credibility of the complainant or witness. As our earlier discussion of "unfounding" indicated, sometimes the officer decides that a reported crime did not, in fact, occur. In this case, she or he would label the complaint "unfounded," and would proceed as if nothing out of the ordinary had happened (Sudnow, 1964).

We refer to detection as a decision process because often what appears to be a decision made on the spur of the moment is actually the culmination of months or years of training or effort. This is particularly true of many of those crimes that are discovered by the police. What seems to be a nearly arbitrary decision to stop and question someone, or to check the license of a particular automobile, is in fact the result of a long process of learning and intelligence gathering.

Harvey Sacks (1978) termed street sense an "incongruity procedure." Street sense is the ability of experienced police officers to "know" who is likely to be a criminal or to be dangerous. Sacks's term is most appropriate because what the police officer relies upon is the fact that something about the individual or circumstances is not right or is incongruous, that is, something does not fit. What appears normal to the average citizen may appear strange to the experienced officer. Police officers are taught to look for certain clues, such as overcoats being worn on warm days, mud splatters on rear license plates, etc. The average citizen either does not notice such things, or does not interpret them as being possibly crime-related. After several years of experience, most officers become quite adept at the use of the incongruity procedure. The detection of crime then often rests on the police officer's perception or interpretation of the incongruous circumstances.

INVESTIGATION

Investigation is a process which continues throughout the law enforcement segment of the criminal justice process, and which often continues into the court segment as well. The decision involved in investigation is split into two parts: first, whether to investigate a suspected crime, and second, how best to proceed with the investigation, if it is initiated. Box 6.1 presents a model of police activity in responding to crime.

An investigation is the accumulation of information and evidence which links a particular person or group of persons to a particular crime or set of crimes. It is the process by which formal criminal charges can be brought against identified individuals. As an evidence gathering activity, the principal tools of investigation are search and interrogation. Other tools and skills are employed, depending on the nature of the offense and the resources that are available to the police, such as forensic analyses, line-ups and surveillance (Palmiotto, 1984).

Search

"Search" involves the seeking-out of evidence of a crime or the location of a suspect. It entails the physical inspection of papers, premises and possessions by the police.

The United States Constitution provides that searches can be conducted only upon the issuance of a warrant based upon probable cause. In practice however, the warrant requirement has proven impractical and problematic. The United States Supreme Court has recognized a number of exceptions to the warrant requirement. Most of these are based on a determination of reasonable behavior by the police under the circumstances. If the police have behaved reasonably, the search will be construed to be valid.

Box 6.1
The Criminal Apprehension Process

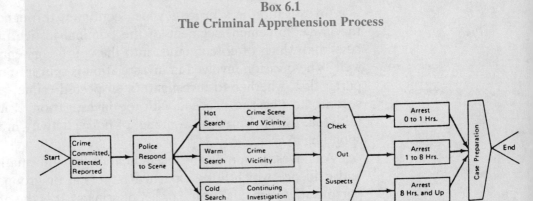

SOURCE: P. Weston & K. Wells (1986), *Criminal Investigation: Basic Perspectives, 4th Ed.* (Englewood Cliffs, NJ: Prentice-Hall):3.

To control unreasonable or improper police behavior in regard to searches, the Supreme Court has adopted the *exclusionary rule*. This rule states that illegally or improperly obtained evidence cannot be used in a trial. The logic of the rule is that the police conduct a search in order to obtain evidence of criminal behavior, and excluding this evidence from trial defeats the purpose of the search. Thus, if the police cannot conduct a legal search, they will not conduct any search.

The Supreme Court developed and imposed an exclusionary rule on federal law enforcement in 1914, in *Weeks v. U.S.*, but refused to apply it to the states, hoping instead that the various state systems would arrive at a better solution to the problem of illegal searches. Finally, in 1961, the Court applied the rule to the states in the case of *Mapp v. Ohio*.

Acting on a tip that a suspect (wanted in connection with a bombing) and gambling apparatus would be found at the home of Ms. Dolree Mapp, Cleveland police went there and asked for admission, which Ms. Mapp refused. Three hours later, more officers arrived and again the police asked to enter. When Ms. Mapp refused, one of the officers displayed papers he claimed were a search warrant and the officers entered the home, searched the premises and discovered pornographic materials in a trunk in the basement of the house. Ms. Mapp was arrested and charged with possession of obscene materials.

The Court ruled that the police behavior in this case was unacceptable and that the evidence (the obscene materials) must be excluded from any future trial of Ms. Mapp. That the police had time to secure a warrant and did not, that the officers claimed to have had a warrant (but never introduced one in Ms. Mapp's trial), and that Ms. Mapp was apparently not guilty of the crimes of which she was suspected, weighed heavily in the Court's decision. In the end, the Court held that the exclusionary rule used to support the Fourth Amendment of the U.S. Constitution was applicable to state cases through the due process clause of the Fourteenth Amendment.

The *Mapp* case and the *Miranda* decision, which is discussed below, led to charges that the Supreme Court was "handcuffing" the police. Critics of the Court launched virulent attacks on this interpretation of the Constitution. They believed that the "overly-liberal" stance characterized these and similar decisions of the Court. Nonetheless, the Supreme Court had interpreted the Constitution, and the exclusionary rule became the law of the land (Wilson, 1988).

Given that the Court would distinguish between the types of searches that would yield admissible evidence and those that would not, it was possible to determine exceptions to the warrant requirement by learning the circumstances under which warrantless searches had been held admissible by the Court. Generally, the Court has identified the following circumstances to be exempt from the warrant requirement: limited protective searches (frisks), searches incident to lawful arrest, searches conducted by police in "hot pursuit" of a suspect, border searches, upon consent of the person being subjected to the search, searches of automobiles, inventory searches, and the seizure of evidence "in plain view" of the officer.

The "frisk" is a traditional police practice which has been upheld by the Supreme Court when conducted under specific circumstances. The Court outlined the requirements for a valid frisk in 1968 when it decided the case of *Terry v. Ohio*. In this case, an experienced Cleveland police officer conducted a limited "pat down" of the outer garments of suspected robbers to insure his safety and that of innocent bystanders.

In the *Terry* case, a 39-year veteran officer observed two suspects repeatedly walk past and look into a store. The officer came to the conclusion that the men were "casing" the store for a robbery, and he approached them to investigate. When the two stopped to confer with another man, the officer approached and asked for their names. When they mumbled in response, he turned one of them around and patted him down, finding a revolver. He frisked the other men and found another gun and placed them under arrest.

The Supreme Court ruled that the officer had acted reasonably under the circumstances and that the evidence (the guns) was taken in a reasonable search. Therefore, the evidence could be used at trial. If an officer has a reasonable suspicion that criminal activity is occurring, the officer has the authority to stop persons and to request identification and information. Further, if the officer has a reasonable belief that these individuals may be armed, and if nothing in the initial investigation dispels this reasonable fear, the officer may conduct a "frisk" to protect himself and others.

The frisk is a protective search limited in scope to only that which is required to assure that the person with whom the officer is dealing is not capable of injuring the officer. Upon a lawful arrest, however, the officer's authority to search is broader. Where frisking is limited to a "pat down" of the outer garments to discover weapons, the arrested person is subject to a full search by the officer. Search that is incident to lawful arrest is designed to protect the officer through discovery of any weapons, and to secure any evidence of the crime which the offender might otherwise be able to destroy. This type of search is limited to the area within the immediate control of the offender (*Chimel v. California*, 1969).

A "hot pursuit" exception to the warrant requirement was recognized by the Court in the case of *Warden v. Hayden* (1967). While the Court would generally prefer that police officers obtain warrants before conducting a search, there are times when this is impractical. In the *Hayden* case, the police were informed of the crime (a robbery) by a cab driver who followed the suspect to a building. The police arrived at the scene within minutes after the suspect

entered the building and were informed by the cab driver
that the suspect had gone inside. The police entered the
building and searched the premises for evidence of the
robbery and for the suspect described to them by the cab
driver. The Court decided that, under the circumstances,
while the police could have cordoned-off the building and
awaited a warrant, the time lag involved might have allowed the suspect to destroy the evidence of the crime, or
to escape. Thus, when in "hot pursuit," the officers may
follow and search for the suspect.

The law regarding search at international borders is
different from the law of searching residences, according to
the Court. As a result of the volume of traffic which
crosses our borders and faces the Customs Service, and the
potential for smuggling, the Court allows searches of persons and possessions at the nation's borders without the
requirement of warrants. Indeed, the U.S. Customs Service periodically conducts random searches at border
points.

It is possible for a competent adult to voluntarily waive
his or her right to be protected from unreasonable
searches. If the suspect consents to the search, any evidence found will be admissible. In the *Mapp* case, for example, if Ms. Mapp had voluntarily allowed the police to
enter her home and search for the bombing suspect, she
would not have been successful in her efforts to have the
evidence excluded from trial.

As a result of the mobility of automobiles, the Court
treats automobile searches differently from searches of
houses or buildings. In *U.S. v. Ross* (1982), the Court ruled
that police officers could conduct a full search of an automobile which the officers had legitimately stopped, as long
as they had probable cause to believe that the automobile
contained contraband. The Court has applied the warrant
standard of probable cause to the search of automobiles.
Thus, as long as the police have probable cause to believe

that an automobile contains contraband or evidence, they may search the vehicle and any containers in it.

A related issue surrounding automobiles in particular is the "inventory" search. If the police seize an automobile or other item, they generally "search" it to determine the contents for the purpose of inventory. They do not want the owner to claim that valuable property is missing after retrieving the car. In *Chambers v. Maroney* (1970), the Court ruled that a search of an automobile shortly after it was seized was permissible. In *Coolidge v. New Hampshire* (1981), however, the Court held that a search of an automobile required that the officers first obtain a warrant. That the police had held the car for a long period before the search negated the possibility that the *Coolidge* case involved an inventory search. As the car was in police custody and could not be moved, the probable cause standard of *Ross* was inapplicable because the officers could have obtained a warrant.

The "plain view" doctrine does not really involve a type of search. What it means is that if an officer sees criminal evidence that is in plain view (that is, the evidence did not have to be "searched" for), the officer may seize that evidence. Thus, if you approach an officer for directions, and you are openly carrying a controlled substance, the officer may seize the substance with no other justification than that it was in plain view.

There are a number of other exceptions to the warrant requirement related to electronic surveillance, emergency situations, and the like, but the exceptions most likely to involve the average police officer are those discussed above. The purpose of the exclusionary rule and the general requirement of a warrant is to protect the liberty of the individual citizen. That there are exceptions indicates the requirements of civility. The police must walk a fine line between what is necessary for the protection of the public and for the control of crime, and what is demanded for the protection of individual liberties. The warrant process, whereby a magistrate reviews the evidence and either confirms the judgment of the police (issues a warrant) or rejects it, and appellate courts rule as to the admissibility of evidence, is an example of how the justice system attempts to check the discretionary powers of the police.

The decisions whether to search, how to search, and what to search are perhaps governed by evidentiary standards such as "reasonable suspicion" or "probable cause," but in practice, the decisions are discretionary. The officer in the street must decide whether to take investigatory steps. This decision is ruled by the evidentiary standards of the courts, but many other factors come into play when the decision is made on the street.

Rubinstein (1973) wrote that the decision to pursue an investigation hinges on the seriousness of the crime reported, the credibility of the witness/complainant, and the circumstances of the event. The less serious the crime, the less likely the police are to invest scarce investigatory resources into solving it. The less believable or sympathetic the witness/complainant, the less likely the police are to investigate, and the busier the police are, the less likely they are to take the time to investigate a given complaint.

Other factors also can affect the decisions of police officers when a crime is detected. A rash of crimes, negative press pressure, the importance or status of the victim, political interference, and the like, can all play roles in the decision whether to investigate. As noted earlier, an analysis of case law is useful in determining the boundaries of police powers, but it is not necessarily determinative of police decisions.

Interrogation

Interrogation of suspects and witnesses has long been a mainstay of criminal investigation. We are all familiar with entertainment-media portrayals of police investigations, where the detectives "grill" the suspect, or where they continually return to the witness to eke out details of the crime. Most often, it is the interrogation which leads the officers to the needed evidence and which ultimately seals the case.

As the Fourth Amendment to the U.S. Constitution protects the homes, papers and possessions of the citizenry from unreasonable searches, the Fifth Amendment protects citizens from overzealous interrogation by the police. The Fifth Amendment states that no one can be compelled to give testimony against himself. Perhaps the most famous of the Court's exclusionary rule cases, *Miranda v. Arizona* (1966) involved the Fifth Amendment.

In the *Miranda* case, as in many other cases preceding it, the police arrested the suspect and held him in custody for several hours while questioning him about the crime. At the conclusion of the interrogation, the suspect had confessed to the crime. Miranda's attorneys appealed the conviction on the grounds that Miranda was not aware that he did not have to speak during the interrogation and that he had a right to an attorney during questioning. Thus, the attorneys contended that the confession was obtained improperly and should not have been allowed as evidence at the trial. The Supreme Court agreed, ruling that when police have a suspect in custody, they must advise the suspect that he or she may remain silent, that what is said may be used against the suspect in court, and that the suspect has the right to either a retained (hired) or appointed attorney during questioning (See Box 6.2).

The *Miranda* decision revolutionized police interrogation practices. One of the reasons the case is so well known is that the Court required that police provide suspects with warnings as to their rights at interrogation, and these required warnings became known as the "*Miranda* Warnings." Traditional practices of "incommunicado" (not permitting the suspect to see or speak with anyone except the investigating officers) and the psychological advantage held by the police in such interrogations were abolished.

> **Box 6.2**
> **Miranda Warnings**
>
> You have the right to remain silent. Anything you say can and will be used against you in a court of law.
>
> You have the right to an attorney during questioning. If you cannot afford an attorney, one will be appointed for you by the court.
>
> Do you understand these rights?

It was the *Miranda* decision, most of all, that led some commentators to charge that the Supreme Court was "handcuffing the police." These critics expressed fears that, as a result of this decision, the police would be unable to obtain confessions, and thereby far fewer offenders would be convicted and far less stolen property would be recovered by the police (Inbau, 1966). Evaluations of the effects of the *Miranda* Warnings on conviction rates and the recovery of stolen property have failed to support these earlier criticisms (Witt, 1977). Box 6.3 shows that, for California cases, evidence problems (including possible exclusionary rule violations) are most common in drug cases. These data do not support critics of the exclusionary rule, who argued that the rule would result in robbers, burglars and other street criminals being released from custody. In part, the critics were wrong in their contention because they probably did not consider the system qualities of the justice process and the ability of systems to resist change and to maintain equilibrium. Several practices developed which may have served to blunt the effect of *Miranda*.

Box 6.3
Felony cases rejected for prosecution
in California (1976-79) for search and seizure problems,
by most serious charge

Most Serious Charge	Number	Percent
Total Cases	4,130 cases	100.0
Drug	2,953	71.5
Other Felonies*	641	15.5
Burglary	217	5.3
Robbery	134	3.2
Assault	88	2.1
Grand Theft Auto	48	1.2
Grand Theft	33	.8
Rape	12	.3
Murder	4	.1

*Includes weapons and other felonies not listed separately

SOURCE: W.R. Burkhart, et al. (1982), *The Effects of the Exclusionary Rule: A Study in California.* (Washington, DC: U.S. Department of Justice):12.

Lewis and Allen (1977) described a post-*Miranda* investigatory style which, they argued, allowed the police to overcome the limits placed upon them by the Court. According to Lewis and Allen, the interrogating officers would give the suspect his or her warnings, but would do so over the course of the interrogation, that is, the warnings were part of the questioning so that *Miranda* "participated" in the interrogation. After several hours, the interrogation would be over, and the warnings would have been given.

As an example, this type of interrogation might proceed as follows:

Officer: You have the right to remain silent, but if you have nothing to hide, we just want to ask a few questions about what you were doing last night. The sooner we can get on with this, the sooner we can all go home. So, tell me, where were you about 10 p.m. last night?

Suspect: (Speaks for a while, answers a few questions.)

Later . . .

Officer: Anything you tell us could be used against you in a court of law, although frankly, I don't think you've done anything. When you were telling us about the car, you mentioned...

Suspect: (Continues speaking and answering questions)

Later . . .

Officer: You have the right to an attorney, but it's late and it would be hard to get an attorney to come down here now. Besides, I don't see any reason why an innocent person would waste money on an attorney...

Over the span of several hours, the entire *Miranda* warning would be given. If the officers obtained a confession, they would have it typed-up for the suspect's signature, along with the waiver of Fifth Amendment rights. Should the suspect complain, the officers need only ask whether the suspect told them what was in the statement, and whether the officers gave the suspect the *Miranda* warnings. The answers to both questions would be *yes*, although the warnings were not given in the way the Court envisioned.

A second practice which enabled police to get around the *Miranda* requirement was "psychological warfare." One effect of the *Miranda* decision may have been to increase the skill of police interrogators. In *Brewer v. Williams* (1977), a suspect in the murder of a little girl finally led police to the body after listening to officers talk about how tragic it was for the girl's parents that they would not be able to provide a proper burial for their daughter. Similar practices were revealed in other cases where police officers preyed upon the guilt of the suspect by speculating about what could happen if neighborhood children found guns that were used in crimes. A guilt-ridden offender often would lead the officers to the guns, thereby providing the police with sufficient evidence to obtain a conviction.

Generally, the Court has determined the admissibility of evidence obtained in these cases on the basis of the intent of the police officers involved. If the officers were consciously trying to provoke the suspect and to obtain evidence, the court usually rules that the interrogation was improper. On the other hand, if the police were merely speaking among themselves, and the suspect, upon overhearing the conversation which was not directed at him or her, volunteers information, it is treated as a valid confession.

Other Investigatory Practices

In addition to search and interrogation, police obtain evidence in a number of ways. Television shows and movies suggest that forensic sciences are a major part of most criminal investigations. The offender's age, race, sex and size can be determined from hairs found at the scene of the crime. The clothes worn by the offender can be identified from fibers collected at the crime scene. The weapon used in the crime can be ascertained from ballistics examinations. These techniques are staples of a forensic scientist's investigation. While rarely employed because of costs and a lack of necessity, the techniques of a forensic scientist sometimes provide the answers to investigators (Peterson, 1987).

Identification of offenders through line-ups and throw-downs are more common practices, whereby the police seek the identity of the suspect from a pool of possibilities by having witnesses examine photographs (throw-downs) or observe possible offenders (line-ups). The major concern of the courts in regard to these practices is that the police not be too suggestive in their behavior. For example, the identification of a white male suspect from a line-up comprised of himself and six black females would be too suggestive. To protect against the possibility that the police would encourage a false identification, the Supreme Court has held that suspects in custody have the right to have an attorney present during line-ups (*Kirby v. Illinois*, 1972). Unless the offender is known to the victim or witness, it is unlikely that these procedures by themselves will yield the offender. More often they are employed after the police already have enough evidence to conclude that the suspect is probably guilty of the offense, and thus these identifications tend to be supporting evidence and not the heart of the case.

Still another investigatory tool is surveillance. Both physical and electronic surveillance are used to gather evidence of criminal activity. "Wire taps," hidden microphones and cameras, and other forms of surreptitious surveillance generally require warrants and are therefore used infrequently. The point of most surveillance is to gather evidence on persons suspected of crimes but against whom insufficient evidence exists to obtain search warrants. Usually, surveillance does not involve tapping telephone lines or watching individual residences. The bulk of surveillance conducted by police agencies is physical surveillance, where officers watch a certain location or follow a suspect to gather evidence.

Surveillance techniques yield evidence of specific criminality and information (or "intelligence") on suspicious persons and places. In the former case, officers generally have reason to believe that a particular person is engaged in criminal activity, or that crimes are occurring at a particular place, and the surveillance is designed to provide evidence about those specific offenses. In "intelligence" gathering, police suspect an individual or location and conduct a surveillance in hopes of obtaining further evidence or information to confirm or reject their suspicions.

Informers are another investigatory tool of the police. To some, the use of informers seems inappropriate as it frequently requires the police to join forces with criminals in order to enforce the law. Nonetheless, informants are extremely useful to police in intelligence gathering. The informer usually is not respected by either the criminals or the police, in keeping with a norm that one should not be a "rat." Yet, informers are able to learn and observe things which an undercover officer would find difficult even after months of work, and which a uniformed officer would find impossible.

Informers do not make particularly good witnesses. Typically, their credibility is questioned either because of their own criminal pasts, or because their information is provided with the expectation of a reward and not as a matter of civic responsibility. Add to this the fact that most informers would not be willing to testify in open court, and this valuable source of information for police becomes less than ideal for the solving of crimes. To combat these weaknesses, many police departments employ "undercover" police officers. These officers are assigned to work in "plain clothes," and are directed to mix with the general public so that their identities as police officers will not be readily apparent.

Undercover Operations

Certain types of crimes, such as the "victimless" offenses associated with vice enforcement, are not likely to yield complainants. The customer who solicits a prostitute or purchases drugs is unlikely to complain to the police because, in so doing, the offender would implicate himself in criminal behavior. Thus, the police must aggressively (proactively) seek evidence of these crimes. Almost every major police department has a vice unit comprised of officers who attempt to uncover instances of victimless crimes. These officers pose either as potential consumers or potential providers of the illicit goods and services, and then they wait to be approached by would-be offenders.

In addition, there are other crimes that are approached in a proactive manner in some places. Robberies, especially street robberies, have been detected through the use of plainclothes "victims." Areas of high incidence of specific crimes are determined through reviews of police reports, and officers disguised as potential victims are assigned to those areas with other officers serving as "back-ups" (Halpher & Ku, 1976). When the criminal strikes, the back-up officers close in and an arrest is made. These types of undercover operations have proven to be very successful with specific types of crimes.

The "sting" is an additional form of undercover operation which has been employed to detect and arrest burglars and other forms of criminal offenders. One of the most famous "sting" operations in recent years is the Federal Bureau of Investigation's ABSCAM operation, in which FBI agents posed as wealthy foreign representatives and attempted to uncover bribery activity among members of Congress and other governmental officials (*Time Magazine*, 1980; Coleman, 1985:104-6).

The most common sting operation involves the establishment of a "fencing" operation, that is, police officers pose as dealers of stolen goods. Burglars and thieves then are photographed when they come to sell (fence) goods they have stolen. Later, these offenders are arrested and charged on the basis of the evidence obtained in the fake fence operation.

There are two commonly-raised criticisms of undercover operations. First, there are those who argue that these operations, especially "sting" operations, create crime because they provide an easily identifiable outlet for stolen property, which encourages people to steal (Langworthy, 1989). Second, and perhaps more important, there are those who suggest that such operations ensnare the innocent through *entrapment*.

Entrapment is a defense to criminal charges because the entrapped offender did not have the inclination to commit a crime absent police enticement. If the police entice an otherwise innocent individual to commit a crime, that individual may have a defense of entrapment (Park, 1976). Assuming that you would not generally think of committing a crime, how would you respond if I offered you one million dollars to transport some drugs across town for me?

For many people (perhaps you and I), this offer is too good to refuse. If you were to say *yes* to my offer and I then wished to arrest you for transporting drugs, you could say you were entrapped. You only committed the crime because I came to you with the idea and offered you an inducement too great to refuse. The same logic applies if an officer suggests a price and activity to a suspected prostitute, whatever the price offered. The law does not question judgment and worth as much as it does motive.

It is important to distinguish between entrapment and encouragement. Unlike entrapment, it is permissible for the police to "encourage" someone to complete a crime the person is already contemplating. An officer who approaches a prostitute and offers to pay for a service may be placing the idea in the mind of the prostitute. Someone contemplating an act of prostitution, however, already has the criminal idea, and the fact that an officer allows a person to make a proposition is not entrapment; it is encouragement.

The investigation of crimes, through whatever means the police employ, is designed to provide a basis for the next decision of importance in the law enforcement segment of the justice process: arrest. When police have probable cause to believe that an individual has committed a crime, they are expected to place that person under arrest. Yet, as with investigation and detection, arrest is a decision process which depends upon a number of factors.

ARREST

The authority to arrest offenders is but one of a number of tools available to the police officer in his or her effort to maintain order. As such, there are times when this authority is the best or most appropriate tool, and other times when it is inappropriate. The decision as to the appropriateness of arrest is often a discretionary one for the officer.

Joseph Goldstein (1960) discussed police discretion in deciding whether to employ the criminal law. He identified the decision not to arrest as "non-invocation discretion" (decision not to invoke the law), and he termed the process "low visibility" decisionmaking. If an officer decides not to make an arrest when an arrest is justified, who knows about the decision? Generally, only the officer and the offender are aware of the failure to arrest. Thus, this decision has "low visibility," that is, most people (including the police administration) do not see it. If an officer decides not to issue a traffic citation to you, no one will know unless the officer or you report his decision. How many times have you reported to the police station that an officer should have issued you a citation but did not?

The other face of non-invocation discretion is, logically, invocation discretion (the decision to invoke the law). This decision is more visible, as the officer must report the arrest, the suspect will have legal counsel, and eventually the case may get into the courts. Yet, the decision to arrest someone is often as discretionary as the decision not to arrest. There are rules of thumb which officers or departments follow in deciding to invoke the criminal law. Occasionally, an officer will opt to enforce the law when the rule of thumb would suggest non-invocation. An example of this is "tolerance limits" in regard to excessive speed. Most departments attempt to avoid bad public relations (and close court decisions) in traffic cases by suggesting that offenders traveling at a rate within a specified difference from the speed limit not be cited. Thus, if the speed limit is 55 mph, traffic officers might be expected to cite only those motorists traveling in excess of 60 mph. A motorist stopped for traveling 58 mph could be cited instead of warned, regardless of the tolerance limit, if the motorist's behavior is deemed inappropriate by the officer.

Similarly, a responding officer might decide that arrest is necessary to separate combatants in a dispute, or that such an arrest might prove more harmful than beneficial in a given situation. An officer might "arrest" an ill child to secure needed medical treatment in the absence of parents, or might fail to arrest a known offender in return for information about other offenses or offenders. In all of these situations, it is apparent that, to the officers involved, arrest is a tool, or a means to an end. To understand the exercise of the arrest power in a particular instance, one must understand the intent of the officer involved.

When an arrest is made, the justice process is fully involved. The arresting officer must file reports, the offender/suspect must be transported to a detention facility and booked (whereby the arrest is entered on official records). Shortly after the arrest, the suspect must be given the opportunity to contact an attorney. The suspect has the right to be considered for pre-trial release. These procedures quickly move the case from the law enforcement segment of the justice system into the courts.

As is evident in the *Miranda* ruling, the behavior of police officers is much more tightly controlled after arrest than before it. Once the suspect is in custody, the procedures designed to protect the liberty of individuals are initiated. Police officers often complain that suspects are returned to freedom on the streets through bail before the officers have completed their paperwork. Typically these officers are expressing frustration with the justice system because it seems to be "stacked" in favor of the suspect.

Booking is designed to prevent the police from holding an offender/suspect incommunicado; anyone can check the booking records to determine if a person is in police custody. Bail or pretrial release is a provision of the Eighth Amendment of the U.S. Constitution which is designed to prevent a suspect from unnecessary confinement prior to conviction, and to allow the defendant to be free to cooperate in his or her own defense. A third stage, the preliminary hearing (which will be discussed in the next chapter), is a review of the evidence and the arrest decision by a magistrate or judge. The hearing is held to determine whether the police had sufficient grounds for placing a person in custody. All of these procedures illustrate the care with which the rights of the individual are guarded in conformity with the presumption of innocence. The frustration felt by police, while they and other actors in the justice system are expected (theoretically at least) to presume that the suspect is innocent, arises from the fact that, in order to do their jobs, the police have to believe in the probable guilt of suspects.

POLICE OFFICERS

Frustration with the courts and with the limitations placed upon the actions of the police by our system of justice are examples of the difficulties experienced by American police officers. The police officer is a very important component of the justice process, and in some ways, he or she is the most important. Police officers decide who will be subjected to justice processing, what crimes will be investigated, and how vigorously laws will be enforced. In addition, as the most numerous and most visible agents of criminal justice, police officers are disproportionately responsible for citizens' opinions about the entire justice system. Finally, police officers are ordinary people entrusted with extraordinary powers, and they are charged with what some have called "an impossible mandate" (Manning, 1978).

Many observers have identified what they have termed "the police personality" (Skolnick, 1966; Niederhoffer, 1967). The suggestion is that police are different from the average citizen. Some have suggested that policing as a career attracts persons who are more cynical, authoritarian, suspicious, brutal, etc. Others argue that the nature of the job changes an average person into the police personality. Whatever the resolution of this debate about what causes the police officer to have this unique personality, it is important to understand the complex set of forces which affects policing activities of the individual officer.

Studies of the police show that officers frequently act as if they are cynical (Regoli, et al, 1987). Some observers say that this apparent cynicism does not mean that police officers do not trust citizens, or that the police do not hope to improve conditions (Langworthy, 1987a & b). Part of the explanation for police cynicism may be the stress of the job (Terry, 1985).

The police officer is a member of an organization and as such must be careful to serve the ends of the organization. She or he is also a bureaucrat and must abide by the rules and regulations of the bureaucracy. Finally, the officer is a member of an occupational group which is larger than his or her individual department. Thus, in any given situation, the behavior of the officer reflects the limits imposed by the department, the goals of the organization, and the prestige of the occupational group. The officer is at least subliminally aware that his or her actions will be judged against all of these criteria.

To this mix of standards must be added the social context of the situation in which the officer is operating. The victim/witness has a set of expectations about how the officer will behave, the officer has expectations about himself or herself, and about the victim/witness, and onlookers have their expectations. The officer is aware of many of these expectations, and they too affect his or her behavior. Thus, while every call to which the police respond is not dangerous or difficult, there are no simple calls.

The complexity of the job facing the individual officer is multiplied several times when we analyze the complexity of policing in society on an organizational level. The department has expectations and goals, the community has expectations and goals, and the prosecutor's office, the courts, the local government all have expectations and goals for the department. Many times, the goals or expectations of the audience of a police department conflict with each other and with those of the department.

For this reason, it is difficult to identify a limited set of important issues in contemporary policing. Almost everything about the police is problematic, and given the dilemma inherent in policing a free society, all of these problems are important. Yet, for our purposes, it is necessary to narrow the field and examine only a few of the problems. Corruption is a traditional problem in policing, and the police are almost always suspected of being corrupt. The use of force, especially deadly force, has been an issue in policing since the first use of force by police. The relationship between the police and the community has traditionally been a source of conflict, and the role of the police in controlling crime remains unclear.

SOME ISSUES IN LAW ENFORCEMENT

American police have a less than flawless tradition. From the beginning, when police were loosely controlled, political patronage and the influence of politicians and criminals on police operations have contributed to a perception among the general public of the police as (at least) corruptible, if not corrupt (Sherman, 1974). The public is aware of past practices, and most people believe that police will treat their friends and political leaders differently than the average citizen. This perception of favoritism supports a view of the police as corrupt. Periodic scandals exposing police acceptance of bribes further reinforce the feeling that the police are corrupt.

The police have broad powers, and yet they operate with decentralized patrols. The discretionary authority of police officers is generally well known (that is, we all hope for a "break" even if we do not get it). This combination of power and lack of accountability makes corruption possible. In fact, given the nature of American policing, it might be more surprising that there is so little widespread corruption than that there is so much of it.

Corruption is an issue, not simply because it means the police are criminal, but because it raises the question of who controls the police. Public fears of police corruption are based more on the fact that a corrupt police department is out of control than on the belief that taking graft is, in itself, morally wrong.

Similar fears surround the issue of justified use of force by the police. Among all of police powers, the ability legitimately to employ physical force to secure compliance with police orders, or with the law, is one of the most problematic issues in law enforcement (Bittner, 1970). Police officers resent having their decisions to employ force "second guessed" by civilians or by the internal affairs unit of the department. Citizens fear the unbridled use of force by the police. The issue revolves around the definition of excessive force, that is, force which is greater than what would be required to achieve the lawful aims of the officer.

The use of deadly force is a case in which fears of excessive police force are clear. No one seriously questions the officer's ability and duty to use deadly force to protect himself or others from death or serious harm. As Box 6.4 illustrates, the need for self defense by police officers is real. Many believe that police officers should be allowed to use deadly force to prevent the escape of dangerous offenders who are likely to injure people again. Questions arise, however, when the officer strikes an offender "too many times," or when the officer shoots and kills an innocent or unarmed person.

The core of the problem is that we have granted our police the power to inflict death and injury without a clear understanding of the fact that the officer must *decide* when to use this power. We are troubled by the decisional aspect of police use of force more so than by the use of force itself. When the evidence reveals that force is not applied randomly and that certain people are more likely to be victims than others, we fear discrimination based on factors other than the threat posed to the officer or to the law. If we could control the decisions of officers to employ deadly force, we would be less troubled by the issue.

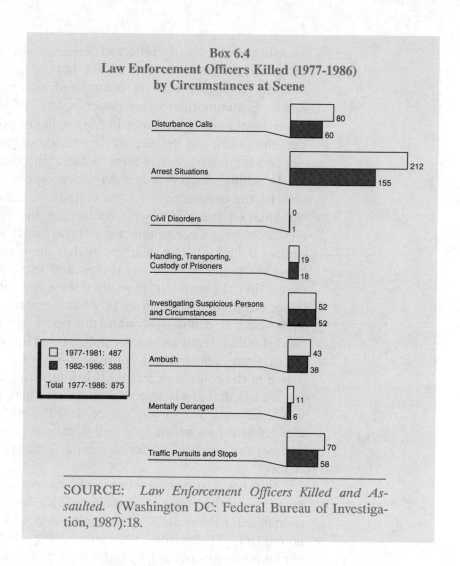

Box 6.4
Law Enforcement Officers Killed (1977-1986)
by Circumstances at Scene

Disturbance Calls: 80 / 60

Arrest Situations: 212 / 155

Civil Disorders: 0 / 1

Handling, Transporting, Custody of Prisoners: 19 / 18

Investigating Suspicious Persons and Circumstances: 52 / 52

Ambush: 43 / 38

Mentally Deranged: 11 / 6

Traffic Pursuits and Stops: 70 / 58

□ 1977-1981: 487
■ 1982-1986: 388
Total 1977-1986: 875

SOURCE: *Law Enforcement Officers Killed and Assaulted.* (Washington DC: Federal Bureau of Investigation, 1987):18.

"Community relations" is a police issue of relatively recent designation; it became an important issue as a result of the civil protests and riots of the late 1960s. Yet, the problem of police and community relations has always plagued the police departments of America. To what extent should the community determine policing policy and priorities? In the early days of American policing, police officers were appointed to serve in their own neighborhoods, and the officers very clearly reflected community standards and norms in the enforcement of the laws. More recently, policing has become more centralized and more impersonal. Communities desire closer control of their police departments and more input in the setting of police policy. Yet, the police are defined as experts about policing matters and oppose what they term "political interference."

In reality, the police are dependent upon, and responsible to, the community. At the same time, the community has charged the police with controlling the behaviors of themselves while complaining about the fact that the police control behavior. The dilemma is that the community has hired the police to do many things, and some of these are things that the community really does not want to see get done. Community relations problems center on those issues where it is not clear who (the police or the community) should directly define the police role (Radelet, 1977).

A final issue for our consideration is the role of the police in the control of crime. It is interesting that the police do not define what behaviors are criminal, do not control their own budget, do not control the social and psychological forces which lead individuals to commit crimes, and yet are responsible for the control and prevention of crime.

In large part, this is what is meant by the "impossible mandate" of the police (Manning, 1978). The police are responsible for the control of something over which they have no control. To control crime, police have adopted a number of strategies over the years which theoretically appear to serve the function of crime control. Many of these, however, have been discovered to be of questionable utility. Rapid response and preventive patrol are but two of these strategies.

For decades, the typical police force has been distributed over the entire jurisdiction for which it is responsible. In part, this distribution has been based on the belief that officers would be able to respond more quickly to calls for aid, and that the quicker response would prove more successful in apprehending offenders. More recent research indicates that this is not true, at least insofar that complainants often do not notify the police soon enough that an offense has occurred. By the time the police are notified, responding within a minute of the call is not normally important (Cordner, Greene & Bynum, 1983).

Another reason for placing the officers out in the community is to provide a "police presence," in order to deter potential violators and reassure law-abiding citizens. Further, when they are not responding to calls for help, the police are expected to patrol and to prevent crime. Recent research has brought this assumption (that patrolling prevents crime) into question. There is little reason to believe that preventive patrol is the crime reduction strategy, that it has traditionally been thought to be (Kelling, et al, 1974). While the effectiveness of preventive patrol requires further study, the general effectiveness of the police in controlling crime has been questioned recently.

The issue involved in the question of police effectiveness would appear to be more one of preventing crime. While there is interest in how to improve police efficiency in apprehending and processing offenders, and there is hope of success in this area, the greatest questions revolve around the ability of the police to prevent crimes. Recent suggestions range from increased technological adaptations through community crime watch and environmental design. In each of these prevention strategies, the role of the police in actual crime prevention is minimal. It may be that the long-held view that police can prevent most crime if they are given sufficient resources must be reconsidered. The question to be decided is whether the police role should continue to cover the dual mandates of crime control and crime prevention.

REVIEW
QUESTIONS

1. Identify and explain the three principal justice system decision points contained in the law enforcement component of the system.

2. Under what circumstances has the U.S. Supreme Court ruled that police need not obtain a warrant prior to conducting a search?

3. What is meant by the "exclusionary rule?"

4. What is the significance of the *Miranda* ruling, and what does it require of the police?

5. Define what is meant by the term "entrapment."

6. What pressures influence the decisions and behavior of police officers?

7. Identify three contemporary issues in American law enforcement.

REFERENCES

Bittner, E. (1970), *The Functions of Police in Modern Society.* (Rockville, MD: National Institute of Mental Health).

Coleman, J.W. (1985), *The Criminal Elite.* (New York: St. Martin's).

Cordner, G.W., J.R. Greene & T.S. Bynum (1983), "The sooner the better: Some effects of police response time," in R.R. Bennett (ed.) *Police at Work: Policy Issues and Analysis.* (Beverly Hills, CA: Sage):145-64.

Goldstein, J. (1960), "Police discretion not to invoke the criminal process: Low visibility decisions in the administration of justice," *Yale Law Journal* 69(March):543-94.

Halpher, A. & R. Ku (1976), *An Exemplary Project: New York Police Department Street Crime Unit.* (Washington, DC: U.S. Government Printing Office).

Inbau, F.E. (1966), "Playing God: Five to four," *Journal of Criminal Law, Criminology & Police Science* 57:377.

Kelling, G., T. Pate, D. Dieckman & C.E. Brown (1974), *The Kansas City Preventive Patrol Experiment--A Summary Report.* (Washington, DC: The Police Foundation).

Langworthy, R.H. (1987a), "Police cynicism: What we know from the Niederhoffer scale," *Journal of Criminal Justice* 15(1):17-36.

Langworthy, R.H. (1987b), "Comment: Have we measured the concept(s) of police cynicism using Niederhoffer's cynicism index?," *Justice Quarterly* 4(2):277-80.

Langworthy, R.H. (1989), "Do stings control crime? An evaluation of a police fencing operation," *Justice Quarterly* (forthcoming).

Lewis, P.W. & H.E. Allen (1977), "Participating *Miranda*: An attempt to subvert certain constitutional safeguards," *Crime & Delinquency* 23(1):75.

Manning, P.K. (1978), "The police: Mandate, strategies and appearances," in P.K. Manning & J. Van Maanen (eds.) *Policing: A View from the Street.* (Santa Monica, CA: Goodyear):7-31.

Niederhoffer, A. (1967), *Behind the Shield: The Police in Urban Society.* (Garden City, NJ: Anchor Books).

Palmiotto, M. (1984), *Critical Issues in Criminal Investigation.* (Cincinnati, OH: Anderson).

Park, R. (1976), "The entrapment controversy," *Minnesota Law Review* 60:163-274.

Peterson, J. L. (1987), *Use of Forensic Evidence by the Police and Courts.* (Washington, DC: National Institute of Justice).

Radelet, L. (1977), *The Police and the Community, 2nd.* (Encino, CA: Glencoe Press).

Regoli, R.M., J.P. Crouch, R.G. Culbertson & E. D. Poole, (1987) "Police professionalism and cynicism reconsidered: An assessment of measurement issues," *Justice Quarterly* 4(2):257-75.

Rubinstein, J. (1973) *City police.* (New York: Farrar, Straus & Giroux).

Sacks, H. (1978), "Notes on police assessment of moral character," in P.K. Manning & J. Maanen (eds.) *Policing: A View from the Street.* (Santa Monica, CA: Goodyear, 1978):187-202.

Sherman, L.W. (ed.) (1974) *Police corruption: A sociological perspective.* (Garden City: Anchor Books).

Skolnick, J. (1966) *Justice without trial.* (New York: John Wiley).

Sudnow, D. (1964), "Normal crimes: Sociological features of the penal code in the public defender's office," *Social Problems* 12:81.

Terry, W. C. (1985), "Police stress as a professional self-image," *Journal of Criminal Justice* 13(6):501-12.

Tiffany, L.P., D.M. McIntyre, J.D. Rotenberg (1967), *Detection of Crime: Stopping and Questioning, Search and Seizure, Encouragement and Entrapment.* (Boston: Little, Brown).

Time Magazine (1980), "The F.B.I. Stings Congress," *Time Magazine* (February 18, 1980): 10-14;18-21.

Van Maanen, J. (1978), "The asshole," in P.K. Manning & J. Van Maanen (eds.), *Policing: A View from the Street.* (Santa Monica: Goodyear):221-38.

Wilson, J. (1988), *The Exclusionary Rule*. Crime file study guide. (Washington, DC: U.S. Department of Justice).

Witt, W. (1977), "Non-coercive interrogation and the administration of criminal justice: The impact of *Miranda* on police effectuality," *Journal of Criminal Law, Criminology and Police Science* 64:320-32.

TABLE
OF CASES

Brewer v. Williams, 430 U.S. 387 (1977).

Chambers v. Maroney, 453 U.S. 42 (1970).

Chimel v. California, 395 U.S. 752 (1969).

Coolidge v. New Hampshire, 403 U.S. 443 (1981).

Kirby v. Illinois, 306 U.S. 682 (1972).

Mapp v. Ohio, 367 U.S. 643 (1961).

Miranda v. Arizona, 384 U.S. 436 (1966).

Terry v. Ohio, 392 U.S. 1 (1968).

United States v. Ross, 456 U.S. 798 (1982).

Warden v. Hayden, 387 U.S. 294 (1967).

Weeks v. United States, 232 U.S. 383 (1914).

7 The Criminal Courts

There are more than 15,000 courts in operation in the United States. Most of these are at the local level in cities and counties across the country. As we saw with police agencies, the large number of individual courts in America is a reflection of our belief in local autonomy. An estimated 84 million cases were filed in American courts in 1983 (Bureau of Justice Statistics, 1984:1). Nearly 70% of all cases filed are for traffic offenses, and more civil cases are filed than non-traffic criminal cases. Less than 2% of all cases filed involved felony offenses.

Almost every county has a felony court (only 19 counties reported having no felony court), but most cases arise in the few populous counties. The 75 largest counties (in terms of population) accounted for more than 25% of felony cases filed in 1985 (Bureau of Justice Statistics, 1987). In terms of crime control, then, American courts mirror the police. Crime control activities are a relatively small part of the total workload of the courts, and criminal cases are concentrated in a few, populous areas.

The work of the courts can be broken into two general categories: *torts* and *crimes*. Torts are "private" wrongs, such as breach of contract or personal injury cases, and with divorce and probate cases, torts comprise the civil court caseload. Crimes are "public" wrongs and are those cases which comprise the criminal justice component of American courts. Thus, for our courts, crime is a part-time function. The basic purpose of the courts is to resolve disputes (Neeley, 1983). As our society becomes more and more complex, we not only encounter more disputes, but informal mechanisms of dispute resolution become less effective. Added to this is the fact that the large and increasing number of attorneys in our society makes it easier for people to obtain legal counsel and to use the courts. Thus, more people are bringing their disputes to the courts each year. Each of these individuals is seeking justice. In discussing the purpose of the courts, Rubin (1983:4) noted:

> If we try to describe the purpose of the courts, someone will usually first suggest that their purpose is to "do justice," to provide individualized justice in individual cases. This is true, but whether justice is done depends typically upon the interests or viewpoints of the affected or interested parties. We are confident that some guilty people have been found innocent in our courts, and that innocent persons have been found guilty. These trials may have been conducted fairly, but was justice done?

The point here is that justice is elusive of definition. Indeed, the courts are perhaps better understood as jugglers attempting to keep many divergent interests in motion without dropping anything. The courts must strike a balance between the rights of disputing parties. In the criminal courts, the principal balance to be maintained is between the rights of an individual (and by extension, all individuals) and those of the state. The resolution of criminal cases more often entails compromise than competition. Perhaps the best example of this "juggling act" quality of the criminal courts is seen in the practice of plea bargaining.

In plea bargaining, the state and the individual defendant compromise, with neither side getting all that it would hope to achieve. The judge serves as the juggler, balancing the interests of the state in securing a conviction and punishing a criminal against the interests of the individual in protecting his or her liberty and constitutional rights. The alternative to plea bargaining is trial. Trial is the epitome of competition. It is filled with costs and uncertainties for both parties involved in the dispute. Either side may "win" the trial, but both sides will have to expend time and money, experience aggravation, and risk losing. Rather than compete in a trial, the prosecutor and defendant often reach a compromise through plea bargaining. In the end, the accused is convicted, but avoids the full measure of punishment for the offense of which he or she was accused. Neither side is completely satisfied with the outcome, but both can accept it.

These compromises, which characterize the workings of the criminal courts, must be understood within the organizational context of the courts. They involve not only a defendant and a prosecutor as two competing parties, but a defense attorney (or defender's office), a prosecutor's office, a judge, witnesses, other court staff, the police, possibly jurors and others. Each actor or set of actors in each criminal case affects the final outcome (Panzarella & Shapiro, 1988). However complex the issues involved in any case, the complexity of the issues is matched or exceeded by the complexity of the court process (Mays & Taggart, 1986).

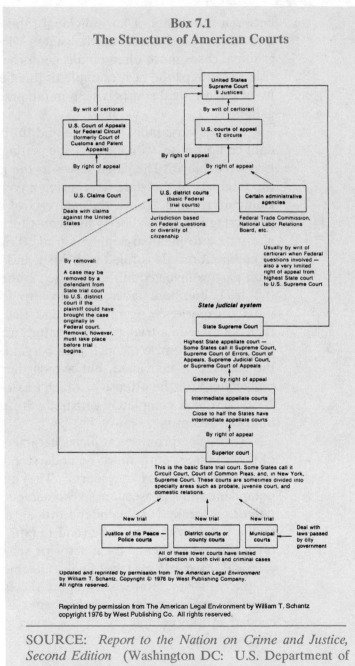

Box 7.1
The Structure of American Courts

SOURCE: *Report to the Nation on Crime and Justice, Second Edition* (Washington DC: U.S. Department of Justice, 1988):81.

THE ORGANIZATION
OF AMERICAN COURTS

The term "courts" covers a wide range of decision-making bodies, ranging from part-time justice of the peace or Mayor's courts, where the "judge" often is not trained in the law, to the nine-member U.S. Supreme Court. There are many different types of courts, and the courts are organized on two basic levels: *federal courts* and *state courts*. The American court process often defies description and in some instances represents an administrative nightmare. Box 7.1 provides a diagram of the American court process.

Federal Courts

The federal judicial system is comprised of the U.S. Supreme Court, 12 U.S. Courts of Appeals, 94 District Courts, more than 400 magistrates assigned to the district courts, and a number of special courts for tax, patent, customs and contract cases. In comparison to most state court systems, the federal courts are relatively simply organized. U.S. magistrates are appointed by District Court judges and are empowered to issue warrants, hear petty cases and conduct the preliminary stages of more serious criminal cases.

U.S. District Courts exist in each of the fifty states, the District of Columbia, and in the federal territories. These courts are trial courts of the federal system and, combined with Magistrates, District Courts form the lower courts in the federal system. They hear both civil and criminal cases involving the federal government or violations of federal laws.

U.S. Courts of Appeals are divided over the fifty states, the District of Columbia, and in the federal territories. Eleven of these courts are identified by number, and the twelfth is the Court of Appeals for the District of

Columbia. These courts receive appeals from the decisions of the District Courts, and also decide appeals from the decisions of many federal administrative agencies. Their decisions become binding on all federal District Courts under their jurisdiction.

The U.S. Supreme Court is the nation's highest court. Its nine justices hear appeals from the U.S. Courts of Appeals and those from state courts of last resort (usually, state supreme courts) which involve questions of federal law or the U.S. Constitution. In most cases, the Supreme Court is not obligated to decide a case and only selects to do so by granting a *writ of certiorari*. This writ is an order to the lower court to send its records of the case so that the Supreme Court can determine if the law has been properly applied. The Court grants *certiorari* in less than 5% of cases brought before it (Neubauer, 1984:47).

State Courts

State court systems mirror the federal courts in general organization into triers of limited or special jurisdiction, general jurisdiction courts, and a court of last resort. From state to state, however, the courts vary greatly in name, number, administration and power. Rubin (1984:11) observed:

> At the state level, courts are created by state constitutions and legislative enactments, and by municipal and county-level legislation. In too many jurisdictions the proliferation of courts has left the citizen unsure of what court to go to for a particular cause of action (divorce, contract dispute, crime, etc.), and for that matter attorneys are not always sure of where to file a particular suit. Some actions can be filed in two or three different courts, and appeals can be taken to several forums.

Indeed, very often the greatest service an attorney can provide his or her client is insuring that the proper papers are filed with the appropriate court. Donald Jackson (1974) described the current structure of American courts as one which would make a "chart-maker collapse in despair." He described the organizational chart of American courts as "a bewildering maze of parallel, perpendicular, crisscrossing, and overlapping lines." Whether, how, and where to enter the courts with any given case are often very ponderous questions.

Suppose that you have a disagreement with a neighbor over parking spaces on the street. For the moment (and because your car is already parked in front of the neighbor's house), you have won. The next morning, you awaken to discover four flat tires. What should you do? The options are many. First, you may "grin and bear it," not knowing for sure who did you wrong, you may opt to repair the tires and try to forget the incident (although you may spend several nights keeping your car under surveillance, or you may be more selective in where you park). Second, you may confront your neighbor because you assume that he is the guilty party (probably a good bet). Of course, if relations between you and your neighbor were better, you would have had an informal mechanism to avoid this incident in the first place. Third, you may seek revenge by slashing your neighbor's tires that evening. Fourth, you may decide to call the police and report the vandalism. Eventually, calling the police could lead to a court appearance. There may be other options, but these appear to be the most likely.

For whatever reasons, let us assume that the first three options are unacceptable. In all probability, you would call the police (this allows you to collect insurance payment for damages) and turn the decision of what to do over to the responding officer. The dispute may then reach the courts as a criminal complaint, but deciding whether, where and how to enter the courts would be someone else's problem.

Unless you have the more expensive all-weather, all-terrain, steel belted tires of a large size, you could take your case to small claims court and sue your neighbor for damages. You could also secure counsel by hiring an attorney or by contacting a legal aid office.

This hypothetical case resulted from a dispute among neighbors over parking privileges. It could go to a number of different courts as a tort (wrongful injury suffered by you, that is, damaged tires), a crime (willful destruction of property by your neighbor), or both. How is the average citizen to know how and where to file a court case?

The general structure of state courts includes courts of limited jurisdiction (over 12,000 of them) which are empowered to hear petty cases such as traffic violations, and to conduct the preliminary stages of more serious cases, much like federal magistrates. A second level of courts is that of general jurisdiction, where trials for civil and criminal cases are conducted. Most states also have a juvenile or family court, which is a special jurisdiction trial court empowered to hear juvenile delinquency cases but is not otherwise involved with criminal matters. Such courts also hear divorce, child custody and related domestic relations cases. Finally, there are frequently other special purpose courts such as probate and surrogate's courts. These types of courts, combined, are referred to as the "lower courts," because they are the first courts in the hierarchy of tribunals to receive cases.

Lower courts decide issues of fact. They conduct trials, receive evidence and establish guilt or innocence. Lower court judges preside over trials and impose criminal sentences upon convicted offenders.

In most states, a third level of appellate courts exists, at which the courts operate like the U.S. Courts of Appeals, that is, they hear appeals from the lower courts. Some states have more than one intermediate appeal level, so that a case may go through two or more appeals before reaching the third level of courts. Each state has a court of last resort or a Supreme Court, which receives appeals from all lower courts in the state and from the intermediate appellate courts. The decisions of these courts are binding on all other courts in the state.

Appellate courts do not decide issues of fact. Rather, appellate courts serve to interpret the law. Appellate courts accept the findings of fact from the lower courts, and then decide whether the lower court judges interpreted and applied the law correctly, resolving questions of law raised by those who lost in the lower courts. The decision of higher courts on the interpretation and application of the law are binding on all the courts beneath them. Thus, when the U.S. Supreme Court decides upon an interpretation of the U.S. Constitution, that interpretation is binding on all other courts in the nation.

THE DEVELOPMENT
OF AMERICAN COURTS

During the colonial period, most of the political power was placed in the hands of the colonial governor (Neubauer, 1984:36). The colonists generally adopted the existing English system of courts and government, but modified the system to fit the less complicated nature of colonial life. The many specialized courts which had evolved in Britain were not fully transplanted to the colonies. Rather, the county court was created as the basic tool of adjudication. Appeals from rulings of the county court were taken directly to the governor. While it was possible to appeal a gubernatorial decision to the English courts, it was seldom done (Glick, 1983:35).

As the colonies grew and commerce developed, the county courts became increasingly less able to handle the number and intricacy of cases that were filed. Each colony created special courts to expedite the handling of cases. New courts of general jurisdiction were also created to reduce the need for litigants to travel great distances to have their cases heard in county courts. The addition and creation of new courts were accomplished on a haphazard basis, that is, new courts were created to resolve specific problems, and not with any grand scheme of court structure in mind. Further, court development occurred independently in each colony. One result of this method of development is that courts performing the same functions often have different names, as is illustrated in Box 7.2.

After the American Revolution, the greatest issues facing the courts were those surrounding the balance between federal and state powers. The nature of the U.S. Constitution, with its limitations on federal powers and reservation of certain governmental powers to the states, insured the continuation of state judicial systems. The Federal Judiciary Act of 1789, designed to create a court system for the resolution of cases arising from federal laws, was a compromise between the Federalists and Antifederalists. The Antifederalists championed states' rights and feared a strong central government. The compromise was that federal courts would be created, but that these courts would not cross state lines. To this day, no U.S. District Court has more than one state within its jurisdiction.

State judges were required to swear an oath of allegiance to the U.S. Constitution, and the Judiciary Act of 1789 gave the Supreme Court of the United States authority to review state decisions involving questions of a constitutional or federal nature. This fact gave the appearance that state courts were subservient to the federal courts (Jacob, 1984:162). Yet, state courts retained tremendous powers. The federal courts did not gain significantly in authority until social changes in America caused state courts to become ineffective.

Box 7.2
Names of Felony Trial Courts, by Jurisdiction

State	Name given to felony court			
	Circuit Court	District Court	Superior Court	Other
Alabama	X			
Alaska			X	
Arizona			X	
Arkansas	X			
California			X	
Colorado		X		
Connecticut			X	
Delaware			X	
Dist. of Columbia			X	
Florida	X			
Georgia			X	
Hawaii	X			
Idaho		X		
Illinois	X			
Indiana	X		X	
Iowa		X		
Kansas		X		
Kentucky	X			
Louisiana		X		
Maine			X	
Maryland	X			
Massachusetts		X	X	X
Michigan	X			
Minnesota		X		
Mississippi	X			
Missouri	X			
Montana		X		
Nebraska		X		
Nevada		X		
New Hampshire			X	
New Jersey			X	
New Mexico		X		
New York				X
North Carolina			X	
North Dakota		X		
Ohio				X
Oklahoma		X		
Oregon	X			
Pennsylvania				X
Rhode Island			X	
South Carolina	X			
South Dakota	X			
Tennessee	X			X
Texas		X		X
Utah		X		
Vermont		X		
Virginia	X			
Washington			X	
West Virginia	X			
Wisconsin	X			
Wyoming		X		

Source: M.L. Clifford and R.T. Roper <u>1984 State Trial Court Jurisdiction Guide for Statistical Reporting</u> (Williamsburg, VA: National Center for State Courts, undated), table 10 and (for Mississippi) table 1.

SOURCE: *State Felony Courts and Felony Laws,* (Washington DC: U.S. Department of Justice) 1987:2.

Throughout the nineteenth century, the development of industry, the completion of the transcontinental railroad, and the growth in interstate commerce created conditions in which state courts were not capable of resolving a large number of cases. In time, federal courts were increasingly called upon to resolve disputes. As Jacob (1984:163) noted:

> Just as state governments in general became less important to national policymaking, so state courts, to a somewhat lesser degree, lost their pre-eminent position in the judicial system and increasingly concentrated on private law cases, which enforce existing norms and affect only the immediate parties to a case.

THE FUNCTIONS OF COURTS

In describing the role of the courts, one of the first goals of the process that we can identify is likely to be "justice" (Rubin, 1984), as previously discussed. That is, the purpose of the courts is to do justice. However, we are not able to agree upon what exactly is "just." Alan Dershowitz (1982:xvi) suggested that, in fact, "nobody wants justice." Rather, parties to a suit are only interested in winning.

It is not possible to understand the operations of the criminal courts without having an appreciation for the complexity of the job performed by the courts. Addressing this issue, Neely (1983:16) noted:

> As long as we are talking only about criminal courts, the questions are relatively simple. As soon, however, as civil courts enter the picture, all bets are off. For while improved funding of the criminal courts would return economic dividends to the public, improved funding of the civil courts has mixed income effects.

Neely continued to cite the example of New York City, where increased funds were given to courts of general jurisdiction to help alleviate caseload backlogs. The creation of more courts and the appointment of more judges opened more opportunities for people to press lawsuits. In many of these accelerated cases, the defendant in the civil suits was none other than the city of New York. In effect, the citizens of New York City had paid more money to create more courts that could then be used by plaintiffs to sue the city for still more money in damages.

Because most courts empowered to hear criminal cases are also authorized to hear civil cases (as is true in New York City), it is not possible to selectively enhance court capacities. Creating new judgeships and courts for the purpose of speeding criminal trials, for example, will necessarily also serve to speed civil trials. Indeed, the civil docket may be so crowded that increased courts will not substantially affect the outcome of criminal cases.

We will focus on the criminal courts for the remainder of this chapter and the next chapter. We must remember, however, that the civil cases and civil caseload lurk in the background and represent the largest portion of workload in the courts (with the exception of traffic cases). The functions of the criminal courts are twofold: the repression of crime and the protection of the rights of individuals accused of crimes.

These goals are served within an environmental context that includes many factors. These factors are the characteristics of the various actors (defendants, witnesses, juries, judges, prosecutors, defense attorneys, etc.), organizational goals of involved agencies, political climate, social forces, and others. The law is only one of several factors which impinge on judicial outcomes. As Glick (1983:18) stated, "Most cases also are settled through informal negotiation, not trials. Personal decision making and compromise are the keys to understanding how disputes are settled."

THE CRIMINAL COURT PROCESS

The basic dispute which is addressed in criminal courts is based on a balance between the need to control criminal behavior and the desire to protect individual rights and liberties. This dispute is at the core of each decision in the court segment of the justice system. After arrest, the suspect is processed into the court stage of the criminal justice process and moves along a series of hearings and decisions which result either in conviction and punishment, or release from custody. The principal decision points in the courts are *initial appearance* (bail determination), *formal charging, arraignment* on charges and *trial*. Sentencing, or punishment, is the subject of Chapter 9.

Initial Appearance

Shortly after arrest, the suspect is taken before a magistrate for the setting of *bail*. Bail is a security posted by the defendant to insure appearance at later court proceedings. The Eighth Amendment to the U.S. Constitution provides that "excessive bail shall not be required." There is some controversy whether this provision creates a right to bail for criminal defendants, or whether it merely protects them from facing an excessive bail. The leading U.S. Supreme Court decision on bail was rendered in the case of *Stack v. Boyle*. Under federal law, defendants in non-capital cases are entitled to bail, and the issue in this case was whether bail set at $50,000 was excessive, given defendant's inability to post that amount. The Court decided that the purpose of bail is to insure appearance at later proceedings and, absent evidence to support an exception, bail which is not reasonably calculated, or which is higher than that normally fixed for similar offenses, is excessive.

Neubauer (1984:213) reported that federal law and the constitutions in most states expressly provide a right to bail in most cases. In the latter part of the 1960s and in the early 1970s, bail was the subject of great scrutiny and debate (Wice, 1974). The Vera Institute of New York City had conducted an experiment on the effects of bail on criminal defendants, which demonstrated that many of those accused of crimes were unable to meet even relatively low bail amounts, and that those who were unable to make bail suffered with higher rates of conviction and incarceration (Ares, Rankin & Sturz, 1963). As a result of this report and of the general interest in bail reform in the United States, a number of "bail projects" were created and implemented across the country. The ways in which a defendant could "make bail" were expanded. In addition to monetary bail, in which the defendant posts cash in the amount specified by the court, a number of alternatives were developed. These were created largely in response to perceived problems with the role of the bail bondsman.

Bail bondsmen are small businessmen who provide bail for criminal defendants for a fee. Usually, the bondsman charges 10% of the bail amount, which is not refundable. Thus, if you face a bail of $2,500, the bondsman will charge you $250 and post the full bond to secure your release. If you appear at the later stages of your trial, the bondsman is refunded the full $2,500, but you are out the $250. Should you fail to appear at later hearings, the bondsman will seek you out and return you to court in order to protect his investment. Observers of the bail process were uncomfortable with profit as the motive behind pretrial release, with the errors made by bondsmen and their agents in apprehending those who "skipped" bail, and with the irregularities in the posting of bond (bondsmen using the same assets to secure release for several defendants) (Goldfarb, 1965; Goldkamp, 1979).

Box 7.3
Pretrial Release Procedure

Both financial bonds and alternative release options are used today *

Financial bond

Fully secured bail—The defendant posts the full amount of bail with the court.

Privately secured bail—A bondsman signs a promissory note to the court for the bail amount and charges the defendant a fee for the service (usually 10% of the bail amount). If the defendant fails to appear, the bondsman must pay the court the full amount. Frequently, the bondsman requires the defendant to post collateral in addition to the fee.

Deposit bail—The courts allow the defendant to deposit a percentage (usually 10%) of the full bail with the court. The full amount of the bail is required if the defendant fails to appear. The percentage bail is returned after disposition of the case, but the court often retains 1% for administrative costs.

Unsecured bail—The defendant pays no money to the court but is liable for the full amount of bail should he or she fail to appear.

Alternative release options

Release on recognizance (ROR)—The court releases the defendant on the promise that he or she will appear in court as required.

Conditional release—The court releases the defendant subject to his or her following specific conditions set by the court, such as attendance at drug treatment therapy or staying away from the complaining witness.

Third party custody—The defendant is released into the custody of an individual or agency that promises to assure his or her appearance in court. No monetary transactions are involved in this type of release.

Citation release—Arrestees are released pending their first court appearance on a written order issued by law enforcement personnel.

The traditional objective of bail or other pretrial release options is to assure appearance at trial * *

In medieval times, the accused was bailed to a third party who would be tried in place of the accused if the accused failed to appear. As the system evolved, the guarantee became the posting of a money bond that was forfeited if the accused failed to appear. In the United States, the Eighth Amendment states that bail shall not be excessive, but it does not grant the right to bail in all cases. The right to bail for many offenses was established by Federal and State laws early in our history.

Most unconvicted jail inmates have had bail set * *

Of 66,936 unconvicted jail inmates surveyed in 1978—
• 81% had bail set
• 46% could not afford the bond that had been set
• 17% had not had bail set
• 6% were held on nonbailable offenses such as murder
• 3% had not yet had a bail hearing
• 2% were held on detainers or warrants.

SOURCES: *Report to the Nation on Crime and Justice, Second Edition*. (Washington, DC: U.S. Department of Justice, 1988):76. **Report to the Nation on Crime and Justice: The Data*. (Washington, DC: U.S. Department of Justice, 1983):59.

In reaction, the Vera Institute and other programs initiated "release on recognizance" (ROR), whereby a defendant with ties to the community (a job, family, stable residence, etc.) would be released on his or her own recognizance without posting bail, as there was reason to believe that he or she would not flee the jurisdiction. In other places, courts allowed defendants to post only 10% of the full amount (because 10% was the amount of money risked by a defendant whose bail was paid by a bondsman), or to post surety rather than cash, that is, surety such as property deeds or automobile titles. Another innovation was the use of issuing citations in lieu of arrest (Kalmanoff, 1976). Here, defendants are issued a summons to appear in court (much like a traffic citation), rather than being arrested. Box 7.3 summarizes the major forms of pretrial release that are available to defendants in our courts.

The central question in bail determinations is to what extent the setting of a bail amount should reflect concern for protecting public safety. While the only constitutionally recognized purpose of bail is to insure appearance by the defendant at later court proceedings, a common concern of police, prosecutors and magistrates (not to mention the general public) is to keep suspected offenders off the streets until they can be convicted and punished. To accomplish this goal, some persons advocate *preventive detention*, in which defendants suspected to be dangerous are denied bail until their cases are tried (Sorin, 1988). There have been many cases in which persons released on bail committed several crimes while on pretrial release, crimes which could have been avoided if the defendant were not released (Ervin, 1971).

In practice, this dilemma is resolved through the establishment of bail schedules and the criteria employed to determine if a defendant is suitable for ROR. Those with prior criminal records, no visible means of support, accused of serious offenses and otherwise thought to be dangerous usually do not qualify for ROR or low-amount bail. As shown in Box 7.4, most jurisdictions have enacted preventive detention statutes, which establish procedures and criteria to follow in order to establish the dangerousness of a defendant and whether to deny pretrial release (Kennedy, 1980).

Whether or not bail or other pretrial release is granted, the next decision point in the court process is the *preliminary hearing*. At this stage, the evidence against the accused is reviewed by a neutral magistrate to determine if the evidence is sufficient to justify binding the defendant over for trial. The preliminary hearing is one method of filing formal charges against a defendant.

Formal Charging

At some point in the pretrial segment of the court process, the state must file *formal charges* against a defendant. These charges are allegations of the specific crimes for which the defendant will stand trial. They are termed "formal charges" to distinguish them from the arrest charge which may not actually reflect the offense for which the accused will be tried. In charging, the prosecutor (or state's attorney or district attorney) applies the criminal law to the facts of the case and identifies which provisions of the criminal code have been violated.

For example, the police may arrest someone who is standing on the porch of a home holding a screwdriver and charge him or her (in the arrest report) with attempted burglary. Upon reviewing the case and the law, the prosecutor may decide that the evidence will not support so serious a charge and opt to charge criminal trespassing and possession of burglar's tools. Similarly, the police may arrest for first degree murder, but the formal charge may be manslaughter.

Box 7.4
Provisions for Pretrial and Preventive Detention
of Defendants in American Courts

**About three-fifths of the States have one or more provisions
to ensure community safety in pretrial release**

Type of provision	States that have enacted the provision
Exclusion of certain crimes from automatic bail eligibility	Colorado, District of Columbia, Florida, Georgia, Michigan, Nebraska, Wisconsin
Definition of the purpose of bail to ensure appearance and safety	Alaska, Arizona, California, Delaware, District of Columbia, Florida, Hawaii, Minnesota, South Carolina, South Dakota, Vermont, Virginia, Wisconsin
Inclusion of crime control factors in the release decision	Alabama, California, Florida, Georgia, Minnesota, South Dakota, Wisconsin
Inclusion of release conditions related to crime control	Alaska, Arkansas, Colorado, Delaware, District of Columbia, Florida, Hawaii, Illinois, Iowa, Minnesota, New Mexico, North Carolina, South Carolina, South Dakota, Vermont, Virginia, Washington, Wisconsin
Limitations on the right to bail for those previously convicted	Colorado, District of Columbia, Florida, Georgia, Hawaii, Indiana, Michigan, New Mexico, Texas, Utah, Wisconsin
Revocation of pretrial release when there is evidence that the accused committed a new crime	Arizona, Arkansas, Colorado, District of Columbia, Georgia, Hawaii, Illinois, Indiana, Maryland, Massachusetts, Michigan, Nevada, New Mexico, New York, Rhode Island, Texas, Utah, Vermont, Wisconsin
Limitations on the right to bail for crimes alleged to have been committed while on release	Arizona, Arkansas, Colorado, District of Columbia, Florida, Georgia, Illinois, Indiana, Maryland, Massachusetts, Michigan, Minnesota, Nevada, New Mexico, New York, Rhode Island, Tennessee, Texas, Utah, Vermont, Wisconsin
Provisions for pretrial detention to ensure safety	Arizona, Arkansas, California, Colorado, District of Columbia, Florida, Georgia, Hawaii, Illinois, Indiana, Maryland, Massachusetts, Michigan, Nebraska, Nevada, New Mexico, New York, Rhode Island, South Dakota, Texas, Utah, Vermont, Virginia, Washington, Wisconsin

Source: Elizabeth Gaynes. *Typology of State laws which permit consideration of danger in the pretrial release decision* (Washington: Pretrial Services Resource Center, 1982) and updated from *Public danger as a factor in pretrial release: A comparative analysis of State laws.* Barbara Gottlieb. National Institute of Justice. July 1985.

SOURCE: *Report to the Nation on Crime and Justice, Second Edition*. (Washington, DC: U.S. Department of Justice, 1988):77.

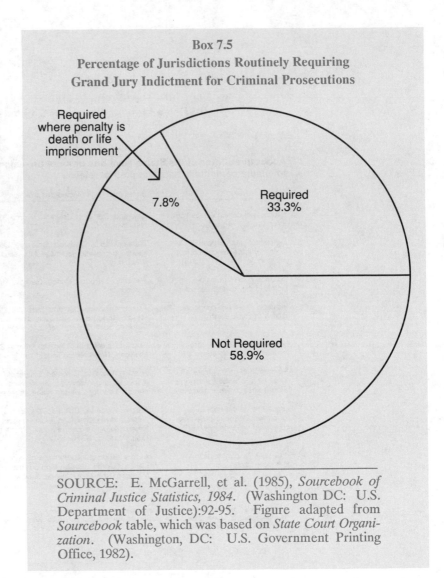

Box 7.5
Percentage of Jurisdictions Routinely Requiring
Grand Jury Indictment for Criminal Prosecutions

Required
where penalty is
death or life
imprisonment

7.8%

Required
33.3%

Not Required
58.9%

SOURCE: E. McGarrell, et al. (1985), *Sourcebook of Criminal Justice Statistics, 1984*. (Washington DC: U.S. Department of Justice):92-95. Figure adapted from *Sourcebook* table, which was based on *State Court Organization*. (Washington, DC: U.S. Government Printing Office, 1982).

The evidentiary standard for charging is the same as that for arrest: probable cause. However, there is a subtle difference in interpretation of probable cause among police and prosecutors. Police tend to be "backward-looking" in attempting to justify an arrest, while the prosecutor is "forward-looking" in attempting to predict the likelihood of successful prosecution (Newman, 1978). That is, the police require probable cause to believe the suspect has committed a crime, while the prosecutor requires probable cause to believe the suspect (now defendant) can be convicted of the crime (Adams, 1983; Boland & Forst, 1985).

There are two methods by which formal charges can be leveled against a defendant. One, previously mentioned, is by the information process through the preliminary hearing. The second is indictment by the grand jury. In about half of the states and in the federal jurisdiction, the grand jury indictment is the normal method of charging. In the remaining states, the information process is the routine manner in which formal charges are brought (Senna & Siegel, 1984:265). Box 7.5 reveals that grand jury charging for felony offenses is required in only one-third of the states.

The *grand jury* is a part of the court processes of all American criminal jurisdictions. It is a panel of citizens (usually 23 citizens, with a quorum of 16) that sits for a month or longer and reviews evidence in criminal cases to determine whether sufficient evidence exists to justify trial of an individual (Newman, 1978). In addition to this charging function, grand juries also have investigatory powers and occasionally are used to investigate suspected criminality and to issue formal charges based on the results of that investigation (Alpert & Petersen, 1985).

The grand jury has been criticized as a "rubber stamp" of the prosecutor. Cases are presented to the grand jury by the prosecutor in secret proceedings without a magistrate or judge to instruct the jury. In 95% of cases the grand jury issues a "true bill," or indictment. In only about 5% of cases does the grand jury go against the wishes of the prosecutor and issue a "no bill," or fail to indict. Thus, it appears that the grand jury does not perform its function of checking the discretion of the prosecutor. The problem with this type of analysis is that the assumption is made that the prosecutor really wants an indictment in every case presented to the grand jury, and that a 5% rejection rate is evidence of inefficiency. These critics thus suggest that prosecutors probably have insufficient evidence for charging in more than the 5% of cases that grand juries reject.

The information process occurs in open court and the defendant and his or her attorney are present and allowed to examine witnesses. The proceedings of the preliminary hearing become part of an official record, and the hearing takes place before a magistrate or judge, who insures that rules of evidence are followed. The result of both processes is the same, that is, either the defendant is bound over for trial on formal charges, or the evidence is found to be insufficient to support the charges and the case is dismissed. The decision as to which charging process to employ is the result of jurisdictional tradition and laws and at the discretion of the prosecutor. In some places, it is the prosecutor's choice as to which process to follow.

The grand jury is more under the control of the prosecutor, but it does not allow a test of evidence sufficiency at trial (i.e., how well witnesses will "hold up" under cross-examination), and it yields no evidence which can be entered into the trial record directly. The grand jury has the advantage of not disclosing the nature of the case or evidence to the defense attorney. The preliminary hearing, on the other hand, allows the state to test the strength of its case and, because the defendant is allowed to face his or her accusers and to cross-examine witnesses, testimony presented at the preliminary hearing can be used at trial if necessary. The disadvantage is that rules of evidence must be more strictly followed and, therefore, the defense is given a good indication of the nature and strength of the case against the defendant. For the defendant, the information process is preferred because of the stricter rules of evidence and the chance to preview the prosecution's case.

Regardless of which method of filing formal charges is employed, once the defendant is bound over for trial on the charges, the next decision point is conviction. The popular media generally depict this decision as being the result of a jury trial filled with strategy and characterized by dignified, formal courtroom demeanor and drama. In reality, most criminal cases are decided at the next stage of the court process, the arraignment, at which the defendant is asked to plead to the charges.

Arraignment

After being formally charged with a crime, the defendant is called into court to be notified of the charges against him or her, and is asked to plead to the charges. In most criminal cases, the defendant will enter a plea of guilty at this point, and avoid a trial of the case on the facts. This high percentage of guilty pleas clearly illustrates the "compromise" nature of the court process. It is most often the result of what is known as "plea bargaining."

At arraignment, the formal charges are read and the defendant is asked, "How do you plead?" The defendant (usually it is the defense attorney who speaks at this point) can answer in one of five ways: not guilty, not guilty by reason of some defense (that is, the defense indicates a special, affirmative defense such as insanity or self-defense), guilty, *nolo contendere*, or the defendant can stand silent. If the defendant is silent, the judge will enter a plea of "not guilty" for the defendant.

The only plea a judge must accept at this point is "not guilty." The plea of *nolo contendere* means that the defendant, by not contesting the charge, will be convicted of the offense. The difference is that the conviction cannot be used against the defendant in other proceedings, especially civil actions. This can be very important, depending upon the nature of the offense, and is a relatively common plea in "white-collar" offenses.

Suppose you drank too much at a party, and while driving home, struck and injured a pedestrian. The responding officer who investigates the accident will probably discover that you are drunk, and charge you with driving under the influence. At arraignment, you plead *nolo contendere* and stand convicted, with all that the conviction entails, such as loss of driving privileges, mandatory jail term, a fine, and the like. The pedestrian you injured files a tort suit against you for pain and suffering, alleging negligence on your part. Conviction of drunken driving would establish your blame for the civil case in itself. By pleading *nolo contendere*, the pedestrian is now required to establish your negligence at the civil trial, without reference to the outcome of your criminal trial.

Certain affirmative defenses involve special pleadings, in which the defense states the reason for asserting innocence, such as "not guilty by reason of insanity." In these cases, the defense generally is not contesting the facts of the case in regards to the criminal act (*actus reus*), but rather is asserting that there is not the requisite mental state (*mens rea* or intention to commit a crime) for the act to be a crime. This special plea serves to give notice to the state that an affirmative defense will be raised, and also shifts the burden of proof from the state to the defense. As we will see, the state generally is required to prove all elements of a criminal offense beyond a reasonable doubt. Failure to do so results in an acquittal. With affirmative defenses, the defense is required to raise a question about the case; for example, the defense may give evidence that the defendant might have been legally "insane" at the time of the crime (Klofas & Weisheit, 1987). Box 7.6 summarizes the requirements and burdens of proof for insanity pleas.

The defense conceivably could remain silent throughout an entire trial and, when all the state's evidence has been entered, move for a directed verdict (dismissal) because the state failed to meet the burden of proof beyond a reasonable doubt. If the state's case is indeed not strong enough, the defendant will be acquitted. With most affirmative defenses, the defendant admits the act, but denies some element crucial to the mental aspect of the crime, such as intent. The burden then falls upon the defense to raise a reasonable doubt about that element, which the state must then prove beyond a reasonable doubt actually existed at the time of the offense.

Box 7.6
Evidentiary Standards and
Burdens of Proof for Insanity Pleas

Test	Legal Standard Because of Mental Illness	Final Burden of Proof	Who Bears Burden of Proof
M'Naghten	"didn't know what he was doing or didn't know it was wrong"	Varies from proof by a balance of probabilities on the defense to proof beyond a reasonable doubt on the prosecutor	
Irresistible Impulse	"could not control his conduct"		
Durham	"the criminal act was caused by his mental illness"	Beyond reasonable doubt	Prosecutor
Brawner– A.L.I.	"lacks substantial capacity to appreciate the wrongfulness of his conduct or to control it"	Beyond reasonable doubt	Prosecutor
Present Federal Law	"lacks capacity to appreciate the wrongfulness of his conduct"	Clear and convincing evidence	Defense

SOURCE: N. Morris (1988), *Insanity Defense*. Crime File Study Guide. (Washington, DC: National Institute of Justice):3.

The "not guilty" plea results in the establishment of a trial date and moving for trial, including jury selection and the filing of pretrial motions for disclosure of evidence, suppression of evidence and the like, in preparation for the trial itself. While this is the normal outcome of arraignment on television and in the movies, it is very rare in the actual operations of the criminal courts.

The "guilty" plea is an admission of the offense and obviates the need for a trial. It is discretionary with the judge whether to accept a plea of guilty, for it entails a waiver of the right to trial, and in many states, a waiver on the right to appeal rulings on the admissibility of the evidence and other controversies. The Federal Rules of Criminal Procedure (Box 7.7) instruct the judge to investigate the factual nature of the plea, the voluntariness of the plea, and the defendant's awareness of the effects of the plea before a guilty plea can be accepted.

Box 7.7
Federal Rules of Criminal Procedure, Rule 11-Pleas

A defendant may plead not guilty, guilty or, with the consent of the court, *nolo contendere*. The court may refuse to accept a plea of guilty, and shall not accept such plea or a plea of *nolo contendere* without first addressing the defendant personally and determining that the plea is made voluntarily with understanding of the nature of the charge and the consequences of the plea. If a defendant refuses to plead or if the court fails to appear, the court shall enter a plea of not guilty. The court shall not enter a judgment upon a plea of guilty unless it is satisfied that there is a factual basis for the plea.

If the defendant does not plead guilty, the next stage of the court process is trial, at which the decision is made about conviction. Here the state presents the case against the defendant, and the defense attempts to discredit or otherwise cast doubt on the case presented by the prosecutor. The act of pleading guilty means that the state's case will go uncontested. While contested trials are the exception in criminal law (if not all law), it is at trial that the full strength of the value placed on individual liberty is evident.

Trial

Although not often used, given the number of available cases, the jury trial is the "balance wheel" (Neubauer, 1984:284) of the court process. It is the possibility of the jury trial that serves to ensure "justice" in the more common plea bargaining. As Jacob (1984:207) explained:

> Although critics focus on plea bargains, bench and jury trials continue to constitute an essential part of the criminal justice process. It is true that only a very small proportion of cases goes to trial, and an especially small proportion go to trial by jury. But the possibility of going to trial constrains the plea bargaining process. No one has to accept a bargain that is worse than the decision that could be obtained at a jury trial. Doubtful cases can be brought to a jury or bench trial, even when the prosecutor would rather close the case with a lenient bargain.

Only the more "celebrated" cases (Walker, 1985:16-17) receive the full panoply of rights, including the jury trial, but the full justice process is available to all. Trials are held in approximately 10% of criminal cases in the United States. These trials are of two types: *jury trials* and *bench trials*.

Box 7.8
State Requirements for Jury Size,
Felony and Misdemeanor Trials

All states require 12-member juries in capital cases.

6 states permit less than 12-member juries in felony trials.

Felonies   **Misdemeanors**

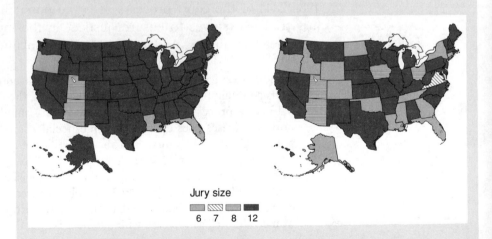

Jury size

6   7   8   12

SOURCE: *Report to the Nation on Crime and Justice, Second Edition.* (Washington, DC: U.S. Department of Justice, 1988):86.

A common form of criminal trial is the bench trial held before a judge sitting alone, with no jury. These trials are routine for petty offenses for which the maximum penalty does not exceed incarceration of six months, and are commonly accepted by defendants in more serious cases in lieu of the more costly and time-consuming jury trials. Jury trials involve a panel of citizens who have the task of determining the facts of the case. The judge rules on questions of law and presides over the trial, but questions of fact, how much weight to give the testimony of a witness, and the final decision about guilt or innocence are the responsibilities of the jury.

The right to trial by jury is rooted in our legal tradition and is firmly established in the U.S. Constitution. The U.S. Supreme Court ruled that any criminal defendant facing a punishment of more than six months incarceration had the right to trial by jury, in the case of *Baldwin v. New York*. Individual states may grant the right to trial by jury for those facing less serious charges if they desire, but they are not required to do so by the U.S. Constitution.

To most of us, the jury is a body of twelve members who come to a unanimous decision about the guilt or innocence of the defendant. To some, the phrase "jury of one's peers" connotes that the members of the jury should be representative of the defendant in age, sex, education, place of residence, race, and in other ways. In fact, "peers" means fellow citizens and thus the jury does not need to reflect the characteristics of the defendant. It may be surprising, however, to learn that the jury does not have to consist of twelve members, and that it does not have to reach a unanimous verdict in all states. Box 7.8 shows state requirements of jury size for felony and misdemeanor cases.

In two cases, the U.S. Supreme Court addressed the unanimity of jury verdicts, and the size of the jury. Many related questions still remain, but the Court decided that it was permissible to use a jury of six members in a robbery trial, in the case of *Williams v. Florida*. The Court has not ruled on whether juries of less than six would be allowed. It has further decided that non-unanimous verdicts are permissible, when the Court upheld convictions based on juror votes of 9-3 (*Johnson v. Louisiana*) and 10-2 (*Apodaca v. Oregon*). Nonetheless, only four states allow non-unanimous verdicts (Neubauer, 1984:287). The Court has not ruled yet on how close a jury vote could be and still be valid, nor has it ruled on the effect of a split vote on a jury of less than twelve members.

If a trial is held, the burden of proving guilt rests with the state, and the rights of the offender are strictly protected. The U.S. Supreme Court ruled that the prosecution must prove every element of the offense "beyond a reasonable doubt," in the case of *In re Winship*. In *Gideon v. Wainwright*, the Court held that an accused must be provided with defense counsel at state expense if he or she is unable to provide for his or her own defense. This case involved a convicted felon who had asked for the assistance of a defense attorney at trial and was denied. The Court ruled that the right to counsel at trial applied to felony cases. In a later case, *Argersinger v. Hamlin*, the Court extended this right to any criminal prosecution where the possible penalty included incarceration of six months or more. Thus, not only does the defendant have a right to contest the state at trial, but if he or she is unable to retain an attorney, the defendant has a right to counsel provided by the state.

While relatively rare, the full jury trial is the center of the court process, and it is the trial of which we most often think when we consider the courts. Our *adversary* system of justice, in which truth is expected to emerge from the arguments of two sides of a question, is epitomized by the jury trial. If acquitted, the defendant is set free and generally cannot be tried again for the offense. (The U.S. Constitution protects criminal defendants from *double jeopardy*, or being subjected to trial or punishment more than once for a single offense.) If convicted, the case proceeds to the next decision point of the justice system: *sentencing*. Sentencing and punishment are the topics addressed in Chapter 9.

REVIEW QUESTIONS

1. Briefly describe the organization of American courts, and explain how this particular court structure developed.

2. Identify the principal decision points in the criminal court process.

3. What is bail and what is its constitutional purpose?

4. Describe two ways in which formal charges may be brought against a defendant.

5. What is meant by "plea bargaining," and why is it important?

6. Differentiate between a bench trial and a jury trial.

REFERENCES

Adams, K. (1983), "The effect of evidentiary factors on charge reduction," *Journal of Criminal Justice* 11(6):525-38.

Adams, K. & C. Cutshall (1987), "Refusing to prosecute minor offenses: The relative influence of legal and extralegal factors," *Justice Quarterly* 4(4):595-609.

Alpert, G. & T.K. Petersen (1985), "The grand jury report: A magic lantern or an agent of social control?," *Justice Quarterly* 2(1):23-50.

Ares, C.E., A. Rankin, and H. Sturz (1963), "The Manhattan Bail Project: An interim report on the use of pre-trial parole," *New York University Law Review* 38(January):71-92.

Boland, B. & B. Forst (1985), "Prosecutors don't always aim to pleas," *Federal Probation* 54(2):10-15.

Bureau of Justice Statistics (1984), *Case Filings in State Courts, 1983* (Washington, DC: U.S. Department of Justice).

_____ (1987), *State Felony Courts and Felony Laws.* (Washington, DC: U.S. Department of Justice).

_____ (1985), *Pretrial Release and Misconduct* (Washington, DC: U.S. Department of Justice).

Dershowitz, A.M. (1982), *The Best Defense.* (New York: Vintage Books).

Ervin, S.J. (1971), *Preventive Detention.* (Chicago: Urban Research Corp.).

Glick, H.R. (1983), *Courts, Politics and Justice.* (New York: McGraw-Hill).

Goldfarb, R. (1965), *Ransom: A Critique of the American Bail System.* (New York: Harper & Row).

Goldkamp, J. (1980), *Two Classes of Accused.* (Lexington: Lexington Books).

Jackson, D.D. (1974), *Judges.* (New York: Atheneum).

Jacob, H. (1984), *Justice in America.* (Boston: Little, Brown).

Kalmanoff, A. (1976), *Criminal Justice: Enforcement and Administration.* (Boston: Little, Brown).

Kennedy, E. (1980), "A new approach to bail release: The proposed federal code and bail reform," *Fordham Law Review* 48:6.

Klofas, J. & R. Weisheit (1987), "Guilty but mentally ill: Reform of the insanity defense in Illinois," *Justice Quarterly* 4(1):39-50.

Mays, G.L. & W.A. Taggart (1986), "Court clerks, court administrators & judges: Conflict in managing the courts," *Journal of
Criminal Justice* 14(1):1-8.

Neely, R. (1983), *Why Courts Don't Work*. (New York: McGraw-
Hill).

Neubauer, D.W. (1984), *America's Courts and the Criminal Justice
System*. (Monterey, CA: Brooks-Cole).

Newman, D.J. (1978), *Introduction to Criminal Justice, 2nd. Edition*,
(Philadelphia: J. B. Lippincott).

Panzarella, R. & I. Shapiro, (1988) "Policy, job practices, and personal values in decision making by court officers," *Journal of Criminal Justice* 16(2):111-120.

Rubin, H.T. (1984), *The Courts: Fulcrum of the Justice System,
2nd. Edition*, (New York: Random House).

Senna, J. & L. Siegel (1984), *Introduction to Criminal Justice, 3rd
Edition*. (St. Paul, MN: West).

Sorin, M.D. (1988), *Out on Bail*. Crime File Study Guide.
(Washington, DC: National Institute of Justice).

Walker, S. (1985), *Sense and Nonsense About Crime*. (Monterey,
CA: Brooks-Cole).

Wice, P.B. (1974), *Freedom for Sale*. (Lexington, MA: Lexington
Books).

TABLE
OF CASES

People and Problems in the Courts

In addition to such persons as bailiffs, victims, witnesses, stenographers, observers, clerks and a number of other actors, four sets of people play major roles in the court segment of the justice system: *defense attorneys, prosecutors, judges* and *jurors*. These are the people who have a direct effect on decision making in the criminal courts. With the exception of jurors, who are usually typical citizens, all are trained in the law and therefore share a common culture (Glick, 1983:2-3). In many ways, prosecutors and defense attorneys mirror each other, except for the fact that they are adversaries at trial. Very often, judges are recruited from the ranks of prosecutors and, to a lesser extent, defense attorneys. As a result, judges not only share a common training and educational experience, they often share common career paths.

DEFENSE ATTORNEYS

In the field of law, criminal law is not a particularly well-respected specialty (Neubauer, 1984:156). Wice

(1978) studied defense attorneys across the country and reported that defense counsel generally were solo practitioners or attorneys working in small offices (2 or 3 associates). They usually began their private practices late in life, and many obtained their criminal law experience and training in prosecutors' offices. Most were not graduates of the nation's best law schools, and their salaries were generally on the lower end of the earnings scale for the legal profession. As Neubauer (1984:157) reported, "[M]ost lawyers view criminal cases as unsavory." Of the hundreds of thousands of attorneys in the United States, fewer than fifty thousand will take criminal cases, and the number of criminal law specialists is probably in the vicinity of only 5,000 (Neubauer, 1984; Glick, 1983; Bartollas, Miller & Wice, 1983).

Of those who routinely do take criminal cases, many do so as a part-time function, to supplement their earnings from a general law practice. Criminal defense services typically are provided by young, inexperienced attorneys, or by older, somewhat less successful attorneys. One result of the *Gideon* and *Argersinger* decisions has been an increase in criminal defense work for attorneys.

Traditional defense services were available to a defendant if he or she could afford to retain the services of an attorney. Privately-retained counsel is still an option for criminal defendants today. This type of arrangement involves the defendant hiring his or her own attorney for a fee. The attorney then represents the defendant at trial and in all other stages of the court process. For those unable to pay an attorney, however, the effect of the Supreme Court's decisions on the right to counsel has been the development of alternative systems for the provision of defense services. The most common are the creation of a public defender's office, or the use of "assigned counsel." Box 8.1 compares these two systems.

Box 8.1
Characteristics of Public Defender
and Assigned Counsel Systems

Summary of public defender system characteristics	Percent of public defender counties
Affiliation	
County government	38%
State executive agency	25
Judiciary	23
Independent nonprofit organization	8
Other	6
Chief public defenders	
Full-time	78
Part-time	22
Number of full-time staff attorneys	
0	24
1–6	59
7–20	10
21–50+	7
Support staffing	
Secretaries	86
Investigators	58
Administrative assistants	18
Law students	16
Paralegal employees	10
Social workers	9
Fiscal officer	6
Training director	3
Salary ranges	
Full-time chief public defenders	
$6,000–66,000 (yearly)	
$20,000–30,000 (modal)	

Summary characteristics of assigned counsel systems	Percent of assigned counsel counties
Administrative	
Ad hoc (appointments made by individual judges, clerks, public defenders, or others)	75%
Coordinated	25
Lists of available attorneys	
● Compiled on basis of:*	
Lawyers who affirmatively volunteer	43
Inclusion of all lawyers	35
Volunteers who qualify	27
Volunteers who participate in continuing legal education	8
● Categorized according to attorneys' specialization in lists	19
● Established procedures for formal removal	15
Caseload	
Cases distributed among most of the attorneys on the list	44
Average of 1 to 10 cases per assigned counsel	75

*Total exceeds 100% because multiple methods are used.

SOURCE: R.L. Spangenberg, et al. (1986), *National Criminal Defense Systems Study: Final Report.* (Washington, DC: U.S. Department of Justice):15,17.

Thus, in addition to privately-retained counsel, these other two forms of defense comprise the three major methods of securing representation for criminal defendants. By far, the most common of these forms is the public defender's office, in terms of the volume of cases handled (Rubin, 1984:201). Larger jurisdictions (those having the heaviest caseloads) are likely to operate a public defender's office that mirrors the prosecutor's office. In many jurisdictions, the public defender is elected and authorized to employ a number of assistant public defenders to serve all indigent defendants. In these systems, the defense attorneys work for the municipality on salary. Young attorneys often seek these positions in order to develop trial experience prior to beginning their own private practices. Older attorneys, weary of the rigors of private practice, also take positions with the public defender's office. Box 8.2 shows the distribution of criminal defense systems by number of counties and size of the populations served. Box 8.3 shows the major form of defense system used in each state.

A second form of defense services is used in the majority of criminal jurisdictions, but serves fewer than half of all indigent criminal defendants. In jurisdictions where there usually are not large enough criminal caseloads to justify the expense of developing and operating public defenders' offices, counsel are placed on a list. Attorneys voluntarily enter their names to be considered for criminal defense work or, in some places, all members of the local bar are enrolled on the defender's list. As indigents come before the court, the judge appoints an attorney from the list, moving down the list of attorney names as cases are initiated. In this system, the assigned counsel generally is paid a fee based on an hourly rate, but with a maximum cap. The fee paid generally is less than an attorney would charge a private client (especially so in places where all members of the bar appear on the list). Again, because of the relatively low fees available under this system, only younger, not yet established attorneys, and those who are not sufficiently busy to provide an adequate income, are likely to seek out assigned counsel appointments.

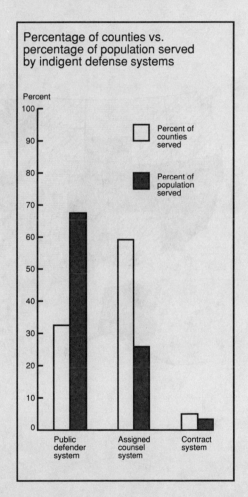

Box 8.2
Distribution of Indigent System Types
by Percentage of Counties
and Percentage of Population Served

Percentage of counties vs. percentage of population served by indigent defense systems

SOURCE: R.L. Spangenberg, et al. (1986), *National Criminal Defense Systems Study: Final Report.* (Washington, DC: U.S. Department of Justice):14.

Box 8.3
Criminal Defense Systems Most Commonly Used
in the States

Predominent system for indigent defense

- Public defender
- Assigned counsel
- Contract

SOURCE: *Report to the Nation on Crime and Justice, Second Edition*. (Washington, DC: U.S. Department of Justice, 1988):75.

There has been some debate about which of these systems provides the best defense services to the accused. Traditionally, and in common sense fashion, it has been expected that privately-retained counsel, as a result of the clear relationship between who is paying for service and who is receiving service, would provide the best defense. Analyses comparing privately-retained counsel with publicly-appointed attorneys have not demonstrated any significant differences in the quality of service provided (Wice & Suwak, 1974; Taylor, et al, 1973).

A final option for defendants in criminal cases is to defend themselves. An interesting question arises when the defendant seeks to represent himself or herself at trial. Given the adage that "a lawyer who represents himself has a fool for a client," do defendants have the right to make fools of themselves? The United States Supreme Court has decided that they do. In *People v. Faretta*, the defendant sought self-representation, but the trial judge denied his request, insisting that Faretta accept the assistance of appointed defense counsel. Faretta appealed, arguing that it was his right to represent himself at trial. The Supreme Court agreed with Faretta that self-representation (*pro se* defense) is a constitutional right of the defendant. What has not yet been decided, however, is whether a *pro se* defendant who loses in court can appeal the conviction on the basis of incompetent representation.

While relatively rare, *pro se* defenses do occur. Occasionally, a defendant feels that no one else can or will present the case as well. More often, these defenses occur when the defendant is interested in using the courtroom as a forum for expressing some viewpoint, rather than as a place for settling a criminal case. Box 8.4 provides some illustrations of the pitfalls that can upset a *pro se* defense.

Box 8.4

Problems with Pro Se Defenses

Defendants often convict themselves, and in a variety of ways:

The Bizarre Defense. In a Chicago case, a burglary suspect stood at the counsel table, stared at the empty witness box and carefully asked a question. Then he darted to the witness chair, buttoned his jacket and waited for spectator giggles to subside before answering. Rushing back to the table, the man inquired of himself, "Where were you the night in question?" After scurrying back to the dock, he replied, "Would you please repeat the question?" So amused, the jury convicted him after deliberating all of two minutes.

The Blooper. Lawyers say that defendant-attorneys typically get too close to their cases and blunder by letting slip information that leads to trouble. Trying to shake an eyewitness's identification of him, one Chicago robbery defendant posed a disastrous question: "How can you be sure? Isn't it true that when I robbed your store I was wearing a ski mask?"

The Ego Trip. A defendant in Boston, pleased at obtaining a hung jury at his trial for the murder of his wife, refused generous offers from the prosecution to plea-bargain for a lesser charge. The second jury convicted him of voluntary manslaughter.

(continued)

PROSECUTORS

Unlike defense services, there is no privately-retained prosecutor. Rather, prosecutors are elected officials whose duty it is to provide legal counsel for the state in criminal trials. Depending on the size of the jurisdiction and the size of its criminal caseload, prosecutors may be either full-time or part-time. Also, depending on the size of the prosecutor's office, the prosecutor (frequently called the state's attorney or district attorney) actually serves as a manager

Self-defense efforts are scorned by veteran attorneys. Asks Boston lawyer-author George Higgins: "If you had a brain tumor, would you operate on yourself?" But there are potential benefits. Judges sometimes tolerantly allow self-defenders to make statements, particularly in summation, for which a lawyer would be ruled in contempt of court. Moreover, by appearing to be bewildered by court procedures, a defendant can occasionally arouse sympathy for the underdog in judge or jury.

In the California trial of Joseph Gesualdo, the judge allowed the lawyer-defendant to reconsider his abandonment of the case--a privilege that probably would not have been granted to an experienced attorney. But Gesualdo continued to encounter difficulties. He recalled a witness to emphasize the man's inability to identify him; the witness suddenly changed his mind and decided he did indeed remember him. Some courtroom observers thought Gesualdo might have obtained at least a hung jury if he had retained a lawyer clever enough to exploit weaknesses in the evidence against him. But after deliberating 50 minutes, the jury found him guilty.

SOURCE: "Fools in Court," *Time Magazine* (May, 1977):45.

and rarely engages in trial preparation or courtroom appearances. Like the public defender described earlier, the prosecutor usually is elected and authorized to employ a number of assistants, who actually provide the legal services of the office. These assistants are salaried employees of the municipality. Again, these positions are attractive to young attorneys seeking trial experience, and to older attorneys who do not wish to engage in private practice or have not been able to secure a position with a larger law firm.

At the federal level, prosecutorial services are provided by United States Attorneys, who are presidential appointees, and who are empowered to employ assistants to handle federal criminal cases. In addition, the federal government (as well as some state and municipal governments) frequently creates an "Office of the Special Prosecutor," whereby an attorney is employed to investigate and prosecute cases arising out of some special circumstance, such as the Watergate investigation during the Nixon administration. Special prosecutors usually are employed when there is concern about possible conflicts of interest, or if the case is so complex that the usual need to perform the ordinary duties of the prosecutor's office would render it impossible for that office to pursue the case adequately.

While similar in many respects, one major difference between the prosecutor's and the public defender's offices is that the prosecutor's office has traditionally been a stepping-stone for political careers. In part as a result of its elective nature, and partly because the prosecutor can garner considerable media coverage by tackling certain cases (pornography, white collar crime, child abuse, etc.), the office of prosecutor enables incumbents to prepare for political advancement. Unlike the prosecutor, the public defender generally does not gain voter support because he earns a living by defending the accused, who are sometimes pornographers or child molesters. An attorney that is interested in a political career as a judge or other elected official often begins in the prosecutor's office.

JUDGES

Glick (1983:74) reported that there are well over 20,000 judgeships in the United States. Judgeships are very prestigious positions, and to many attorneys, becoming a judge represents the pinnacle of a legal career. (Neely,

1983). Compared to the general practice of law, being a judge is more prestigious, more secure, and less stressful. The overwhelming majority of the nation's judges achieve their offices through election. Unfortunately, judicial elections, at least as measured by voter turnout, generally do not provoke much citizen interest. Yet, the selection of judges is important because the characteristics of the judge are often what determine the outcome of a case, more so than does the nature of the case itself (Jackson, 1974; Eisenstein & Jacob, 1977; Levin, 1977). There are two basic methods by which judges are selected in the United States: *election* and *appointment*. In the case of elections, states determine whether judicial races can be partisan or must be non-partisan. In elections, judges run for office much the same as mayors or state legislators. In states having appointment processes, the governor or state legislature is empowered to appoint judges to office. For years there has been debate over how best to ensure that those selected for judicial positions have the requisite qualifications for the job. Generally, the debate has focused on either the election of judges or on the *Missouri Plan*.

In the Missouri Plan (so named because it originated in the state of Missouri), a panel of the bar association rates the qualifications of candidates and the executive then appoints someone from the list of qualified candidates. The appointed judge must then periodically face an uncontested "retention election," in which the sole question before the voters is whether the judge should be retained in office. Should the voters decide to oust the judge, the executive then appoints another from a list of qualified candidates, and the process is repeated. Supporters of this system of judicial selection argue that it provides the best of all worlds, that is, the system includes direct voter input in the selection of judges through the retention election, yet it insures that only qualified candidates become judges and that those judges are at least somewhat insulated from political pressure and are isolated from partisan politics. The evidence is not clear that this method of choosing judges is "better" than direct election, however (Nagel, 1973). Box 8.5 describes the methods by which judges are selected in the United States.

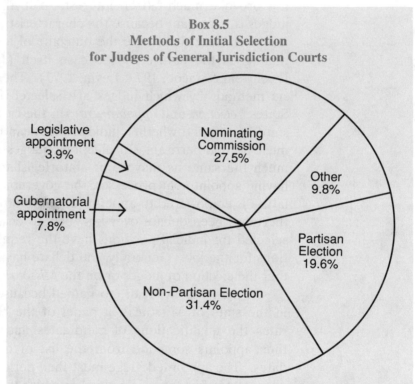

Box 8.5
Methods of Initial Selection
for Judges of General Jurisdiction Courts

Source: E. McGarrell, et al (1985 *Sourcebook of criminal justice statistics, 1984,* (Washington, D.C.: U.S. Department of Justice): 88-89. Figure adapted from *Sourcebook* table based on L. Berkson, S. Beller & N. Grimaldi (1980) *Judicial selection in the United States.* (Chicago: American Judicature Society), updated by American Judicature Society, 1989.

Non-Partisan Election—GA, ID, KY, LA, MN, MT, NV, ND, OH, OK, OR, SD.

Nominating Commission—AK, CO, CT, DC, HI, IA, NE, NM, UT, VT, WY, and DE, MA, MD by governor's executive order.

Partisan Election—AL, AR, IL, MS, NC, NY, PA, TN, TX, WV.

Gubernatorial Appointment—ME, NH, NJ, RI.

Other—AZ (Counties of 150,000+ population use nominating commission, others use non-partisan election for Superior Court), CA (Local electors choose gubernatorial appointment or non-partisan election for Superior Court), IN, KS, MO (Some counties use nominating commission for general jurisdiction court, others use partisan election).

The federal judicial system operates differently in that federal judges are appointed by the President for life terms. The President generally accepts nominations from the senators of the state in which the district court judge will serve, but he is not required to do so. The candidate is then nominated by the President, whose final appointment of the judge is subject to the advice and consent of the Senate. Recent controversy over the appointment of Supreme Court justices during the Reagan administration illustrates the hazards of Senate confirmation faced by federal judicial nominees.

In the autumn of 1987, the President nominated three candidates before he was able to obtain the consent of the Senate. Seeking conservative justices who would be strict constructionists in their interpretation of constitutional issues, the President nominated Judge Robert Bork, followed by Judge Douglas Ginsburg. An active senatorial committee dominated by Democrats closely investigated both candidates. Judge Bork was found unacceptable on the basis of his record in equal rights issues. Judge Ginsburg removed his name from consideration after acknowledging that he had experimented with marijuana in his youth (*Criminal Justice Newsletter*, 1987). The third nominee, Judge Anthony M. Kennedy, won senate approval.

The principal difference between the federal and state judiciaries is the tenure of judicial office in each. State judges, no matter how selected, undergo periodic review and face possible removal without impeachment. Lifetime tenure insulates the federal judge from improper political or other influence, but it means that incompetent or corrupt judges cannot easily be removed from office. The removal of a federal judge can be accomplished only through impeachment.

JURORS

The last important set of decision-makers in the criminal courts is the *jury*. The jury is a panel of citizens selected through the process of *voir dire* (literally, to speak the truth) who are charged with hearing the cases and determining guilt or innocence. While rarely used, the criminal trial jury is at least symbolically important as evidence that the citizenry reigns, and is provided for in the Constitution of the United States, and in the state constitutions. Regardless of the testimony and other evidence presented at trial, the verdict of the jury is almost totally within its discretion and binding on the court. Only in very rare instances can the defense attorney succeed in convincing the judge to order a directed verdict of acquittal. This occurs when, at the conclusion of presenting its case, the prosecution has failed to provide enough evidence about some important element of the offense. In such cases, the defense counsel requests that charges be dropped because the prosecution has failed to establish its case.

Because of the tremendous discretionary power of the jury, prosecutors and defense attorneys are very careful in the jury selection or *voir dire* process. Each side is awarded a number of *peremptory challenges* which allow them to remove otherwise qualified jurors from service. In addition, each side may challenge any number of prospective jurors for cause. Thus, when selecting jurors, prospective jurors may be asked about how they feel about the defendant, if they know about the case, etc. Any answer is cause for a "challenge." Peremptory challenges are used by attorneys when they cannot establish a just cause for keeping someone off the jury, yet they believe that the individual will not be receptive to their case.

Both the prosecution and the defense seek to seat jurors whom they believe will support their respective presentations of the case. In many ways, jury selection is the most important part of the trial process (Fried, et al, 1975). Just as judicial decisions reflect the characteristics of the judge, jury decisions reflect the characteristics of the jury (Simon, 1980; Kalven & Zeisel, 1966). Turner, et al (1986) reported that prosecutors and defense attorneys agree, for example, that black jurors are more likely to vote for acquittal, while white jurors are usually in favor of conviction.

PROBLEMS IN THE CRIMINAL COURTS

As with every stage of the justice system, the court process is plagued with problems and issues that defy easy resolution. Some have been touched upon earlier in this chapter, such as the best mechanism for the provision of defense counsel, the effects of judicial selection, and the selection of jurors. Three additional issues have been identified for further consideration in this section. Currently, the debate about plea bargaining continues and has resulted in some jurisdictions attempting to eliminate or control the practice. The role of the press in trials is still unresolved and, while this was a particularly important issue during the "political" trials of the student anti-war and civil rights activists in the early 1970s, it has resurfaced and again gained prominence. Finally, with severe overcrowding in the nation's jails, the right to a speedy trial is again an important practical and constitutional issue.

Speedy Trial

The issue embodied in the title "Speedy Trial" is most often thought of as court delay. That is, speedy trial is the solution to the problem of what some perceive as unacceptable delays in the processing of criminal cases from arrest to disposition. The concern over court delay is founded on three related, but different perspectives (Bureau of Justice Statistics, 1986). First, there are those who advocate speedy trials for the protection of the rights of the defendant. Then, there are those who see speedy trials as the solution to some of the mistreatment of crime victims by the justice system. Finally, there are those who propose speedy trials as a crime-control strategy.

Lengthy delays between arrest and trial (or between charging and trial) can serve to the disadvantage of criminal defendants. Especially in those cases in which the defendant is unable to make bail, denial of a speedy trial amounts to incarceration prior to conviction. By virtue of their inability to obtain pretrial release, defendants awaiting trial for long periods of time are likely to suffer such further losses as loss of income (if not loss of job), possible loss of residence, separation from family and friends, and upon conviction, higher rates of incarceration. Thus, at least one group proposes speedy trial as a protected right of the defendant (American Bar Association, 1968).

Crime victims frequently are ignored by the justice system. Indeed, the role of the victim in the justice process is generally that of witness, if anything. The justice system is not designed to alleviate the suffering of crime victims. Lengthy court proceedings, especially in which the victim is involved as a witness, result in lost work days, mental anguish while awaiting resolution of the case, delays in recouping stolen property, and other costs to the victim. While speedy trial acts to the advantage of the accused (especially the innocent accused), it is also suggested that the crime victim has a stake in early resolution of criminal cases (Walker, 1985:141).

Yet another reason for speedy trials is the desire to control crime. Pretrial delays are often blamed for high rates of plea bargaining. Plea bargaining, in turn, is blamed for the lack of deterrent effect of the criminal law. A more quantifiable effect of case processing delays on crime, however, may be the amount of crime committed by criminal defendants who are free on bail and at large in the community. The longer a defendant is at liberty on bail, the greater the likelihood that he or she will commit a new crime while awaiting trial (Bureau of Justice Statistics, 1985). Speedier trial and convictions (especially those resulting in incarceration) would reduce at least this one form of crime (Walker, 1985:53). Finally, the longer the period between when a crime occurs and when the trial is held, the more difficult it is to secure a conviction. Witnesses move or die, memories fail, outrage at the offense lessens, and general interest in the case wanes. Indeed, defense attorneys often use delay strategies to win cases, that is, they seek repeated continuances in hopes that witnesses eventually will fail to appear. Box 8.6 presents information on case processing time and the right to a speedy trial.

Regardless of the relatively widespread support for speedy trials, this is not a reform likely to be easily realized. Speedy trials are not in the best interests of the guilty defendant, nor are they always in the best interests of the prosecutor. Especially when the defendant is incarcerated and awaiting trial, the length of time between arrest and trial serves as an inducement to the defendant to engage in plea bargaining, thereby assuring conviction. Klemm (1986) reported that case processing time in five cities was more dependent upon the type of plea than other factors. Thus, defendants pleading not guilty and going to trial experienced longer court delays than did those pleading guilty. A report from the Bureau of Justice Statistics (1986), based on courts in 12 jurisdictions, echoed Klemm's findings. Further, as Feeley (1983) recognized, reforms that aim to promote speedy trials are subject to the desires of the courtroom work force. The judges, prosecutors and defense attorneys who regularly work in America's courts realize that speedy trials will disrupt their operations and, therefore, they oppose such a reform, even if the opposition is not knowingly and openly voiced. The opposition is usually enough to render the reform ineffective. Case processing delays are, in fact, more likely to be products of this work group and the legal culture of a community than the result of caseload pressures, trial rates, or other factors (Klemm, 1986).

Box 8.6
Felony Case Processing Times and Speedy Trial

	Average elapsed time from arrest to disposition for:	
	Cases filed in court	Cases indicted and bound over for trial
Total (mean)	3.5 mos.	4.9 mos.
Type of disposition		
Dismissal	2.8	5.3
Guilty plea	3.4	4.5
Trial	7.1	7.4
Most serious charge		
Homicide	6.2	7.1
Sexual assault	4.2	6.0
Robbery	3.5	4.4
Burglary	3.2	4.1
Larceny	3.2	4.7

Note: Data are derived from 12 different jurisdictions and represent median case processing times within jurisdictions averaged using the mean across all jurisdictions with available data. Data for "total" and "type of disposition" were available from all 12 jurisdictions; data for "most serious charge" were available for 9 jurisdictions. The elapsed time in months was computed by dividing the elapsed time in days by 30.4 (the average number of days per month in a nonleap year).

Right to a Speedy Trial

A criminal defendant's right to a speedy trial is guaranteed by the Sixth Amendment to the U.S. Constitution: "In all criminal prosecutions, the accused shall enjoy the right to a speedy and public trial...." Determining when this right has been violated, however, is rarely a matter of simple objective fact. In *Barker v. Wingo* (407 U.S. 514, 530-33 (1972)) the Supreme Court spelled out four factors for courts to weigh in determining if a defendant's constitutional right to a speedy trial has been denied. The *length of the delay* is the most important consideration, but it must be judged in light of the *reasons for the delay*. Deliberate attempts to delay by the government weigh heavily in favor of the defendant. Certain reasons, such as the absence of a key witness, are considered valid. The court must also determine *if the defendant asserted his rights to a speedy trial* and *if the delay prejudiced the case against the defendant.*

SOURCE: *Felony Case Processing Time.* (Washington, DC: U.S. Department of Justice, 1986):2.

Free Press and Fair Trial

While the issue of media compromising the trial process is relatively rare, it is an important concern because it deals with a balance of rights, that is, the right of the defendant to a fair and impartial hearing, and the right of the press to report on operations of the government (or, as members of the news media may state it, "the public's right to know"). Press coverage of criminal trials may affect court processes in two ways. First, the effects of pretrial publicity may make it difficult, if not impossible, to select a jury which has not been exposed to prejudicial coverage of the case (Brady, 1983). Second, in cases where members of the press are allowed into the courtroom, it is possible that the entire trial will take on a "circus atmosphere." That is, not only will the behavior of reporters disrupt court proceedings, but the very presence of reporters may alter the behavior of the judge, prosecutor, defendant, jury and others (Giglio, 1982).

Because this issue involves two constitutional guarantees, free press and fair trial, the courts generally have adopted a "totality of circumstances" test, wherein they attempt to balance the rights of the media to cover trials against the rights of the state and the accused to proceed in an orderly fashion. The issue only becomes important in those cases which receive the lion's share of media attention, that is, cases that involve particularly gruesome offenses, or the otherwise newsworthy cases (those involving well-known victims or defendants).

It is instructive to compare the American handling of news media coverage of criminal trials with that of England. In England, the press is strictly forbidden from reporting on pending criminal cases, under penalty of contempt of court. That is, once a criminal case has been opened, the British press are banned from commenting on it. Violation of this ban can (and usually does) result in the offending reporter being incarcerated for contempt of court. In the United States, such a ban on reporting would violate the First Amendment's prohibition against "prior restraint" (censoring "free speech" before it occurs). Rather, American courts have relied upon post-trial remedies, such as declaring convictions invalid and ordering new trials, as in *Sheppard v. Maxwell* and *Estes v. Texas*.

The strong American value placed on individual rights, such as free speech, and our commitment to the sovereignty of the citizen prevent us from banning press coverage of trials. The other side of the dilemma is our commitment to fairness and a recognition that media coverage of criminal cases can bias juries and result in unfair verdicts. The American solution of post-trial remedies, like the British use of prior restraint, reflect the different values of the two societies. As Giglio (1982:349) stated it, "The British emphasis, therefore, is on justice being done, rather than witnessed." Conversely, the American emphasis is on justice being witnessed, in order to insure that justice is done.

In practice, much of the problem of balancing the rights to free press and fair trial has been resolved in American courts through the development of norms of doing business. Occasionally, explicit policies and agreements have been reached among judges, attorneys and the press, and more often, understandings of what is appropriate and inappropriate reporting develop tacitly. The reliance on post-trial remedies to possibly prejudicial media coverage of criminal cases allows the courts and the press to learn from experience and develop such policies to avoid future controversies.

The question of fair trial versus free press is complex because the coverage of criminal cases by the media, while sometimes misleading (as by presenting the jury trial as the norm), leads to a better understanding of criminal justice processes for the citizenry. Further, media coverage of criminal cases supports ultimate accountability of justice system officers to the public. On the other hand, the possible biasing effects of media commentary about criminal cases cannot be denied. In comparing the American and British practices, Giglio concluded that one result of freer press coverage of criminal cases in the United States is that American citizens have a better understanding of their system of justice than do citizens of Britain. The difficulty inherent in balancing the good against the bad of media coverage of criminal cases insures that this issue will remain relevant for some time to come.

Plea Bargaining

As shown in Box 8.7, the overwhelming majority of criminal convictions come as a result of a negotiated plea of guilty. In a study of the processing of felony cases in New York City, the Vera Institute reported that 98% of felony arrests resulted in guilty pleas (Vera Institute, 1977). The Bureau of Justice Statistics (1984) reported that 90% of felony arrests resulted in guilty pleas by those going to court disposition of their cases. The fact of plea bargaining, and its importance in the court process, cannot be denied. Opinion is divided, however, as to the appropriateness of pleading guilty for considerations (Newman, 1966).

On the one hand, there are those who argue that plea bargaining violates the rights of the accused. Especially in cases where possible penalties are very severe, or when the defendant is in jail awaiting trial, the incentives to plead guilty are thought to be too enticing. By pleading guilty, in most jurisdictions, the defendant has waived his or her right not only to a jury trial, but also to appeal questions of evidence admissibility. On the other hand, there are those who suggest that plea negotiations are unfair to the state and the victim. These critics argue that plea bargains serve to "let the guilty off" without sufficient punishment. They feel that negotiated guilty pleas serve to lessen the deterrent effect of the law, as offenders are allowed to avoid their due penalties. Further, the idea that "justice is open to negotiation" is repugnant to these critics of plea bargaining.

Box 8.7
Case Dispositions of Typical
Felony Arrests and Indictments

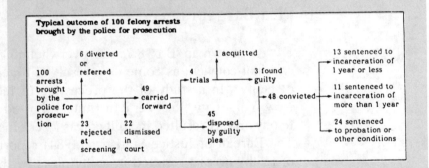

Typical outcome of 100 felony arrests brought by the police for prosecution

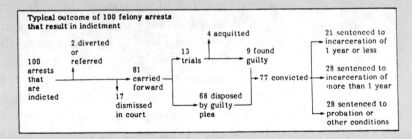

Typical outcome of 100 felony arrests that result in indictment

SOURCE: F. Foland & R. Sones (1986), *The Prosecution of Felony Arrest, 1981.* (Washington, DC: U.S. Department of Justice):2.

Yet, plea negotiations have some supporters. It has been suggested that the criminal justice system could not possibly provide the number of trials required if every criminal defendant were to demand one. The justice system would collapse under the burden of so many trials. The plea bargain results in a sure conviction of the offender, which a jury trial may not, and the defendant who pleads guilty is entitled to a sentence concession as a result of his honesty in admitting guilt, his demonstration of remorse in pleading guilty, or his cooperation with the state (Champion, 1987). Indeed, in *Santobello v. New York*, the U.S. Supreme Court declared that plea bargaining, when properly carried out, is something to be encouraged.

In an ideal world, perhaps it would be best if every criminal defendant were given a trial and plea bargaining were not allowed. In reality, however, this is unlikely to occur. The caseload-pressure argument, which explains high levels of plea bargaining on the basis of necessity, has not been supported by empirical study (Parnas, 1980; Klemm, 1986). The abolition of plea bargaining in some jurisdictions, such as Alaska, for example, has not resulted in a tremendous decrease in the number of cases that are concluded as a result of guilty pleas (Rubinstein & White, 1980; Call, et al, 1983). Thus, not only does it appear that plea bargaining is not associated with limited ability to provide trials, it further appears that plea bargaining is not a practice which can be easily abolished. Similar results were obtained in an analysis of the abolition of plea bargaining in trials within the U.S. Coast Guard.

Whatever else may be said about plea bargaining, it appears to be a practice which is functional. Again, the concept of a courtroom work group is important. Whether or not pleas of guilty result from formal negotiations between the prosecution and defense, those "negotiations" will continue, as will the pleas of guilty. Failure to recognize the informal structure of the courthouse and the professional relationships that exist among the prosecutors, judges and defense attorneys, leads reformers to believe that plea negotiations are somehow aberrant. Rather, given the purpose of the court to resolve disputes, it is only natural that a certain amount of compromise develops among the set of actors that engages in this dispute resolution daily. Indeed, the history of plea bargaining indicates that it is a useful, and traditional, practice (Sanborn, 1986). Plea bargaining is a good example of the effect of people on the justice system. In assessing the operations of the justice process, it is important to remember that the system is comprised of people and operates through people (Champion, 1987).

REVIEW QUESTIONS

1. Identify three ways in which defendants in criminal cases may obtain defense counsel.

2. Summarize the case of *Gideon v. Wainwright* and explain how it relates to *Argersinger v. Hamlin*.

3. Compare criminal defense attorneys with prosecutors. In what ways are their jobs similar?

4. Tell which method of judicial selection you feel is most likely to yield competent judges who are responsive to the public, and explain how the system you select will accomplish this goal.

5. Describe the *voir dire* process and explain how it allows attorneys to protect the interests of their clients.

6. How can "speedy trial" be expected to reduce strains in other areas of the justice system?

7. The conflict between a free press and a fair trial reflects one of the ideological dilemmas of American criminal justice. Explain this conflict, and propose a solution.

8. Take a position on the issue of plea bargaining, that is, either support or oppose the practice, and give arguments against those who take the opposing position to that which you have taken.

REFERENCES

American Bar Association (1968), *Standards Relating to Speedy Trial.* (New York: Institute of Judicial Administration).

Bartollas, C., S. Miller & P. Wice (1983), *Participants in American Criminal Justice: The Promise and the Performance.* (Englewood Cliffs, NJ: Prentice-Hall).

Brady, J. (1983), "Fair and impartial railroad: The jury, the media, and political trials," *Journal of Criminal Justice* 11(3):241-64.

Bureau of Justice Statistics (1984), *The Prevalence of Guilty Pleas.* (Washington, DC: U.S. Department of Justice).

_____ (1985), *Pretrial Release and Misconduct.* (Washington, DC: U.S. Department of Justice).

_____ (1986), *Felony Case-Processing Time.* (Washington, DC: U.S. Department of Justice).

Call, J., D. England, & S. Talarico (1983), "The abolition of plea bargaining in the Coast Guard," *Journal of Criminal Justice* 11(4):351-58.

Champion, D. (1987), "Felony offenders, plea bargaining, and probation: A case of extra-legal exigencies in sentencing practices," *Justice Professional* 2(2):1-18.

Criminal Justice Newsletter, "President cites crime issue in choosing Kennedy for high court," *Criminal Justice Newsletter* 18(22):4.

Eisenstein, J. & H. Jacob (1977), *Felony Justice.* (Boston: Little, Brown).

Feeley, M. (1983), *Court Reform on Trial.* (New York: Basic Books).

Fried, M., K. Kaplan & K. Klein (1975), "Juror selection: An analysis of *voir dire*," in R. Simon (ed.), *The Jury System in America.* (Beverly Hills, CA: Sage).

Giglio, E. (1982), "Free press--fair trial in Britain and America," *Journal of Criminal Justice* 10(5):341-58.

Glick, H. (1983), *Courts, Politics and Justice.* (New York: Mc-Graw-Hill).

Jackson, D. (1974), *Judges.* (New York: Atheneum).

Kalven, H. & H. Zeisel (1966), *The American Jury.* (Boston: Little, Brown).

Klemm, M. (1986), "A look at case processing time in five cities," *Journal of Criminal Justice* 14(1):9-23.

Levin, M. (1977), *Urban Politics and Criminal Courts.* (Chicago: University of Chicago Press).

Nagel, S. (1973), *Comparing Elected and Appointed Judicial Systems.* (Beverly Hills, CA: Sage).

Neely, R. (1983), *Why Courts Don't Work.* (New York: McGraw-Hill).

Neubauer, D. (1984), *America's Courts and the Criminal Justice System.* (Monterey, CA: Brooks-Cole).

Newman, D. (1966), *Conviction: The Determination of Guilt or Innocence without Trial.* (Boston: Little, Brown).

Parnas, R. (1980), "Empirical data, tentative conclusions, and difficult questions about plea bargaining in three California counties," *Federal Probation* 44(2):12.

Rubenstein, M. & T. White (1979), "Plea bargaining: Can Alaska live without it?," *Judicature* 62:266.

Rubin, H. (1984), *The Courts: Fulcrum of the Justice System, 2nd. Edition.* (New York: Random House).

Sanborn, J.B. (1986), "A historical sketch of plea bargaining," *Justice Quarterly* 3(2):111-38.

Simon, R. (1980), *The Jury: Its Role in American Society.* (Lexington, MA: Lexington Books).

Taylor, J., et al. (1973), "Analysis of defense counsel in the processing of felony defendants in Denver, Colorado," *Denver Law Journal* (1973):9.

Turner, B., R. Lovell, J. Young & W. Denny (1986), "Race and peremptory challenge during *voir dire*: Do prosecution and defense agree?," *Journal of Criminal Justice* 14(1):61-70.

Vera Institute of Justice (1977), *Felony Arrests: Their Prosecution and Disposition in New York City's Courts.* (New York: Vera Institute of Justice).

Walker, S. (1985), *Sense and Nonsense About Crime.* (Monterey, CA: Brooks-Cole).

Wice, P. (1978), *Criminal Lawyers: An Endangered Species.* (Beverly Hills, CA: Sage).

Wice, P. & P. Suwak (1974), "Current realities of public defender programs," *Criminal Law Bulletin* 10(March):163.

TABLE
OF CASES

Estes v. Texas, 381 U.S. 532.

People v. Faretta, 422 U.S. 806.

Santobello v. New York, 404 U.S. 257.

Sheppard v. Maxwell, 384 U.S. 333.

9 Sentencing: The Goals and Process of Punishment

After conviction, the next major decision point in the criminal justice system is *sentencing*, which represents the decision about punishment. In many ways the sentencing decision represents the crux of the justice system, for it is at sentencing that we determine what will be done to, for, with, or about the criminal offender.

Criminal sentences involve the imposition of fines, community supervision, or incarceration. In some cases, a criminal sentence includes a combination of all of these. Excluding fines and incarceration in a local jail, over one million people each year receive criminal sentences of probation or imprisonment. If we include punishments for all sorts of offenses, including traffic citations, sentences are imposed on over ten million people each year. In 1986, an estimated 583,000 people were convicted of felonies in state courts, only 46% of whom were sentenced to prison (Bureau of Justice Statistics, 1989).

Understanding how the distinction is drawn between who is incarcerated and who is allowed to remain in the community under supervision requires an understanding of the purposes of the punishment and the motivations of the people who make the punishment decision. This chapter will examine these factors.

THE PURPOSES OF PUNISHMENT

Traditionally, four purposes or justifications for criminal penalties have been advanced: *deterrence*, *incapacitation*, *treatment* (or rehabilitation) and *desert* (or retribution). These theories of punishment answer the question: why punish at all? This is a question the average citizen does not often hear in the context of criminal law. Yet, most of us have heard the expression that "two wrongs do not make a right." That expression, if applied to the criminal law, would imply that imposing a punishment on someone who has broken the law is a "second wrong," and does not make it "right." If I steal your television and am sent to prison for a year because of it, have things turned out right? You are deprived of your television, I am deprived of a year of my life, and we (all of us) pay the costs of trial and imprisonment.

From this point of view, the punishment of crime seems useless, if not wasteful. However, we usually do not think of punishment for crime in this way. Rather, it seems almost automatic that someone who breaks the law will be punished (von Hirsch, 1976). What can justify a system of penalties which can be argued to involve nothing but costs to everyone affected?

Deterrence is one purpose of punishment that is based on the idea that punishment of the individual offender produces benefits for the future by making the idea of criminal behavior less attractive. Deterrence has two parts: *specific deterrence*, in which the object of the deterrent effect is the specific offender, and *general deterrence*, in which the object of the deterrent effect is a wider audience (the general public). In deterrence, punishment is an example of what awaits law violators and serves to educate would-be offenders, so that they will weigh the costs of crime against its benefits (Paternoster, 1987).

With specific deterrence, after I am released from prison, I will think twice before I steal another television because I now know that I will face a year in prison if I steal and am caught. With general deterrence, after seeing what happened to me, you will rethink your plan to replace your missing television by stealing your neighbor's set. In both cases, the punishment serves to prevent future crimes. If society does not punish, there is no reason for us to obey the law.

Deterrence has a certain intuitive appeal. On the surface, it makes sense that deterrence will "work." Unfortunately, the evidence of its effectiveness is not that clear (Newman, 1983:101-05). Few (if any) criminals believe they will be caught and punished (indeed, if they expected to be caught, they most probably would not commit the offense). While we have used the term "educate," deterrence is based on fear. Would-be offenders must fear the penalty, and thus we are left with a society in which behavior is based on fear, which is a basis that most of us do not favor. Finally, when someone has thought about and decided not to commit a crime, it is unclear whether the person made the decision based on fear of punishment, fear of public ridicule, fear of eternal damnation, or whether the decision was based on some other factor. Deterrence has strong appeal, but it is difficult to prove.

The theory of deterrence assumes that man is a rational being guided by a pleasure principal. That is, humans do things that please them, and avoid things that hurt them. Further, we are able to assess the likely effects of our behavior and guide ourselves according to these assessments. As rational beings, we will avoid "bad" behaviors, such as committing crimes, when the behaviors will produce unpleasant results (punishments). Rationality, of course, is difficult to establish. Indeed, many crimes, especially violent offenses among friends and family, are more emotional than rational.

In order for a punishment to deter a would-be offender, two conditions must be met. First, the penalty must be severe enough that the pain of the punishment will outweigh the pleasure of the criminal act. Using an economic example, if the penalty for theft were a $100 fine, it may be severe enough to stop us from stealing $50. Given the opportunity to steal $500, however, the rational man may take the money and pay the fine, keeping a $400 profit. Thus, deterrence depends in part on the severity of punishment.

The second condition is whether the punishment is certain to be imposed. Not only must the punishment be severe enough to outweigh the gain realized by crime, but the likelihood of being punished must be high enough that the offender takes the threat seriously. If the punishment for theft were ten years in prison, but the chance of being caught and punished were only one in a million, the threat of punishment probably would not deter. The lower the risk of punishment, the higher the likelihood that a crime will be committed.

Research has indicated that, of these two conditions, certainty of punishment is the more important aspect of deterrence. Given a rational offender, uncertainty of punishment makes deterrence even more troublesome. The offender will assess the likelihood of being caught, and then take steps to reduce the chance of detection before committing an offense. Deterrence may serve best to make offenders more cautious rather than less criminal. In a review of the deterrence literature, Paternoster (1987) suggested that neither certainty nor severity appear to affect the behaviors of deterrence research samples. He warned deterrence researchers to prepare for the possibility that people who commit crimes may not be acting rationally. It may well be that people are not motivated by their perceptions of either the certainty or the severity of punishment.

Incapacitation, like deterrence, suggests that punishment serves to prevent future crime, but not by education or fear. An incapacitative punishment prevents future crimes by the offender (like specific deterrence) by removing opportunities for crime (unlike specific deterrence). One good reason to imprison a criminal is to insure that he or she does not have the chance to break the law again. I cannot steal your television if I am in prison. Probably the most effective incapacitative penalty is capital punishment. Not only do dead men tell no tales, but they also commit no crimes.

The major drawbacks to incapacitation as a justification for criminal punishment are the difficulties in predicting who is likely to commit an offense in the future, and the costs of incapacitating offenders. At the current level of sophistication, it is not possible for social and behavioral scientists to identify precisely those persons likely to pose a threat of serious crime in the future (Visher, 1987). The prediction problem is simply too complex.

In any attempt to predict "dangerousness" among a population of criminal offenders (not to mention the general population), one runs a risk of making two types of errors: *false positives* and *false negatives*. A false positive is someone who is predicted to be dangerous (positive on danger), but who turns out not to be a threat (false). A false negative is someone who is predicted to be safe (negative on danger), but who turns out to be dangerous (false). False positives are incapacitated as if they were dangerous, and thus prison resources are wasted and individual freedoms are needlessly infringed. False negatives are not incapacitated and, thus, free to victimize others. Every crime-prediction scheme available makes both types of errors. Under the best of circumstances, the likelihood is that roughly eight false positives will be incapacitated for each truly dangerous offender imprisoned, and that nearly half of the dangerous offenders will be classed as posing little danger and released (Wenk, Robison & Smith, 1972).

Largely as a result of the numerous false positives, incapacitation entails a significant increase in prison space (Van Dine, Conrad & Dinitz, 1979; Greenwood, 1982). If we work with the 8:1 ratio of false positives to "true positives" (or actually dangerous offenders), for us to incapacitate 100 more dangerous offenders each year, we also will need to incarcerate 800 more non-dangerous offenders. That is, the prison populations increase nine times as fast as the population of dangerous offenders. In order to provide sufficient prison capacities for these larger populations, it would be necessary to build four to six times as many prisons as are currently in operation. Walker (1985) estimated that it would cost $120 billion over five years in construction and operating expenses to realize a 27% reduction in violent crime. Incapacitation is ultimately rational, but determination of its effectiveness must await the development of accurate prediction devices. Upon reviewing the available evidence about incapacitation, Visher (1987) concluded, "These findings indicate that "lock 'em up" strategies...are only slightly more effective against crime than current practice."

Treatment (also called rehabilitation) is also a rationale based on a reduction of future crime. Unlike deterrence or incapacitation, treatment is concerned with the offender as an individual (Cullen & Gilbert, 1982). Here the punishment imposed is one which fits the individual and is most likely to result in a change in the individual's desire to commit crime. Treatment suggests that individuals commit crimes for a variety of reasons and that the solution to the problem of crime will be achieved through changing individuals so that they will not wish to engage in crime, and by having other options available to them that will allow them to avoid criminality.

As with prediction in incapacitation, the behavioral sciences do not yet have a level of sophistication that allows treatment programs imposed as criminal sentences to be successful. Partly as a result of pragmatic need, the treatment options available for criminal offenders are limited. Generally, offenders receive some type of counseling, which is applied to a wide range of offenders. While designed to deal with individuals, the realities of large numbers of offenders and limited treatment resources mean that treatment is applied to groups and tailored (often not very well) to individuals. Adams (1961) reported that such approaches may be very good for some, of no effect for others, and very bad for others. The net result is that, for the total group, the treatment leads to no marked improvement when those for whom the treatment was harmful cancel out those for whom it was beneficial.

Studies of the effects of treatment suggest that treatments for criminal offenders generally are not effective (Martinson, 1974; Bailey, 1966). Like incapacitation, treatment is eminently plausible, but must await greater sophistication in the design and delivery of services to offenders, and the investment of sufficient resources, in order to meet in practice what is expected in theory.

Despite discouraging results from many attempts at rehabilitation, the efforts to treat criminal offenders continues, and may be increasing (Gendreau & Ross, 1987). Several treatment programs show promise of being effective answers to the criminality of specific populations of offenders. Completing a review of the evidence on rehabilitation effectiveness, Gendreau and Ross (1987) argued that we have successful programs. What is lacking, they contended, is an ability to translate experimental treatments into routine, effective programs for offenders.

Desert (sometimes called retribution) is the only justification for criminal punishment that is not "forward-looking." That is, it does not offer a reduction in future crime as the principal justification for the imposition of a punishment. Rather, desert is based on the belief that whoever breaks the law "deserves" to be punished. Breaking the law in itself is justification for punishment, whether that punishment reduces, increases, or has no effect on future levels of crime. Essentially, the criminal law is a promise wherein we (the state) promise to punish anyone who violates the law, and in the desert rationale, the promise must be kept.

As a justification for punishment, desert places limits on the degree to which someone may be punished. Punishment is expected to be commensurate with (proportionate to) the severity of the crime committed. Thus, public torture and execution of parking violators would deter most of us from parking illegally (if not from driving altogether), and these methods would be acceptable in a purely deterrent system of punishment. In contrast, these extreme forms of punishment for parking violations would be unthinkable in a desert scheme. Further, while a purely deterrent system of punishment does not require that the person being punished be convicted first, the desert rationale is that only convicted offenders are punished.

Partly because it is so difficult to alter the certainty of punishment, compared to the relative ease of increasing the severity of punishment, supporters of deterrence often engage in "penalty escalation" (Newman, 1983). In this case, the penalty for a given offense, say five years imprisonment for theft, is increased (perhaps to ten years). It is easier to increase penalty severity than to become more efficient at catching and punishing thieves. Further, deterrence rests on an argument that the good of the penalty (in terms of crimes prevented) must outweigh its harm in terms of injury to the punished. It is possible, then, for a deterrent penalty to be imposed on an innocent person, as long as the social good outweighs the individual harm.

Incapacitative penalties also can be argued to have the effect of punishing the innocent. The determination of how severe a penalty should be for incapacitation does not rest on the seriousness of the crime committed. Rather, incapacitative penalties depend upon a prediction that the offender will commit another crime. Like the queen in *Alice in Wonderland*, proponents of incapacitation invoke the penalty first, and the crime comes last, after the penalty is served. And, if there in fact is no crime, so much the better.

Treatment penalties assume an "identity of interest" between the state and the offender. The state wants what is best for the offender, that is, to improve his or her chances in life and to reduce the offender's desire to commit crimes. The offender either wants the same thing, or would want it if he or she were competent. Thus, the imposition of a punishment is for the offender's own good. A sanction that seems disproportionate to the seriousness of the offense is not a problem, as long as it is "good" for the offender.

The desert justification for punishment is often stated in biblical terms as "an eye for an eye." It fits rather well with our beliefs that, regardless of the reason, those who break the law should be punished. The difficulty with desert is that we cannot yet precisely measure levels of crime severity, or of punishment severity (Durham, 1988). Additionally, we are uncomfortable with the idea that punishment can (or should) be imposed simply for the sake of punishment.

These four rationales for the imposition of criminal punishment have been presented separately and analyzed as if they were required to stand alone. In practice, however, operating sentencing systems are founded on many purposes. It is not unusual, for example, for the sentencing judge to "throw the book" at a defendant for deterrent purposes, while correctional authorities seek to "treat" the offender's problems and rehabilitate him or her, only to have a paroling authority refuse to release the offender because of a fear that the offender will commit a new crime and, therefore, must be incapacitated.

Not only do most sentencing systems expressly serve all four of these functions, but the decision-makers in those sentencing systems (judges, parole authority members, correctional workers and administrators) favor different justifications for punishment. To further complicate matters, these different actors favor different rationales for punishment of different offenders at different points in time. Further, each criminal jurisdiction has its own structure for the determination and implementation of criminal sentences.

SENTENCING STRUCTURES IN THE UNITED STATES

There are substantial differences among the states as to how they go about the sentencing of criminals. As the Bureau of Justice Statistics (1984:1) reported:

> It requires more than 200 pages to describe the basic features of the sentencing laws in each state. In addition to the different laws that govern sentencing, there are differences in how specific offenses are defined and classified by the criminal code in each state.

Criminal sentencing has been the topic of a great deal of interest and debate in recent years (Travis, 1982; Zalman, 1987). Since 1975, many states have adopted changes in the structures they used for criminal sentencing. The result has been the addition of a number of innovative formats for sentencing. Nonetheless, the traditional distinction made between *determinate* and *indeterminate* sentencing is useful.

Determinate sentencing structures are those in which each offender knows the exact length and nature of his or her punishment at the time it is imposed. Indeterminate sentencing structures are those in which the precise length of the penalty is unknown until some time has passed since the imposition of the penalty. Within each of these classes, there are several types of sentencing structures. Each sentencing structure represents a balance of power among the legislative, judicial, and executive branches of government. The structure of sentencing reflects varying emphasis on each of the goals of criminal sentencing, and it affects how sentencing is conducted.

Box 9.1 depicts sentencing structures found across the United States. The majority of sentencing authority rests with the legislature, which establishes criminal penalties and defines crimes. There has traditionally been a certain level of sentencing power vested in the executive branch in the form of clemency. The governor of a state or President of the United States can grant pardons, commutations, reprieves and other forms of mercy. What sentencing power is granted to parole authorities and sentencing judges is generally delegated to these offices by the legislature.

In indeterminate sentencing systems, the legislature establishes a range of penalties (minimum to maximum), and the sentencing judge is then authorized to impose a sentence which is not less than the minimum and not more than the maximum. In some cases, the legislature establishes a minimum term and then allows the judge to set a maximum within some absolute outer limit. In other cases, the legislature sets a minimum term that is some fraction of the maximum term decreed by the judge. In any indeterminate sentencing system, a paroling authority is authorized to grant release sometime between the end of the minimum term and that of the maximum term. Thus, the judge has powers delegated by the legislature, and the paroling authority has power that is limited both by the legislature and by the decision of the judge.

Box 9.1
Basic Sentencing Structures in the United States

The basic difference in sentencing systems is the apportioning of discretion between the judge and parole authorities

Indeterminate sentencing—the judge specifies minimum and maximum sentence lengths. These set upper and lower bounds on the time to be served. The actual release date (and therefore the time actually served) is determined later by parole authorities within those limits.

Partially indeterminate sentencing—a variation of indeterminate sentencing in which the judge specifies only the maximum sentence length. An associated minimum automatically is implied, but is not within the judge's discretion. The implied minimum may be a fixed time (such as 1 year) for all sentences or a fixed proportion of the maximum. In some States the implied minimum is zero; thus the parole board is empowered to release the prisoner at any time.

Determinate sentencing—the judge specifies a fixed term of incarceration, which must be served in full (less any "goodtime" earned in prison). There is no discretionary parole release.

Since 1975 many States have adopted determinate sentencing, but most still use Indeterminate sentencing

In 1976 Maine was the first State to adopt determinate sentencing. The sentencing system is entirely or predominantly determinate in these 10 states:

California	Maine
Connecticut	Minnesota
Florida	New Mexico
Illinois	North Carolina
Indiana	Washington

The other States and the District of Columbia use indeterminate sentencing in its various forms. One State, Colorado, after changing to determinate sentencing in 1979, went back to indeterminate sentencing in 1985. The Federal justice system has adopted determinate sentencing through a system of sentencing guidelines.

States employ other sentencing features in conjunction with their basic strategies

Mandatory sentencing—Law requires the judge to impose a sentence of incarceration, often of specified length, for certain crimes or certain categories of offenders. There is no option of probation or a suspended sentence.

Mandatory sentencing laws are in force in 46 States (all except Maine, Minnesota, Nebraska, and Rhode Island) and the District of Columbia. In 25 States imprisonment is mandatory for certain repeat felony offenders. In 30 States imprisonment is mandatory if a firearm was involved in the commission of a crime. In 45 States conviction for certain offenses or classes of offenses leads to mandatory imprisonment; most such offenses are serious, violent crimes, and drug trafficking is included in 18 of the States. Many States have recently made drunk driving an offense for which incarceration is mandated (usually for relatively short periods in a local jail rather than a State prison).

Presumptive sentencing—The discretion of a judge who imposes a prison sentence is constrained by a specific sentence length set by law for each offense or class of offense. That sentence must be imposed in all unexceptional cases. In response to mitigating or aggravating circumstances, the judge may shorten or lengthen the sentence within specified boundaries, usually with written justification being required.

Presumptive sentencing is used, at least to some degree, in about 12 States.

Sentencing guidelines—Explicit policies and procedures are specified for deciding on individual sentences. The decision is usually based on the nature of the offense and the offender's criminal record. For example, the prescribed sentence for a certain offense might be probation if the offender has no previous felony convictions, a short term of incarceration if the offender has one prior conviction, and progressively longer prison terms if the offender's criminal history is more extensive.

Sentencing guidelines came into use in the late 1970s. They are—
• used in 13 States and the Federal criminal justice system
• written into statute in the Federal system and in Florida, Louisiana, Maryland, Minnesota, New Jersey, Ohio, Pennsylvania, and Tennessee
• used systemwide, but not mandated by law, in Utah
• applied selectively in Massachusetts, Michigan, Rhode Island, and Wisconsin
• being considered for adoption in other States and the District of Columbia.

Sentence enhancements—In nearly all States, the judge may lengthen the prison term for an offender with prior felony convictions. The lengths of such enhancements and the criteria for imposing them vary among the States.

In some States that group felonies according to their seriousness, the repeat offender may be given a sentence ordinarily imposed for a higher seriousness category. Some States prescribe lengthening the sentences of habitual offenders by specified amounts or imposing a mandatory minimum term that must be served before parole can be considered. In other States the guidelines provide for sentences that reflect the offender's criminal history as well as the seriousness of the offense. Many States prescribe conditions under which parole eligibility is limited or eliminated. For example, a person with three or more prior felony convictions, if convicted of a serious violent offense, might be sentenced to life imprisonment without parole.

Sources: Surveys conducted for the Bureau of Justice Statistics by the U.S. Bureau of the Census in 1985 and by the Pennsylvania Commission on Crime and Delinquency in 1986.

SOURCE: *Report to the Nation on Crime and Justice, Second Edition.* (Washington, DC: U.S. Department of Justice, 1988):91.

In determinate sentencing systems, the legislature generally reserves most of the sentencing power to itself. In some cases, the legislature actually will determine the sentence to be imposed on persons convicted of a specific offense. Here, the judge and parole authority have no sentencing power. More common is the model in which the legislature describes the expected or normal penalty for an offense, and then allows the sentencing judge to modify (with reasons given). This is a presumptive sentence system, that is, the law establishes what the legislature "presumes" will be the sentence, and then requires the judge to explain any case in which the presumed term is not imposed. In determinate sentencing systems, the parole authority typically has no sentencing power.

In most cases, the legislature grants the sentencing judge the ability to choose between a sentence of incarceration and one of community supervision. This is considerable sentencing power, even in a system in which the power of the judge to determine the length of a prison sentence has been strictly curtailed. The decision as to what decision-maker receives how much sentencing power reflects a different emphasis on each of the four purposes of criminal sentencing.

Deterrent sentences are best defined and imposed by the legislature, so that it is clear to everyone beforehand that a specific punishment will follow a certain criminal conviction. This is the rationale behind what are known as "mandatory minimum" sentences. In these sentences, the legislature decrees that anyone convicted of a particular offense (say, use of a handgun in the commission of a crime or drunk driving) will be sentenced to a minimum number of days or years of incarceration. The prison sentence is mandatory and is expected to deter offenders.

Desert, or retributive, sentencing is perhaps best accomplished by granting limited sentencing power to the judge. The legislature sets an expectation or limit on how severe a penalty may be imposed for a particular criminal act, but the judge is expected to "fine tune" the sentence so that the severity of the sentence matches the severity of the offense.

Rehabilitative (treatment) and incapacitative sentences are probably best imposed by granting substantial control in sentencing to the paroling authority. This authority can then determine when the offender is safe for release (cured of criminal tendencies), and adjust the sentence accordingly. The legislature and sentencing judge are ill-suited to this task because they either do not deal directly with the offender, or their roles occur too early in the process. Both of these rationales require that someone continually monitors the offender for progress.

SENTENCING IN THE JUSTICE SYSTEM

Criminal sentencing is the final decision point in the court segment of the criminal justice system (with the possible exception of probation revocation, which is discussed in Chapter 12). It represents a transitional decision point where the fate of the offender is determined jointly by correctional and judicial officials. In cases of negotiated pleas of guilty, the prosecutor also plays a large role in determining the sentence (Alschuler, 1978).

The decision about sentence is bifurcated (Wilkins, et al, 1976), that is, it is made in two stages. First, the sentencing judge decides whether to incarcerate the convicted offender. Next, the conditions of sentence are determined. These conditions range from the restrictions and obligations placed upon those who are given probation to the length of term for those incarcerated.

Historically, sentencing judges had a greater voice in setting the conditions of prison confinement for sentenced offenders. The judge used to be able to specify the institution to which an offender would be sent, or to require that

the sentence be served "at hard labor." Today, most jurisdictions restrict the judge to setting the term of confinement, and leave to the correctional authorities the discretionary power to establish the place and conditions of confinement.

Especially in indeterminate sentencing systems based
on a rehabilitative rationale, the sentencing decision is expected to be based on the results of a presentence investigation (PSI) conducted by a probation officer. This report
describes the offense and offender, and in many jurisdictions includes a recommendation of sentence from the reporting officer (Czajkoski, 1973). Presentence investigations are common in most felony cases across the nation,
thereby involving probation officers in the sentencing decision.

Presentence Investigation

After conviction, the judge generally sets a date for
sentencing that is delayed long enough to allow the probation department to conclude a presentence investigation.
This investigation includes a detailed assessment of the offense and the offender's criminal and social background. A
report on the investigation (the PSI) is then submitted to
the sentencing judge so that it can be relied upon in arriving at an appropriate sentence. In addition to its usefulness at the sentencing stage, the PSI serves many other
purposes. It is a basic information source for the correctional programming used in developing probation plans
and institutional classification, it provides background data
used by parole boards in their decisions, and it serves as a
basic resource document for research on correctional authorities, offenders and corrections (U.S. Division of Probation, 1974).

The typical presentence report includes a "face sheet,"
which contains basic offense and offender demographic in-

formation. The textual part of the report generally covers the offense, that is, it gives the official (police) version and the offender's version of the facts (occasionally the victim's version is also added), the social history of the defendant (describing his or her childhood) and current family, employment, economic and educational situations, and the prior criminal record of the offender. Much of this information is obtained through interviews with the offender, members of the offender's family, and others who know the offender. The material in the report is not held to the strict evidentiary standards of trial.

Traditionally, the PSI did not have to be disclosed to the defendant. In 1949, the U.S. Supreme Court decided the case of *Williams v. New York*, which dealt with the issue of disclosure of the presentence investigation report. Williams had been convicted of capital murder, but the jury had recommended leniency. After reviewing the PSI, the judge imposed the death penalty. Williams' attorney was not allowed to see the report and verify its accuracy. The Court ruled that there was no constitutional right to review the report. However, in 1977 the Court ruled in *Gardner v. Florida* that when the death penalty is imposed as a result of information contained in a presentence report, the defense has a right to review that report. Therefore, at least in a capital case, the contents of the PSI must be disclosed to defense counsel.

In jurisdictions where probation officers are allowed to make recommendations to the sentencing judge, sentencing judges have been found to concur with these recommendations in the great majority of cases (Carter & Wilkins, 1967). This is one of the principal reasons why some argue that the defendant should be allowed to review the document. Disclosure of the PSI, however, is opposed by others, who argue that letting the defendant see the report will cause those interviewed to withhold information, or that disclosure might jeopardize the rehabilitation of the offender, should he or she learn things from the report which would be detrimental to rehabilitative programming.

In many jurisdictions, this issue has been resolved, either through disclosure of the entire report (Dubois, 1981), or more likely, through partial disclosure. In partial disclosure, the judge either summarizes the facts and the reasons for sentence, allowing the defense to contest any errors, or provides a copy of the body of the report to the defense. In jurisdictions where a copy is provided, often there is a "confidential" addendum which is not disclosed.

The Sentencing Hearing

There is no constitutional right to a separate hearing, although a sentencing hearing is generally held for felony defendants and, in some places, there are statutory provisions for sentencing hearings (Kittrie & Zenoff, 1981). In jurisdictions or cases in which there is no presentence investigation, sentencing typically follows conviction. Although there is not a separate hearing, the defendant is afforded the opportunity to speak on his or her own behalf (usually through counsel), and the state (prosecutor) is also asked to comment on sentencing. Sometimes the victim is present and allowed to speak or submit a written statement for consideration at sentencing.

At the point of sentencing, whether or not there is a separate hearing for that purpose, the defendant has the right to counsel. In 1967, the U.S. Supreme Court ruled that sentencing was a "critical stage" of the justice system, at which the defendant stands to lose protected rights and interests. In *Mempa v. Rhay*, the Court held that the offender had the right to be represented at sentencing.

The Parole Hearing

In cases in which the offender is sentenced to incarceration in prison under an indeterminate sentence model, the final sentencing decision is rendered by a parole authority. In these cases, the judge imposes a sentence that has a minimum and maximum term, but the actual duration of the penalty is not known. The paroling authority has the power to grant release (limit the duration of confinement) at some point between the end of the minimum term and the end of the maximum term. This decision usually is made by the entire board, or by a "panel" of board members, and after a hearing with the inmate.

At the parole hearing, the paroling authority reviews the criminal and social history of the offender, assesses his or her adjustment to prison, and evaluates the offender's potential for success under parole supervision. The inmate is allowed to speak at this hearing, and to present whatever evidence he or she feels relevant. There is no right to counsel at the parole release hearing (O'Leary & Hanrahan, 1976).

CONDITIONS OF SENTENCE

Whichever disposition (probation or imprisonment) the judge initially decides upon, the second decision in sentencing relates to the conditions of sentence. In cases of probation, the judge retains broad discretionary power to set the conditions of supervision. In incarcerative sentences, the power is shared between the legislature and correctional authorities.

Probation

Probation, as a punishment for criminal behavior, is conditional liberty. The convicted offender is allowed to remain in the community under the supervision of a probation officer, provided that he or she abides by certain conditions of conduct established by the judge. Should the probationer violate the conditions of release, he or she may be taken before the court for a hearing, at which time probation may be revoked and the probationer sentenced to prison.

Probation sentences generally are regarded by offenders and the public as leniency (Newman, 1983; Gibbs, 1985). Probation may be imposed in a variety of ways. The most common way in which probation is imposed is when a pronounced prison sentence is ordered suspended, that is, the execution of sentence (actually taking the offender to prison) is suspended. Another very common practice is suspended sentencing, in which the offender is placed on probation before a sentence (prison term) is actually pronounced. A third method entails a direct sentence to probation, in which the sentence is a probation term, but surprisingly few jurisdictions actually have statutes that specifically recognize and authorize probation as a criminal sentence. Other less formal mechanisms for probation may also be used, but these more closely mirror "diversion" programs than criminal sentences. That is, there are some jurisdictions in which the conviction will not be entered if the defendant successfully completes the probation term (Newman, 1986).

The offender on probation is supervised by a probation officer who works for the court, but the probationer is responsible to the judge. The judge establishes the conditions of release, including such things as "punish lessons," curfews, partial incarceration and community service (Parisi, 1980; Umbreit, 1981). Because of the large number of judges, and their individual discretion, probation conditions include a wide variety of restrictions and prescriptions (Jaffe, 1979). These will be discussed more fully in Chapter 12.

Incarceration

Later we will discuss incarceration in greater detail, but the conditions of the sentence of incarceration involve two dimensions: the type of facility and the length of term. In any jurisdiction with more than one correctional facility, there will be differences in the experience of being imprisoned, depending upon where one is incarcerated. Prisons differ in terms of population (hardened, dangerous criminals or young, first offenders), type of programs (educational and vocational, or industrial), and level of custody (maximum, medium or minimum security). As an example of the variance in prison experiences, serving three years by working outside on a prison farm for half of a day and attending school for the other half of the day is qualitatively different from spending the same amount of time locked inside a huge maximum-security prison making automobile tags all day.

The decision as to where an offender will serve his or her sentence is sometimes controlled by statute, so that offenders over a certain age, or those that were convicted of a specified crime, must be incarcerated in a maximum-security prison. What the offender will do while incarcerated, and where he or she will be incarcerated, however, are questions that often are left to the discretion of correctional authorities.

The length of sentence is controlled by statutory provisions, which define parole eligibility (minimum term), and by the "good time" policies and laws of the jurisdiction. Most states shorten prison terms for good behavior while incarcerated. In some states, this "good time" is credited only against the maximum term, that is, by advancing the date of mandatory release. In others, it is counted against the minimum term, that is, by advancing the date of parole eligibility. Finally, in still others, it is credited against both the minimum and maximum terms. Thus, the legislature, judge, and parole board all have some power in regard to sentence length, but correctional administrators who award and revoke "good time" also share in this decision.

ISSUES IN SENTENCING

Like the rest of the justice system, sentencing is fraught with questions and unresolved issues. The sentencing process is constantly emerging and evolving, sometimes returning to earlier practices and procedures that had previously been abandoned as inappropriate. Today, as perhaps only once before in our history, sentencing is undergoing considerable scrutiny and reform. In the latter part of the nineteenth century, we began to abandon corporal and capital penalties and long, harsh prison terms in favor of rehabilitative strategies. Today, we may be moving away from indeterminate, rehabilitative sentences towards an unclear future.

Three core issues can be identified that allow us to better understand the complex problems of criminal sentencing. Disparity is a central issue today and the concern which is at the base of most recent efforts to change criminal sentencing. Corporal and capital punishment have reemerged (perhaps continued) as issues in sentencing. Finally, the calculation of prison time is still a point of contention.

Disparity

Disparity refers to the unequal treatment of similar offenders at sentencing (Gottfredson, 1979). Most of us would agree that offenders convicted of the same offense, with similar criminal histories, ought to receive similar penalties. When differences in sentences appear among similar offenders, the differences generally are termed disparity. Yet, disparity actually refers to "unwarranted" differences (Gottfredson, et al, 1978).

For example, if a jurisdiction follows an incapacitative sentencing model and has two first-offender burglars, it would not be disparity if one, who posed a great risk of further crime, was imprisoned while the other, posing little risk, was granted probation. Under the concerns of incapacitation, these are not similar offenders. The current debate over disparity hinges, in large measure, on the definition of "similar" (Vining, 1983).

Since 1976, several states and the federal jurisdictions have enacted legislation which alters their sentencing structures. In large measure, these changes are aimed at increasing equity (reducing disparity) in criminal sentences (LaGoy, et al, 1978; von Hirsch & Hanrahan, 1979; Goodstein & Hepburn, 1983). Several states have implemented presumptive or determinate sentencing to insure that similarly situated offenders receive similar sanctions. The results of these reforms are now being studied and the evaluation of their success is unclear (Griswold, 1987).

One type of determinate sentencing which legislatures have adopted in hopes of controlling disparity and insuring more certainty in punishment is based on the use of sentencing guidelines. Guidelines identify the factors which judges should consider in sentencing and give an indication of what would be an acceptable penalty for each of many different types of cases. The federal government adopted a sentencing guideline system in November 1987, and it will abolish the federal parole commission sometime in 1992 (Criminal Justice Newsletter, 1987).

At least nine states have abandoned parole release as a part of their sentencing structures (Bureau of Justice Statistics, 1984). Instead, there is increasing emphasis placed on linking sentence severity directly to offense seriousness, generally with some modification for seriousness of prior criminal record. These reforms are designed to remove as much discretionary authority from sentencing as possible (Forst, 1982).

The culprit has been identified as the individual whims of justice system officials (judges, parole board members, etc.), which come out in the exercise of discretionary authority. To combat these disparate decisions, reformers have moved to give legislatures tighter control over sentencing power by more closely defining sentences and the factors to be relied upon in determining punishments. The effects of reform are unclear, and may involve changes in the rates at which people are incarcerated, in the types of crimes for which offenders are imprisoned, and in the lengths of terms. More recently, the movement to reform sentencing has slowed, as states increasingly are exercising more caution before altering their sentencing structures, but the issue remains current.

Corporal and Capital Punishment

In America, from colonial times through the early part of the nineteenth century, most punishments for serious offenses involved physical pain, such as branding, maiming, flogging, and death. In recent history, we have abandoned those forms of punishment in favor of the more humane alternative of incarceration. Yet, more recently, there has been a rebirth of support for physical punishment (Foucault, 1977; Newman, 1978; Newman, 1983). The death penalty is back; in 1987, 25 inmates were executed

and nearly 2,000 inmates were on death row in the United
States. Since 1976, there have been 93 executions in this
country (Bureau of Justice Statistics, 1988). The types of
offenses for which the death penalty may be imposed are
described in Box 9.2.

Box 9.2
Types of Offenses for Which the Death Penalty is Authorized

*What types of murder are most often cited in State capital
punishment laws?*

Type of murder for which death penalty is authorized	Number of States
Murder during another crime	
Sexual offense (such as rape)	35
Kidnaping	34
Robbery	33
Burglary	32
Arson	29
Murder of a certain type of victim	
Police or other law enforcement officer	34
Corrections employee	26
Firefighter	22
Murder by a person with a criminal history or criminal justice status	
Defendant was in custody	27
Defendant was previously convicted of murder	20
Murder carried out in a particular way	
Defendant created a grave risk of death to others	26
Murder was especially heinous, atrocious, cruel, vile, etc.	23

Murder carried out for a
particular purpose

For pecuniary gain (contract murder, murder for hire)	35
To effect an escape	26
To avoid or prevent an arrest	20

Other

Multiple murders	22
Hiring another to kill	21

SOURCE: BJS analysis of State capital punishment laws, 1986.

Who is on death row?

Of the 1,591 inmates on death row in 1985:

* All had been convicted of murder, 2 out of 3 had at least one prior felony conviction, 1 out of 11 had a prior murder conviction, and 2 out of 5 had a legal status (on bail, probation, or parole) at the time of the capital murder.

* 1,574 were male and 17 were female.

* 903 were white, 672 were black, 11 were American Indian, 5 were Asian, and 99 were of Hispanic origin.

* The median elapsed time since death sentence was imposed was 36 months.

SOURCE: *Report to the Nation on Crime and Justice, Second Edition.* (Washington, DC: U.S. Department of Justice, 1988):99.

Flogging or whipping as a sanction for offenses was finally abandoned in this country in the 1970s, when the state of Delaware removed the whipping post from its penitentiary. The constitutionality of corporal and capital punishment is always subject to question. The U.S. Supreme Court has not ruled the death penalty to be cruel and unusual punishment or to be otherwise unconstitutional. In the 1976 case of *Gregg v. Georgia*, the Court held that the death penalty, per se, is not unconstitutional. Earlier, in 1972, the Court had focused on the procedures by which the death penalty was imposed in *Furman v. Georgia*. Having found then existing procedures too vague and unstructured, the Court did not address the issue of the death penalty itself. The *Gregg* decision was the first of several where revised procedures for imposing the death penalty were reviewed by the Court. Given an acceptable procedure (jury recommendation based on a presentation of aggravating and mitigating factors identified in the statute), the Court also addressed the constitutionality of the death penalty itself.

Some support the death penalty as an incapacitative sanction, saying that murderers pose too great a risk to society. Vito and Wilson (1988) addressed this issue and found that most prisoners in their sample who were sentenced to death were not particularly dangerous, as is shown in Box 9.3. Opponents suggest that an alternative to capital punishment is to impose life sentences without possibility of parole (Cheatwood, 1988). The debate over capital punishment continues. The public, it appears, specifically supports capital punishment, and generally is in favor of harsher criminal sanctions (Flanagan, 1987).

Those supporting corporal punishment argue that physical pain, properly administered, is less destructive, less costly and more effective than lengthy incarceration (Newman, 1983). Those who are opposed to corporal punishment suggest that such penalties will continue to be considered cruel and unusual and, therefore, unconstitutional. If the issue were raised, it is not clear how the Court would decide the question. A principal rationale in support of corporal punishment is that our current practices are not effective in controlling crime and that our prisons and jails are too crowded to accommodate many more prisoners. Added to this is the reasoning that death is allowed as a penalty for crime, and thus penalties less than death should not be considered too severe.

Box 9.3
"Back from the Dead;"
Parole Outcome for Death-Row Inmates

Following the Supreme Court decision in *Furman v. Georgia*, 21 convicted murderers on death row in Kentucky had their sentences commuted to life imprisonment. Professors Gennaro Vito and Deborah Wilson of the University of Louisville kept track of what happened to 17 of these murderers, who were eventually granted parole. None of these people committed another murder. One parolee was returned for violating the conditions of parole, and four others were convicted of new crimes. The status report of the death-row parolees at the time Vito and Wilson completed their study follows:

Granted Final Release (Successful completion of parole)	1
Placed on inactive supervision (technically on parole, but not closely supervised)	11
Violated Parole (without new conviction)	1
Convicted of New Crime (2 for robbery, 1 for burglary, 1 for possession of drugs)	4
TOTAL	17

"Reprinted with permission of the Academy of Criminal Justice Sciences."

SOURCE: G. Vito & D. Wilson (1968) "Back from the dead: Tracking the progress of Kentucky's *Furman*-commuted death row population," *Justice Quarterly* 5(1):105-6.

Box 9.4
Felony Sentencing Limits, by Jurisdiction

Jurisdiction	Minimum	Maximum
Alabama	Greater than 1 year	Death
Alaska	Greater than 1 year	99 years
Arizona	Greater than 1½ years	Death
Arkansas	No minimum exists	Death
California	Greater than 1 year	Death
Colorado	Minimum of 1 year	Death
Connecticut	Minimum of 1 year	Death
Delaware	No minimum exists	Death
District of Columbia[a]	Greater than 1 year	Life
Florida	Greater than 1 year	Death
Georgia	Greater than 1 year	Death
Hawaii	Greater than 1 year	Life
Idaho	No minimum exists	Death
Illinois	Minimum of 1 year	Death
Indiana	Minimum of 1 year	Death
Iowa[b]	Greater than 1 year	Life
Kansas	Minimum of 1 year	Life
Kentucky	Minimum of 1 year	Death
Louisiana	Minimum of 1 year, hard labor	Death
Main[a]	No minimum exists	Life
Maryland	Minimum of 1 year	Death
Massachusetts	Greater than 2½ years	Life
Michigan[b]	Greater than 1 year	Life
Minnesota	Greater than 1 year	Life
Mississippi	Minimum of 1 year	Death
Missouri	Greater than 1 year	Death
Montana	Greater than 1 year	Death
Nebraska	No minimum exists	Death
Nevada	Minimum of 1 year	Death
New Hampshire	Greater than 1 year	Death
New Jersey[a]	Minimum of 3 years	Death
New Mexico	Minimum of 1 year	Death
New York[c]	Minimum of 1 year	Life
North Carolina	Minimum of 1 year	Death
North Dakota	Greater than 1 year	Life
Ohio	Greater than 1 year	Death
Oklahoma	Minimum of 1 year	Death
Oregon	Greater than 1 year	Death
Pennsylvania	Minimum of 3½ years[d]	Death
Rhode Island	Greater than 1 year	Life
South Carolina	Minimum of 3 months	Death
South Dakota	No minimum exists	Death
Tennessee	Minimum of 1 year	Death
Texas	Minimum of 2 years	Death
Utah	Greater than 1 year	Death
Vermont	No minimum exists	Death
Virginia	Minimum of 1 year	Death
Washington	No minimum exists	Death
West Virginia	Minimum of 1 year	Life
Wisconsin	Minimum of 1 year	Life
Wyoming	Greater than 1 year	Death

Note: Minimums reported here refer to statutorily defined minimum sentences for those receiving a prison term. Any potential effect of aggravating or mitigating circumstances in sentences imposed is not reflected in this table. Other types of sentences—jail, fines, probation—may also be given.
[a] These jurisdictions do not use the term felony, but a working definition has been constructed here for the purposes of cross-jurisdictional analysis.
[b] These States contain classifications referred to as "aggravated" or "serious" misdemeanors, with penalties that exceed felony minimums. They resemble felonies in procedural terms, essentially constituting misdemeanor status in name only.
[c] Although the New York State Penal Code authorizes the death penalty for first degree murder, the capital statute was ruled unconstitutional by the State Supreme Court in 1984. The statute has never been repealed by the New York State legislature.
[d] The minimum term derives from the Pennsylvania judicial code which stipulates that the minimum be half the maximum sentence for third degree felonies.
Source: Annotated code of each State, 1986, and State officials.

SOURCE: *State Felony Courts and Felony Laws.* (Washington, DC: U.S. Department of Justice) 1987:5.

It is difficult to predict how this recent suggestion for a return to corporal punishment will turn out. On the one hand, it could be seen as a practical alternative to incarceration for those convicted of serious offenses for which probation seems too lenient. On the other hand, it is entirely likely that, if accepted, corporal punishment would be added to current penalties, resulting in sentences to prison with corporal punishment, or bodily punishment as a condition of probation. Whatever the result, the resurgence of this once-discredited response to criminality illustrates the intractable nature of the issues involved in sentencing.

Calculation of Prison Time

We have already seen how provisions for "good time" affect sentencing decisions by adding correctional administrators to the list of officials who exercise authority in sentencing decisions. What is not as clear is the complexity of using time as a penalty. Although the death penalty can be used for heinous murders, the basic limitation on criminal penalties in the United States is time (see Box 9.4). While conditions of confinement vary, for the individual offender, the length of term is critical. How long an offender serves is dependent on several factors, each of which has importance for the severity of punishment and the operation of correctional institutions.

Prison time is typically measured in days, although sentences are generally imposed in months and years. Most states that have provisions for good-time reductions of sentence award good time on a "per days served" basis. Good time is expected to be an incentive to encourage inmates to obey prison rules. James Emshoff and William Davidson (1987) recognized that sentence reductions may affect inmate behavior, but contended that other factors are at least as important. A typical model awards ten days of good time for every thirty served, so that after serving twenty days, ten days are added to complete the month. A six-year sentence is then reduced to four years (1/3 reduction). In some states, good time is awarded on a "sliding scale," that is, the longer the sentence, or the longer the term served, the more good-time days received. Thus, an inmate could earn ten days for every thirty for the first three years, and fifteen days for every thirty for the next three years, and so on, "sliding" up the scale of good-time award. To this sentence may be added "meritorious" good time, earned by the inmate for special accomplishments such as exceptional industry, donating blood, and the like. Reductions for "good behavior," then, can be substantial.

Whatever the reductions for good behavior, there are other time calculations that are questionable. For an offender unable to secure pretrial release on bail, what part of his pretrial time counts as time served? The time spent in jail after conviction, but before going to prison, generally counts against a prison sentence. The decision whether to count the time spent in jail prior to conviction is generally left to the discretion of the judge or correctional authorities. Thus, an offender who is in jail for six months prior to conviction (and three months after conviction) prior to transport to the prison, may be granted nine months off of his or her sentence, and generally must be granted three months. A question remains, however, as to whether the offender also should be granted good time for time served before going to prison. Generally, sentence reductions for jail time are not awarded.

A final consideration is the ability of the judge to impose terms for multiple convictions to run either consecutively or concurrently. A consecutive term is one in which each sentence must be served in order, one following the other. A concurrent term is one in which all the sentences run at the same time. Two five-year terms imposed consecutively total ten years; the same terms imposed concurrently total five years.

Box 9.5
Average Time Served in State Prison
for Specified Offenses

Most serious offense	1984 Percent of first releases	1984 Time served in jail and prison Median	1984 Time served in jail and prison Mean	1983 Percent of first releases	1983 Time served in jail and prison Median	1983 Time served in jail and prison Mean
All offenses	100%	17 months	23.4 months	100%	19 months	25.1 months
Violent offenses	31.4	28	35.7	37.4	30	37.6
Murder	1.8	78	85.3	2.4	82	91.4
Manslaughter	2.7	32	35.2	3.1	33	36.0
Kidnaping	.6	31	38.4	1.0	35	41.8
Rape	1.7	44	49.2	2.1	48	55.0
Other sexual assault	2.7	26	31.3	3.1	30	34.7
Robbery	13.7	30	35.4	16.5	30	35.3
Assault	7.2	22	26.2	7.3	25	27.6
Other violent	1.1	16	19.6	1.9	15	18.2
Property offenses	47.4	15	18.5	46.1	15	18.2
Burglary	22.0	17	20.6	25.1	17	19.9
Larceny/theft	13.2	12	16.1	10.7	12	15.1
Motor vehicle theft	1.8	14	16.4	1.7	16	17.4
Arson	.9	19	23.1	.8	22	24.5
Fraud	5.7	13	16.3	5.6	15	17.6
Stolen property	2.7	13	16.9	1.2	12	15.6
Other property	1.2	12	16.6	1.0	11	14.0
Drug offenses	10.5	14	16.7	8.9	15	18.3
Possession	2.2	12	13.9	2.3	12	14.8
Trafficking	5.5	16	18.0	5.5	16	19.1
Other drug	2.7	13	16.6	1.1	17	23.2
Public-order offenses	8.7	9	13.2	5.7	9	12.0
Weapons	1.6	15	18.0	1.4	16	18.5
Other public-order	7.1	7	11.5	4.4	7	9.8
Other offenses	2.0	15	17.8	1.9	17	17.6
Number of releases	90,041	64,973		48,374	38,922	

Note: Data on offense distribution in 1984 are based on 99.3% of the 90,687 first releases from prison with sentences of more than a year. Data on time served in jail and prison are based on 64,973 first releases for which conviction offense, time served in local jails credited to the prison sentence, and time served in prison were all reported.

SOURCE: S. Minor-Harper & C. Innes (1987), *Time Served in Prison and on Parole, 1984.* (Washington, DC: U.S. Department of Justice):2.

The unresolved problem in the calculation of prison time is that the imposed sentence generally is not the same as the actual term served, as can be seen in Box 9.5. Von Hirsch and Hanrahan (1979) suggested that one of the major difficulties faced in sentencing reform is that we do not sentence offenders in "real time." The public sees the sentence imposed as being the maximum term ordered by the judge, without reference to "good time" or to the fact that concurrent terms are imposed frequently. Thus, if an offender sentenced to three concurrent five-year terms is released in two years, the public may begin to believe that the law does not mean what it says. The Bureau of Justice Statistics (1989), for example, estimates that felons sentenced to prison in state courts will serve only between 32 and 44 percent of their sentences before being released.

Perhaps the major obstacle to reforming criminal sentencing in the United States lies not in sentencing's considerable complexity of operation and calculation, but more in the lack of effort among our citizens to achieve understanding of the sentencing process. In order to achieve a rational and workable system of sentencing, it may first be necessary to be more open and honest about the meaning of criminal sentences, and more consistent in our purposes served by criminal sanctions.

REVIEW QUESTIONS

1. Identify the four traditional purposes of criminal penalties.

2. What types of errors are involved in the prediction of dangerousness at sentencing?

3. Distinguish between determinate and indeterminate criminal sentencing structures.

4. What is the presentence investigation and what purposes does it serve?

5. What is the sentencing hearing, and what takes place at one?

6. Identify two principal types of sanctions imposed on serious criminal offenders.

7. What is meant by sentencing disparity?

8. Besides sentencing disparity, identify two other current issues in criminal sentencing.

REFERENCES

Adams, S. (1961), *Effectiveness of Interview Therapy with Older Youth Authority Wards: An Interim Evaluation of the PICO Project.* (Sacramento, CA: California Youth Authority).

Alschuler, A.W. (1978), "Sentencing reform and prosecutorial power: A critique of recent proposals for 'fixed' and 'presumptive' sentencing," in, U.S. Department of Justice, *Determinate Sentencing: Reform or Regression?* (Washington, DC: U.S. Government Printing Office):59-88.

Bailey, W. (1966), "Correctional outcome: An evaluation of 100 reports," *Journal of Criminal Law, Criminology, & Police Science* 57:153-60.

Bureau of Justice Statistics (1984), *Sentencing Practices in 13 States.* (Washington, DC: U.S. Department of Justice).

_____ (1985a), *The Prevalence of Imprisonment.* (Washington, DC: U.S. Department of Justice).

_____ (1985b), *Capital Punishment in 1984.* (Washington, DC: U.S. Department of Justice).

_____ (1988), *Capital Punishment, 1987.* (Washington, DC: U.S. Department of Justice).

_____ (1989), *Felony Sentences in State Courts, 1986.* (Washington DC: U.S. Department of Justice).

Carter, R.M. & L.T. Wilkins (1967), "Some factors in sentencing policy," *Journal of Criminal Law, Criminology, & Police Science* 58:503.

Cheatwood, D. (1988), "The life-without-parole sanction: Its current status and a research agenda," *Crime & Delinquency* 34(1):43-59.

Criminal Justice Newsletter (1987), "Despite warnings of 'chaos,' no delay on sentencing reforms," *Criminal Justice Newsletter* 18(21):1, November 2, 1987.

Criminal Justice Newsletter (1987), "Sentencing reforms are expected to go into effect on November 1," *Criminal Justice Newsletter* 18(20):1, October 15, 1987.

Cullen, F.T. & K.E. Gilbert (1982), *Reaffirming Rehabilitation.* (Cincinnati, OH: Anderson).

Czajkoski, E.H. (1973), "Exposing the quasi-judicial role of the probation officer," *Federal Probation* 37:9.

Dubois, P.L. (1981), "Disclosure of presentence reports in the United States District Courts," *Federal Probation* 45(1):3-9.

Durham, A.M. (1988), "Crime seriousness and punitive severity: An assessment of social attitudes," *Justice Quarterly* 5(1):131-53.

Emshoff, J.G. & W.S. Davidson (1987), "The effect of 'good time' credit on inmate behavior: A quasi-experiment," *Criminal Justice and Behavior* 14(3):335-51.

Flanagan, T.J. (1987), "Change and influence in popular criminology: Public attributions of crime causation," *Journal of Criminal Justice* 15(3):231-43.

Forst, M.L. (ed.) (1982), *Sentencing Reform.* (Beverly Hills, CA: Sage).

Foucault, M. (1977), *Discipline and Punish.* (New York: Pantheon).

Gendreau, P. & R. Ross (1987), "Revivification of rehabilitation: Evidence from the 1980s," *Justice Quarterly* 4(3):349-407.

Gibbs, J.J. (1985), "Clients' views of community corrections," in L.F. Travis III (ed.) *Probation, Parole, and Community Corrections.* (Prospect Heights, IL: Waveland).

Goodstein, L. & J. Hepburn (1983), *Determinate Sentencing and Imprisonment.* (Cincinnati, OH: Anderson).

Gottfredson, D.M., C.A. Cosgrove, L.T. Wilkins, J. Wallersteing, & C. Rauh (1978), *Classification for Parole Decision Policy.* (Washington, DC: U.S. Government Printing Office).

Gottfredson, M.R. (1979), "Parole guidelines and the reduction of sentencing disparity: A preliminary study," *Journal of Research in Crime & Delinquency* 16(2):218-31.

Greenwood, P. (1982), *Selective Incapacitation.* (Santa Monica, CA: RAND).

Griswold, D. B. (1987), "Deviation from sentencing guidelines: The issue of unwarranted disparity," *Journal of Criminal Justice* 15(4):317-29.

Jaffe, H.J. (1979), "Probation with a flair: A look at some out-of-the ordinary conditions," *Federal Probation* 43(1):25-36.

Kittrie, N.N. & E.H. Zenoff (1981), *Sanctions, sentencing, and corrections* (Mineola, NY: Foundation Press).

LaGoy, S.P., F.A. Hussey & J.H. Kramer (1978) "A comparative assessment of determinate sentencing in the four pioneer states," *Crime & Delinquency* 24:385-400.

Martinson, R.M. (1974), "What works?" *The Public Interest* (Spring):22.

Newman, D.J. (1986), *Introduction to Criminal Justice, 3rd* (New York: Random House).

Newman, G.R. (1983) *Just and Painful* (New York: McMillan).

Newman, G.R. (1978), *The Punishment Response* (Philadelphia: J.B. Lippincott).

O'Leary, V. & K.J. Hanrahan (1976) *Parole Systems in the U.S.* (Hackensack, NJ: National Council on Crime & Delinquency).

Parisi, N. (1980), "Combining incarceration and probation" *Federal Probation* 44(2):3-12.

Paternoster, R. (1987), "The deterrent effect of the perceived certainty and severity of punishment: A review of the evidence and issues," *Justice Quarterly* 4(2):173-217.

Travis III, L.F. (1982), "The politics of sentencing reform," in M.L. Forst (ed.) *Sentencing Reform* (Beverly Hills, CA: Sage):59-89.

Umbreit, M.S. (1981), "Community service sentencing: Jail alternative or added sanction?" *Federal Probation* 45(3):3-14.

U.S. Division of Probation (1974), "The selective presentence investigation report" *Federal Probation* 38(4):52-3.

Van Dine, S., J.P. Conrad & S. Dinitz (1979), "The incapacitation of the chronic thug" *Journal of Criminal Law & Criminology* 65:535.

Vining, A.R. (1983), "Developing aggregate measures of disparity" *Criminology* 21(2):233-52.

Visher, C. (1987), "Incapacitation and crime control: Does a 'lock 'em up' strategy reduce crime?" *Justice Quarterly* 4(4):513-43.

Vito, G.F. & D.G. Wilson (1988), "Back from the dead: Tracking the progress of Kentucky's Furman commuted death row population," *Justice quarterly* 5(1):101-111.

von Hirsch, A. (1976), *Doing Justice* (New York: Hill & Wang).

von Hirsch, A. & K.J. Hanrahan (1978), *Abolish Parole?* (Washington, DC: U.S. Government Printing Office).

von Hirsch, A. & K.J. Hanrahan (1979), *The Question of Parole* (Cambridge, MA: Ballinger).

Walker, S. (1985), *Sense and Nonsense About Crime* (Monterey, CA: Brooks-Cole).

Wenk, E.A., J.O. Robison & G.W. Smith (1972), "Can violence be predicted?," *Crime & Delinquency* 18(3):393-402.

Wilkins, L.T., J.M. Kress, D. Gottfredson, J.C. Calpin & A. Gelman (1976), *Sentencing Guidelines: Structuring Judicial Discretion*. (Albany, NY: Criminal Justice Research Center).

Zalman, M. (1987), "Sentencing in a free society: The failure of the President's crime commission to influence sentencing policy," *Justice Quarterly* 4(4):545-69.

TABLE
OF CASES

Furman v. Georgia, 408 U.S. 238 (1972).

Gardner v. Florida, 430 U.S. 349 (1977).

Gregg v. Georgia, 428 U.S. 153 (1976).

Mempa v. Rhay, 389 U.S. 128 (1967).

Williams v. New York, 377 U.S. 241 (1949).

10 Incarceration

On any given day there are more than three-quarters of a million people incarcerated in thousands of jails and hundreds of prisons across the United States (Bureau of Justice Statistics, 1983; 1987a; 1987b; 1988). The overwhelming majority of those incarcerated are male, and the U.S. Department of Justice estimates that the average American male has a 3-5% chance of serving a prison or jail term over the course of his lifetime. For a variety of reasons, the prison is traditionally seen as our response to crime.

Non-incarcerative sanctions are often viewed by the public as leniency (Newman, 1983). Prisons, as punishment for serious criminal behavior, are an American invention. Most of us view incarceration as the most appropriate penalty to impose on those who violate the criminal laws. While most offenders are not sentenced to terms of imprisonment, it seems to be our belief that the prisons are the core of American corrections.

Box 10.1
Characteristics of Prisons and Jails

What are the characteristics of prisons?

	Federal	State
Number of prisons	38	521
Security level		
Maximum	13	140
Medium	17	207
Minimum	8	174
Inmate population		
Less than 500	10	366
500–999	18	80
1,000 or more	10	75
Year built		
Before 1875	0	25
1875–1924	3	76
1925–1949	16	125
1950–1969	8	156
1970–1978	11	139
Prisoners housed		
Males	31	460
Females	2	40
Coed	5	21
Prison employees		
Number	8,626	83,535
% administrative	2.2	2.2
% custodial	42.4	62.9
% service	23.0	15.9
% other	32.4	19.0

What are the characteristics of jails?

Number of jails	3,493
Facilities with populations of—	
Less than 10	1,538
10–249	1,825
250 +	130
Year built	
Before 1875	156
1875–1924	732
1925–1949	768
1950–1969	1,182
1970–1978	655
Employees	70,517
% administration	25
% custodial	53
% service	9
% other	13

Jails house diverse populations

Nationally, the jail population is composed of a mix of persons in various stages of criminal justice processing.

Among the jail inmates are persons who—
• Are awaiting arraignment or trial (the unconvicted)
• Have been sentenced to a term in jail
• Have been sentenced to prison but are awaiting transport
• Are being held in jail because of prison crowding; there were more than 8,200 such persons in 1982
• Have been convicted of a violation of probation or parole.

It is estimated that in 1982, 57% of all jail inmates were unconvicted; the other 43% had been convicted.

Prisons are often classified by the level of security

• **Maximum or close custody prisons** are typically surrounded by a double fence or wall (usually 18 to 25 feet high) with armed guards in observation towers. Such facilities usually have large interior cell blocks for inmate housing areas. About 41% of the maximum security prisons were built before 1925.

• **Medium custody prisons** typically have double fences topped with barbed wire to enclose the facility. Housing architecture is quite varied, consisting of outside cell blocks in units of 150 cells or less, dormitories, and cubicles. More than 87% of the medium-custody prisons were built after 1925.

• **Minimum custody prisons** typically do not have armed posts and may or may not have fences to enclose the institution. To a large degree, housing consists of open dormitories. More than 60% of the minimum security prisons were built after 1950.

SOURCE: *Report to the Nation on Crime and Justice: The Data*. (Washington, DC: U.S. Department of Justice, 1983):78-79.

There is good reason to believe that prisons are central to American corrections. By virtue of their size, history and cost, prisons receive the lion's share of attention from correctional administrators (and until recently, from persons studying corrections as well). Further, the threat of imprisonment is considered necessary in order to make less severe sanctions workable (Connolly, 1975). The argument is that without the threat of imprisonment such sanctions as fines or probation would not be taken seriously by offenders.

Incarceration of criminals (and those accused of criminal behavior) takes place in prisons and jails, two distinct types of institutions that are compared in Box 10.1. Prisons are state or federally run facilities that are generally segregated according to the sex of inmates and that house persons convicted of felonies who are serving sentences of one year or more. Jails are usually operated by municipal governments, and they house a variety of people who are convicted of misdemeanors or are at various stages of felony case processing. As might be expected, there are far more jails in the country than prisons, but most of the jails are small in size and experience a greater turnover in population (Bureau of Justice Statistics, 1983).

This chapter examines incarceration in the American criminal justice system. We will describe the history, organization and practice of incarceration in both prisons and jails. Several contemporary issues in the operation of prisons and jails will be addressed in the next chapter.

THE ORIGIN
OF AMERICAN INCARCERATION

The jail was established in England during the reign of Alfred the Great. Its purpose was to serve as a detention facility for those accused of seriously breaching the peace.

As mentioned earlier, in addition to tax collecting and other duties, the Shire Reeve (Sheriff) was responsible for maintaining the jail. Then, as now, the jail operated on a local level in holding prisoners for a centralized authority.

The American colonists brought the jail with them to the New World, but generally did not need to use it within their small, close-knit communities. As had happened earlier in England, towns grew in the colonies, and jails received more use. Those incarcerated in jails were not yet convicted, or they were debtors or people who failed to pay fines. Incarceration was not yet used as a punishment for criminal behavior (Moynahan & Steward, 1980).

Incarceration as a response to criminal behavior developed as part of a larger "discovery" of the asylum in American society in the early 1800s (Rothman, 1971). After the American Revolution, the nature of American society was altered. No longer was it common for people to know all of their neighbors and to maintain a sense of small community in their dealings with others. Mobility (caused by the war), the beginnings of industrialism and immigration, and the growth of commerce and cities led to a more impersonal, less intimate social climate. Problems of poverty, dependency and crime increasingly came to be seen as requiring a more centralized solution than had been characteristic of the colonial response. The solution to the social problems of poverty, insanity, and crime was found in the "asylum," or institution. Poorhouses, insane asylums and jails became more common around the nation in the latter part of the 1700s.

The penitentiary as a response to crime was particularly attractive. The harsh criminal code of England had been transported to the colonies with the result that most offenses were punished with what Langbein termed "blood punishments" (1976). It was common practice to torture, mutilate, or execute offenders. These "barbaric" penalties violated the assumptions of the Enlightenment, which underlay the New Republic. When Patrick Henry addressed the Virginia House of Burgesses and declared, "Give me liberty or give me death!" he unwittingly identified the perfect penalty. Incarceration gives the convicted offender neither liberty nor death.

Pragmatically, incarceration solved a pressing problem of administration for penal codes that provided for severe punishments. When the penalties for offenses were perceived as being too harsh (lashes or branding for petty theft, death for repeat offenses), juries dealt with the dilemma by failing to convict the offenders. Some observers saw this as a major obstacle to meeting the deterrent functions of the law. Further, in a rational penalty system, it was difficult to grade penalties to offenses when physical pain was the standard. Incarceration seemed more humane and likely to result in higher conviction rates. It also made an easier task of matching lengths of term to seriousness of offense.

The problem of harsh penalties was very troublesome. If the penalty for stealing a pig was death, what should be the penalty for stealing a cow? If a burglar faced hanging, what would deter him from killing the homeowner? Jurors faced tough decisions as well. Convicting a hungry offender who stole a loaf of bread could insure that the offender suffered branding, mutilation, or death. By establishing time as a punishment, and describing the prison as a harsh, but humane environment, it was possible to better match penalties to offenses, such as one year for stealing a pig or three years for stealing a cow. The availability of incarceration as a sentencing option also led to a higher rate of conviction, as juries were less adverse to seeing a hungry thief spend a few months in prison (where he would be fed and clothed).

Box 10.2
Comparison of Segregate and Congregate Systems

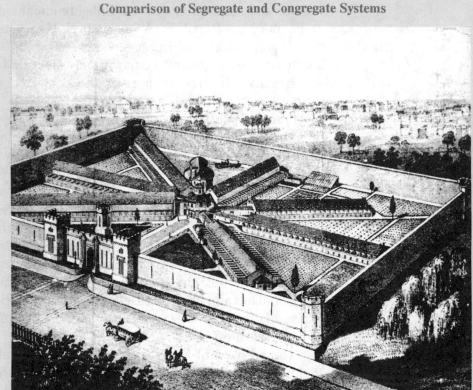

The Eastern State Penitentiary, designed by John Haviland and completed in 1829, became the model and primary exponent of the Pennsylvania "separate" system. The prison had seven original cell blocks radiating from the hub-like center, a rotunda with an observatory tower, and an alarm bell.

A corridor ran down the center of each block with the cells at right angles to the corridor. Each cell had a back door to a small, uncovered exercise yard and double front doors, the outer one made of wood, and the other of grated iron with a trap so that meals could be passed to prisoners.

SOURCE: American Correctional Association (1983), *The American Prison: From the Beginning...A Pictorial History.* (College Park, MD: ACA):39, 48.

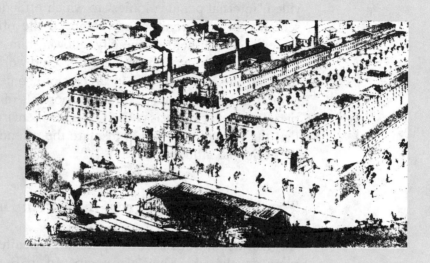

In 1816, New York began the construction of a new prison at Auburn. It was patterned after other early American prisons with a few solitary cells to conform to the law of solitary confinement to be used for punishment, and with sizeable night rooms to accommodate most prisoners.

To test the efficiency of the Pennsylvania system, an experiment was tried in 1821 with a group of inmates who were confined to their cells without labor. Many of these inmates became insane and sick. The experiment was abandoned as a failure in 1823, and most of the inmates studied were pardoned.

A new plan was adopted whereby all inmates were locked in separate cells at night, but worked and ate together in congregate settings in silence under penalty of punishment.

Ideologically, incarceration appeared well-suited to the needs of offender reform. Without the opportunity to transport prisoners to penal colonies, penitentiaries provided "internal penal colonies" to which offenders could be sentenced. The penitentiary removed the offender from the evil environment of the city, allowed him to reflect on the error of his ways, and taught him good work habits. Indeed, in the early days of incarceration, some viewed the penitentiary as a "utopia." Most proponents of the penitentiary felt that crime was caused by an evil environment, and that the penitentiary would insulate the offender from further criminal influences.

The Congregate/Segregate System Debate

During the 1820s, two systems of penitentiary discipline developed. They are compared in Box 10.2. The first, in Pennsylvania, was known as the *segregate* or *Pennsylvania system*. Here, inmates were housed separately in individual cells, took their meals in their cells, exercised in separate yards, and never interacted with other offenders. What industry was conducted was "cottage" industry, in which inmates completed the entire product in their cells.

This system had the advantage of insuring that offenders were protected from the corrupting influence of other offenders. The major disadvantages were that offenders suffered psychologically from isolation, and that the prison was expensive to operate and was not always able to produce a profit from its industry. Nonetheless, the Pennsylvania system had its supporters because it was true to an ideal of penance and isolation.

In contrast, the second penitentiary in the United States was developed in Auburn, New York. This system came to be known as the *congregate* or *Auburn system* of prison discipline. Here, inmates were housed in separate cells, but the inmates ate, worked, and exercised in groups.

"Isolation" was maintained by a strict rule of silence which prohibited inmates from conversing with each other. This organization reduced costs as a result of mass movement and feeding of prisoners. Further, the ability to work offenders in groups allowed assembly-line methods of production and a wider variety of prison-made products.

The strengths of this system were the more humane mingling of prisoners (even if they were silent, inmates at least were able to see each other), and the cost-effectiveness of the system. The disadvantages were that the congregate system required closer surveillance of inmates to enforce silence, and that prison administrators were unable to keep inmates isolated. Also, in the congregate system, there was greater potential for riots and fights among inmates.

For several decades, a debate raged over which of these systems was the "better" method for handling inmates. In the end, the cost-effectiveness of the congregate system emerged the "victor" of the debate, at least in the United States. Later generations of American penitentiaries most often operated under the Auburn system of congregate feeding, work and exercise.

The experience of the Virginia Penitentiary illustrates this point. In an attempt to benefit from both the congregate and segregate systems, Virginia law required that inmates, who were initially housed in larger dormitories under a "silent system," spend their last three months in solitary confinement. Keve (1986:41) cited the 1832 report of a legislative study committee, which found the solitary confinement requirement of Virginia prison terms counterproductive:

> Upon the subject of the three month's solitary confinement required by law to be inflicted upon convicts immediately preceding their discharge, the committee have had much reflection; and they have come to the conclusion that this portion of the close confinement ought to be

abolished. They believe that it is productive of no substantial benefit, but is on the contrary, decidedly injuri-
ous. It obliterates the habits of industry previously acquired. Upon the score of more interest to the state it is
inexpedient because it abstracts from the institution the
most valuable portion of the time and labor of the convicts. It exceeds the requisitions of stern justice...But
above all it ruins the health of the victim and indirectly
takes away human life...In any aspect which it may be
viewed experience proves its inexpediency, if not its absolute inhumanity and injustice.

The Changing Purposes of Prison

Initially, it was believed that the experience of incarceration alone would lead to improved behavior on the part
of offenders. The learning of good work habits, the removal from contaminating influences, and other benefits of
incarceration would result in better citizens. Over time, it
became clear that the reform (prison) was itself in need of
reform. By the middle of the nineteenth century, penitentiaries were replaced with reformatories in which offenders
were trained to be law-abiding citizens and released from
incarceration as soon as it was clear that they had been reformed.

Created as a humanitarian and practical alternative to
the corporal and capital punishments of the eighteenth century and earlier, the penitentiary soon came to be recognized as flawed. The early developers of the penitentiary
supported isolation of prisoners because they sincerely believed that criminality was caused when people were
tempted by their environment. A lack of adequate discipline and training from the family, combined with the lure
of taverns and "bawdy houses," led otherwise law-abiding
citizens into a life of crime. Isolation, solitary contempla-
tion on right and wrong, and the discipline of hard work in
a "sanitized" environment free from criminal temptations

would work to improve offenders and prepare them for lawful living.

By the Civil War period, observers came to believe that simple incarceration was not enough. The penitentiary lacked an incentive to offenders to make them want to change. Further, the imposition of a definite term of confinement seemed counter-productive. If a prisoner with a five-year term had reformed in one year, these observers saw no reason to continue his or her confinement for an additional four years. It was important that prisons take active steps to reform criminals. These steps would include instilling discipline and industry as habits in the inmates, and offering the possibility of early release from incarceration as an incentive to reform.

In the reformatory, inmates were raw materials that were to be shaped into law-abiding citizens. Upon entering the reformatory, the prisoner lost his civilian identity, contact with the outside world, and nearly all of his rights. The reformatory was a factory producing useful citizens. The process through which this production was to be accomplished was training. Prisoners were conditioned to industry and discipline in the belief that once the habits were established in the prison, they would not be broken after release. As an ex-convict, author Malcolm Braly (1976:202) noted that the habits acquired in the penitentiary did endure, at least for a while. Describing his first few days of freedom after release from San Quentin, Braly wrote, "That first morning and every morning for several weeks I woke exactly at six-thirty when the big bell had begun to pound in the blocks. Rise and shine. It's daylight in the swamps."

Within fifty years of the creation of reformatories, a new correctional ideology developed (O'Leary & Duffee, 1971). The mere training of offenders was not sufficient. Rather, offenders were "ill" and in need of treatment to cure them of their proclivities towards crime. The rehabilitative correctional institution had arrived with a treatment staff in addition to the custody and industry staffs.

Several problems had plagued the "reformatory ideal." First, the habits established in prison did not last long for many prisoners after they were released. Second, over time, early release was used increasingly as a prison management tool rather than a recognition of inmate reformation. If the prison became crowded, inmates would be released. If a particular inmate was needed (for example, if he or she was the only barber in the institution), he or she might not be released, no matter how reformed he or she became. Finally, the view of the cause of criminality also changed.

The growth of the social and behavioral sciences, and the development of service professions related to these disciplines fostered a re-examination of institutional corrections. In 1897, Warren Spalding, Secretary of the Massachusetts Prison Association, remarked (1897:47), "The State is not an avenger, with a mission to right the wrong which the criminal has done, but is to try to right the criminal, that he may cease to do wrong." The emphasis on the individual offender, and on the motives and causes of the individual's criminality, grew in the early twentieth century (Fogel, 1979:50-61). This was the Progressive Era, when there was a general trust in the ability of the state to do good for individuals, and when reformers wanted prisons that met the needs of individual criminals, rather than the general needs of society (Rothman, 1980).

In the middle 1960s, yet another shift occurred in correctional ideology. Prisons themselves were now viewed as part of the problem of crime. The best solution to reforming criminal offenders was thought to rest in keeping the criminal in the community where he could learn how to live a law-abiding life. Prison populations fell, and those kept in prison increasingly were able to take advantage of furlough programs and to enjoy increased contact with the outside world. Observers of the nation's prisons came to believe that attempts at individualizing treatment, and the focus on the cause of crime as being inside the offender, were ineffective. Rather, to succeed in changing offenders into law-abiding citizens, it would be necessary to deal with the criminal in society.

Another prison writer, Lou Torok (1974:91), succinctly summarized the arguments in favor of the re-integration philosophy of corrections, which flourished for a decade from the middle 1960s:

> It costs the taxpayer up to six thousand dollars each year to keep one convict locked up uselessly in prison. On the other hand, it would only cost about three hundred dollars a year to keep the same man in the community, under close supervision, on parole or probation, where he will pay his own way, earn a salary, keep his family off welfare and live a law-abiding life. Both society and the offender would benefit from this approach but so many people are unwilling to examine the facts and figures objectively. They continue to pour millions of dollars of tax money into an archaic prison system which does not correct, does not reform, simply does not, in any sense work.

Again, in the middle 1970s, correctional ideology shifted. The purpose of imprisonment came to be defined principally as punishment. Inmates served time as punishment for criminal offenses. Whatever programs and industries were available to inmates were there for voluntary usage. Release from incarceration was based on service of sentence, not on evidence of reform or rehabilitation. Further, more offenders were expected to serve prison sentences as punishment, although the length of terms for most offenders was reduced (Twentieth Century Fund, 1976).

One of the arguments in favor of this newest purpose of prisons was that, in the end, the only purpose that the tradition of the prison had shown incarceration could serve was that of punishment. Torok (1974:88) wrote, "In actual practice, prisons do little more than punish." Similarly, Braly (1976:362) wrote of the new prisons, "The old timers scorned these new prisons and dismissed them as Holiday Motels. We couldn't be conned by *departmental* [Department of Corrections] window dressing. We were still under the Man, and the Man still had a gun locked away somewhere nearby...Essentially, it was only Folsom with Muzak."

The American prison was developed as a humane alternative to the harsh punishments of colonial justice. In a history of slightly more than 150 years, the purpose of prisons has been redefined several times in accord with changing public and social attitudes regarding crime and human behavior. Through it all, the prison has survived. It is instructive to recognize that one of the first prisons ever erected, Auburn Penitentiary, is still in operation today. It has undergone several renovations and name changes, yet it still houses inmates.

The history of prisons in America reveals that these institutions are enduring (Travis, et al, 1983). The prison represents the core of our views on how to respond to criminal behavior. It is likely to do so for the foreseeable future, if not longer.

THE ORGANIZATION
OF AMERICAN INCARCERATION

Given the distinct, if related, natures and functions of jails and prisons, it is necessary to describe the organizations of the two separately. While both types of institutions hold convicted offenders, their widely divergent structures cannot be combined easily.

Jail Organization

Local control, multiple functions, and a transient, hetero-
geneous population have shaped the major organizational
characteristics of jails. Typically they are under the jurisdiction of county government. In most instances, the local area has neither the necessary tax base from which to
finance a jail adequately nor sufficient size to justify even
the most rudimentary correctional programs. Local control has inevitably meant involvement with local politics.
Jails are left in a paradoxical situation: localities cling
tenaciously to them but are unwilling or unable to meet
even minimal standards. (National Advisory Commission, 1973:274)

Most jails in the United States are operated by county
sheriffs' offices. Of nearly 3,500 jails in the nation, more
than 80% are operated at the county level, and more than
16% are city jails. Less than 1.5% of jails are classified as
multi-jurisdictional. All but six states (Alaska, Connecticut,
Delaware, Hawaii, Rhode Island, and Vermont) have local
jails. Even in Alaska, six of the state's jails are administered by cities (Bureau of Justice Statistics, 1981).

As local institutions, jails must compete within a larger
sheriff's or police department (and with other municipal
services such as public works, sanitation, health, education,
and the like) for resources. Further, the majority of
American jails are designed to house fewer than 21 inmates; less than 4% of jails are capable of housing over 250
inmates (Bureau of Justice Statistics, 1981:2). Yet, nearly
three-quarters of all jail inmates are held in the institutions
of 358 jurisdictions. Thus, the majority of inmates are held
in about 20% of the nation's jails, which means that most
inmates are held in large institutions (Bureau of Justice
Statistics, 1988:1).

On any given day, nearly 300,000 inmates are being
held in our nation's jails (Bureau of Justice Statistics,

1988).   Annually, millions of prisoners are processed through the jails, and estimates show that up to 10 million persons each year enter jails. The Bureau of Justice Statistics reported that approximately 8 million persons entered, and nearly 8 million left jails in 1985 (BJS, 1987c). Roughly half of those incarcerated in jails have not yet been convicted of a criminal offense and are awaiting trial. Those serving sentences in jail generally face short terms, and the jail population experiences a rapid turnover.

Most jail inmates are male, under the age of 30, unmarried, and did not graduate from high school. Less than 10% of jail inmates are female (Bureau of Justice Statistics, 1985; 1988). As a result of short terms and small total population sizes, programs for jail inmates generally do not exist or are inadequate. Much of a jail inmate's incarceration time is spent in idleness, viewing television or otherwise attempting to pass the hours.

The majority of jail staff are custodial officers, and as a result of the administration of jails by sheriffs and police, many custodial officers are sworn police officers who would rather not be serving in jails. Fewer than 10% of jail personnel are service staff members, such as doctors, social workers and teachers.

The organization and administration of jails has remained relatively unchanged over the years, and there is little hope that speedy change in jail organization will occur (Skoler, 1978:11). Jails have historically been criticized for their lack of programs for inmates, poor physical condition, and inadequate staffing (Fishman, 1923; McGee,1971; Goldfarb, 1975). Although there has been some improvement in jails over the past decade, much remains to be done (Katsampes & Neil, 1981).

Prison Organization

Prisons are organized on a state or federal level. Unlike the jail, prisons suffer from problems associated with their large size. The National Advisory Commission on Criminal Justice Standards and Goals observed the detrimental consequences of overly large institutions (1973: 355):

> The usual response to bigness has been regimentation and uniformity. Individuals become subjugated to the needs generated by the institution. Uniformity is translated into depersonalization. A human being ceases to be identified by the usual points of reference, such as his name, his job, or family role. He becomes a number, identified by the cellblock where he sleeps. Such practices reflect maladaptation resulting from size.

The majority of prisons in the United States are operated by state governments. Of the more than 600 prisons in America, less than 50 are federal prisons (Bureau of Justice Statistics, 1983:79). Every state has at least one prison, or state confinement facility, and several states operate more than ten each (Bureau of Justice Statistics, 1982:3). Most state facilities house fewer than 500 inmates but, like those in jails, most prison inmates are housed in large prisons.

At the end of 1984, the Bureau of Justice Statistics (1985) reported that more than 480,000 offenders were being held in American prisons. That population increased over 17% by the end of 1986, when there were 546,659 prison inmates in America (Bureau of Justice Statistics, 1987a:1). Most of these offenders are housed in single-sex facilities. Because prisons have a much lower turnover rate than jails, probably no more than 700,000 inmates are processed through prisons each year.

Most prison inmates, like their counterparts in jails, are male, unmarried, young, and have not graduated from high school (Bureau of Justice Statistics, 1982). Because of the longer terms of confinement, and generally larger populations, prisons are able to provide a wide range of programs to inmates, including educational, vocational, recreational, social and psychological counseling programs.

Similar to jails, the majority of prison staff hold custodial positions. There are, however, higher percentages of prison staff that hold administrative (2.2%), service (16%), and other (20%) job titles. Unlike jails, correctional personnel in prisons are hired solely as correctional personnel. The organization and administration of prisons has changed little over the years and it is not likely to change much in the future.

DOING TIME

Incarceration is the foundation of American corrections. With the exception of capital punishment, it is the most severe sanction available to the state, and as such, incarceration is the "stick" that supports community corrections programs, such as halfway houses, probation and parole (Reasons & Kaplan, 1975). Prisons are an American invention, and Americans rely upon the use of incarceration as a response to criminal behavior.

The experience of incarceration differs, depending upon where an inmate is incarcerated, yet in large measure, it is the same wherever and whenever it occurs. The inmate in either prison or jail is typically under control and is not a contributing member of any policy-making body. This fact leads to a similarity of experience for all inmates. The experience of "doing time" is painful. The pains of imprisonment were identified by Gresham Sykes (1969) as: *Deprivation of Liberty, Deprivation of Goods and Services, Deprivation of Heterosexual Relations, Deprivation of Autonomy* and *Deprivation of Security*.

Deprivation of Liberty

By definition, those confined in correctional institutions do not have any liberty of movement. Yet, even within the institution, the inmate is not at liberty to move around. As Sykes observed (1969:65), "In short, the prisoner's loss of liberty is a double one: first, by confinement to the institution and second, by confinement within the institution."

The prison (or jail) inmate generally is not allowed freedom of movement. Prisoners are moved *en masse* from cell block to activity, to dining facility, to activity, to cell block. Few inmates are allowed the privilege of moving about the institution without an escort. Inmates also are not free to choose to whom they may write, or with whom they may otherwise interact. The net effect of this deprivation is isolation from the outside community, and this loss of liberty is symbolic of a loss of status as a trusted member of society. As one inmate put it (Wright, 1973:146):

> Freedom is the only meaningful thing to a human. Without freedom things lose meaning. The whole system in prison is designed to degenerate a human being, to break him as a man. They take away all of his freedom, his freedom to express himself and his feelings. How can you be human if you can't express yourself?...

Deprivation of Goods and Services

While options have been increased since Sykes made his observations, inmates today are still deprived of access to, and ownership of, a wide variety of goods and services. Most prisons do not allow inmates to possess money, and most require standardization of clothing and other possessions.

Upon admission to a prison or jail, the "civilian" possessions of inmates (i.e., jewelry, money, clothing, etc.) are confiscated, and they are either stored until release or shipped to a destination chosen by the inmate (usually "home"). All of the fittings of free society by which we make a statement about who we are, such as the clothes we wear, the way we wear our hair, the car we drive, and the like, are removed from the inmate. Instead, the inmate is issued a uniform, given a prison haircut, and generally not allowed to exercise personal taste in the selection and purchase of goods and services.

Most penal facilities now have commissaries, where inmates are allowed to purchase toiletries, candy bars and other small items. Some prisons allow inmates to wear certain articles of civilian clothing, such as hats or tee shirts, but the range of options available to the inmate is very restricted. The effect of this deprivation is that the inmate feels impoverished. His or her self-worth is lessened by reason of the reduced "net worth."

> In prison the slightest distinction is cherished and enlarged...Bob, since he had bad feet, had been allowed to keep his own shoes rather than wear the Santa Rosa hightops which were standard issue. He had polished these shoes until they glittered, and, as we spoke, he continued to rub one shoe and then the other against his pants leg. He also wore the watch Big John had given him, and he glanced at it frequently as if he had an important appointment and wasn't just standing around, as I was, killing time until lunch (Braly, 1976:156)

Deprivation of Heterosexual Relations

As noted earlier, most American penal facilities segregate by sex. The inmate is not only denied liberty and impoverished by reason of incarceration, but is also forced to endure involuntary celibacy. The lack of members of the opposite sex in the prison society leads to anxieties about sexual identity among inmates.

The effect of sex segregation is not only physical, but also psychological in that the inmate has lost half of the audience and comparison group from whom he or she receives a validation of sexual identity. That is, it is more difficult to be masculine or feminine in an all-male or all-female society (respectively) than in mixed company. One of the principle ways in which we know who we are sexually is by comparison with members of the opposite sex. In prison, these comparisons are largely absent (Nacci & Kane, 1984).

> Some men look feminine and looks are enough alone for a man behind these walls to try and get him. It is a hell of a thing to say, but here you are another man and you are behind these walls and before long another man begins to look like a woman to you (Lockwood, 1982:54).

Deprivation of Autonomy

The prison is a "total institution," as described by Goffman (1961). The total institution provides all the necessities for the individual, and makes all the decisions for its residents. This fact leads to what has been called "institutionalization," which is the creation of individuals who are almost wholly dependent upon the institution and incapable of caring for themselves in the free society.

The prison inmate is not allowed to decide when to eat, what to eat, when or how often to take a shower, when to go to sleep, when to awaken, what job to do, and how to make other seemingly trivial decisions. Rather, the inmate is subjected to a life in which all major, and most minor, decisions are made for him by others. The refusal of inmate requests is generally not accompanied by any explanation, thereby adding insult to injury.

The net effect of the loss of autonomy is a reduction in feelings of self-worth, as inmates come to recognize that they are no longer in control of their own destinies. The inmate is reduced to a state of childlike dependency upon the parent (the state). As Sykes (1969:76) explained, "But for the adult who has escaped such helplessness with the passage of years, to be thrust back into childhood's helplessness is even more painful..."

In the words of an inmate at San Quentin (Wright, 1973:146):

> The worst thing here is the way your life is regulated, always regulated, day in and day out. They tell you what to do almost every moment of the day. You become a robot just following instructions. They do this, they say, so that you can learn to be free on the outside.

Deprivation of Security

The final pain of imprisonment mentioned by Sykes is paradoxical: the loss of security. In a prison, even one classified as "maximum security," the prisoner experiences a real loss of personal security. Prisons are not safe places in which to reside. Consider living in a neighborhood where all of those around you are accused criminals, convicted felons and other criminal offenders. How many people would move voluntarily into such a neighborhood?

At any time, the prisoner must be prepared to fight to protect his or her belongings and personal safety. Living with the constant threat of victimization is stressful, and this constant stress adds to the pain of imprisonment. The cell doors serve not only to lock in the inmate, but also to lock out others who may harm the prisoner. It is not uncommon for prison inmates to request placement in segregation (solitary confinement) for personal safety. Existing in the general prison population is generally a frightening experience.

> It used to be a pastime of mine to watch the change in men, to observe the blackening of their hearts. It takes place before your eyes. They enter prison more bewildered than afraid. Every step after that, the fear creeps into them...No one is prepared for it.

> *Everyone* is afraid. It is not an emotional, psychological fear. It is a practical matter. If you do not threaten someone, at the very least, someone will threaten you (Abbott, 1981:144).

THE OTHER INMATES: CORRECTIONAL OFFICERS

If imprisonment is frustrating and painful to inmates, it is not much less so for those whose job it is to work within the walls of penal facilities each day. In recent years, there has been increasing attention paid to the stressful role of custodial officers in prisons and jails (Moracco, 1985; Philliber, 1987). While they may be able to leave the institution at the end of their shifts, most correctional officers, over the span of their careers, will spend more time in prison or jail than will the inmates. They too suffer several pains of imprisonment.

The correctional officer serves a dual role: manager of inmates, and line-level worker within the prison. As a line worker, the officer is subjected to frequent "shake-downs" (to control the possibility of officers smuggling contraband into the prison), supervision and disciplinary action by superior officers, and other controls, which make the occupation of correctional officer similar to the role of prison inmate (Clear & Cole, 1986:306).

Starting pay for correctional officers is generally low, between $12,000 and $17,000 per year, and there is little hope for advancement to managerial positions (Fogel, 1979:95-96). Requirements for officers are also minimal, and turnover in the custodial ranks is high. By virtue of the low entrance criteria, relatively low pay, and low status associated with the job of custodial officer, these individuals suffer many of the same kinds of deprivations as do inmates.

While over 60% of the prison staff hold correctional officer positions, the role of correctional officer has been ignored until very recently (Hawkins, 1976). Recent investigations of the correctional officer's role have identified the importance of the officer to the operation of the prison (Jacobs & Crotty, 1978; Lombardo, 1989). Guards have the greatest contact with prison inmates, and are most directly responsible for the smooth operation of the prison. Box 10.3 compares correctional officers to inmates.

A recent survey of correctional officers in New Jersey (Cheek & Miller, 1983) identified twenty-one items that the officers felt were the most stressful aspects of the job. The most important of these can be classified into the categories of organizational or administrative problems. The officers reported being most troubled by a lack of clear job description, absence of support from superiors, and not being able to exercise personal judgment. Cheek & Miller (1983:19) concluded:

> The officer gets no respect from anyone. Not from the outside community, which sees him as the brute portrayed in the old James Cagney movies, not from the inmates who use him as a dumping ground for their hostility, not from prison administrators who expect him to play the tin soldier....A stressful job indeed!

As with any occupational group, it is difficult to generalize about guards, for they differ widely among themselves in terms of how they perceive and perform their jobs. Toch and Klofas (1982) reported that perhaps one-fourth of all custodial officers fit the movie image of the brutal, uncaring guard. They called this type of officer the "smug hack." However, this estimate means that 75% of the custodial force does not fit the stereotype. Johnson (1987:184) suggested that most guards are not "hacks," but play an important role in providing services to inmates. The guards do this, Johnson argued, at least partly in response to their need to make the job more challenging and important than either the public or the prison administration believes it to be.

Box 10.3
Characteristics of Correctional Officers and Inmates

	OFFICERS	INMATES
RACE:		
White	69.6%	54.0%
Non-White	30.4%	46.0%
SEX:		
Male	85.6%	95.2%
Female	14.4%	4.8%

SOURCE: Camp, G.M. & C.G. Camp (1988), *The Corrections Yearbook.* (New York: Criminal Justice Institute, Inc.):5, 43.

Many officers, however, try to solve the problem of alienation by expanding their roles and making them more substantial and rewarding. These officers discover that in the process of helping inmates and thereby giving them more autonomy, security, and emotional support, the officers gain the same benefits: more control over their environment, more security in their daily interactions with prisoners, and a sense of community, however inchoate or ill-defined, with at least some of the men under their care. In solving inmate adjustment problems, in other words, staff solve their own problems as well.

Custodial officers in prison then, like the inmates, and like police in the community, are affected by the nature of their positions within the justice system. In a classic experiment on the effects of incarceration, Philip Zimbardo (1972) concluded that incarceration profoundly affected both the inmates and the guards. He concluded that the social situation (role definitions of guard or prisoner, presence or absence of power, etc.) determines how people will act. Whether because of the media stereotype of the "hack," a lack of training, or administrative rules, prison officers have a limited range of actions open to them. As part-time prison inmates, correctional officers too are deprived of liberty, autonomy and security. What these officers seem to want is not just more respect or support from the public and superiors, but more options. That is, officers seem to believe that they will achieve greater security in the prison if they are granted the liberty to perform their jobs in a more autonomous fashion (Hepburn, 1987).

INCARCERATION IN THE CRIMINAL JUSTICE SYSTEM

As the "backbone" of American corrections, incarceration holds a central role in the American system of criminal justice. For years, the operations of penal facilities were not open to public or court scrutiny. Rather, the prisons and jails were assumed to require no supervision by outsiders, and indeed, it was believed that outside interference would be more harmful than beneficial. In the past two decades, however, this condition has changed with the emergence of prisoners' rights.

David Fogel (1979) suggested that our perceptions of prison inmates have traveled along a continuum, from the earliest days when the offender was seen as a pariah, through periods of viewing the offender as penitent, prisoner, and patient, to the current view of the prisoner as a "peer." This shift to seeing prisoners as "peers" has been status-costly to correctional authorities, for they must now deal with inmates as individuals who retain certain rights. The unreviewed, nearly total power over inmates that traditionally rested with correctional authorities is now subject to judicial review upon the filing of suits by the inmates themselves. In 1941, the U.S. Supreme Court ruled that inmates had the right to access of the courts in the case of *Ex parte Hull*. Initially, this right of access was more theoretical than practical. For years, appellate courts adopted a "hands off" doctrine in deciding cases concerning the rights of inmates (Vito & Kaci, 1982). In a series of appellate court decisions, rights of inmates have been identified, and due process controls have been placed on the exercise of discretion by prison authorities.

In 1964, The U.S. Supreme Court decided the case of *Cooper v. Pate*, ruling that prisoners in state and federal institutions were protected from arbitrary and capricious violations of their civil rights. Prison inmates were entitled to the protections of the Civil Rights Act of 1871. In deciding the case, the Court provided a vehicle by which inmates could challenge conditions of confinement in the nation's courts. A later decision, *Johnson v. Avery*, further strengthened the position of inmates. In this case, the Court ruled that prison authorities must either allow inmates the use of "jailhouse lawyers" (inmates who assist others in the preparation of court documents) or provide an adequate alternative. In combination, these two rulings meant that inmates were not only entitled to certain rights, but that they were also to be provided with the necessary resources to secure those rights in court. As Cohen (1972:862) noted, "To hold, for example, that a prisoner must be guaranteed reasonable access to the courts, that he must suffer no reprisals for his efforts, and that there is a right to some form of assistance, recognizes the prisoner as a jural entity."

With access to the courts thus ensured, the next stage in the development of prisoners' rights was entered. It was now time for prisoners to seek protections from the more onerous conditions of confinement. In a flurry of litigation, this is precisely what happened. The more important developments in prisoners' rights occurred in three areas: the First, Eighth and Fourteenth Amendment protections.

In deciding questions of prisoners' rights, the courts have generally applied three tests to the reasonableness of prison conditions and regulations: compelling state interest, least restrictive alternative, and clear and present danger. A *compelling state interest* is any concern of the state (prison administration) that is so important that it overrides the protections afforded in the Constitution. Such an interest, for example, would be evident if an inmate were to request the right to go on a pilgrimage for religious reasons; the state "interest" in custody is compelling and justifies the denial of the right to go on a pilgrimage. The *least restrictive alternative* refers to the desire to be no more oppressive than is necessary to meet the needs of the state. For example, a rule punishing an inmate for possession of lewd photographs would probably be too restrictive, given that a rule prohibiting display of the material would meet the state's interests in not arousing other inmates. Finally, *clear and present danger* refers to controls on the activities of inmates that pose a direct threat to the smooth operation of the institution. For example, rules prohibiting inmates from assembling and making inflammatory speeches will be upheld, as such activities pose a clear and present danger of instigating riots.

...ctions

> f their civil rights
>
> Johnson vs. Avery
> (later)
> ison authorities must
> ow use of "jailhouse
> lawyers" or an ade-
> quate alternative
> prisoners must have
> cess to the courts
> be able to sue

o the U.S. Constitution pro-
, speech, the press, assembly,
ent for redress of grievances.
y prisoners' cases focused on
religion, although other First
o litigated.   The examples
kinds of issues that have been

garding freedom of religion
spread of Islam in the pris-
s were initially (and perhaps
spicion by prison administra-
n more as a political group
sts for special diets, spiritual
to the Koran, and the like,
son authority rather than at-
The Muslims were required
involved in the practice of

quired to clarify other First
cess to the media, censorship
ation of prisoners' unions and
e three reasonableness tests
ve decided hundreds of cases
dealing with First Amendment rights of prisoners.

Eighth Amendment Protections

The Eighth Amendment to the U.S. Constitution provides that cruel and unusual punishments will not be in-
flicted upon offenders. Prisoners have brought suits under
this amendment to protest perceived deficiencies in nearly

every aspect of prison life, from food to medical treatment. With the recent surge in prison populations, these suits have become more controversial as inmates seek relief from overcrowded prisons and overburdened prison resources. In *Chapman v. Rhodes*, the U.S. Supreme Court ruled that crowding (housing two inmates in cells designed for one) by itself does not constitute cruel and unusual punishment.

Eighth Amendment suits have been responsible for the cessation of corporal punishment and a general improvement in prison conditions. There is evidence, however, that the courts are reluctant to interfere in the operation of prisons. A leading case in prison conditions is *Holt v. Sarver*, on which the movie "Brubaker" was based. In this case, inmates in Arkansas protested a wide range of prison conditions, from poor sanitary facilities to the use of inmate trustees (including allegations of inadequate medical care, food, sleeping quarters, and almost everything else). The court found that many of the specific allegations did not constitute cruel and unusual punishment, but when it considered the claims together (the totality of the circumstances), the court decided that conditions at the prison combined to make life there cruel and unusual. Later cases similar to this have led to the appointment of "masters," who are charged by the court with the responsibility of bringing a prison or entire prison system into compliance with the Constitution.

Fourteenth Amendment Protections

The third major area of development in prisoners' rights lies within the purview of the Fourteenth Amendment, which provides that no state may deprive any citizen of life, liberty or property without due process of law. This amendment also insures that the federal courts can apply the requirements of the U.S. Constitution to the states.

Perhaps the most important "due process" case in the area of prisoners' rights was decided by the U.S. Supreme Court in 1974. In *Wolff v. McDonnell*, the Court determined what due process rights applied to prison disciplinary hearings. Prior to this decision, it was not uncommon for prisoners to face a "presumption of guilt" and be granted no constitutional protections in disciplinary hearings. The *Wolff* decision required that correctional authorities provide to any prisoner charged with a rules violation written notice of the charges, a hearing within 72 hours of notice, warnings of possible criminal proceedings that could result from the hearing, a written statement of the findings and evidence, and the right to appeal within five days.

While prisons are still not "country clubs" by any stretch of the imagination, one effect of the prisoners' rights movement has been to make prisons less oppressive than they had been. While the pains of imprisonment mentioned before still do exist, inmates today have somewhat more freedom and autonomy within the institution than did inmates at the time Sykes identified the five "Deprivations" associated with prison life.

REVIEW QUESTIONS

1. Why can incarceration be considered the cornerstone of American corrections?

2. Briefly relate the history of American prisons and jails. Distinguish between the Auburn and Pennsylvania systems of incarceration.

3. With reference to organizational and legal differences, distinguish between prisons and jails.

4. Identify the "pains of imprisonment."

5. Who are the "other inmates"?

6. Explain what is meant by the "hands-off doctrine."

7. Identify three areas in which prisoners' rights have been granted or expanded in recent years.

REFERENCES

Abbott, J.H. (1981), *In the Belly of the Beast: Letters from Prison.* (New York: Vintage).

Braly, M. (1976), *False Starts: A Memoir of San Quentin and Other Prisons.* (New York: Penguin Books).

Bureau of Justice Statistics (1981), *Census of Jails: Vols. I-IV.* (Washington, DC: U.S. Department of Justice).

_____ (1982), *Prisons and Prisoners.* (Washington, DC: U.S. Department of Justice).

_____ (1983), *Report to the Nation on Crime and Justice.* (Washington, DC: U.S. Department of Justice).

_____ (1984), *The 1983 Jail Census.* (Washington, DC: U.S. Department of Justice).

_____ (1985), *Jail Inmates 1983.* (Washington, DC: U.S. Department of Justice).

_____ (1986), *Population Density in State Prisons.* (Washington, DC: U.S. Department of Justice).

_____ (1987a), *Prisoners in 1986.* (Washington, DC: U.S. Department of Justice).

_____ (1987c), *BJS Data Report, 1986.* (Washington, DC: U.S. Department of Justice).

_____ (1988), *Jail Inmates, 1987.* (Washington, DC: U.S. Department of Justice).

_____ (1987c), *Jail Inmates, 1985.* (Washington, DC: U.S. Department of Justice).

Cheek, F.E. & M.D. Miller (1983), "The experience of stress for correction officers: A double-bind theory of correctional stress," *Journal of Criminal Justice* 11(2):105-20.

Clear, T.R. & G.F. Cole (1986), *American Corrections.* (Monterey, CA: Brooks-Cole).

Cohen, F. (1972), "The discovery of prison reform," *Buffalo Law Review* 21(3):855-87.

Connolly, P.K. (1975), "The possibility of a prison sentence is a necessity," *Crime & Delinquency* 21(4):356-59.

Fishman, J.F. (1923), *Crucibles of Crime: The Shocking Story of the American Jail.* (Montclair, NJ: Patterson-Smith, 1969).

Fogel, D.F. (1979), *We Are the Living Proof...* (Cincinnati, OH: Anderson).

Goffman, E. (1961), *Asylums: Essays on the Social Situations of Mental Patients and Other Inmates.* (Chicago: Aldine).

Goldfarb, R. (1975), *Jails: The Ultimate Ghetto.* (New York: Anchor-Doubleday).

Hawkins, G. (1976), *The Prison: Policy and Practice.* (Chicago: University of Chicago Press).

Hepburn, J. (1987), "The prison control structure and its effects on work attitudes: The perceptions and attitudes of prison guards," *Journal of Criminal Justice* 15(1):49-64.

Jacobs, J.B. & N. Crotty (1978), *Guard Unions and the Future of Prisons.* (Ithaca, NY: New York State School of Industrial and Labor Relations).

Johnson, R. (1987), *Hard Time: Understanding and Reforming the Prison.* (Monterey, CA: Brooks-Cole).

Katsampes, P & T.C. Neil (1981), "A decade of improvement for Our Sick Jails," *Federal Probation* 45(3):45-48.

Keve, P.W. (1986), *The History of Corrections in Virginia.* (Charlottesville, VA: University Press of Virginia).

Langbein, J.H. (1976), "The historical origins of the sanction of imprisonment for serious crime," *Journal of Legal Studies* 5.

Lockwood, D. (1982), "The contribution of sexual harrassment to stress and coping in confinement," in N. Parisi (ed.), *Coping with Imprisonment.* (Beverly Hills, CA: Sage, 1982):45-64.

Lombardo, L.X. (1989), *Guards Imprisoned, Second Edition.* (Cincinnati, OH: Anderson).

McGee, R. (1971), "Our sick jails," *Federal Probation* 35(1):3-8.

Moracco, J.C. (1985), "Stress: How corrections personnel can anticipate, manage, and reduce stress on the job," *Corrections Today* 47(7):22-26.

Moynahan, J.M. & E. Steward (1980), *The American Jail.* (Chicago: Nelson-Hall).

Nacci, P.L. & T.R. Kane (1984), "Sex and sexual aggression in federal prisons: Inmate involvement and employee impact," *Federal Probation* 48(1):46-53.

National Advisory Commission on Criminal Justice Standards and Goals (1973), *Corrections.* (Washington, DC: Government Printing Office).

Newman, G.R. (1983) *Just and Painful.* (New York: MacMillan).

O'Leary, V. & D. Duffee (1971), "Correctional policy: A classification of goals designed for change," *Crime and Delinquency* 17(4):373-86.

Philliber, S. (1987), "Thy brother's keeper: A review of the literature on correctional officers," *Justice Quarterly* 4(1):9-37.

Reasons, C.E. & R.L. Kaplan (1975), "Tear down the walls? Some functions of prisons" *Crime and Delinquency* 21(4):360-72.

Rothman, D. (1971), *The Discovery of the Asylum.* (Boston: Little, Brown).

_____ (1980), *Conscience and Convenience: The Asylum and Its Alternatives in Progressive America.* (Boston: Little, Brown).

Skoler, D.L. (1978), *Governmental Structuring of Criminal Justice Services: Organizing the Non-system.* (Washington, DC: Government Printing Office).

Spalding, W.F. (1897), "Indeterminate sentences," in *Proceedings of the National Conference of Charities and Correction at the 24th Annual Sesion Held in Toronto, Canada, July 7-14, 1897*, pp. 46-51.

Sykes, G.M. (1969), *The Society of Captives.* (Princeton, NJ: Princeton University Press).

Toch, H. & J. Klofas (1982), "Alienation and desire for job enrichment among correctional officers," *Federal Probation* 36:35-47.

Torok, L. (1974), *Straight Talk from Prison: A Convict Reflects on Youth, Crime and Society.* (New York: Human Sciences Press).

Travis, L.F., M.D. Schwartz & T.R. Clear (eds.) (1983), *Corrections: An Issues Approach, Second Edition.* (Cincinnati, OH: Anderson).

Twentieth Century Fund (1976), *Fair and Certain Punishment.* (New York: McGraw-Hill).

Vito, G.F. & J.H. Kaci (1982), "Hands on or hands off? The use of judicial intervention to establish prisoners' rights," in N. Parisi (ed.) *Coping with Imprisonment.* (Beverly Hills, CA: Sage):79-100.

Wright, E.O. (ed.) (1973), *The Politics of Punishment: A Critical Analysis of Prisons in America.* (New York: Harper Torchbooks).

Zimbardo, P.G. (1972), "The pathology of imprisonment," *Society* 9(2).

TABLE
OF CASES

Chapman v. Rhodes, 452 U.S. 337 (1982).

Cooper v. Pate, 378 U.S. 546 (1964).

Ex parte Hull, 312 U.S. 546 (1941).

Holt v. Sarver, 309 F.Supp. 362 (1970).

Johnson v. Avery, 393 U.S. 483 (1969).

Wolff v. McDonnell, 418 U.S. 539 (1974).

11 Problems and Issues in Incarceration

The development of prisoners' rights is a core issue in the use of incarceration. Like other areas of the justice system, however, incarceration of offenders is filled with controversy. Indeed, the concept of incarceration, especially the way it is practiced in the United States, is itself controversial. Critics often note that, among all the nations in Western civilization, the United States has the highest rate of imprisonment, and imposes the longest prison terms on offenders (Doleschal, 1971).

It is clear that, as a society, we incarcerate a large number of individuals. Little is known about whom we incarcerate, and how patterns of incarceration change over time. Those who are incarcerated most often come from the lower classes in society. Jail inmate populations tend to reflect the ethnic composition of our lower and working classes (Stojkovic, Pope & Feyerherm, 1987). In addition, jail use varies by community (Klofas, 1987). As it is for the police and courts, some of the explanation for incarceration is found in community attitudes and values.

Reacting to this observation, several commentators have suggested that the most appropriate strategy for the control of criminal offenders is one that reduces reliance on incarceration (Rector, 1975; National Council on Crime & Delinquency, 1972; Nagel, 1973; McDonald, 1986). Norval Morris (1974) took a middle-ground approach in suggesting that prisons are necessary and useful in the control of the small percentage of dangerous offenders, but that the United States currently overuses incarceration.

Other observers believe that the problem with American prisons is that they are under used. There are those who suggest that the solution to the crime problem will be found in the incarceration of offenders for incapacitative purposes (Wilson, 1975; Greenwood, 1981). The approach taken by these observers mirrors that of Morris in that they view prison as a scarce resource. They suggest the method of identifying those criminals who commit the most offenses and reserving prison sentences for them. Other observers are less discriminating, and would impose incarceration on a much wider range of offenders.

Fox (1983:299) reported, "The viewpoint taken by the majority of correctional administrators is that prisons are overused and that many people in prison today do not need to be there." Yet, it is also true that abolition of the prison is not likely to occur in the near future. Whether because of its long tradition as a criminal sanction or, as Johnson (1987) suggests, because the urge to incarcerate may be "natural," the continued use of prisons seems assured. Assuming that we will continue to employ incarceration as a sanction for criminal offenses, the issues and controversies surrounding prison and jail operations today are significant.

We will discuss four current issues in American incarceration. While it is safe to say that there may be no *new* issues in American prisons and jails, as the history of incarceration has been one of problems (Schwartz, et al, 1980:212), two of the four issues represent new twists on old issues: *privatization* and *crowding*. The other pair of issues more closely resemble continuations of traditional problems: *prison industries* and *violence* in the institution. At base, these four contemporary concerns reveal the structural limitations on the ability of correctional institutions to change, and the effects of broader social changes on criminal justice system operations.

Box 11.1
Private Operation of Correctional Facilities in 1984

Facility management contracting activity in early 1984[a]

Federal contracts	State corrections contracts	Local jail contracts
Immigration and Naturalization Service	**Secondary adult facilities**	• Legislation enabling private jail operations was pending in Colorado and had passed in New Mexico and Texas.
• Four facility contracts for aliens awaiting deportation were operating in San Diego, Los Angeles, Houston, and Denver. Capacity: 625 beds.	• A total of 28 States reported use of privately operated prerelease, work-release, or halfway house facilities. Largest private facility networks found in California, Massachusetts, Michigan, New York, Ohio, Texas, and Washington.	• Corporate providers reported significant interest, and there were a number of pending proposals for jail operations in the South and West, in spite of the formal opposition of the National Sheriffs' Association.
• Three facility contracts were nearing award in Las Vegas, Phoenix, and San Francisco. Capacity: 225 beds.	**Primary adult facilities**	• In Hamilton County, Tennessee, a private contractor took over operation of a local workhouse for 300 men and women awaiting trial or serving sentences of up to 6 years.
• Two facility contracts were planned in the near term in Laredo and El Paso, Texas. Capacity: 270 beds.	• Kentucky Corrections Cabinet issued an RFP in late 1984 to contract for minimum security housing for 200 sentenced felons. However, no contracts for the confinement of mainstream adult populations were reported in operation.	**Shared facilities**
U.S. Marshals Service	• Two interstate facilities for protective custody prisoners were planned by private contractor.	• One private organization in Texas was planning to construct and operate a facility to serve both local detention needs and the needs of Federal agencies responsible for confining illegal aliens.
• Two small facilities were operating under contract in California. Capacity: 30 beds.	**Juvenile facilities**	• Other proposals called for the development of regional jail facilities to serve multicounty detention needs.
• One contracted facility for alien material witnesses was planned in Los Angeles. Capacity: 100-150 beds.	• A 1982-83 survey of private juvenile facilities found 1,877 privately operated residential programs holding a total of 31,390 juveniles, of whom 10,712 were held for delinquency. Only 47 institutions were classified as strict security and 426 as medium security. The rest were primarily small, less secure facilities.[b]	
Federal Bureau of Prisons		
• One contracted facility for sentenced aliens was planned in the Southwest region. (Project delayed due to siting difficulties.) Capacity: 400-600 beds.	• An exception was Florida's Okeechobee Training School for 400 to 500 serious juvenile offenders, operated by a private contractor.	
• One contracted facility for offenders under the Federal Youth Corrections Act was operating in La Honda, California. Capacity: 60 beds.		

[a] Reported in telephone contacts made in January and February 1984, with additional followup at later points in 1984.

[b] Unpublished tables from *Children in Custody: Advance Report on the 1982-83 Census of Private Facilities*, U.S. Department of Justice, Office of Juvenile Justice and Delinquency Prevention, Washington, D.C.

SOURCE: J. Mullen (1985), "Corrections and the private sector," *NIJ Reports* (May:4).

Privatization

For years, correctional institutions have contracted for services with private corporations, ranging from facility design and construction, to the provision of medical care or food service for the inmate population. In more recent years, there has been a movement to contracting with a private vendor for the entire operation of a prison or jail (Ericson, McMahon & Evans, 1987). Peter Greenwood (1981) suggested that private enterprise could do a better job of running the nation's prisons, at less cost. In 1985, the delegate assembly of the American Correctional Association passed a policy statement that was generally supportive of further privatization (Controversial ACA Policy, 1985:1-2).

Several detention facilities are currently operated by private businesses (Krajick, 1984). Most of these institutions deal with special offender populations, such as illegal aliens or juvenile offenders. There is now the growing suggestion that private companies be allowed to operate general purpose prisons and jails (Logan, 1987). The effects of private operation are unclear. Box 11.1 describes current contracts for private operation of penal facilities.

The National Institute of Justice (1985) reported on *The Privatization of Corrections*. As of February 1984, every state had some correctional service provided under contract. The most common contract service was medical or psychiatric care for state prisoners (33 states). The private operation of halfway houses, pre-release centers, or related transitional residential programming was reported in 28 states. These residential programs were reported to have the capacity to house between 7,500 and 8,000 inmates in total. Only three states reported that they had contracting for the operations of institutions for adults under state jurisdiction, with a total of 61 beds. Obviously, private operation of penal institutions was limited at that time.

By 1987, however, privatization had spread. Hackett, et al (1987) reported that, by the end of 1986, about 1,200 adults were housed in secure facilities operated by private organizations. The state of Kentucky had contracted for the operation of a 200-bed minimum-security facility which opened in January 1986. As the authors concluded, "State and local experience in contracting for the entire operation and management of a secure adult institution is still quite limited."

Nonetheless, privatization has emerged as a potential alternative form of providing incarceration for all jurisdictions. Shover and Einstadter (1988) suggested that privatization has come to the fore in the 1980s because it is congruent with a national social view that the private sector and the "marketplace" are proper forums for the resolution of social problems. Thus, corrections again reflects changes in social and political ideology.

In an assessment of the benefits and drawbacks of private prisons and jails, Travis, Latessa and Vito (1985) identified problems with private involvement in three areas. First, it is not clear what is the legal authority of private contractors. Second, there is no solid evidence that privatization will prove to be less costly than state operation. And finally, there are unresolved questions about accountability.

Is a private company and its agents authorized to exercise force (including deadly force) to prevent escapes, quell riots, and otherwise control an inmate population? Perhaps more basic is the question of whether a private company can be empowered to deprive citizens of their liberty. Related legal issues surround the question of liability. If an inmate is injured through negligence of a private company, would the committing state or local government also be liable for damages? These questions need to be answered before any large-scale movement to private prisons can take place. In a later assessment, Charles Logan (1987) suggested that the right of the state to imprison derives ultimately from the citizens, and could be delegated properly to a private company. Further, he astutely suggested that the motives of state agencies cannot be assumed to be any better than the profit motive of a private firm.

With many services, contracting with private agencies appears to be more cost-efficient than governmental operation (Camp & Camp, 1984). Yet, the question of cost is less clear when discussing the possibility of an entire institution being run by a contractor. What cost savings are realized may be attained by lowering quality control. Might a private company hire custodial officers at minimum wage, thereby limit the pool from which candidates might be drawn, and enhance the likelihood of employee turnover?

A third set of concerns deals with accountability for the operation of the institution. If a prison or jail is "contracted," the contracting governmental authority is still accountable for the delivery of incarceration services. The task changes from that of managing the facility to that of overseeing and managing the contract. In addition, other problems of accountability arise because a new layer of administration has been created.

Would the manager of a privately operated prison be allowed to "cap" the population of the facility? Or could the private facility refuse to accept inmates suspected of being "trouble-makers?" At bottom, it is most likely that the governmental agency contracting for the private prison would still be held accountable for its operation, but would be forced to negotiate with the contractor over most aspects of institutional operation. Until these and other issues are resolved, privatization will pose as many problems as it does solutions (Bowditch & Everett, 1987).

Crowding

As mentioned earlier, perhaps the most pressing concern of correctional administrators today is the crisis of crowding in the nation's prisons and jails. The Bureau of

Justice Statistics (1984) reported that five of the nation's ten largest jails were under court order to reduce overcrowding in June 1983. Further, nearly 20% of American jails were holding inmates as a result of crowding at other facilities, and almost 10,000 jail inmates in June 1983 were being held as a result of crowding in prisons. The situation did not improve, but worsened over time. In 1987, the Bureau reported that, at the end of 1986, nearly 14,000 state prison inmates were housed in local jails because of prison crowding.

A similar picture can be painted for prisons. In 1983 eight state prison systems (Alabama, Florida, Michigan, Mississippi, Oklahoma, Rhode Island, Tennessee and Texas) were operating under court order or had been declared to be unconstitutional. In addition, the District of Columbia and 21 states had one or more institutions operating under court order, while nine others had litigation pending, and two states were operating under consent decrees. Thus, the majority of prison systems in the United States were crowded to the point that court intervention had occurred or was sought.

In 1986, the Bureau of Justice Statistics reported that 32 of the 51 (fifty states and the federal) jurisdictions were housing more inmates than their highest capacity. That is, these jurisdictions were crowded. Using a different estimate of capacity, it was reported that as many as 41 jurisdictions could be classified as crowded. The Bureau reported, "Jurisdictions have employed many methods to alleviate crowding. Construction of permanent and temporary facilities, backups in local jails, double-bunking, intensive community supervision programs, accelerated parole release, and sentence rollbacks have all been used to make room for new inmates." One of the difficulties in assessing prison crowding is the determination of prison population capacity. Box 11.2 presents three definitions of prison capacity: *rated*, *operational* and *design capacity*.

Box 11.2
Definitions of Prison Capacity

Estimating prison capacity

The extent of crowding in the Nation's prisons is difficult to determine precisely because of the absence of uniform measures for defining capacity. A wide variety of capacity measures are in use among the 52 reporting jurisdictions since capacity may reflect both available space to house inmates as well as the ability to staff and operate an institution. To estimate the capacity of the Nation's prisons, States were asked to supply up to three measures for year-end 1986--rated, operational, and design capacities. These measures were defined as follows:

* Rated capacity is the number of beds or inmates assigned by a rating official to institutions within the State.

* Operational capacity is the number of inmates that can be accommodated based on a facility's staff, existing programs, and services.

* Design capacity is the number of inmates that planners or architects intended for the facility.

SOURCE: *Prisoners in 1986.* (Washington, DC: U.S. Department of Justice, 1987):4.

In response to the crisis of crowding, many states are developing ways to reduce their prison populations, or are engaging in construction programs to create more prison space. By late 1986, more than $3 billion had been allocated for the construction of prison space for 59,000 inmates (ACA, 1986:3). The National Institute of Corrections has operated a program in several states that involves the use of prison crowding policy teams to assist the states in responding to the crowding problem. Some states have passed legislation enabling correctional administrators to accelerate release dates for certain inmates whenever the prison population reaches the point of crowding. There has been an increased interest in probation and parole (to be discussed in the next chapter) as alternatives to incarceration (Latessa, 1985).

Crowding in correctional institutions poses several problems for inmates, correctional staff, and correctional administrators. For these reasons, it is simply not acceptable to jam more prisoners into existing space, at least not as a long-term response to crowding. Rather, alternatives must be developed that insure adequate capacity to house the large numbers of offenders now populating the nation's prisons and jails.

For inmates, crowding places severe demands upon available resources. Simple things, such as hot water for showers, that are generally taken for granted, become scarce resources. Privacy, always at a premium in penal facilities, becomes almost totally beyond the reach of most inmates. A crowded facility generally lacks the ability to provide activities for inmates (or "meaningful" work experiences for them), which fill the long hours of each day. There are more inmates with whom recreational, educational, vocational, and other resources must be shared. If the institution is sufficiently crowded, it may even become difficult to find a seat from which to view television.

Research indicates that crowding leads to irritability and increased violence among inmates. Thus, the crowded institution is also a more dangerous place to be. Disease and illness spread more rapidly in a crowded institution. The effect of all of these pressures is to make the experience of imprisonment even more painful for inmates, and this increase in pain often breeds resentment towards the prison (resentment that may be expressed in the form of riots, or assault on prison staff).

Prison staff also feel the pressures of crowding. In addition to the increased tension in the institution and the perceived increase in the likelihood of attack by inmates, the workload of staff increases. Doubling the inmate population means doubling the caseloads of correctional counselors, increasing the class sizes of educational staff, doubling the demands upon food-service staff and increased activity for the custody staff. There are twice as many inmates to count, escort, search, counsel, and watch. Correctional officers can be overwhelmed by the sheer numbers of inmates. The crowded institution becomes more anonymous and impersonal, making it difficult for officers to recognize and know inmates, or to provide adequate service and protection to them. As a result, correctional officers in crowded institutions are likely to be less attuned to the population and more distant from it. As Box 11.3 shows, justice system officials identify prison and jail crowding as one of their most pressing problems.

Correctional managers must provide for the needs of larger numbers of inmates with a constant level of resources. Managers become more concerned with tranquility and bed space than with the provision of services and opportunities. As Johnson (1987:182) noted, "When prisons become overcrowded, moreover, the temptation to warehouse inmates *as a matter of policy*, rather than as a failure of policy, is strong." That is, correctional managers facing crowded prisons seek to survive without disruption, rather than to improve either their institutions or the lives of inmates. For example, several jurisdictions are using what is euphemistically called "bus housing." It has been estimated that large states, like California, may have 1,000 or more inmates "in transit" between prisons at any time. Inmates on a bus do not require cells.

Box 11.3
Justice System Problems Identified by Justice Officials

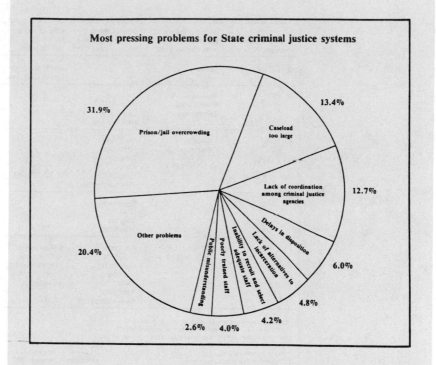

Most pressing problems for State criminal justice systems

31.9% Prison/jail overcrowding

13.4% Caseload too large

12.7% Lack of coordination among criminal justice agencies

Delays in disposition 6.0%

Lack of alternatives to incarceration 4.8%

Inability to recruit and select adequate staff 4.2%

Poorly trained staff 4.0%

Public misunderstanding 2.6%

Other problems 20.4%

SOURCE: S. Gettinger (1984), *Assessing Criminal Justice Needs.* (Washington, DC: U.S. Department of Justice):3.

Box 11.4
Status of Prisoner Litigation
Over Prison Crowding, 1982

% of crowded inmates*	Entire prison system declared unconstitutional	One or more facilities under court order	One or more facilities in litigation	No litigation on crowding pending
80-100%	Texas		North Carolina South Carolina	
60-79%	Florida Mississippi Tennessee	Georgia Illinois Louisiana New Mexico		Nebraska
40-59%	Alabama Oklahoma	Maryland Missouri Nevada Ohio Oregon Washington		Alaska Arkansas
20-39%		Delaware Utah Virginia Wyoming		Hawaii Idaho Kansas New York
Less than 19%	Michigan** Rhode Island	Arizona Colorado Connecticut Indiana Iowa Kentucky New Hampshire	California Maine Massachusetts West Virginia Wisconsin	Minnesota Montana New Jersey North Dakota Pennsylvania South Dakota Vermont***

*Crowded inmates are defined as those inmates in multiple-inmate confinement units that provide less than 60 square feet of floor space per person as of March 1978.
**Male prisoners only.
***Vermont State prison closed.

Sources: *American prisons and jails,* vol. III, *ACLU Newsletter,* January 1983.

SOURCE: *Report to the Nation on Crime and Justice: The Data.* (Washington, DC: U.S. Department of Justice, 1983):80.

Surely, routine transfers for the sake of bed space do not serve well the needs of prisoners (or of the prison system). Yet, faced with severe crowding, it is one strategy that allows correctional managers to retain custody over inmates when there is insufficient space to house them.

Correctional managers face yet another pressure from overcrowding, and that is court intervention. Box 11.4 provides an overview of crowding related lawsuits filed by prisoners. Schlesinger (1986) reported,

> Four out of five states have been found to be operating prison facilities under conditions that violate the Eighth Amendment. Courts have placed entire correctional systems in receivership, appointed masters to operate state systems, and ordered the early release of thousands of offenders. Some state officials were even threatened with fines and jail terms for noncompliance with court orders to relieve prison conditions.

How to resolve the problem of prison crowding is a question that lacks a ready answer. The solution to crowding depends upon conditions in the jurisdiction. Benton and Silberstein (1983) suggested that the policy a jurisdiction adopts for dealing with crowding depends upon the size of the prison system, court rulings, the nature of the increase in population, prevailing political sentiment, and economic conditions, among other factors. Thus, the decision whether to build more prisons, to grant early releases, to divert convicted offenders from prison, or to deal with crowding in another manner varies from state to state. The response to prison and jail crowding in any jurisdiction, then, depends upon the nature and characteristics of the justice system and its environment in that jurisdiction. John Klofas (1987) observed that similar factors influence the use of incarceration in a jurisdiction. Thus, the solutions to the crowding problem in a jurisdiction reflect the way that a jurisdiction views incarceration as a response to crime.

Prison Industries

In the early days of prisons in America, inmates were expected to pay for the costs of incarceration by working in prison industries. Indeed, the early proponents of incarceration hoped that prisons would not only be self-sufficient, but that they might even become profit centers for the state. After decades of prison industry, including both contracting prison labor with private companies, and state-run industries, prison factories were not considered to be profitable.

"Self-sufficiency was a goal pursued by all states where prisons were instituted. Legislators persistently demanded that their penitentiaries pay their way, even though private industries lobbied against prison manufacturing," observed Keve (1986:28). Prison industry is believed to have a number of beneficial effects. First, especially in the early years of the penitentiary, it was hoped that convict labor could be used to defray the expense of constructing and operating prisons and jails, that is, that inmates could be made to pay for their own punishment. Second, it was believed that the activity of work would occupy inmates and keep them from breaking prison rules. Finally, it was hoped that a regimen of work for inmates would serve to instill in them good habits. As Johnson (1987:26-27) summarized the approach,

> It was hoped that silent laboring days and solitary contemplative nights would encourage communion with God and effect a transformation of at least some of the wayward prisoner's souls. But simple conformity to the prison routine, a life of pure habits if not pure intentions, was enough to get a prisoner by in the congregate systems.

Fox (1983) reported that prison industry has been organized in many ways over time. Six of the more common of these are piece price, contract, lease, public account, state use and public works. Each has its strengths and weaknesses. The *piece price system* was common in the early years of prisons. The manufacturer supplied the raw materials to the prison, and inmates constructed the finished product, which the manufacturer bought at an established price. The *contract system* involved the entrepreneur contracting with the prison for labor and the use of prison shops for the production of goods. The highest bidder won the right to use prison labor and shops. The *lease system* was common in southern prisons after the Civil War. The prison simply leased its convicts to a contractor who produced goods with convict labor. All of these involved having a private contractor.

The other common methods of organizing prison industry relied upon prison-run operations. *Public account systems* were those in which prisoners in correctional industries produced goods and sold them on the open market. There have traditionally been severe restrictions on what prisons may produce, or to whom the products may be sold. *State-use industries* allowed the prison to produce almost any product, but limit the sale or distribution of the product to governmental agencies. The state-use method of organization does not allow the prison industry to compete on the open market. *Public works systems* use inmate labor for public service projects, such as road maintenance, construction of parks, and other government services. Sing Sing Prison in the state of New York was an early public works prison project; it was constructed largely through the labors of inmates brought from the penitentiary at Auburn.

Opposition to the use of "slave" convict labor and the unfair advantage given to manufacturers employing convicts led to the passage of several laws limiting the sale of prison-made goods across state lines, and within states to non-governmental units (Cullen & Travis, 1984). The resulting decline in markets as well as the lack of capital investment in prison industries rendered most prison factories non-competitive with free-world enterprises. More recently, however, there has been a resurgence in prison industry competing in free-world markets.

The new prison industries are designed to be more similar to free-world production than were prison industries in the past. Inmate participation in prison industries is generally voluntary. The inmates receive wages comparable to those paid on the free market, and they pay taxes, child support and other expenses. Local unions are consulted prior to the development of industries to insure that the new prison jobs do not cause unemployment among law-abiding citizens (Auerbach, 1982). An experimental program using inmates in state-of-the-art production for private businesses, called the Free Venture Program, has been established in a number of prisons and appears to be very promising (Fedo, 1981).

The cycle of prison industry progressing from the production of goods for the open market, through restricted public use, and back again to the free market, shows how difficult it is to resolve the issue of what to do with prison inmates. Recent analyses have suggested that introducing free-market practices and pay scales into prison industry programs will benefit both the inmates (Schwarz, 1986) and the general economy of the state (Lonski, 1986:52). Still, there is opposition to the idea of prisoners manufacturing and selling goods. Finally, the old hopes for prison industry have not been changed. Those advocating the expansion of prison industry programs still suggest that the results of these efforts will be, as identified by Demos and Lucas (1986:63), the goals of the Prison Industry Enhancement Certification Program:

    *   To generate products and services that produce income so that inmates can make a contribution to society, their own costs, and victims of crime, and

    *   To provide purposeful work for inmates, thereby reducing prison tensions, increasing job skills, and providing some marginal opportunity for inmate rehabilitation.

As is apparent from these goals, when compared to the history of prison industries, the only change has been that the supporters of industries no longer expect full self-sufficiency or complete rehabilitation to result from convict labor.

The resurgence of prison industries is a reflection of the current efforts to improve incarceration. Having learned from past problems, correctional administrators are attempting to accentuate the positive of past efforts while controlling the negative effects (Cullen & Travis, 1984). In a sense, the revitalization of prison industries represents a general return to incarceration as a preferred criminal sanction, which is an effect that has occurred since the early 1970s. The appeal of putting prisoners to work, both for their own good, and for the good of the state, is strong. The question is whether it is possible to overcome objections to convict labor and to obtain the expected benefits of prison industries.

Violence

Violence has long been a part of the incarceration experience (Braswell, Dillingham & Montgomery, 1985). The earliest prison riot in the United States occurred in 1774, when inmates at Newgate revolted (Fox, 1983:114). Newgate was an abandoned copper mine where offenders were sentenced to terms in the old underground mine shafts. Riots and non-violent strikes by inmates have occurred throughout the history of prisons and jails. In addition, violence on a smaller scale, between inmates and officers, and among inmates, has a long tradition. Prison violence occurs in many forms. We shall briefly examine interpersonal assaults and homicide, sexual assaults and violence, and riots.

Interpersonal Assaults and Homicide

John Conrad (1982) suggested that prison violence results from five factors: violence-prone inmates; the "lower class value system," which emphasizes masculinity, toughness and violence; the use of violence by correctional administrators to control inmates; the anonymity of large (especially crowded) prisons; and the utility of violence in furthering inmate objectives. Given that prisons are places where aggressive, often violent people are locked in close proximity to each other, it is not so surprising that so much violence occurs in prisons. Rather, it is surprising that so little violence occurs.

Whether or not a high level of violence exists in any particular institution, the potential for violence is there, and the threat of harm colors the behavior of inmates and staff alike. Jack Abbott (1981:150), a convict-writer who expressed his experiences in prison in his book, titled *In the Belly of the Beast*, wrote, "Everyone in prison has an ideal of violence, murder. Beneath all relationships between prisoners in prison is the ever-present fact of murder. It ultimately *defines* our relationship among ourselves." Abbott suggested that life in a modern prison is akin to life in the jungle. The rule is "kill or be killed." Correctional officers are not immune to the constant threat of violence inside the institution, as evidenced by the growing interest in and market for "body armor" for correctional officers (Kaplan, 1987).

In 1984, 111 prison inmates were killed by other inmates in the United States (Jamieson & Flanagan,
1987:427), and 59 such homicides occurred in the first six
months of 1985. This number of homicides translates to a
rate of roughly 24.6 homicides per 100,000 inmates. The
homicide rate for the nation, as reported in the Uniform
Crime Reports for 1985, was 7.9 per 100,000 people. The
murder rate for prisoners then is more than three times
that for the general public. The level of violence in institutions becomes more evident when assaults on officers
(6,047 in 1984) and inmate-caused deaths of correctional
staff (7 in 1984) are added to the analysis. These numbers,
of course, do not include inmate assaults on other inmates.
Fox (1983:107) wrote, "Homicides in prison appear to be
grossly underreported." He further estimated that the official statistics should be doubled to approach a more accurate figure.

Sexual Assaults and Violence

Sexual assaults in prison are a special case of individual
violence among inmates. The first reported study of sexual
assaults among inmates was made by Alan Davis (1968).
Davis studied this type of inmate violence in the Philadelphia prison system and in sheriff's vans transporting prisoners. He included verbal assaults with actual physical attacks in his definition of sexual assault. As a result, Davis
concluded that nearly 5% of the prison population had
been victims of sexual assaults.

Based on this conclusion, the academic literature and
popular media has portrayed sexual violence in correctional institutions as widespread (Lockwood, 1985). The
image of such violence, however, has been that of the homosexual rape. In fact, later studies (Lockwood, 1980;
Nacci, 1988) revealed that rape is a relatively rare event,

with estimates of less than 1% of the inmate population being victims of physical sexual assaults.

That the actual incidence of homosexual rape is low, however, tells only part of the story. The impact of sexual assault, or the threat of sexual assault, is a general increase in the level of violence in prisons. The fear of victimization leads otherwise peaceful inmates to commit acts of violence to deter attackers.

Toch (1965) reported that 25% of inmate assaults in six California prisons were attributed to homosexual activity. Of these, nearly half involved cases of rivalry (jealousy, unrequited love), and the remainder were cases of forced sexual contact (rape). Lockwood (1980) argued that the reactions of inmates to sexual harassment probably contributed to the total level of prison violence beyond those cases with a clearly homosexual cause.

One positive result of fighting in prison is self-defense. Especially given the media portrayal of widespread rape and sexual victimization in prison, inmates may attempt to build a "reputation" in the institution to insure that they will not become targets of sexual aggressors. Thus, some inmates may assault others in non-sexual circumstances for the purpose of avoiding sexual attack.

One inmate interviewed by Lockwood (1980:95-6) explained an assault on another in the dining hall as self-defense. The inmate Lockwood interviewed had been the victim of a sexual assault, and attacking another inmate in the dining hall was designed to prevent future sexual victimization. As the inmate explained his actions:

> They had a code in the prison on the chow line that said no man should cut ahead of you in the chow line. And this one man passed me a couple of times in the line, and he knew that I was aware of what he was doing. If I failed to do what I was supposed to do here, then I was lost again (would be a sexual victim again). So the next day, when they come through the chow line, when this guy cut in front of me, I hit him in the head with a tray as

hard as I could. And when he went to the ground, I hit him several more times before the guard could reach me. It is regrettable but it is the only way that you can handle it. And I didn't want to do it, but I did what I had to do to protect myself.

As Lockwood suggested, the importance of sexual violence in prisons may come more from the perception than the reality of sexual assaults. It appears that, in reality, there are relatively few cases of actual sexual assault in prisons. It also appears, however, that inmates believe the threat of sexual assault is both real and great. Many instances of individual violence in prisons, therefore, may result from the fear of sexual assault. In this way, it is possible that most prison violence is a form of sexual violence.

Riots

To the relatively high level of violence among individuals must be added the danger of riot. In the past twenty years, three large-scale prison riots have captured media attention and illustrated the potential violence in prison riots. While similar in some respects, each of these riots had different outcomes. The riots at Attica and the New Mexico State Penitentiary in Santa Fe were among the bloodiest in history, while the riots by Cuban detainees at the federal institutions in Atlanta and Oakdale, Louisiana resulted in only one inmate death.

On September 9, 1971, inmates rioted at the New York State Correctional Facility at Attica, and took control of a large part of the prison. On September 13, state police and prison authorities stormed the prison and took command. When the smoke cleared, 43 persons were dead, most of whom were inmates killed during the attack (30). It was the bloodiest prison riot in American history. Nine years later, on February 15 and 16, 1980, inmates rioted for 36 hours at the New Mexico State Penitentiary. When the incident was over, it was learned that the rioting inmates had killed 33 prisoners, and many of these deaths occurred after the victims had been barbarically tortured (Serrill & Katel, 1980). In late 1987, Cuban detainees rioted at the Federal Detention Center in Oakdale, Louisiana, and two days later, Cuban inmates also rioted at the Federal Penitentiary in Atlanta (*Newsweek*, 1987). Two weeks after the beginning of the Oakdale disturbance, the Atlanta rioters finally surrendered.

The riots by the Cuban detainees did not involve anything near the level of personal violence that characterized the Attica and Santa Fe uprisings, as only one inmate was killed. But the extent of property damage caused by the rioting Oakdale and Atlanta detainees was massive (Nacci, 1988). The two institutions were almost completely destroyed. In this respect, the federal riots mirrored the Santa Fe experience, in which inmates also caused extensive damage to the facility, in addition to the killings. At Attica, damage to the institution was much less severe.

Because of the intensity of riots, and the numbers of inmates and staff who are at risk, as well as the possibility of damage to the facility itself, riots are a major concern of correctional administrators. The problem is that not enough is known about the causes of prison riots to allow adequate planning to avoid them (Mahan, 1982). The paradoxical nature of prison violence, including riots, is that the violence may be the result of efforts to reform the prison and improve the quality of life for prison inmates.

What makes prison violence a contemporary issue, although it has always been a part of the prison experience, is that there is evidence to suggest that violence in prisons today is qualitatively different from such violence in the past. As Johnson (1987:75) stated the issue, "Violence has always been a salient aspect of the convict world. In many of today's prisons, however, the convict culture of violence is unusually pronounced." The question remains: "Why is this violent culture so much more pronounced today?"

Observers point to many factors that they believe have changed the nature of American prisons and jails (Conrad, 1982). Two of the more important have been the emergence of professional prison administrators (Mahan, 1982; Conrad, 1982; Fox, 1983; Johnson, 1987) and the effect of court intervention on prison operations (Jacobs, 1977; Marquart & Crouch, 1984). In effect, the prisoners' rights movement and the prevalence of "professional" prison administrators have lessened the authority of correctional staff by humanizing the prison.

Recognizing the prisoner as an individual who deserves to be considered and listened to in making decisions about the running of the institution has the effect of lessening the power of correctional personnel. In regard to the prisoners' rights movement, the success of inmates in court was identified by Fogel (1979) as being "status costly" to correctional staff, as it reduced the staff's position of social and physical superiority over inmates. Perhaps what this means is that a decrease in control over prisons and prisoners by correctional authorities has created a "power vacuum" in our institutions. The perceived increase in prison violence then represents a "power struggle" among inmates to fill that vacuum. As Johnson (1987:81) concluded this argument, "Today's prisons are, as a result, more relaxed in their discipline but more dangerous in their daily operation. The iron hand of the custodian has given way to a "rule of the cruel," with the hard-core convicts now setting the tone of prison life."

The dilemma we face in attempting to solve the problem of violence in our prisons is to solve the problem, if possible, without resorting to the oppressive conditions characteristic of prison life prior to the 1970s. The question is whether it is possible to grant legal rights and protections to prison inmates, as well as giving inmates some level of self-determination, while maintaining control over the operation of the prison? If that question can be answered in the affirmative, there is a chance that we can reduce the current level of prison violence and still retain the progress that has been made in conditions of confinement.

REVIEW QUESTIONS

1. Tell what is meant by privatization in institutional corrections, and identify at least three unresolved issues in the trend of privatization.

2. Explain how the current crisis of crowding in American prisons has affected our jail populations.

3. Identify three solutions a state may employ to deal with prison crowding, and name some factors which may help explain why a particular state selects a specific option.

4. Identify the effects of prison crowding on inmates, staff, and prison administrators.

5. Identify five of the six ways in which prison industry has been organized over the years.

6. What positive benefits are expected from successful prison industry programs for the state and for inmates?

7. Briefly describe three recent prison riots.

8. Some observers believe that recent changes in prison administration which have improved conditions for inmates vis-a-vis prison staff have contributed to increased violence. Briefly explain this argument.

REFERENCES

Abbott, J.H. (1981), *In the Belly of the Beast: Letters from Prison.* (New York: Vintage).

American Correctional Association (1986), "Construction tops $3 billion," *On the Line* 9(3):1.

Auerbach, B. (1982), "New prison industries legislation: The private sector re-enters the field," *The Prison Journal* 62(2):25-36.

Benton, F.W. & J.A. Silberstein (1983), "State prison expansion: An explanatory model," *Journal of Criminal Justice* 11(2):121-28.

Bowditch, C. & R. Everett (1987), "Private prisons: Problems within the solution," *Justice Quarterly* 4(3):441-453.

Bowker, L.H. (1980), *Prison Victimization.* (New York: Elsevier).

Braswell, M., S. Dillingham & R. Montgomery (eds.) (1985), *Prison Violence in America.* (Cincinnati, OH: Anderson).

Bureau of Justice Statistics (1982), *Prisons and Prisoners.* (Washington, DC: U.S. Department of Justice).

_____ (1984), *The 1983 Jail Census.* (Washington, DC: U.S. Department of Justice).

_____ (1986), *Population Density in State Prisons.* (Washington, DC: U.S. Department of Justice).

_____ (1987), *Prisoners in 1986.* (Washington, DC: U.S. Department of Justice).

Camp, C.C. & G.M. Camp (1984), *Private Sector Involvement in Prison Services and Operations.* (Washington, DC: U.S. Department of Justice).

Conrad, J. (1982), "What do the undeserving deserve?" in R. Johnson & H. Toch (eds.) *The Pains of Imprisonment.* (Beverly Hills, CA: Sage):313-30.

"Controversial A.C.A. policy calls for 'privatization'" (1985), *Criminal Justice Newsletter* 16(3):1-3.

Cullen, F.T. & L.F. Travis (1984), "Work as an avenue of prison reform," *New England Journal on Criminal and Civil Confinement* 10(1):45-64.

Davis, A. (1968), "Sexual assaults in the Philadelphia prison system and sheriff's vans," *Transaction* 6:13.

Demos, N.L. & L.S. Lucas (1986), "Industries initiative--PIE: Inmates work free-world style," *Corrections Today* 48(7):62-65;73.

Doleschal, E. (1971), "Rate and length of imprisonment," *Crime & Delinquency* 23:51.

Ericson, R., M. McMahon & D. Evans (1987), "Punishment for profit: Reflections on the revival of privatization in corrections," *Canadian Journal of Criminology* 29(4):355-88.

Fedo, M. (1981), "Free enterprise goes to prison," *Corrections Magazine* 7(2):5-13.

Fogel, D.F. (1979), *"We Are the Living Proof..."* (Cincinnati, OH: Anderson).

Fox, V. (1983), *Correctional Institutions.* (Englewood Cliffs, NJ: Prentice-Hall).

Greenwood, P. (1981), *Private Enterprise Prisons? Why not? The Job Would Be Done Better and at Less Cost.* (Santa Monica, CA: RAND).

_____ (1982), *Selective Incapacitation.* (Santa Monica, CA: RAND).

Hackett, J.C., H.P. Hatry, R.B. Levinson, J. Allen, K. Chi & E.D. Feigenbaum (1987), *Contracting for the Operation of Prisons and Jails.* (Washington, DC: U.S. Department of Justice).

Jacobs, J. (1977), *Stateville: The Penitentiary in Mass Society.* (Chicago: University of Chicago Press).

Jamieson, K.M. & T.J. Flanagan (1987), *Sourcebook of Criminal Justice Statistics--1986.* (Washington, DC: U.S. Department of Justice).

Johnson, R. (1987), *Hard Time: Understanding and Reforming the Prison.* (Monterey, CA: Brooks-Cole).

Kaplan, S. (1987), "Solid protection--New advances in body armor," *Corrections Today* 49(4):80-82.

Keve, P. (1986), *The History of Corrections in Virginia.* (Charlottesville, VA: University of Virginia Press).

Klofas, J. (1987), "Patterns of jail use," *Journal of Criminal Justice* 15(5):403-12.

Krajick, K. (1984), "Punishment for Profit" *Across the Board* (March):20-27.

Latessa, E.J. (1985), "Community corrections as diversion," in L. Travis (ed.), *Probation, Parole, and Community Corrections.* (Prospect Heights, IL: Waveland, 1985):81-93.

Lockwood, D. (1985), "Issues in prison sexual violence," in M. Braswell, S. Dillingham & R. Montgomery (eds.) *Prison Violence in America.* (Cincinnati: Anderson, 1985):89-97.

Lockwood, D. (1980), *Prison Sexual Violence.* (New York: Elsevier).

Logan, C.H. (1987), "The propriety of proprietary prisons," *Federal Probation* 51(3):35-40.

Lonski, P.D. (1986), "Illinois shatters myth--Industries boost local economy," *Corrections Today* 48(7):52-56.

Mahan, S. (1982), "An 'Orgy of Brutality' at Attica and the 'Killing Ground' at Santa Fe: A comparison of prison riots," in N. Parisi (ed.) *Coping With Imprisonment.* (Beverly Hills, CA: Sage):65-78.

Marquart, J.W. & B.M. Crouch (1984), "Coopting the kept: Using inmates for social control in a southern prison," *Justice Quarterly* 1(4):491-509.

McDonald, D.C. (1986), *Punishment Without Walls: Community Service Sentences in New York City.* (New Brunswick, NJ: Rutgers University Press).

Morris, N. (1974), *The Future of Imprisonment.* (Chicago: University of Chicago Press).

Nacci, P.L. (1988), "The Oakdale-Atlanta prison disturbances: The events, the results," *Federal Probation* 52(4): 3-12

Nagel, W.G. (1973), *The New Red Barn: A Critical Look at the Modern American Prison.* (New York: Walker & Co.).

National Council on Crime & Delinquency (1972), "Institutional construction" *Crime & Delinquency* 18(3):331.

National Institute of Justice (1985), *The Privatization of Corrections.* (Washington, DC: U.S. Department of Justice).

Newsweek (1987), "A Cuban explosion," *Newsweek* (23), December 7, 1987:38-40.

Rector, M. (1975), "The extravagance of imprisonment," *Crime & Delinquency* 21(3):323-30.

Schlesinger, S. (1986), "So how does it all add up? -- A look at the statistics," *Corrections Today* 48(8):32-36.

Schwartz, M.D., L.F. Travis & T.R. Clear (eds.) (1980), *Corrections: An Issues Approach, Second Edition.* (Cincinnati: Anderson).

Schwarz, R.J. (1986), "Pay off--Enriching lives through correctional industries," *Corrections Today* 48(7):18-20.

Serrill, M. & P. Katel (1980), "New Mexicao: The anatomy of a riot," *Corrections Magazine* 6(2):6-24.

Shover, N. & W. Einstadter (1988), *Analyzing American Corrections.* (Belmont, CA: Wadsworth).

Stojkovic, S., C. Pope & W. Feyerherm (1987), "Confinement patterns in the Milwaukee county house of correction: 1907-1965," *Journal of Criminal Justice* 15(4):301-316.

Toch, H. (1965), in *Task Force for Institutional Violence, 1965*, unpublished manuscript. (Sacramento, CA: California Dept. of Corrections).

Travis, L.F., E.J. Latessa & G.F. Vito (1985), "Private enterprise in institutional corrections: A call for caution," *Federal Probation* 49(4):11-16.

Wilson, J.Q. (1975), *Thinking About Crime.* (New York: Basic Books).

12 Probation, Parole and Community Corrections

The Bureau of Justice Statistics (1984:1) reported that the combined population of offenders under probation and parole supervision in 1983 was greater than 1.75 million. At any given time, there are roughly three times as many people under probation and parole supervision as there are people incarcerated in the United States. As of December 31, 1983, almost 1% of the adult population of the United States was either on probation or parole. While incarceration may be the cornerstone of American corrections, the majority of criminal offenders are sentenced to probation.

By the end of 1985, the Bureau of Justice Statistics (1987:1) indicated that more than 2.9 million persons were under community supervision, and 74% of all those were under correctional authority (on probation or parole). With reference to adults, the Bureau reported that there were 1,222 probationers and parolees for every 100,000 persons, that is, 1.22% of the adult population was comprised of probationers and parolees. By 1987, there were more than 2.6 million offenders on probation and parole, or 1.45% of the adult population (Bureau of Justice Statistics, 1988:1).

Like the prison, probation and parole supervision, as currently operated, are American inventions. Both involve the conditional release of convicted offenders into the community under supervision. Probationers and parolees experience similar treatment, but as we shall see, there are important differences between the two. Probation and parole can be considered to be the "bookends" of imprisonment (See Box 12.1).

Probation is a sanction generally imposed in lieu of incarceration, and thus, it occurs before imprisonment. Parole involves those who are released early from incarceration sentences, and thus, it occurs after a period of imprisonment. Therefore, probation and parole "flank" imprisonment as criminal sanctions.

This chapter examines community supervision in the American criminal justice system. We will describe both probation and parole supervision and other forms of community control of offenders. The chapter will address the history, population and practice of probation and parole, other community-based sanctions, and final discharge from the justice process.

THE ORIGIN OF
COMMUNITY SUPERVISION

Probation and parole developed in the nineteenth century in America, although each had precursors in western civilization. An examination of the history of community supervision shows how the justice system has changed with the social and intellectual currents in the larger society. Shortly after the creation of the penitentiary, many people came to view incarceration as a less-than-adequate response to all offenders. Probation and parole developed as alternatives to incarceration for select groups of offenders.

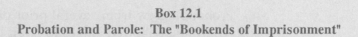

Box 12.1
Probation and Parole: The "Bookends of Imprisonment"

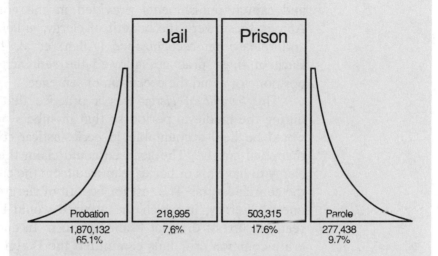

Probation	218,995	503,315	Parole
1,870,132	7.6%	17.6%	277,438
65.1%			9.7%

Probation—The sentencing of an offender to community supervision by a probation agency, often as a result of suspending a sentence to confinement. Such supervision normally entails specific rules of conduct while in the community. If the rules are violated a sentence to confinement may be imposed. Probation is the most widely used correctional disposition in the United States.

Incarceration—The confinement of a convicted criminal in a Federal or State prison or a local jail to serve a court-imposed sentence. Confinement is usually in a jail, administered locally, or a prison, operated by the State or Federal Government. In many States offenders sentenced to 1 year or less are held in a jail; those sentenced to longer terms are committed to a State prison.

Release from prison generally occurs as the result of a decision of a paroling authority, mandatory release, or expiration of sentence. In 1984 half of all releases from prison were by a parole board decision.

• **Parole** is the release of a prisoner by the decision of a paroling authority. The offender is placed under the supervision of a parole officer who monitors the offender's compliance with rules of conduct imposed by the paroling authority. Violations of these rules may result in reimprisonment for the balance of the unexpired sentence.

• **Mandatory release** is based on earned "goodtime" (days earned for good behavior) or other statutory sentence-reduction measures and, though supervision is required after release, does not usually depend on the discretionary decision of a parole board. Supervision rules of conduct, if violated, may result in a return to prison for the time remaining on the sentence.

SOURCE: Bureau of Justice Statistics (1988), *Report to the Nation on Crime and Justice, Second Edition.* (Washington, DC: U.S. Department of Justice):96, 100, 102.

Probation grew from several prior practices in the English courts that allowed judges to grant leniency to offenders who would otherwise be subjected to the harsh corporal and capital punishments provided in the common law. Among these were the benefit of clergy, judicial reprieve, and release on recognizance (Allen, et al, 1985:37-40). Each of these practices allowed the sentencing judge to postpone or avoid the execution of sentence.

The *benefit of clergy* was a practice that developed during the medieval period so that members of the clergy would be held accountable in ecclesiastical courts rather than civil courts. The accused could claim the benefit of clergy to have his or her case moved from the civil courts to the church courts. The test for benefit of clergy came to be one of literacy, in which the accused would be asked to read the text of the 51st Psalm in court. In due time, illiterate common criminals committed the Psalm to memory so that they could pretend to read it and thus avoid the punishments of the king's courts (Clear & Cole, 1986:232).

The 51st Psalm, because it allowed many offenders to avoid hanging as the penalty for their crimes, came to be known as "the neck verse" (See Box 12.2). After a period of expansion of the benefit of clergy, from the 14th through the 18th centuries, the practice was disallowed by statute in 1827. No longer was it possible to escape to the less severe sanctions of the church courts.

Box 12.2
51st Psalm:
The Neck Verse

Have mercy upon me, O God,
    according to thy loving kindness,
According to the multitude of thy tender mercies
    blot out my transgressions.

Judicial reprieve was a common practice in England in the nineteenth century. Under this practice, the offender could apply to the judge for a reprieve, which would require that sentencing of the offender be delayed under condition of good behavior, for a specific period of time. After the allotted time period, the offender would be allowed to ask for a pardon from the king. Here we see the addition of two components of contemporary probation: a set time period, and the requirement that the offender abide by conditions of good behavior.

Release on recognizance was a practice (combined with peace bonds) that was a forerunner to bail. While awaiting the arrival of the circuit magistrate, an accused offender obtained release by posting a surety or by having someone vouch for him. It was this practice that most directly led to the development of contemporary probation, as it was practiced in Massachusetts.

John Augustus, a Boston bootmaker, is generally credited as the "father of probation." It was common practice in Massachusetts courts to allow offenders to be released on the recognizance of a third party. Augustus began a nearly twenty-year career as a voluntary probation officer by posting bail in the Boston Police Court in 1841 for a man accused of drunkeness. He similarly supervised nearly 2,000 people between 1841 and 1858. He was so successful that the state of Massachusetts passed legislation authorizing probation as a disposition and provided for the first paid probation officer. Over time, the Massachusetts practice was emulated by other states. Today, probation is the most common disposition of criminal cases.

Parole also developed in the middle 1800s. By the 1850s, observers of the penitentiary system grew dissatisfied with the effectiveness of incarceration in preventing further criminal behavior by offenders. These critics began to call for a reform of incarceration practices that would serve to "reform" inmates and produce law-abiding citizens. The outcome of this reform movement was *parole release and supervision*.

In England and other European countries, several practices were already in place that laid the groundwork for the creation of parole. The term "parole" was taken from the French phrase *parole de honeur*, which meant "word of honor." Prisoners of war were released on their "parole" that they would not again take up arms against their captors. This term was later applied to the procedure for allowing prison inmates to return to society prior to the expiration of their prison terms. Essentially, the prisoners were expected to vow that they would not violate the law, in return for which they were released.

Banishment and transportation have been discussed as precursors to parole in that these procedures essentially allowed an offender to avoid a more harsh penalty upon condition that he not return to the land of his original crime (Barnes & Teeters, 1959). Closer to modern parole practice, however, were release procedures developed by Walter Crofton and Capt. Alexander Maconochie. As superintendents of penal facilities, each of these men created a system of inmate discipline that allowed the prisoners to earn early release.

Crofton devised a "ticket of leave" for inmates in the Irish prison system. Prisoners were classified into three stages of treatment, ranging from segregated confinement, through work on public projects increasingly free of supervision, until final release "on license." Successful inmates earned their "ticket of leave" through hard work and good behavior. When Crofton believed an inmate to be ready for release, he would issue a ticket authorizing the inmate to return to his home and report his return to the local police. There was no supervision of the released inmate.

Maconochie is called the "father of parole." His system was very similar to that of Crofton. Maconochie operated the British penal colony on Norfolk Island off the coast of Australia. There he classified offenders into three groups and instituted a "mark" system. All inmates began at the "penal stage," which involved close supervision while engaging in hard labor with a large group of fellow prisoners. Good behavior and industry earned marks for an inmate, and upon acquiring enough marks, the prisoner was moved to the next stage. The "social stage" involved working and living in groups of about seven prisoners, with less supervision than the penal stage. Again, marks were earned leading to promotion to the "individual stage," during which the prisoner was allowed his own cottage and individual work. Prisoners were liable to being moved back to earlier stages for misconduct or laziness. Those in the individual stage who continued to demonstrate good behavior and industry were eventually rewarded with a ticket of leave or conditional pardon. Often they were apprenticed to citizens on mainland Australia (Travis, 1985).

The apparent success of these programs did not go unnoticed in the United States. In 1870, the American Prison Association in Cincinnati provided the forum for reformers to push for the creation of parole and a system of reformatory discipline in America (Lindsey, 1925). As a result of the growing support for early release and reformatory discipline, New York enacted legislation creating a reformatory at Elmira, where first offenders would be sentenced to terms that would last "until reformation, not to exceed five years." Parole release had been born in the United States.

Over the next seventy years, a number of legal challenges to parole were raised, and the practice of discretionary, early release from incarceration was finally accepted. Also, during the Progressive Era, increasing attention was focused on the role of post-release supervision of offenders (as well as probation supervision), leading eventually to the current system of parole involving both early release and supervision in the community (Rothman, 1980).

THE ORGANIZATION OF COMMUNITY SUPERVISION

Probation and parole are very similar. In organization, however, there are some differences. While many states charge supervising officers with the responsibility of serving both parolees and probationers, there are other states where the two tasks are administratively separate, as indicated in Box 12.3. Probation tends to be organized as a county and municipal function. Parole, on the other hand, usually is a state function, even in states where parolees are supervised by probation officers (U.S. Department of Justice, 1978).

Parole supervision was exclusively a state function in 44 states, and 7 states (this total included the District of Columbia) supplemented state-level authority with local systems. Probation supervision is attached to the criminal court, but in most cases, probation officers are employees of the executive branch of the state government. About 27.9% of agencies responsible for the supervision of adult and juvenile probationers only are state level, while nearly 70% are organized at the county level. The remaining 4% of probation agencies are city and municipal organizations. For parole supervision, the numbers are reversed, that is, more than 99% of agencies charged solely with the supervision of parolees are organized at the state level. In places where the same agency supervises both probationers and parolees, more than 90% of the organizations are administered at the state level. Thus, for the most part, probation is a local function and parole is a state function.

Probationers are under the jurisdiction of the sentencing court, and are held to a set of conditions imposed by the sentencing judge. Probation officers are responsible for carrying out the wishes of the sentencing judge. Parolees are under the jurisdiction of the state paroling authority, and are held to a set of conditions imposed by that authority. Parole officers are responsible for carrying out the wishes of the parole authority. In jurisdictions where the same officers supervise both parole and probation, the officers wear two hats, and their behavior is contingent upon the legal status (probationer or parolee) of the client.

Box 12.3
Number of State and Local
Probation and Parole Agencies
by Function(s) and Level of Government,
September 1, 1976

Function(s) of agencies	Level of government			
	State-local total	State	County	Munic-ipal
Total agencies	3,868	2,364	1,430	74
Agencies with a single function	1,628	827	758	43
Adult probation only	340	103	212	25
Juvenile probation only	808	249	543	16
Adult parole only	121	118	2	1
Juvenile parole only	359	357	1	1
Agencies with dual functions	1,832	1,270	532	30
Adult and juvenile probation	546	121	400	25
Adult and juvenile parole	20	20	—	—
Adult probation and parole	702	657	41	4
Juvenile probation and parole	564	472	91	1
Agencies with three or four functions	343	203	140	—
Parole authorities	65	64	—	1

—Represents zero.

SOURCE: *State and Local Probation and Parole Systems.* (Washington, DC: U.S. Department of Justice, 1978):2.

Little data exist on the characteristics of probationers and parolees. It is generally safe to say that probationers, for the most part, are less serious offenders who have less extensive criminal records than do prisoners. Parolees, on the other hand, were prisoners themselves, and therefore, they can be expected to mirror the prison population. If anything, in those states where release is discretionary, we can expect parolees to be slightly less "dangerous" than the general prison population, but this is speculation.

What is clear is that the two populations differ from one another. Parole populations tend to be comprised of offenders with more serious criminal records. Further, largely as a result of incarceration, parolees tend to have greater needs in the areas of housing, employment, and personal relations than do probationers. One major difference is that parole caseloads tend to be significantly smaller than those served by probation officers. However, even though the parole caseloads are smaller, the greater needs of the parole population often make them more difficult to supervise than the probation population.

OTHER FORMS OF COMMUNITY SUPERVISION

While probation and parole are the major components of community supervision of criminal offenders, there are other programs that play a role in the non-incarcerative treatment of convicted offenders. These programs include halfway houses, community service, furlough, home incarceration and various diversion programs. Very frequently, these programs are achieved through their imposition as conditions of release under probation or parole. Nonetheless, we will briefly discuss each of these separately.

Halfway Houses

Halfway houses are generally small residential programs that are based in the community and serve populations of less than thirty people (Wilson, 1985). While these houses have a long tradition, their application to criminal corrections has experienced tremendous growth in the past three decades (Allen, et al, 1978). Changes in our thinking about the role of the community in the development of socially acceptable behavior has spurred the development of halfway houses for both criminal offenders and the mentally ill (Beha, 1975).

Halfway houses are so named because they represent an intermediate step, that is, halfway between incarceration and community supervision. They can be either "halfway-out" houses dealing with parolees and other ex-inmates, or "halfway-in" houses for probationers and others not imprisoned (Keller & Alper, 1970). In either case, "treatment" is a part of the halfway-house routine.

In addition to providing room and board, halfway houses generally offer counseling services that include group and individual counseling sessions. Some halfway houses restrict their client population to "special needs" offenders, such as drug and alcohol abusers. Other houses accept a wider range of persons, and provide or contract for a wider range of services.

Community-Service Programs

Community-service orders are a relatively new addition to the arsenal of criminal punishments (Perrier & Pink, 1985). In these programs, convicted offenders are sentenced to a number of hours of service to community organizations or governmental agencies. The work takes place in the community, and the offender is generally at liberty except for the scheduled work hours. The work of the convicted offender is supervised (Umbreit, 1981).

These programs are not yet widely used, but appear to be gaining in popularity. Community service is often seen as symbolically retributive in that the offender is typically sentenced to render some service related to his offense. For example, drunk drivers may be ordered to assist in a hospital emergency room, vandals may be ordered to clean and repair damaged buildings, and similar reflective penalties may be imposed on other offenders. Those completing community service sentences are generally supervised by probation officers and, frequently, community service is imposed as a condition of probation (Hurd & Miller, 1981).

One of the most ambitious community-service sentencing programs reported to date is operated by the Vera Institute of Justice in New York City (McDonald, 1986). In this program, minor offenders were sentenced to perform 70 hours of community service work, such as cleaning and maintaining parks and senior citizen centers, or restoring buildings for low-income housing. The community-service sanction was to be imposed on those offenders that were likely to receive jail terms of 90 days or less, and on those who were likely to receive no sanction because of the pettiness of their offenses. In about five years, nearly 3,500 offenders had served community-service sentences in three boroughs of New York.

Furlough

Furlough programs are also relatively recent alternatives to the traditional sanction of incarceration. At base, a furlough program allows an inmate to leave the penal facility for a specified period to perform an identified function. Several prisons and jails operate work and educational furlough programs. Inmates are released, without escort, to participate in educational programs or to report to work.

After work or school, they return to the institution where they are incarcerated.

These programs are designed to eliminate some of the more debilitating effects of incarceration, such as the loss of a job or the severance of community ties. Furloughs also are employed to help inmates prepare for re-entry to the community by gradual exposure to release (Doleschal, 1971). Inmates on these types of furloughs are expected to seek work and housing, which they will need upon release from the institution.

Furloughs have a relatively long history in American corrections, but their use has changed and grown in recent years. Traditionally, furloughs were available to prison inmates in cases of family emergencies, that is, to visit seriously ill relatives or to attend funerals. In these traditional furloughs, the inmate and the inmate's family were required to pay all expenses, including the cost of an escorting officer (Fox, 1983:147). In the 1960s, several states began granting furloughs to qualifying inmates for social visits, that is, these states issued weekend passes to certain inmates. Today, many states use furlough programs to allow inmates that are near the time of their release on parole to seek employment or arrange for residences.

Home Incarceration

As a response to crowded prisons and jails, there has been a resurgence of interest in the practice of "house arrest" (Petersilia, 1986). Offenders sentenced to home incarceration are essentially "grounded." They are ordered to remain at home except for approved absences, such as attending school, going to work, or keeping medical appointments. While thus incarcerated, the offender is kept out of society yet is not confined in a jail. Ties to family and the community are retained, costs to the state are reduced, and the conditions of confinement for the offender are generally better than would exist in a penal facility.

Proponents of home incarceration argue that this practice is more humane and less costly than incarceration (Corbett & Fersch, 1985). Box 12.4 compares the costs of home incarceration (house arrest) with other possible sanctions. These proponents suggest that, for many offenders, home incarceration represents a more satisfactory alternative to incarceration than do the traditional practices of fines or probation. With home incarceration, someone (usually a probation officer) must be responsible for monitoring the offender to insure that he or she stays home.

Box 12.4
Comparison of Costs for House Arrest
and Other Sanctions

—ANNUAL COST OF HOUSE ARREST VS.
ALTERNATIVE SENTENCES

Routine Probation	$300—$2,000
Intensive Probation	$2,000—$7,000
House Arrest (w/o electronics)	$2,000—$7,000
With Telephonic Call Back System	$2,500—$5,500
With Passive Electronic Monitoring	$2,500—$6,500
With Active Electronic Monitoring	$4,500—$8,500
Local Jail	$8,000—$12,000
Local Detention Center	$5,000—$15,000
State Prison	$9,000—$20,000

Reprinted with permission from Pergamon Press, Inc.

SOURCE: J. Petersilia (1986), "Exploring the option of house arrest," *Federal Probation* 50(2):52.

Diversion

The general rubric of diversion incorporates a wide variety of programs that occur at all stages of the justice system. Diversion is included in the discussion of community supervision because its most common formal application is at some point in the court process prior to conviction or sentencing. In most places, supervision of both diverted and sentenced offenders is conducted by the same office: the probation department (McSparron, 1980).

Diversion programs are designed to prevent some offenders from being processed through the justice system or to minimize the extent of their processing. It is hoped that diverting offenders from the system will enable them to avoid the stigma of a criminal label and the other negative effects of justice-system processing. While used for adults in many jurisdictions, diversion programs are more commonly used with juvenile offenders (Latessa, et al, 1984).

BEING "ON PAPER"

As already mentioned, community supervision is the punishment of choice for most offenders. Thus, community supervision plays a large role in the justice system. This role has been enhanced lately, as a result of overcrowded prisons. The core of community supervision is conditional release as an alternative to imprisonment. Offenders under community supervision are generally held to a higher moral standard than are members of the free society, by virtue of the conditions of release. Probationers and parolees often speak of their status as being "on paper," in reference to their probation or parole agreements, which set out the conditions of release.

Box 12.5
Parole Conditions in Effect in the United States in 1982

	Federal Parole	D.C.	Alabama	Alaska	Arizona	Arkansas	California	Colorado	Connecticut	Delaware	Florida	Georgia	Hawaii	Idaho	Illinois	Indiana	Iowa	Kansas	Kentucky	Louisiana	Maine	Maryland	Massachusetts	Michigan	Minnesota	Mississippi	Missouri	Montana
1. Out of State Travel	1	1	1	1	1	1	1	1	1	1	1	1	1	1	1	1	1	1	1	1	1		1a	1	1	1	1	1
2. Comply with Law	3	3	3	3	3	3	3	3	3	3	3	3	3	3	3	3	3	3	3	3	3	3	3	3	3	3	3	3
3. Regular Reporting	3b		3b	3b	3		3b	3	3	3	3b	3b	3	3	3b	3	3	3	3b	3b	3	3b		3b	3	3	3	3b
4. Weapons	1	2	2	1	2	2	2	2	2		1	2	2	2	2	2	2	2	2c	2		1			2	2	2	2
5. Change Residence	6f	6d	1	1	1	1	1	1			6f	6g	1	1	1	1	1	1	6e	1	1	1	6e	6e	6	1	6f	1
6. Employment		6d	1	1		6d	6g		6f	6g	1	1	1	1	1	1	6		1	1	1	1	6e	6e		1	1	
7. First Arrival Report	3	3	3	3	3	3	3	3	3		3	3		3		3			3	3	3		3		3	3	3	3
8. Maintain Gainful Employment	3	3	3	3	3				3		3	3	3	3	3	3	3	3	3	3		3	3	3	3		3	3
9. Narcotics (Controlled Substance) Usage	2	2	2	2	2	2			2		2	2	2			2		2	2	2		2			2	2	2	2
10. Undesirable Associations/ Correspondence	1		2					2			2	2	1		2	2		2	2	2		2	2	2		2	2	
11. Report if Arrested	6f	6	6e			6c		6f	6d		6d			6e				6e	6		6a	6d	6e	6e			6f	
12. Waive Extradition			3	3	3	3					3	3							3	3	3			3	3			3
13. Support Dependents	3	3	3	3		3					3	3	3	3	3				3	3			3					
14. Liquor Usage	4				4	4					4	4			4			4									2	4
15. Permit Home/Job Visits (Searches)		3						3	3	3				3		3			3									3
16. General Conduct		3		3					3		3			3		3			3	3			3	3		3		3
17. Motor Vehicle Registration And License			1	1								1					1	1									1	1
18. Approval of Marriage (or Divorce)			1		1	1		6f															1			1	1	
19. Act as Informer	2	2	1																				2					
20. Indebtedness					1	1					2			2														1
21. Participation in Drug/ Alcohol/Psychological Program			3		3																		3					
22. Curfew												3i	3h															
23. Civil Rights/Suffrage																				2								
24. Frequenting Illicit/ Immoral Locations	2	2	2			2					2	2										2				2		

SOURCE: L.F. Travis, III and E.J. Latessa (1984), "'A summary of parole rules--thirteen years later': Revisited thirteen years later," *Journal of Criminal Justice* 12(6):594-5.

	Nebraska	Nevada	New Hampshire	New Jersey	New Mexico	New York	North Carolina	North Dakota	Ohio	Oklahoma	Oregon	Pennsylvania	Rhode Island	South Carolina	South Dakota	Tennessee	Texas	Utah	Vermont	Virginia	Washington	West Virginia	Wisconsin	Wyoming	Total
1. Out of State Travel	1	1	1	1a	1	1	1	1	1	1	1	1	1	1	1	1	1	1	1	1	1	1	1	1	52
2. Comply with Law	3		3	3		3	3	3	3	3	3	3	3	3	3	3	3	3	3	3	3	3	3	3	50
3. Regular Reporting	3b	3b	3b	3	3b	3	3	3b	3b	3b	3	3		3	3b	3	3b	3b	3b	3b	3	3b	3b	3b	49
4. Weapons	2	2	2c	1c	2	2	1	2	2	2c	2	2	2	2c	1	2	2c	2	2	2c	2	2	1	2c	48
5. Change Residence	1	1	1	1	1	1	1			6d	1	1	1	1	1	1	1	1	2	1		1	1	1	48
6. Employment	1	1	1	1	1	1	1	1		6d	1	6f	1	1	1	1	1	1	2	6		1	1	1	45
7. First Arrival Report	3	3	3	3		3			3	3	3	3	3	3		3	3				3	3	3	3	39
8. Maintain Gainful Employment	3	3	3		3		3	3		3	3	3	3		3	3		3	3	3	3		3	3	38
9. Narcotics (Controlled Substance) Usage	2	2	2		2	2	2			2		2	2	2		2	2	2		2		2			33
10. Undesirable Associations/ Correspondence	1	1	2		1	2				1		1		2		1	2			1					26
11. Report if Arrested	6			6d	6f		6e			6d		6f	6d			6d		6f		6f			6f		26
12. Waive Extradition	3		3		3	3	3					3	3	3		3	3	3	3			3		3	26
13. Support Dependents	3		3				3					3	3			3	3		3	3		3			23
14. Liquor Usage	4	4	4		4		4				2		2	2	2	4	4		4	4		4			23
15. Permit Home/Job Visits (Searches)		3	3		3	3	3			3			3	3	3	3	3	3		3			3		22
16. General Conduct		3			3	3	3		3			3			3	3	3		3	3			3		19
17. Motor Vehicle Registration And License	1	1							1				1		1					1	1	1	1		16
18. Approval of Marriage (or Divorce)	1	1				1				6d		1			1				1			1		1	16
19. Act as Informer			2	1	1		1									1		2				1		1	12
20. Indebtedness	1	1		1			1									1									8
21. Participation in Drug/ Alcohol/Psychological Program											3				3								1	1	8
22. Curfew		3j														3i									5
23. Civil Rights/Suffrage																									4
24. Frequenting Illicit/ Immoral Locations		2								2		2	2	2		2						2			15

KEY:
1. Must have permission 2. Prohibited 3. Compulsory 4. Allowed, but not to excess
5. May receive 6. Must report
a. If over 24 hours *b.* Monthly *c.* Firearms *d.* Immediately *e.* Within 24 hours
f. Within 48 hours *g.* Within 72 hours *h.* 11 PM to 6 AM *i.* Midnight to 6 AM *j.* Set P O

Supervision Conditions

In the final analysis, probation and parole represent an agreement between the offender and the state. In return for the decision not to incarcerate (or for the decision to release from incarceration), the offender agrees to abide by several conditions while at liberty in the community. Violation of any of these conditions can be used as the basis for revocation of liberty and subsequent incarceration of the offender.

Probation and parole conditions cover a wide variety of behavior, and serve a number of purposes (Travis & Latessa, 1984:599). The primary goal of supervision conditions is to prevent future criminality on the part of probationers and parolees. Conditions can be classified into two general types: standard conditions that are imposed on everyone under supervision in a jurisdiction, and special conditions that are imposed on individual offenders and that relate directly to status and characteristics.

Standard conditions of parole and probation vary across jurisdictions, but usually include restrictions on travel and on the freedom to change addresses or jobs, and instructions on reporting to the supervising officer. These conditions insure that the probation or parole officer will be able to monitor the offender. Box 12.5 presents standard conditions of parole in the United States. Special conditions vary greatly (Jaffe, 1979). They include restrictions on association with particular people, requirements of attending treatment programs, restrictions on the consumption of alcoholic beverages, restitution orders, and the like.

Client Perspectives

The experience of being "on paper" reflects the number and content of conditions as well as the characteristics of the probation or parole officer. A probationer facing conditions that include a curfew, restriction on associating with friends, requirements of restitution, and some period of incarceration will have a qualitatively different experience than will a probationer under less restrictive conditions. Similarly, a parolee whose supervising officer is rule-oriented and unsympathetic will experience a different sanction than one whose officer is flexible and empathetic.

The ability to impose special conditions of probation has led to the use of probation to accomplish many correctional goals that are not necessarily authorized by statute. For example, in a jurisdiction where there is no law authorizing "split sentences," (Talarico & Myers, 1987) a judge wishing to impose such a sentence can place the offender on probation on condition that he serves some time in jail. In a like fashion, absent a statutory authority to impose restitution, a judge can simply make restitution a condition of probation. Probation and (to a lesser extent) parole are the most flexible of sanctions, and this may account, in part, for their popularity among justice system officials.

Recently, criminal justice scholars have begun to ask probationers and parolees for their views on community supervision (Gibbs, 1985; McCleary, 1978; and Allen, 1985). In large part, these offenders prefer probation or parole to any form of incarceration. Many feel fortunate to have been granted an opportunity to prove themselves in the community. Yet, most also identify problems associated with being under supervision.

Probationers and parolees most often complain about what they perceive as the pettiness and unfairness of some conditions of release. They also dislike the requirement that they seek approval of their supervising officers for many minor decisions. Finally, many are dissatisfied with their officers. Many probationers and parolees feel that their officers do not act as advocates for them, and many believe their officers to be too intrusive.

Officer Perspectives

Probation and parole officers lead a schizophrenic existence in relation to their jobs. For years, research into the role of the community supervision officer has identified conflicting dimensions of the responsibilities to help and to control (Clear & Cole, 1986). The officer is expected both to befriend and assist his or her clients, as well as monitor and control them. With reference to parole officers, Studt (1973) identified officer "style" as critical to an understanding of the supervision process, and observed two basic styles: service and surveillance.

Crean (1985:118) reported, "Within a typical work week, a line officer is usually called upon to be an investigator, a biographer, a watchdog, counselor, friend, confidant, reporter, expert witness and broker of outside services." The line officer is a public employee and responsible to the authority that placed the offender under the officer's supervision. Further, the officer must interact on a regular basis with the offender, the offender's family, law enforcement officials, and representatives of community agencies (Sigler, 1988).

As with most criminal justice jobs, the task of community supervision involves a rather large degree of discretion and responsibility. It also entails a tremendous amount of paperwork. While there are psychological, monetary and social rewards in being a probation or parole officer, there are the concomitant costs of dealing with offenders, danger, and bureaucracy. In the end, to most probation and parole officers, the job is just that, a job. Nevertheless, probation and parole officers exhibit the characteristics of professionals, and they frequently do not work steady hours. Those who remain at their positions learn to separate work from the other aspects of their lives.

Probation and (to a lesser extent) parole are correctional interventions that often employ citizen volunteers. Probation was originated by a volunteer, and thus volunteer involvement is not surprising. As the primary task of community supervision is to see that offenders can reside in the community safely, there are good reasons for using volunteers. Volunteers can perform many functions for probation and parole officers. The use of volunteers also helps clients by connecting them with law-abiding citizens (Lucas, 1987).

The dual roles of service and surveillance, coupled with heavy caseloads and frequently inadequate community services, often frustrate probation and parole officers and managers. Recent areas of inquiry are burnout and job satisfaction among the ranks of probation and parole officers (Whitehead, 1986). While there are many demoralizing facets of the job of community supervision agent, most officers report that the benefits outweigh the drawbacks of the job.

COMMUNITY SUPERVISION
IN THE CRIMINAL JUSTICE SYSTEM

In previous chapters, we have discussed several areas of overlap between community supervision and other components of the justice system. Pre-trial release, diversion from court, prosecutorial charging, incarceration, and the size of the prison population all involve decisions that depend (more or less) directly on the operation of community supervision. For example, if probation and parole were not available as alternatives to incarceration, absent the development of other practices, the prison and jail population would increase four-fold.

Probation and parole are normally considered privileges and not rights, thus the offender has no right to be granted probation or parole (del Carmen, 1985). Once placed on probation or parole, however, the offender does have a constitutionally protected interest in retaining that status, as opposed to being incarcerated. To date, there have been relatively few U.S. Supreme Court decisions dealing with the acceptability of various conditions of release and supervision practices. Most of the existing cases in this area were decided by state or federal appellate courts.

Essentially, courts have supported all types of probation and parole conditions as long as those conditions were constitutional, reasonably related to criminality, clearly written, or contributed to the rehabilitation of the offender. The decisions of courts vary across jurisdictions, and they are indeed case-specific. For example, a prohibition against the consumption of alcoholic beverages is likely to be upheld in a case in which the offender's criminality stemmed from drunkenness, and likely to be voided in a case in which the offender has no history of alcohol abuse.

Probation and parole conditions often serve as an arsenal of the prosecutor for correctional authorities. Because violation of any of the conditions of parole or probation constitutes grounds for revocation and incarceration, the conditions provide the officer with "leverage" for the control of the offender. As to the point of revocation, however, the U.S. Supreme Court has set forth due process protections for probationers and parolees.

In 1972, the Court decided *Morrissey v. Brewer*, in which a parolee sought relief after his parole had been revoked.

The Court ruled that parolees facing revocation must be granted the following protections: written notice of the claimed violations, disclosure of evidence against the parolee, the opportunity to be heard and to present evidence, a limited right to confront and cross-examine witnesses, a hearing before a neutral body, and a written statement of the decision and evidence upon which it was based.

The following year, the Court decided *Gagnon v. Scarpelli*, which dealt with probation revocation. In this case, the Court stated that, at least in regard to revocation procedures, there was no substantial difference between probationers and parolees. They granted probationers the same protections as those given the previous year to parolees.

Those under community supervision generally are less restricted and suffer fewer "pains" than those incarcerated. Nonetheless, community supervision is a punishment for crime, and the status of conviction and being under sentence sets probationers and parolees apart from free citizens. Even with the protections afforded by the *Morrissey* and *Gagnon* decisions, probationers and parolees may have their liberty revoked and be incarcerated for "offenses" that would not carry similar penalties for free citizens, and incarceration may follow hearings for which the burden of proof is not as high as the trial standard of proof beyond a reasonable doubt.

REVIEW QUESTIONS

1. Distinguish between probation and parole.

2. Briefly trace the origins of community supervision in corrections.

3. Describe the organization of community supervision.

4. Identify five forms of community supervision, excluding probation and parole.

5. Distinguish between the "standard" and "special" conditions of probation or parole.

6. Describe the role and importance of community supervision in the criminal justice system.

7. Identify the due process rights of probationers and parolees at revocation.

8. Discuss recent innovations in community supervision.

REFERENCES

Allen, G.F. (1985), "The probationers speak: Analysis of probationer's experiences and attitudes," *Federal Probation* 49(3):67-75.

Allen, H.E., E.W. Carlson, E.C. Parks & R.P. Seiter (1978), *Halfway Houses* (Washington, DC: U.S. Government Printing Office).

Allen, H.E., C.W. Eskridge, E.J. Latessa & G.F. Vito (1985), *Probation and Parole in America* (Monterey, CA: Brooks-Cole).

Barnes, H.E. & N.D. Teeters (1959), *New Horizons in Criminology* (Englewood Cliffs, NJ: Prentice-Hall).

Beha, J.A. (1975), "Halfway houses in adult corrections: The law, practice, and results," *Criminal Law Bulletin* 11(4).

Bureau of Justice Statistics (1984), *Probation and parole in 1983* (Washington, DC: U.S. Department of Justice).

_____ (1987), *Probation and Parole, 1985.* (Washington, DC: U.S. Department of Justice).

_____ (1988), *Probation and Parole, 1987.* (Washington, DC: U.S. Department of Justice).

Clear, T.R. & G.F. Cole (1986), *American Corrections.* (Monterey, CA: Brooks-Cole).

Corbett, R.P. & E.A. I. Fersch (1985), "Home as prison: The use of house arrest," *Federal Probation* 49(1):13-17.

Crean, D.M. (1985), "Community corrections: On the line," in L.F. Travis III (ed.), *Probation, Parole and Community Corrections.* (Prospect Heights, IL: Waveland):109-24.

del Carmen, R.V. (1985), "Legal issues and liabilities in community corrections," in L.F. Travis III (ed.), *Probation, Parole and Community Corrections.* (Prospect Heights, IL: Waveland):47-70.

Doleschal, E. (1971), *Graduated Release.* (Rockville, MD: NIMH).

Fox, V. (1983), *Correctional Institutions.* (Englewood Cliffs, NJ: Prentice-Hall).

Gibbs, J.J. (1985), "Client's views of community corrections," in L.F. Travis III (ed.), *Probation, Parole and Community Corrections.* (Prospect Heights, IL:Waveland):97-108.

Hurd, J.L. & K.D. Miller (1981), "Community service: What, why, and how," *Federal Probation* 45(4):39-41.

Jaffe, H.J. (1979), "Probation with a flair: A look at some out-of-the-ordinary conditions," *Federal Probation* 43(1)25-36.

Keller, O. & B. Alper (1970), *Halfway Houses: Community Centered Corrections and Treatment*. (Lexington, MA: D.C. Heath).

Latessa, E.J., L.F. Travis III & G.P. Wilson (1984), "Juvenile diversion: Factors related to decision making and outcome," in S.H. Decker (ed), *Juvenile Justice Policy* (Beverly Hills,CA: Sage):145-65.

Lindsey, E. (1925), "Historical sketch of the indeterminate sentence and parole system," *Journal of Criminal Law & Criminology* 16(1925):9-126.

Lucas, W. (1987), "Perceptions of the volunteer role," *Journal of Offender Counseling, Services & Rehabilitation* 12(1):141-46.

McCleary, R. (1978), *Dangerous Men*. (Beverly Hills, CA: Sage).

McDonald, D. (1986), *Punishment without Walls: Community Service Sentences in New York City*. (New Brunswick, NJ: Rutgers University Press).

McSparron, J. (1980), "Community corrections and diversion: Cost and benefit, subsidy models, and start-up recommendations," *Crime and Delinquency* 26(2):226-47.

Perrier, D.C. & F.S. Pink (1985), "Community service: All things to all people," *Federal Probation* 49(2):32-38.

Rothman, D.J. (1980), *Conscience and Convenience*. (Boston: Little, Brown).

Sigler, R. (1988), "Role conflict for adult probation and parole officers: Fact or myth?" *Journal of Criminal Justice* 16(2):121-30.

Studt, E. (1973), *Surveillance and Service in Parole*. (Washington, DC: U.S. Government Printing Office).

Talarico, S. & M. Myers (1987), "Split sentencing in Georgia: A test of two empirical assumptions," *Justice Quarterly* 4(4):611-29.

Travis III, L.F. (1984), "Intensive supervision in probation and parole," *Corrections Today* 46(4):34.

_____ (1985), "The development of American parole," in H.E. Allen, et al, *Probation and Parole in America*. (New York: Free Press):19-35.

Travis III, L.F. & E.J. Latessa (1984), "'A summary of parole rules--Thirteen years later': Revisited thirteen years later," *Journal of Criminal Justice* 12(6):591-600.

Umbreit, M.S. (1981), "Community service sentencing: Jail alternative or added sanction?" *Federal Probation* 45(3):3-14.

U.S. Department of Justice (1978), *State and local probation and parole systems*. (Washington, DC: U.S. Government Printing Office).

Vito, G.F. (1985), "Probation as punishment: New directions," in L.F. Travis III (ed), *Probation, Parole and Community Corrections* (Prospect Heights, IL: Waveland):73-80.

Vito, G.F. & F.H. Marshall (1983), "The administrative caseload project," *Federal Probation* 46(3):33-41.

Whitehead, J. (1986), "Job burnout and job satisfaction among probation managers," *Journal of Criminal Justice* 14(1):25-36.

Wilson, G.P. (1985), "Halfway house programs for offenders," in L.F. Travis III (ed.), *Probation, Parole and Community Corrections*. (Prospect Heights, IL: Waveland):151-64.

TABLE
OF CASES

Gagnon v. Scarpelli, 411 U.S. 778 (1973).

Morrissey v. Brewer, 408 U.S. 471 (1972).

13 Issues in Community Supervision

Many important issues in community supervision center around innovations in the financing, management, and practice of probation and parole. Largely as a result of crowded institutions, there is renewed interest in community supervision as an alternative to incarceration. Many recent developments are attempts to improve and enhance the effectiveness and economy of probation and parole. In the past few years, however, the central practices of community supervision (probation and parole supervision) have themselves come under attack. This chapter examines the current controversy over community supervision, and discusses specific attempts to improve the efficiency of community corrections.

DOES COMMUNITY SUPERVISION WORK?

In 1978, Andrew von Hirsch and Kathleen Hanrahan published a report to the U.S. Department of Justice titled,

Abolish Parole?. In this brief document, they suggested that parole supervision might be useless. On both rational (practical) and philosophical grounds, the authors concluded that there was little reason to continue the practice of parole supervision. Philosophically speaking, they saw a period of supervision under conditions as an *added* penalty. That is, assuming the offender served a prison sentence as punishment, there was no reason to impose conditional release in addition to incarceration. From a practical standpoint, they argued that the research to date did not support parole supervision as a crime-control strategy. The authors also argued that parole officers were not very effective in providing needed services to parolees. In short, they felt that there was no evidence to support parole supervision.

Von Hirsch and Hanrahan were not the first to question the parole supervision, but they may have been the most eloquent critics. Later reports (Gottfredson, et al, 1982) showed that success of supervision in preventing crimes by parolees often depends on how "new crimes" are defined. If a parolee that is returned to prison for violating the conditions of release without committing a new crime is counted as a "failure," parole supervision may be less effective in preventing recidivism than is no supervision at all. Because parolees must obey the conditions of release, they may be returned to prison for reasons such as violating curfew, failing to report to their parole officers, and other non-criminal behavior. If returns to prison for violation of these conditions are counted as "failures," parolees have more chances to "fail" than do non-parolees, who must be convicted of new crimes to be incarcerated. The research reports show mixed findings. It is difficult, if not impossible, to decide whether parole supervision is an effective crime-prevention method (Flanagan, 1985).

Other critics have raised similar concerns about probation supervision. With the increased use of both probation and parole in response to prison crowding, these concerns have grown. Observers believe that not only are more offenders being placed under community supervision, but that probation and parole now include more serious and more dangerous offenders (Guynes, 1988). Critics are beginning to re-examine the degree to which community supervision protects public safety.

Joan Petersilia (1985) studied probationers convicted of felonies in two large California counties. Her conclusions raised serious questions about the ability of community supervision to control crime. Petersilia and her colleagues concluded that a 65% rate of new criminality among their sample showed that granting probation to those convicted of felonies was not in the best interests of public safety. She later summarized the results of this study (1986:2):

> These results would seem to support the contention that routine probation is not an appropriate or effective sanction for convicted felons. It evidently could not provide the kind of supervision that might have prevented the majority of our sample of felony offenders from returning to crime.

The importance of Petersilia's study was exaggerated by news media attention (Goldstein, et al, 1985). In the weeks following the release of her report by the RAND Corporation, newspapers across the country reported the story. They summarized the research, often with forbidding headlines telling of the dangers posed by felony probation. Reactions to the report were quick, but failed to achieve the same level of media coverage.

Vito (1986) replicated the RAND study on a sample of Kentucky probationers. He reported that felons on probation in Kentucky were much less likely to commit new crimes than were those studied by Petersilia. Similarly, McGaha, et al (1987) replicated the study with probationers in Missouri. They found results similar to those found by Vito. Goldstein (1985) concluded that probationers in New Jersey did not pose as great a threat to public safety as those examined in Petersilia's study in California. The results of Petersilia's study may have been unique to California, as they are different from findings in other states.

Petersilia's findings of risk of future criminality among probationers may not be accurate for the nation. The question that she raised about the ability of probation supervision to provide for community safety remains critical. At a minimum, the perception exists that probation populations are more dangerous today than ever before. There is growing concern about the risk posed by offenders placed under community supervision. One result of the recognition that probation and parole populations now include more dangerous offenders can be seen in that probation and parole officers, in order to better insure public safety, are changing the way that they do their jobs. Other changes involve making both probation and parole more "punitive," such as the increasing use of "shock" and "intensive supervision."

Relatively new practices in community supervision, the programs of "shock" and "intensive supervision" have affected the operation of traditional probation and parole. They illustrate most clearly how community supervision serves as an alternative to incarceration. In both programs, the attempt is made to use community supervision to meet sentencing goals normally associated with incarceration. Specifically, the desired result is the enhancement of both the deterrent and incapacitative effects of community supervision.

Shock probation and parole attempt to deter offenders from continued criminality by imposing a prison sentence that is later "commuted" to a period of supervision. The initial incarceration is expected to "shock" the offender by the severity of the punishment. It also informs offenders what to expect if they continue to break the law (Vito, 1985). Thus, with shock probation, the judge might sentence the offender to a long prison term but, within six months, alter the sentence to a probation period. In some states, such as Ohio, the inmate can petition the court for shock probation. In other states, such as Texas, shock probation is solely at the discretion of the judge.

Shock parole is similar to shock probation in that it involves an early release from a relatively long prison term. The difference here is that it is the parole authority that grants an early release from incarceration to parole supervision, rather than the judge granting probation. For example, a convicted forger that receives a ten-year prison sentence may receive shock probation from the judge after four or five months. If shock probation is not granted, in several states the parole authority is empowered to grant early or shock parole to the offender at his or her first hearing before the board. Like shock probation, states differ as to whether inmates must petition the parole board for shock parole consideration.

In practice, the effectiveness of shock programs is unclear. Many of the programs provide no shock value because offenders expect to be released. Ideally, the incarcerated offender is "shocked" when released. In practice, however, the only shock may come if the offender is not granted an early release. Through a combination of a short prison term followed by community supervision, shock programs attempt to gain the benefits of both incarceration and supervision as sanctions. The offender is expected to be deterred. In theory, shock probation and parole provide a stern warning to the inmate. Without the kindness of the judge or parole authority, the offender would be serving a long prison term. In effect, the released inmate is expected to realize that he or she is living "on borrowed time," and will face a long term if supervision is unsuccessful.

Another practice which is somewhat akin to shock probation is the imposition of "split sentences." A split sentence is a penalty that is divided (split) between a period of incarceration and a period of probationary supervision.

Because of the great flexibility that judges are allowed in determining the conditions of probation, split sentences are relatively widely used. This is true even in jurisdictions where there is no law that specifically allows the judge to use split sentencing.

Parisi (1980) described four historical methods of imposing split sentences, including shock probation as it is practiced in several states. If a defendant is convicted of several offenses or counts, the judge may order incarceration for some offenses and probation for others. Thus, a defendant convicted of two counts of theft may be sentenced to ninety days on the first count and two years of probation on the second. In shock probation, the same offender may receive an initial five-year prison term, and be "shocked" to probation in ninety days. Another way to impose split sentences can be seen in legislation that allows the judge to combine incarceration and probation in one sentence, such as a sentence of ninety days of incarceration followed by two years of probation. Finally, most states have legislation allowing the judge to use incarceration as a condition of probation. In this case, the offender might receive two years probation with the condition that the first ninety days be spent in jail. Regardless of the method used to impose split sentences, the outcomes are the same.

Probation is often seen by judges, offenders, and the general public as a lenient sanction. The use of split or combination sentences allows judges to increase the harshness of the penalty. A judge may not wish to send a minor offender to prison for a long period, but may want the offender to spend some time in jail. Split sentences allow judges to adjust the severity of sanctions.

"Intensive supervision" programs seek to provide more control and service to offenders who otherwise would be incarcerated (Travis, 1984). In practice, these programs rely upon lower client-to-officer ratios, and thus, they assume a higher level of supervision and service delivery (Latessa, 1980). Evaluations to date of intensive supervision programs show some promise of their effectiveness. They do not show that intensive supervision yields better results for the intensive populations than does regular supervision for the regular caseload.

In the intensive supervision programs in which the level of service delivery actually increased, intensive supervision programs do appear to be modestly effective. In any event, intensive supervision appears to effect the release of many offenders who otherwise would be incarcerated. What is perhaps more important is that the mental picture caused by the label "intensive supervision" may make it politically possible to retain a number of relatively serious or persistent offenders under community supervision, as opposed to incarcerating them (Clear & Shapiro, 1986). This is consistent with the traditional role of community supervision as the "overflow" valve for incarceration.

Several states have implemented intensive supervision programs (ISPs). The state of Georgia, perhaps the leader in ISPs, began a program in 1982 that has supervised nearly 3,000 offenders to date (Erwin, 1986). Evaluations of programs in several states (Petersilia, 1986:41) show that these programs may be successful in preventing criminality among probationers, at least during periods of supervision.

Typically, an intensive supervision program requires the probationer to have more contacts with his or her probation officer. By reducing the size of caseloads, we expect officers to be more vigilant in intensive supervision programs (Byrne, 1986). The net effect of these differences is to make the penalty more painful. The probationer experiences more intrusions by the officer. The penalty is also more incapacitative. The offender is more closely watched, and thus he or she is prevented from relapsing into crime.

Shock probation and parole, split sentencing, and intensive supervision programs blur the distinction between incarceration and community supervision. The experience of being "on paper" becomes much more like that of being incarcerated. In these programs, the probationer or parolee faces additional deprivations of autonomy, liberty, and the like. It is difficult to determine whether the development of these programs has led to the increasing use of community supervision for felons and dangerous offenders. It is possible that these developments are in response to a changing population.

SOME OTHER ISSUES IN COMMUNITY SUPERVISION

As prison populations have increased over the past decade, so have the numbers of people under community supervision. The change in types of offenders being placed on probation and parole supervision is an important factor in understanding changes in community supervision. The simple growth in the size of the population, regardless of its characteristics, has also led to changes. Three areas in which such changes can be seen are the financing, management, and practice of probation and parole. These changes merit attention, regardless of whether they involve special programs such as shock or intensive supervision.

Innovative Financing

Several states have implemented "community corrections" legislation, which includes various funding formulas, to support community supervision activities. These laws provide financial incentive to counties to reduce their prison commitments and to retain offenders in the community. The typical law either authorizes a subsidy for counties that reduce their commitment rates, or provides financial support for improved and increased community corrections. The state reduces the subsidy if the commitment rate is increased (Clear & Cole, 1986:399-400; National Advisory Commission, 1973:315).

The first state to employ an incentive program in order to encourage communities to keep offenders out of the prison system was California. In 1965, the California legislature passed the "Probation Subsidy Act," which paid counties $4,000 for each offender that was not sentenced to prison in each county. The state developed a formula that estimated the number of offenders expected to be sentenced to prison, and then paid $4,000 to the county for each offender less than that number that was not sentenced to prison. If a county was expected to commit 1,000 offenders to prison, but actually committed only 900, the county received a subsidy of $400,000 ($4,000 x 100). Subsidy funds were to be used to improve local correctional services. Other states developed similar models.

The California subsidy program faced several obstacles (Clear & Cole, 1986). There was no subsidy assistance to law enforcement, although the effect of the program was to keep offenders in the community. There was no inflation factor included, so that within ten years, the purchasing power of the subsidy declined by over one third. There also was no adjustment for counties that historically had kept offenders in local correctional custody. For example, a county traditionally may have kept non-violent offenders in the community on probation. Under the subsidy formula, that county had a lower estimate of commitments. Another county may have traditionally incarcerated nearly every felony offender. Under the subsidy program, the first county could only receive aid by keeping violent or more serious offenders in the community. The second county could begin to use probation for minor, non-violent offenders, and it could reap a large subsidy.

Later funding formulas for community corrections attempted to overcome some of the original difficulties in the California subsidy program. Minnesota, Oregon, and Colorado passed community-corrections legislation that included more options for counties. These states also tried to adjust for crime and incarceration rates, and they included inflation factors. Other states, such as Ohio, have begun subsidy programs for specific practices that counties could adopt to reduce prison commitments. In each of these cases, funding is tied to the development and expansion of community programs. The effects are to support probation and other community services and to assist the counties in handling their increasing caseloads.

Another recent development is in the charging of "supervision fees." Several state parole authorities and probation offices now require that the client make a monthly payment to the agency to offset the costs of supervision (Wheeler, et al, 1989). This requirement further increases the cost advantage of probation and parole over incarceration. Similarly, it is common for a condition of supervision to be the payment of court costs. This requires that probation and parole officers serve (at least part time) as bill collectors for the courts. Box 13.1 illustrates the kinds of financial conditions imposed on probationers today.

Box 13.1
Financial Conditions Imposed on Probationers
in 16 Jurisdictions

Condition	Average Amount	No. Jurisdictions
Fine	$ 625	14
Court Costs	$ 130	15
Supervision Fees	$ 356	12
Restitution	$1,817	16
Victim Compensation Fund Contribution	$ 226	12
Other	$ 270	11

SOURCE: M. Cunniff (1986), *A Sentencing Postscript: Felony Probationers Under Supervision in the Community*. (Washington, DC: National Association of Criminal Justice Planners):57.

A related financial alteration in the operation of probation and parole is the growing use of restitution. Offenders on probation and parole are increasingly being ordered to make restitution to the victims of their crimes. Probation and parole officers are then required to manage the payment process for restitution (Clear & Cole, 1986: 110-11).

On the one hand, these developments assist community supervision by providing enhanced resources and by reducing costs of operation. On the other hand, these programs also add to the burden of probation and parole officers, who generally dislike working as "bill collectors." In the end, these practices reflect the tradition of experimentation with correctional practices in probation and parole.

Innovations in Management

The traditional approach to probation and parole supervision consisted of the "casework" model. In casework, each officer was responsible for a caseload of offenders. The officer was a generalist expected to supervise a variety of persons with a variety of needs. The casework model expected the single officer to be capable of providing needed services to all of the offenders.

More recently, several different models of organization and caseload management have been proposed and adopted. Several jurisdictions now use teams of officers responsible for large groups of offenders. In team supervision, officers can take advantage of their varied strengths and skills. Box 13.2 demonstrates how probation teams may be organized. Thus, an officer who is particularly effective with offenders that require employment services can concentrate on that type of case for the entire team (Dell'Appa, et al, 1976).

Another development involves the classification of offenders by objectives of supervision, rather than the general assignment of offenders to officers. This process clarifies the goals of supervision for the officer, and it allows officers to set priorities in responding to the needs of offenders (Clear & O'Leary, 1983).

Box 13.2
Team Probation in Milwaukee, Wisconsin

Probation officer tasks are split into surveillance/risk control, and delivery of services. Each of these teams has one officer assigned to perform legal tasks, such as violation investigations and revocation hearings.

SUPERVISOR

Green Team	Blue Team
Legal Facilitator	Legal Facilitator
Casework Control Institution Liaison	Developmentally Disabled/ Clinical Service Liaison/ Institution Liaison
Environmental Structure/ Frederick Douglas Center Liaison	Alcohol/Drug Abuse Specialist
Limit Setters/Bridge Halfway House Liaison	Employment/Financial Collection Specialist

---

SOURCE: J. Husz, B. Davis & D. Danner (1985), "The team revolution: Survival in the '80s," *Perspective* 10 Fall(1):16.

A related adaptation involves identifying the offenders that are least in need of supervision and service, and assigning them to a very low level of monitoring. This practice reduces the caseloads of officers who are providing service, and it maximizes (at least in theory) utilization of supervision resources (Vito & Marshall, 1983). As with objectives-based supervision classification, recent practice involves the identification of supervision levels on the basis of assessments of both the needs and risk of offenders.

The National Institute of Corrections has developed a "Model Case Management System" (NIC, 1981). The system relies upon two case-assessment instruments: a risk assessment and a needs assessment. Each supervising officer completes these two questionnaires and then reviews them with the offender. From discussion of the instruments, the officer and the offender develop a plan for dealing with needs. They develop case objectives from that plan. This system helps identify concrete actions that the officer should take, and it provides an ability to assess case progress.

As a management system, the Model Program involves three components. The first, *classification*, is accomplished through the assessments mentioned above. Depending upon the levels of need or risk, or upon combinations of the two, the offender is placed in a supervision category that is somewhere between "high" (frequent officer attention) and "low" (little or no direct contact by officer). Second, *case planning*, which is based upon a structured interview with the client, leads to writing case objectives. The officers' supervisors review the objectives and approve or modify them. Finally, cases are assigned varying "degrees of difficulty," or *workload units*. These units describe how much of an officer's time the case will consume. In this manner, the officer and his or her supervisor know how much effort to expend on that case, and they know how much effort is being spent on the total caseload.

From the information derived through individual case planning, it is possible for the agency or office to assess its needs, objectives, and progress. If 35% of the agency's caseload has high employment needs, administrators can see the utility in providing officers with employment development training. The agency would assign some officers as employment specialists. If a large enough percentage of the caseload has high risk scores, administrators may want to create special "surveillance" units. These units will serve risk-control goals that are distinct from service delivery (Clear & O'Leary, 1983).

The National Institute of Corrections has devoted considerable resources to the development and dissemination of this case management program. Training, technical assistance, and the provision of written documentation have spread the model program to probation and parole agencies across the country. With some adaptation for local considerations, the model program may have revolutionized the organization and administration of community supervision.

Emerging Technologies

The last area of recent innovations in community supervision that we shall discuss involves the application of communications and other technologies to supervision. These applications have taken a number of forms, but we shall discuss only two in detail: *substance abuse testing* and *electronic surveillance*. Other developments, such as word processing, telecommunications and video recording have had some effects, and can be expected to play a larger role in the future. For the present, however, these two important technological advances for community supervision have strengthened the ability of probation and parole agencies to supervise and control an increasingly dangerous population.

Substance Abuse Testing

Drug testing is currently a "hot topic" throughout all of our society. The "Just Say No" campaign, increasingly tough drunk-driving laws, deaths of celebrities from drug-related causes, and transportation accidents attributed to drug use have focused attention on substance abuse. There are today a number of relatively simple technologies for the detection of drug and alcohol consumption. They range from the breathalyzer test to determine if a person has been driving "under the influence" of alcohol, to blood tests to determine drug or alcohol content. Urine testing is becoming an increasingly common component of community supervision conditions.

Judges and parole boards hope to reduce the incidence of substance abuse among convicted offenders, in the hopes of reducing future criminality. Judges and parole boards have traditionally prohibited probationers and parolees from the consumption of excessive amounts of alcohol or the use of drugs. When the author worked for the Oregon Board of Parole, a standard condition of parole limited drinking for all parolees. Parolees were either not allowed to drink alcohol to excess, not allowed to drink alcohol at all, or required to take antabuse. *Antabuse* is a drug that reacts with alcohol to produce very unpleasant symptoms in the drinker. These symptoms include nausea, shortness of breath, dizziness and other sensations, which are generally unpleasant enough to deter the drinker.

Regardless of the attempts to control substance abuse, probationers and parolees continue to acquire and use drugs and alcohol. The development of easily administered detection tests has strengthened the ability of probation and parole officers to control substance abuse among their clients. Many believe that merely testing for use will deter offenders. As Atmore & Bauchiero (1987) reported:

We have noted significant behavioral improvements when we test regularly, because it serves as a deterrent. Therefore, we are returning less people to higher security for positive urines because they know they are taking a huge risk by substance use. In other words, test regularly! You need to have a consistent policy for testing and sanctions for positive results, or else word will get around quickly that one should not take this seriously.

There are some easy to use and very reliable machines for urine testing now available...Any probation or parole officer could be trained to use basic urinalysis equipment in a short period of time...

In addition to the urine test described by Atmore and Bauchiero, probation and parole officers have a wide array of other testing technologies available to them. These include the breathalyzer and blood tests, and also some newer developments, such as a saliva test for alcohol use. With this test, the subject's saliva is placed on a "blotter" that is actually a form of litmus paper. If the subject has recently used alcohol, the paper will change colors. Efforts are currently underway to develop similar saliva tests for drug use.

Substance abuse testing technologies enhance the ability of officers to control the risks of crime posed by their clients. These procedures also may change the nature of the job. The officers must now "test" their clients, serve as medical technicians, and otherwise assume the role of cop and not as helper. In the Georgia Intensive Supervision program, special officers were designated as "surveillance officers" and charged with conducting urine tests and investigations. Using special officers protected the helping relationship between the probation or parole officer and the offender (Erwin & Clear, 1987). The net effect of testing may not be a change in the role of the officer, but some believe that testing does alter the nature of the officer's job and his or her relationship with offenders.

Electronic Surveillance

Another recent development is electronic surveillance, which appears "tailor-made" as a solution for the current problems of agencies in controlling dangerous offenders. Most of us are aware of the possibilities of telemetric tracking. The physical condition of astronauts, for example, can be monitored from thousands of miles away. The technology of "homing devices" has recently been applied to the supervision of offenders in the community. It has added to the options available for the control of offenders on probation and parole (Schmidt, 1986). Box 13.3 describes available electronic monitoring systems.

Annesley Schmidt (1989) reported a survey of electronic monitor usage that showed programs existing in 33 states. It is likely that, in the near future, electronic monitoring will be employed in the supervision of thousands of offenders in hundreds of jurisdictions. Huskey (1987) also reported on electronic monitoring, and estimated that the technology had great potential for reducing jail and prison incarceration costs. Ford and Schmidt (1985) reported that the first operational use of electronic surveillance for monitoring convicted offenders occurred in early 1983. Judge Jack Love in Albuquerque, New Mexico ordered a probation violator to be monitored in April 1983. He later sentenced four other offenders to home confinement under electronic surveillance. In Monroe County, Florida, Judge J. Allison DeFoor II sentenced a dozen offenders over a six-month period to monitored house arrest. Ball and Lilly (1986) reported on the development and operation of a monitoring program in Kentucky.

Box 13.3
Systems for Electronic Monitoring of Offenders

(Purpose: To monitor an offender's presence in a given environment where the offender is required to remain)

Devices that use a telephone at the monitored location		Devices that do not use a telephone	
Continuously signaling	**Programmed contact**	**Continuously signaling**	**Radio signaling**
A miniaturized **transmitter** is strapped to the offender and it broadcasts an encoded signal at regular intervals over a range.	A **computer** is programmed to call the offender during the hours being monitored either randomly or at specifically selected times. It prepares reports on the results of the calls.	A **transmitter** is strapped to the offender which sends out a constant signal.	The **link** is a small transmitter worn by the offender.
A **receiver-dialer**, located in the offender's home, detects signals from the transmitter and reports to a central computer when it stops receiving the signal from the transmitter and when it starts receiving the signal again; it also provides periodic checks.	Strapped on the offender's arm is a **wristlet**, a black plastic module.	A **portable receiver**, in the car of the officer who is monitoring the offender, is tuned to receive the signal from the specific transmitter when the officer drives within one block of the offender's home.	The **locator unit**, placed in the offender's home or other approved location, receives the signal from the link, records it and relays the information by radio signals to the local area monitor.
A central **computer** or **receiver** accepts reports from the receiver-dialer over the telephone lines, compares them with the offender's curfew schedule, and alerts correctional officials to unauthorized absences.	When the computer calls, the wristlet is inserted into a **verifier box** connected to the telephone to verify that the call is being answered by the offender being monitored.	Manufacturer/Distributor:	The **local area monitor** is a microcomputer and information management system. This equipment is placed with the network manager (the leader of a small group of people who supervise the offender and
Manufacturers/Distributors:	Manufacturer/Distributor:	**Cost-Effective Monitoring System.** Dr. Walter W. McMahon, 2207 Grange Circle, Urbana, IL 61801. Telephone Day 217-333-4579 or Evening 217-367-3990.	encourage him to succeed). It receives information from the offender and coordinates communications among the network members. Each local network can handle 15 to 25 people.
CSD Home Escort. Corrections Systems, Control Data Corporation, 7600 France Avenue, Edina, MN 55435. Telephone 612-921-6835.	**On Guard System.** Digital Products Corporation, 4021 Northeast 5th Terrace, Ft. Lauderdale, FL 33334. Telephone 305-564-0521.		If required, a **central base station** can be added to provide increased security and back-up functions.
Supervisor. CONTRAC. Controlled Activities Corp., 93351 Overseas Highway, Tavernier, FL 33070. Telephone 305-852-9507.	The computer functions similarly to that described above, calling the offender and preparing reports on the results of the call.		Manufacturer/Distributor:
In-House Arrest System. Correctional Services Inc., P.O. Box 2941, West Palm Beach, FL 33402. Telephone 305-683-7166	However, **voice verification** technology assures that the telephone is answered by the offender being monitored.		**LENS System.** Life Sciences Research Group, 515 Fargo Street, Thousand Oaks, CA 91360. Telephone 805-492-4406.
Contac. Computrac Systems, Inc., 420 East South Temple, Suite 340, Salt Lake City, UT 84111. Telephone 801-531-0500.	Manufacturer/Distributor:		
Prisoner Monitoring System. Controlec, Inc., Box 48132, Niles, IL 60648. Telephone 312-966-8435.	**Provotron.** VoxTron Systems Inc., 190 Seguin St., New Braunfels, TX 78130. Telephone 512-629-4807.		
ASC II b.* Advanced Signal Concepts, P.O. Box 1856, Clewiston, FL 33440. Telephone 813-983-2073.			
Home Incarceration Unit.* American Security Communications, P.O. Box 5238, Norman, OK 73070. Telephone 405-360-6605.	***This device can transmit to the central unit over either** telephone lines or long-range wireless repeater system.		

SOURCE: A. Schmidt (1986), "Electronic Monitors," *Federal Probation* 50(2):59.

While the use of surveillance technology to monitor criminal offenders is relatively new, the potential of such technology for crime control has long been recognized. As early as 1966, Ralph Schwitzgebel described a potential telemetric monitoring system for probationers and parolees. In 1968, a prototype of the system was developed and tested. An assessment of the legal ramifications of electronic monitoring was published in *The Harvard Law Review* in 1966. Later, Robert Schwitzgebel, Ralph's brother, experimented with telemetric monitoring with volunteers in California (Schwitzgebel, 1969). For years, a debate over the acceptability of electronic monitoring continued, and the debate periodically found expression in commentary (Ingraham & Smith, 1972; Szasz, 1975). The debate continues today (del Carmen & Vaughn, 1986), but the sheer practicality of the technology has meant that, while many important issues remain to be solved, electronic monitoring of criminal offenders is an on-going practice.

Currently, there are two basic types of electronic surveillance systems in use (Schmidt, 1987; Huskey, 1987; Ford & Schmidt, 1985). These systems were termed either *active* or *passive surveillance*. As the term implies, in an active system, the supervising agency takes positive steps to monitor the offender. Generally, this system involves fitting the offender with a transmitting device. The transmitter sends a tone over the telephone. A computer program randomly calls offenders at times when they are supposed to be at home. The offender must answer the phone, and place the transmitter in a special telephone connection, so that the transmitter sends a message to the computer. In the passive system, a transmitter attached to the offender emits a continuous signal. The transmitter must be kept within range of an amplifier/transmitter or the signal will not reach a monitoring computer. This continuously signaling system requires the offender to remain within 150-200 feet of the fixed amplifier, which is usually installed in the offender's home (Huskey, 1987:19-20).

Both systems have tamper alarms that signal a warning to monitors if the devices are removed or altered. The random calling system allows for both voice identification and the transmission of a monitoring signal. As it operates over telephone lines, this system is unaffected by interruptions in transmission caused by walls, structural steel, or other radio transmissions. Therefore, the random calling system appears to have a lower false-alarm rate. The continuous transmission system, while more prone to false alarms, provides a continuous monitoring of the offender's whereabouts.

Most jurisdictions have adopted one or the other form of monitoring technology, but a few have used both. The random calling system allows somewhat greater freedom, such as, the offender could be next door at a neighbor's house and still be called to the telephone. The use of both systems could provide a gradation in the severity of monitoring. Thus, a probationer who is given the random calling monitor and then misses a call could be "punished" by being issued a continuous transmission monitor. The possibility of varying the level of restriction within a category of penalty called "monitoring" adds to the attractiveness of this sanction.

Thus far, electronic monitoring has been limited to telephone and radio communication. Obviously, we now possess the technology to use television monitoring for the control of offender populations. Many banks, prisons, businesses and apartment buildings employ closed-circuit television monitoring. It does not take a giant leap of the imagination to conjure uses of this technology in monitoring offenders. It may be possible to reverse the transmission on television cable lines to allow video surveillance of offenders at home or in the workplace.

In 1949, George Orwell's book *1984* was published. In that book, Orwell assessed the future of the human race under the conditions of the arms race. He suggested that society would become increasingly bureaucratized and governments would become more totalitarian. The leader of one government, "Big Brother," would retain power through torture and brainwashing. The dominant aspect of life in this society would be that everyone was under surveillance by the government. It was in *1984* that Orwell coined the slogan, "Big Brother is watching." Because of the time period in which he wrote the book, much of what he described appeared to be science fiction. However, as evidenced by our current level of sophistication, it appears that George Orwell only missed by a few years when he titled his book *1984*.

The issues involved in electronic surveillance are reminiscent of the questions raised about the development of probation and parole supervision. On the one hand are critics who suggest monitoring is an insufficient penalty for many offenders. They contend that this leniency reduces the deterrent effect of the law. Other critics argue that the use of monitoring technology to allow the release from incarceration of "dangerous" offenders poses too great a risk to the community. On the other hand are those who criticize this technology as too oppressive, that is, it violates current standards of privacy and infringes on constitutional rights to protection against unreasonable searches and seizures. Finally, some critics fear that electronic monitoring, in practice, will be used to increase the severity of community supervision for those who would have been released to traditional probation or parole.

Proponents of surveillance argue that the technology enhances public safety by insuring supervision of offenders in the community. Further, surveillance itself deters offenders from committing crimes. Similarly, the proponents suggest that the ability to monitor offenders results in a lessening of penalty severity. They argue that some offenders are sent to prison who do not actually need to be incarcerated. Continual supervision will allow judges and parole boards to leave these offenders in the community. While the current focus may be on the electronics of contemporary surveillance, at base, the questions and criticisms are the same ones that have always surrounded community supervision.

REVIEW QUESTIONS

1. How have probation and parole populations changed in recent years?

2. Name and describe two innovations in probation and parole that allow community supervision to approximate more closely the severity of incarceration.

3. What are "split sentences," and how may they be imposed by a judge?

4. Take a position on the question of whether or not community supervision is "effective," including public risk, cost, and other relevant factors in arguments for your position.

5. Describe funding approaches that serve to encourage communities to keep offenders out of state prisons, and argue either in favor or in opposition to them.

6. How can classification of probationers and parolees aid in the use of community supervision resources?

7. Describe two ways in which emerging technologies have affected the ability of probation and parole agencies to supervise offenders in the community.

REFERENCES

Atmore, T. & E. Bauchiero (1987), "Substance abusers: Identification and treatment," *Corrections Today* 49(7):22-24, et seq.

Ball, R. & J.R. Lilly (1986), "A theoretical examination of home incarceration," *Federal Probation* 50(1):17-24.

Byrne, J. (1986), "The control controversy: A preliminary examination of intensive probation supervision programs in the United States," *Federal Probation* 50(2):4-16.

Clear, T.R. & G.F. Cole (1986), *American Corrections*. (Monterey, CA: Brooks-Cole).

Clear, T.R. & V. O'Leary (1983), *Controlling the Offender in the Community*. (Lexington, MA: Lexington).

Clear, T.R. & C. Shapiro (1986), "Identifying high risk probationers for supervision in the community: The Oregon model," *Federal Probation* 50(2):42-49.

del Carmen, R. & J. Vaughn (1986), "Legal issues in the use of electronic surveillance in probation," *Federal Probation* 50(2):60-69.

Dell'Appa, F., et al (1976), "Advocacy, brokerage, community: The ABC's of probation and parole," *Federal Probation* 40(4):3-8.

Erwin, B. (1986), "Turning up the heat on probationers in Georgia," *Federal Probation* 50(2):17-24.

Erwin, B. & T. Clear (1987), "Rethinking role conflict in community supervision," *Perspectives* 11(2):21-24.

Flanagan, T. (1985), "Questioning the other parole: The effectiveness of community supervision of offenders," in L. Travis (ed.), *Probation, Parole, and Community Corrections: A Reader.* (Prospect Heights, IL: Waveland):167-83.

Ford, D. & A. Schmidt (1985), "Electronically monitored home confinement," *NCJRS Update* (November, 1985).

Goldstein, H., W. Burrell & R. Talty (1985), "Probation: The Rand report and beyond," *Perspectives* 9(2):11-12, *et seq*.

Gottfredson, M., S. Mitchell-Herzfeld & T. Flanagan (1982), "Another look at the effectiveness of parole supervision," *Journal of Research in Crime & Delinquency* 18(2):277-98.

Guynes, R. (1988), *Difficult Clients, Large Caseloads Plague Probation, Parole Agencies*. (Washington, DC: U.S. Department of Justice).

Huskey, B. (1987), "Electronic monitoring: An evolving alternative," *Perspectives* 11(3):19-23.

Ingraham, B. & G. Smith (1972), "Electronic surveillance and control of behavior and its possible use in rehabilitation and parole," in *Issues in Criminology, Vol. 7*. (Beverly Hills, CA: Sage):35-52.

Latessa, E.J. (1980), "Intensive diversion unit: An evaluation," in B. Price & P. J. Baunach (eds.), *Criminal Justice Research*. (Beverly Hills, CA: Sage):101-24.

McGaha, J., M. Fichter & P. Hirschburg (1987), "Felony probation: A re-examination of public risk," *American Journal of Criminal Justice* (forthcoming).

National Advisory Commission on Criminal Justice Standards and Goals, *Corrections*. (Washington, DC: U.S. Government Printing Office).

National Institute of Corrections (1981), *Model Probation and Parole Management Project*. (Washington, DC: National Institute of Corrections).

Note (1966), "Anthropotelemetry: Dr. Schwitzgebel's machine," *Harvard Law Review* 80:403.

Parisi, N. (1980), "Combining incarceration and probation," *Federal Probation* 44(2):3-11.

Petersilia, J. (1985), *Probation and Felony Offenders*. (Washington, DC: U.S. Department of Justice).

Petersilia, J., S. Turner & J. Peterson (1985), *Granting Felons Probation: Public Risks and Alternatives.* (Santa Monica, CA: RAND Corporation).

_____ (1986), *Prison Versus Probation in California: Implications for Crime and Offender Recidivism.* (Santa Monica, CA: RAND Corporation).

Schmidt, A. (1989), "Electronic monitoring of offenders increases," *NIJ Reports* (January/February):2-5).

_____ (1987), "Electronic monitoring: Who uses it? How much does it cost? Does it work?" *Corrections Today* 49(7):28-34.

_____ (1986), "Electronic monitors," *Federal Probation* 50(2):56-59.

Schwitzgebel, R. (1969), "A belt from Big Brother," *Psychology Today* 2(11):45-47,65.

Szasz, T. (1975), "The control of conduct: Authority vs. autonomy," *Criminal Law Bulletin* 11.

Travis III, L.F. (1984), "Intensive supervision in probation and parole," *Corrections Today* 46(4):34.

Vito, G.F. (1986), "Felony probation and recidivism: Replication and response," *Federal Probation* 50(4):17-25.

_____ (1985), "Probation as punishment: New directions," in L.F. Travis III (ed), *Probation, Parole and Community Corrections.* (Prospect Heights, IL: Waveland):73-80.

Vito, G.F. & F.H. Marshall (1983), "The administrative caseload project," *Federal Probation* 46(3):33-41.

von Hirsch, A. & K. Hanrahan (1978), *Abolish Parole?* (Washington, DC: U.S. Department of Justice).

Wheeler, G.R., T.M. Macam, R.V. Hissong and M.P. Slusher (1989), "The effects of probation service fees on case management strategy and sanctions," *Journal of Criminal Justice* 17(1):15-24.

14 Discharge and Developments

In 1985, an estimated 1.2 million persons were released from some form of correctional supervision (Bureau of Justice Statistics, 1987). More than one million of these were released from probation supervision, while the remainder were either discharged from prison or released from parole supervision. Assuming that one-third were failures from probation or parole who were returned to prison and thus not actually released from custody, approximately 750,000 persons were discharged from custody in that year. Burton, et al (1987) estimated that more than 14 million convicted felons live in the population at large.

This chapter examines what happens to those people who progress through the justice system to the point of discharge from custody, or to where the justice system stops. In doing so, we see that, for many released offenders, the effects of justice system processing do not stop, but start anew. We will also examine changes in the criminal justice system that can be anticipated, or that seem to be beginning now.

DISCHARGE

The last major point in the criminal justice process is the discharge of offenders. In many cases, discharge is not actually a decision point, but rather is an event that occurs at a point in time. For example, if you were convicted of theft and sentenced to five years in prison on January 1, 1989, at midnight on December 31, 1993, the sentence would expire. You would have to be discharged from custody at that point, as there would no longer be a legal justification for custody. In many states, however, discharge itself is a decision.

Traditionally, a convicted offender was considered to be under the custody of the justice system until his or her sentence had expired. With the imposition of relatively long sentences, this meant that a person sentenced to a life term could be in custody for his or her entire lifetime. Most states developed mechanisms for limiting the period of custody, and empowered the parole authority to grant a discharge from sentence after a period of successful parole supervision. As a pragmatic alternative, many parole authorities created a custody class of "unsupervised parole," in which the offender was no longer required to report to a parole officer, and was no longer subjected to supervision. Unsupervised parole allowed an offender to "serve" a sentence until discharge without actually being restricted. Further, many states have specifically empowered correctional officials to grant final releases or discharges from sentence. Box 14.1 compares the distribution of time served in prison or jail with the period spent under parole supervision for different types of offenses.

In still other states, the practice was to allow offenders to apply for *executive clemency*. That is, a convict could ask the governor for a commutation or pardon. If the request was granted, the prisoner would receive a discharge from sentence. Someone serving a twenty-year term, for example, might be imprisoned for two years, serve an additional two years under parole supervision, and still "owe" sixteen years on the sentence. That offender could ask the governor to commute the sentence to four years, and receive a discharge, or the offender could be pardoned for the offense.

Box 14.1
Average Time Under Correctional Custody
and Percentage on Parole for 1984 Parolees,
by Most Serious Offense

| Most serious offense | Mean time under correctional supervision | | | Percent of total time spent on parole |
	Total	Jail and prison	Parole	
All offenses	46 months	27 months	19 months	41%
Violent offenses	60	36	24	40
Murder	115	77	38	33
Manslaughter	63	37	26	41
Kidnaping	58	35	23	40
Rape	74	48	26	35
Other sexual assault	54	34	20	37
Robbery	60	35	25	42
Assault	46	28	18	39
Other violent	41	25	16	39
Property offenses	37	21	16	43
Burglary	38	21	17	45
Larceny/theft	33	18	15	45
Motor vehicle theft	42	25	17	40
Arson	47	28	19	40
Fraud	38	22	16	42
Stolen property	34	19	15	44
Other property	33	16	17	52
Drug offenses	42	24	18	43
Possession	34	18	16	47
Trafficking	46	27	19	41
Other drug	37	21	16	43
Public-order offenses	34	20	14	41
Weapons	43	26	17	40
Other public-order	29	16	13	45
Other offenses	37	20	17	46

Note: Data on offense distribution and mean time served are based on the 41,514 successful parole releases who had entered prison with sentences of more than a year. Data include those on supervised release even if not technically termed "parole."

SOURCE: S. Minor-Harper & C. Innes (1987). *Served in Prison and on Parole, 1984.* (Washing... U.S. Department of Justice);7.

Box 14.2
Collateral Consequences of Felony Convictions in American Jurisdictions

RESTRICTIONS OF FELONY OFFENDERS' CIVIL RIGHTS
Restrictive vs. Less Restrictive, by Right & Jurisdiction

Jurisdiction	Voting Permanently Lost vs. Restorable	Parental Yes vs. No	Divorce Yes vs. No	Public Employment Permanently Lost vs. Restorable	Juror Permanently Lost vs. Restorable	Holding Office Permanently Lost vs. Restorable	Firearm "Violent" Felony vs. "Any" Felony	Criminal Registration Yes vs. No	Civil Death Yes vs. No
Alabama	X	X	X	X	X	X		X	
Alaska			X		X		X		
Arizona		X					X	X	
Arkansas	X		X		X	X	X		
California		X			X	X¹	X	X	
Colorado		X							
Connecticut			X				X		
Delaware				X	X	X	X		
D.C.			X		X	X¹	X		
Florida	X				X	X	X	X	
Georgia			X		X	X	X		
Hawaii					X		X		
Idaho			X		X				X
Illinois			X				X		
Indiana		X	X		X		X		
Iowa	X			X	X	X	X		
Kansas		X					X		
Kentucky	X				X	X	X		
Louisiana			X						
Maine						X¹	X		
Maryland		X			X				
Massachusetts		X				X¹	X		
Michigan		X					X		
Minnesota			X						
Mississippi	X	X	X	X		X	X	X	X
Missouri					X				
Montana					X		X		
Nebraska					X		X		
Nevada	X	X			X	X	X	X	
New Hampshire			X				X		
New Jersey			X		X	X			
New Mexico	X				X	X	X		
New York			X		X	X	X		X
North Carolina									
North Dakota			X						
Ohio			X		X	X			
Oklahoma			X		X		X		
Oregon		X					X		
Pennsylvania			X		X		X		
Rhode Island	X	X	X	X	X	X			X
South Carolina				X	X	X			
South Dakota		X	X						
Tennessee	X	X	X		X	X		X	
Texas			X		X	X	X		
Utah			X		X			X	
Vermont			X						
Virginia	X		X		X	X			
Washington									
West Virginia			X				X		
Wisconsin		X				X	X		
Wyoming		X			X				

X = right is restricted or jeopardized
1 = right is restricted for specific offenses

SOURCE: V. Burton, F. Cullen & L. Travis (1987), "The collateral consequences of a felony conviction: A national survey of state statutes," *Federal Probation* 51(3):55.

Regardless of the method, the fact remains that, at some time, most offenders will be discharged from sentence. At the point of discharge, whether by a discretionary decision made by a justice system official, or at the expiration of sentence, the offender is free from direct intervention by the criminal justice system. The effects of conviction, however, will linger.

Collateral Consequences of Conviction

Once convicted of a criminal offense, an individual experiences several negative effects. The sentence imposed for crime is a direct consequence of conviction, and is intentionally painful. Other effects result from conviction and are, therefore, additional or collateral consequences. In many ways, these effects can be more disturbing and painful than the sentence imposed. Box 14.2 identifies some of the collateral consequences of a felony conviction.

There is a stigma that attaches to a person who has been convicted of a crime. The label of "ex-con" is difficult to overcome. If you were hiring people to work for a company, and had two equally qualified candidates, one of whom was an ex-con, which applicant would you hire? At a party, how would you react when meeting someone who was an ex-con? The fact that we can discuss a set of people simply by using the label "ex-con" illustrates the point of stigma. The fact of a prior conviction is meaningful to us in our dealings with ex-cons. Robert Homant and Daniel Kennedy (1982) assessed the stigma of ex-cons relative to that of ex-mental patients, obese people, and neutral or non-stigmatized people. They found that there was little difference in how the four groups were treated by their subjects. Earlier research, however, has shown that ex-offenders do suffer the stigma associated with their convictions (Schwartz & Skolnick, 1962; Reed, 1979).

In addition to the stigma of having a criminal record, other collateral consequences attend criminal conviction. Some avenues of employment are closed to offenders (Finn & Fontaine, 1985). Many jobs in our society require that the employee be "bonded" (insured), and ex-offenders normally are not considered good risks by bonding companies. Thus, an ex-offender may even have difficulty obtaining employment as a cashier in a convenience store. Other occupations, such as barbers, beauticians, teachers, physicians, nurses and attorneys require licensure. In many cases, a felony conviction is a bar to licensure (Davidenas, 1983).

Assuming the offender served a prison term, he or she may have a particularly difficult time in securing credit or employment because of the incarceration. How does an ex-inmate answer questions about where he or she was employed for the past two years, or about where he or she resided? One of the author's students, an ex-convict, routinely answered such questions by saying that he had "worked for the state" for the past seven years.

As if the natural consequences of conviction were not severe enough, most states impose specific limitations on the rights of those convicted of felonies. These limitations are added to whatever sentence may be ordered (Burton, et al, 1987; Vile, 1981). Only two states, North Carolina and Washington, do not routinely restrict a convicted offender's rights. Four states have provisions allowing certain offenders (generally, those receiving life sentences) to be declared civilly dead. That is, as far as civil rights (contracting, marriage, voting, etc.) are concerned, the offender is "dead." Most states restrict some civil rights for at least as long as the offender is serving his or her sentence. In most jurisdictions, conviction of a felony carries the permanent loss of some civil rights. Given these collateral consequences of conviction, for many offenders, criminal justice processing never ends.

Restoration of Rights

Most states today have provisions for the restoration of all, or most, of the civil rights that are lost upon conviction of a felony. In many states, such as Ohio, the parole authority is empowered to grant a full restoration of rights upon discharge from parole supervision and sentence. In other places, like California (Allen & Simonsen, 1986), the ex-convict may apply for a restoration of rights after certain conditions are met. The California provisions require that the offender petition the court for a pardon. To qualify for the pardon, the ex-offender must have led a crime-free life for ten years after final release from parole. The court then conducts a formal hearing, at which it receives opinions from the district attorney and law enforcement officials. The probation department investigates the petitioner and reports to the court. If all of the evidence is favorable, the court approves the application and forwards it to the governor. The governor instructs the parole authority to investigate and then to recommend a pardon decision. In the end, based on this recommendation from the parole authority, the governor decides whether to grant the pardon.

Other states have less involved restoration processes, but even these processes generally include a petition by the ex-offender, and an investigation. These states also require some period of good behavior after discharge from sentence (usually five or ten years). While the ex-convict may eventually be restored to full citizenship, the effect of the conviction will last through the sentence and for many years afterward.

Burton, et al (1987) suggested that there is a movement afoot for states to become less restrictive of the rights of convicted offenders. With the exception of parental rights and the right to possess firearms, most of the restrictions on civil rights that were traditionally imposed by states have been relaxed. The commentators contended that this reduction in restrictiveness represents an extension of the "due process movement," in which courts are more likely to require the state to provide reasons for restrictions. They also summarized the arguments in favor of, and in opposition to, the restriction of civil rights.

Those opposed to the imposition of collateral consequences of felony conviction argue that restrictions may be counterproductive. Adding to penalties by limiting rights may cause ex-offenders to become bitter toward society in general, and the justice system in particular. Especially in regard to employment rights, restrictions may be harmful. They limit an ex-offender's ability to lead a law-abiding life by closing opportunities for socially accepted means of earning a living. Also, many restrictions on civil rights, such as restrictions on the voting rights of someone with a prior conviction for theft, are unrelated to the offender's crime. Finally, there are those who argue that the imposition of additional restrictions after the sentence has been served means that the offender can never pay his or her debt to society.

Those favoring the restriction of civil rights for people convicted of criminal offenses argue that such restrictions serve several purposes. First, rights are balanced by duties and, by failing to meet the duty of obeying the law, offenders have lost the privilege of exercising their rights (Vile, 1981). Others suggest that a "principle of least eligibility" applies, in that ex-offenders are least eligible to be protected in their rights to vote, work, etc. Others suggest that conviction evidences unacceptable character flaws, so that restricting offenders from holding public office, serving on juries, and voting actually protects law-abiding citizens from possible election fraud and malfeasance in office by offenders. Other restrictions on rights are justified by proponents as pragmatic concessions. In many states, incarceration is grounds for divorce; it is justified by the argument that it is not fair to require the spouse to stand by an absent mate. Loss of parental rights has been justified because a felony conviction is said to represent proof of being an unfit parent. Finally, civil death has been justified to enable family members to dispose of the convicted offender's debts and property.

RECIDIVISM

Ex-convict Malcolm Braly wrote his autobiography, which he aptly titled *False Starts*. In the book, Braly recalled twenty years of criminal justice experience, during which he spent time in and out of reform school and prison. His first incarceration was in a reform school before he had turned eighteen. Describing his years as an offender, Braly remembered his "false starts" at living a conventional, law-abiding life. Through four releases from custody, three of which became failed paroles, Braly learned how to live in the free world, and finally was successfully rehabilitated after his fifth release, when he was forty. The data presented in Box 14.3 indicate that Braly's experience may be typical of repeat offenders.

Box 14.3
Cumulative Rates of Return to Prison for
Releases Over a Seven-Year Period, by Age at Release

Number of years after prison release	Age at last release from State prison				
	18-24	25-34	35-44	45+	All ages
1 year	21.8%	12.1%	7.1%	2.1%	14.0%
2	34.2	21.3	14.0	3.7	23.4
3	41.1	27.9	18.3	5.7	29.4
4	44.8	32.7	22.4	7.9	33.5
5	47.8	37.0	26.3	9.7	37.1
6	49.4	40.8	30.2	10.8	40.0
7	49.9	42.8	34.0	12.4	41.7

SOURCE: L.A. Greenfield (1985), *Examining Recidivism*. (Washington, DC: U.S. Department of Justice):4.

As a "business," the criminal justice system is not supposed to encourage repeat "customers." If the system operated at peak effectiveness, anyone that committed a crime most assuredly would not commit a second offense. Unfortunately, the data indicate that the justice system produces many "customers" who return again and again. These repeat offenders are often called *recidivists*.

Defining Recidivism

Perhaps no other concept in criminal justice has been as fully studied and debated as has recidivism. In fact, the notion of recidivism is so controversial that contemporary writers tend to use other labels for it, like "failure" or "return." At base, recidivism means repetition of crime. The term is confusing because it is not exactly clear what "repetition" should include. For example, if a convicted robber is released from custody and commits a theft, has the offender repeated? If the offender is arrested, but not convicted, is it recidivism? If the offender's parole is revoked for failing to report to the supervising officer, is the offender a recidivist? On the surface, these seem to be technical distinctions, but they can be very important.

Whatever definition one adopts for "recidivism," the concept is crucial to evaluations of the effectiveness of criminal justice processing. Gottfredson, et al (1982), suggested that the definition employed has an effect on the level of recidivism that will be detected. For example, if technical violations of probation or parole rules are counted as recidivism, the rate of return to crime will be higher. Counting arrests yields higher recidivism rates than counting only convictions. Counting only returns to prison as repeat offenses leads to still lower rates of recidivism, and counting only repeated convictions for the same crime yields the lowest rates of recidivism.

Flanagan (1985) argued that time is yet another important component of the definition of recidivism. The longer the period over which offenders are tracked, the higher the total level of recidivism. Hoffman and Stone-Meierhoffer (1979) indicated that, for federal parolees at least, rates of return remain relatively stable for up to three years after release. This finding means that, if recidivism is measured for only one year, the rate of return might be 20%. Extending the time frame to three years might yield a total return rate of 48%. As Box 14.4 indicates, it is important to measure not only the total number of returns to prison, but the percentage of failure of the "at-risk" population for each year. While most offenders who return may fail in the first year or two, the rate of return of those at risk may not change for three or more years.

Box 14.4
Rate of Return to Prison as Percentages
of the "At-Risk" Population

At-Risk Population	Returns	% of Those at Risk	Cumulative % Returned
1,000	200	20%	20.0%
800	160	20%	36.0%
640	128	20%	48.8%
512	51	10%	53.9%

From this example, the rate of return to prison for those at risk remains stable for three years and then decreases. While most of those who return to prison do so within two years (36%), the rate of return for the population at risk remains the same for the third year as well (20%).

Recidivism and Criminal Justice Policy

The problem with recidivism is that it is an important concept, but one that is very difficult to measure. Obviously, knowledge of the effectiveness of correctional programs and judicial sentencing decisions based on the rate of return to crime can help us to design crime control policies. The fact that recidivism depends so heavily on what is counted, and for how long, means that we must be especially careful in interpreting and using recidivism statistics as the basis for policy decisions.

The Rand study of probation supervision effectiveness (discussed in Chapter 12) illustrates this point. Without sufficient care in interpreting the results of that study, a wise policy decision might be to ban felons from receiving probation. After all, Petersilia, et al (1986) reported that nearly two-thirds (65%) of their sample were arrested for new offenses. However, only about one-third (34%) were sentenced to jail or prison terms, and less than one-fifth (19%) of the probation sample were sentenced to new prison terms. As a policy maker, what does this information tell you about the use of probation for felons?

Unfortunately, it tells us little. Paradoxically, it also tells us much. Ultimately, the decision about using probation supervision with convicted felons will depend upon this and other information, and upon the attitudes of the policymakers themselves. If they count new prison terms as "recidivism," 80% of felony probationers are successes, and probation is a useful disposition for felons. If the policymakers count arrests as failures, 65% of felony probationers fail, and probation may not be an appropriate disposition for felons. What is important is that in order to make an informed judgment, the decision-makers need to know not only the statistics (65% or 19% "failures"), but also what the statistics *mean*.

A recently released study of parolee recidivism (Beck & Shipley, 1987) reported that nearly 70% of a group of young parolees released in 1978 had been re-arrested for a serious crime within six years. Based on this finding and a similar recidivism rate for the probationers in the Rand study in California, it appears likely that most offenders will again be subjected to criminal justice processing. Yet, other research indicates that the criminal justice system can have a positive effect on the lives of offenders (Sechrest, et al, 1979). There is some evidence to suggest, as may have been the case with Malcolm Braly, that some offenders simply mature and grow out of crime as they get older (Hoffman & Beck, 1984). Still, for many offenders, the end of the justice system represents a continuation in their lives of crime, which eventually leads them back into the justice system. However, for many others (between one-third and one-half of all convicted offenders), discharge means the start of a law-abiding life.

DEVELOPMENTS
IN CRIMINAL JUSTICE

Bennett (1987) coined a phrase to describe what she saw as changes in the future of criminal justice in the United States. That phrase, "crime-warps," described the alterations that Bennett expected to occur in our definitions of crime as well as our responses to crime. As "warp" implies, she anticipated that the form, if not the substance, of crime will take on new shapes in the future. Consequently, the justice system will need to adapt to these new developments as well.

Bennett identified six crime-warps, ranging from new types of criminals to changes in the balance between the protection of individual liberties and the requirements of social defense. Increasingly, those committing crimes will be female, older, and more affluent than criminals in the past. Further, there will be increasing emphasis on white-

collar and computer crimes. Bennett also expects legaliza-
tion of many "victimless" crimes such as prostitution, ho-
mosexuality, gambling and drug abuse. Other offenses,
such as manufacturing and distributing pornography, will
be subjected to greater restrictions. Bennett predicted that
traditional street crime will move from the cities to the
suburbs and rural areas, and from the Northeast to the Sun
Belt. In response to increasing fear of crime, and new
definitions of crime, she anticipated greater technological
development in criminal justice, an enhanced role for private enterprise and a reduction in privacy. Civil liberties
will be increasingly threatened as citizens are subjected to
increasing surveillance by both justice officials and their
neighbors, according to her predictions.

It is always risky to predict the future. As we have
seen, criminal justice practices and policies are the products of a complex set of forces. Ideological shifts, economic
changes, demographic variations, organizational goals, and
the attitudes of individual agents and offenders all affect
criminal justice decision-making. Attempting to predict
how these factors will change and develop, and how they
will interact, to produce different decisions and patterns of
criminal justice practice is hazardous and error-prone.
Nonetheless, it is incumbent upon us to attempt to foresee
the future, that we can try to shape it. If we fail in that attempt, at least we may be able to understand the future.

In an effort to discern the future of criminal justice in
America, we shall examine two trends and project possible
futures. In doing so, our attention must be drawn to the
forces that gave rise to the trends, and to the powerful
forces opposing any real change in the operation of the
criminal justice system. Hedging our bets, we shall call
these trends "possibilities." It should be remembered, of
course, that it is likely that nothing will change in the foreseeable future. The possibilities that we shall examine are
private justice and *technological justice*.

Private Justice

In earlier chapters, we have discussed developments that tend toward the privatization of criminal justice. These include, but are not limited to, contracted services for the operation of correctional programs and institutions, citizen crime prevention, private security, and alternative dispute resolutions. Additionally, recent developments in victims' rights may be considered to be indicative of trends toward a privatization of justice.

Historically, the criminal justice system evolved from a tradition of private retaliation for wrongdoing. If a member of my family should injure a member of yours, our families would settle the dispute. Either you and your kin would seek revenge, or my kin and I would pay reparations. With the emergence of stronger leaders and central governments, offenses came to be defined as crimes against the state, rather than as wrongs to individuals. With a growing division of labor within society, the duty to prevent and control crime came to be the province of a set of defined agents and organizations. This relieved the average citizen of the necessity to intercede in criminal matters. Over time, both the definition of crimes and the response to them became matters of public domain.

Today we can see the beginnings of a reversal of that trend. Increasingly, crime and crime control are becoming defined as private concerns. This new definition goes beyond acceptance of private industry provision of criminal justice services, such as the contract prisons discussed earlier. There is a recognition that private individuals are harmed by crimes, and that private individuals must be involved in solving the problem of crime.

Rosenbaum, Lurigio and Lavrakas (1986) reported that, between 1978 and 1986, the number of "Crime Stoppers" programs in the United States grew from 5 to over 600. (See Box 14.5.)

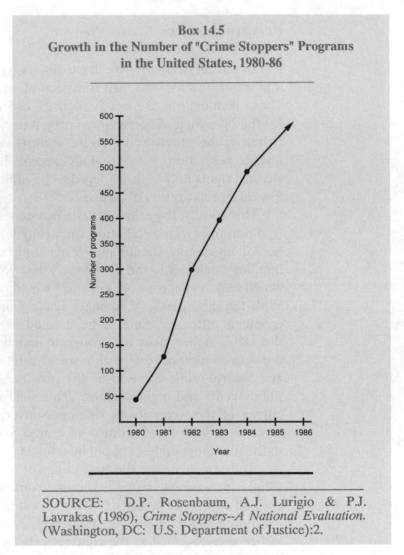

Box 14.5
Growth in the Number of "Crime Stoppers" Programs
in the United States, 1980-86

SOURCE: D.P. Rosenbaum, A.J. Lurigio & P.J.
Lavrakas (1986), *Crime Stoppers--A National Evaluation.*
(Washington, DC: U.S. Department of Justice):2.

These programs encourage citizens to provide information
to the police by granting anonymity and cash rewards for
tips that lead to arrests and convictions in criminal cases.
The programs rely upon private citizens to provide leads
and evidence to the public law enforcement agencies. Further, the majority of funding for these programs comes

from private (usually business and industry) donations. In short, the past decade has seen a tremendous growth in this form of private crime control, which essentially uses the police to process cases that are detected and solved privately (Kelling, Edwards & Moore, 1986).

Neighborhood watch programs have experienced similar growth (Latessa & Travis, 1987). Beginning in 1967, criminal justice observers noted the importance of citizen involvement in assisting the police to control crime. Projects designed to increase citizen cooperation with the police began across the country. Variously named, the most common of these projects are "neighborhood watch" or "crime watch" programs. They rely upon citizen volunteers to act as "the eyes and ears" of the police. Again, the effect of these programs is that private citizens are taking responsibility for crime control. One interesting product of a crime watch program studied by Latessa and Travis (1987:48) was that less citizens believed that the police were successful in controlling crime. It may be that crime watch programs lead citizens to appreciate their role in crime control, and therefore, to devalue the role of the police. These programs may develop a "they-couldn't-do-it-without-us" attitude toward the police.

Dispute resolution is yet another area where there is a movement away from the criminal justice system as the solution to crime. Dispute resolution programs generally attempt to take less serious offenses and citizen disputes out of the criminal justice arena, and put them into a private negotiation format. Rather than neighbors pressing criminal charges or landlords bringing charges against tenants, these programs provide a forum in which the conflicting parties can resolve their differences without recourse to the criminal law. As indicated in Box 14.6, dispute resolution centers appear to provide alternatives to criminal justice processing, and participants seem satisfied with the programs.

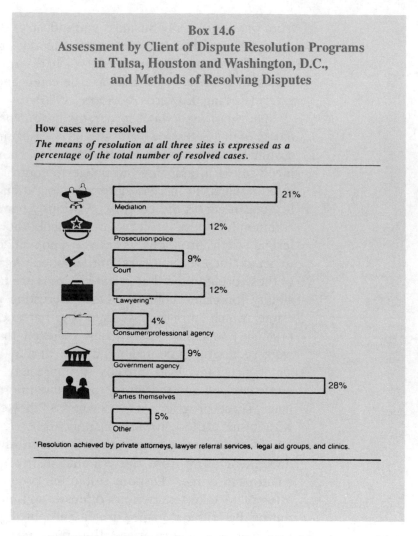

Box 14.6
Assessment by Client of Dispute Resolution Programs
in Tulsa, Houston and Washington, D.C.,
and Methods of Resolving Disputes

How cases were resolved
The means of resolution at all three sites is expressed as a
percentage of the total number of resolved cases.

Mediation — 21%
Prosecution/police — 12%
Court — 9%
"Lawyering"* — 12%
Consumer/professional agency — 4%
Government agency — 9%
Parties themselves — 28%
Other — 5%

*Resolution achieved by private attorneys, lawyer referral services, legal aid groups, and clinics.

McGillis (1986) reported the results of a survey of 29 dispute resolution centers. His report included information on the growth and widespread use of these programs. Though they were intended to increase access to justice and to reduce the number of cases filed in criminal and civil courts, a major difficulty faced by these programs was a lack of citizen participation. The solution, according to

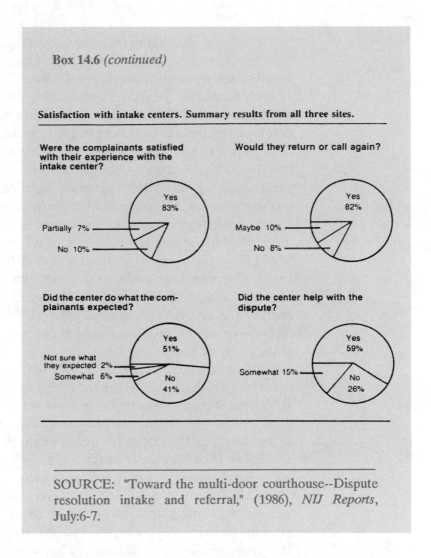

Box 14.6 *(continued)*

Satisfaction with intake centers. Summary results from all three sites.

Were the complainants satisfied with their experience with the intake center?

Yes 83%
Partially 7%
No 10%

Would they return or call again?

Yes 82%
Maybe 10%
No 8%

Did the center do what the complainants expected?

Yes 51%
Not sure what they expected 2%
Somewhat 6%
No 41%

Did the center help with the dispute?

Yes 59%
Somewhat 15%
No 26%

SOURCE: "Toward the multi-door courthouse--Dispute resolution intake and referral," (1986), *NIJ Reports*, July:6-7.

McGillis, lies in encouraging greater participation, that is, increasing the private (or at least semi-public) resolution of disputes. Television shows based on dispute resolution (such as *The People's Court*) illustrate this trend. Another example of the trend is evident in the increasing number of "trouble shooters" who investigate consumer complaints as part of local news programs (Pfuhl & Altheide, 1987).

A related development involves what are known as "victim/offender mediation" programs (Umbreit, 1986). In a recent survey of such programs, Umbreit identified over 32 such mediation projects in operation; the first of these was begun in 1974. The majority of these programs were developed by private sector organizations. The major goals of such projects are to provide sentencing alternatives, allow the victim a voice in the justice process, reduce the harm done to the victim (generally through restitution), and increase the offender's accountability to the victim.

In mediation programs, the offender and the victim meet, face to face, in the presence of a trained mediator. These programs operate in the criminal justice system, not in the civil courts. In addition to restitution, the programs also seek to allow the victim and offender to reconcile their conflict arising from the criminal event (Umbreit, 1986:54). Two-thirds of the programs hold these meetings prior to sentencing, although three-fourths of the programs also schedule reconciliation meetings after sentencing.

The growth and development in restitution also reflects the increasing emphasis on the private wrongs that accompany crime. In restitution programs, the offender is directed to repay the victim for losses incurred as a result of the crime (Galaway & Hudson, 1978). While restitution had always been a traditional practice (Schwartz, et al, 1980:268-70), in the middle 1970s, several jurisdictions began experimenting with restitution as an official part of a criminal sanction (Galaway, 1977). The age-old practice of the offender paying restitution or reparation to erase or minimize the crime before sentencing became a part of the official sentence itself.

Perhaps the clearest indication of a movement towards private justice today can be found in the development and spread of programs for crime victims. Until very recently, the victim of crime was generally ignored by the criminal justice system. At best, the victim was treated as an important witness; at worst, the victim was treated almost as if he or she were the offender. In the 1980s, the separate threads of restitution, dispute resolution, and victim/offender mediation programs have come together in comprehensive crime victim legislation.

Davis (1987) wrote that future historians may declare the 1980s as the period when crime victims were finally recognized by the justice system. He reported that more than thirty states have passed victims' rights legislation. Programs for crime victims run the gamut from counseling to compensation. Once again, the victims of crime have come to be defined as the injured parties in the criminal acts. Technically, the offense may still be against the state, but today, the state is beginning to accept a responsibility to protect the individual interests of the victim.

In many jurisdictions, legislation has been passed that allows the victim to address the court at sentencing, or the parole authority at release determinations. It is increasingly common for presentence investigation reports to include a section on "victim impact." One of the most far-reaching of these laws that provide for victim input is California's "Victim's Bill of Rights," which was passed in 1982. This law allows the victim to appear before the court and parole authorities. Other states have adopted similar procedures that allow victims to speak at critical decision points in the justice process. As Walker (1985:183) observed, "The great danger is that the presence of the victim would add a note of vengeance to the criminal process, or at least a greater one than presently exists."

As is true whenever we attempt to predict the future, it is unclear where we are headed with our current privatization of justice. In many ways, current trends can be easily dismissed as a natural reaction to the due process revolution of the 1960s, which, according to many observers, "handcuffed the police." It is quite possible that what we see today is an effort to return the justice process to a point of equilibrium. Perhaps one result of the Supreme Court's decisions on criminal matters in the 1960s was to tip the scales too far in favor of offenders, and the contemporary focus on the victim is an effort to restore the previous balance.

It may also be that those who proclaim the 1980s to be the "me generation," are correct. It could be that a fundamental shift in our perceptions of government and its duty to the citizenry is reflected in criminal justice processes. Paradoxically, government today is expected to leave us alone as much as possible, yet it is supposed to protect our interests to the maximum. Insured loans to business, like that to the Chrysler Corporation, are expected as a function of government, yet government is also expected not to tax too greatly or regulate too strictly. The justice system, then, should not control our behavior too closely, yet it should serve our individual needs should we become victims.

One can predict that the next several years will be a period of adjustment. Evidence thus far indicates that most victims of crime do not want a direct voice in criminal justice processing (Forer, 1980; Davis, 1987); less than 3% of all victims actually exercise their rights to speak at sentencing and parole hearings. In the end, it appears that the results of the privatization of criminal justice will be mixed. Victims will be treated more humanely, services and compensation to reduce the traumatic effects of victimization will be maintained, but decisions about the handling of offenders will revert to the detached, professional judgments of criminal justice agents and officers. In short, over a span of years, we will learn the limits to privatization, both practical and philosophical, and the system will be adjusted accordingly.

Technological Justice

Earlier we devoted considerable attention to the development and impact of surveillance technologies on community supervision. In all aspects of life, technological changes have caused adjustments in behavior. We take for granted such advances as household electricity, inside plumbing, telephones, automobiles, and other commonplace technological conveniences. Yet, as recently as fifty years ago, these technologies were unavailable to large segments of our population. The computer age is now upon us, but fifty years ago we still used vacuum tubes in large, complicated computing devices. One hundred years ago, we did not even have aircraft (other than hot air balloons).

The effects of technological advances on criminal justice have been staggering, as they have been on other areas of life. The telephone and the automobile changed the nature of policing. No longer did the neighborhood cop walk a beat and know everyone. Now a simple telephone call to an impersonal dispatcher results in the arrival, by automobile, of an equally impersonal police officer. In the past, offenders could simply give the police an alias, or cross a state line to avoid prosecution. Today, computerized criminal records and fingerprint checks lead to quick identifications. A simple traffic stop may lead to a felony arrest when a computer check yields outstanding warrants.

Warehouses full of paper documents have been reduced to a few boxes of microfiche. Some observers anticipate "paperless" criminal justice (Duffie & Graham, 1986), with records and documents stored on computer files. Television, videotapes, and computer simulations can be used to great effect in investigations and at trial to present and test evidence and to reduce delays and costs. "Teleconferencing" can be used to replace on-site hearings for parole or probation revocation, or even for parole release hearings; this recent advance reduces costs and increases efficiency.

Modern prisons and jails are making use of a variety of technological innovations to improve custody and services. Electronic perimeter security (microwave, electric eye, and vibration sensors are increasingly replacing towers and stone walls) has reduced construction costs and accelerated construction schedules for new prisons (Camp & Camp, 1987; Latessa, et al, 1988). Closed-circuit television, automatic locking devices and careful planning have reduced the need for custodial staff in prisons and jails.

Automatic tellers, computerized scanning cash registers, and the telephone have revolutionized banking, retailing and marketing in much the same way as previously mentioned developments have altered the criminal justice system. The justice system now is able to detect, apprehend and process offenders more quickly and economically. The technologies have allowed us to conduct business as usual, but in a more efficient manner. In addition, other technologies have arisen that may alter the conduct of criminal justice business in more significant ways.

One way criminal justice has been altered is in the effect that new technologies have had on the types of crimes that will be the focus of criminal justice efforts. Another alteration is from the effect of new technologies on the delicate balance between the rights of individuals and those of the community. The future of crime seems more easily predictable than does the outcome of the balance of state and individual interests.

Johnson (1981) explained that changes in police organization and operation were partly due to the changes in the nature and extent of crime. Similarly, Lundman (1980) explained the development of police, in part, as a result in changes in the rates and images of crime. That is, the police (and by extension, the entire criminal justice system) must be responsive to those acts that we view as seriously threatening public order and safety.

Willie Sutton, a famous bank robber, is credited with a witty response to a question about his actions. When asked why he committed bank robberies, Sutton is said to have replied, "Because that's where the money is." If we look at crimes throughout American history, we see that, very of-

ten, they also take place "where the money is." Highway-
men, like Jesse James, robbed stagecoaches because these
coaches carried large sums of money (corporate payments,
payrolls, etc.). These men became train robbers when cash
began to be transported by rail. Bank robberies became
more common when cash transactions were replaced by
checks and fund transfers. Today's offender might well be
described as a "lineman," that is, he or she often steals by
computer. Box 14.7 indicates that fraud with computerized
banking is already a problem and is likely to become more
important in the future.

Box 14.7
Bank Officers' Estimates of Dollar Losses
from Fraudulent Electronic Fund Transfers

Loss	Low	Average	High
Loss estimates:			
Current annual net loss per bank[a]	$100	$23,327	$215,000
Anticipated loss per bank in 5 years[b]	$100	$39,548	$500,000

[a] Based on 35 banks that sustained a loss.
[b] Based on 28 banks that responded to this question and assuming that no new fraud prevention measures are adopted.

SOURCE: *Electronic Fund Transfer Fraud.* (Washington, DC: U.S. Department of Justice, 1985):4.

Not only is money itself at risk in an increasingly computerized commercial system, but information is also more
often the target of theft. Trade secrets, customer lists,

business records, and all sorts of other information, including national defense secrets, are stored in computer data bases. Theft of such information often is more damaging (and more profitable for the thief) than fraudulent fund transfers. As quoted by Bennett (1987:109), Marvin Wolfgang predicted, "By the turn of the century, the main concern of criminal justice will be information crime."

Detection of computer crime (and enforcement of laws against it) will require a different type of law enforcement response than that required by traditional street crime. The officer in the patrol car may be replaced by the systems analyst at the terminal. This does not mean that street crime will disappear, but that computer-related offenses will increase in frequency and importance, which will lead to justice system adaptations to combat them.

During the 1970s, especially in the Carter administration, the beginnings of a shift to the newer crimes could be detected in changes in federal law enforcement. In that time period, the FBI sought agents with the skills required to track white-collar crime; recruits were trained in accounting, computers or law. These backgrounds would prepare the agents for the shifting emphasis of federal law enforcement to corporate and white-collar crimes. Since then, the re-emergence of drug-related crimes and the increased concern about terrorism resulted, at least partially, in a return of federal law enforcement to more traditional practices during the Reagan administration.

A change in social attitudes about the responsibilities and duties of businesses and corporations has led to increasing concern over what has been termed corporate and white-collar crime (Cullen, et al, 1987; Clinard & Yeager, 1980). As recently as fifty years ago, white-collar crime was virtually unknown. Businesses and businessmen committed wrongs against the public, but these acts were not necessarily considered crimes. The consumer protection movement, which developed in the 1960s, was responsible for the identification of white-collar crime as a serious criminal justice problem.

Technology affects the types of crimes that can be, and are, committed. In response, the qualifications of justice system officials, the nature of cases in the criminal justice process, and responses to offenders will be altered. There is little doubt that, similar to the shift from stagecoach robbery to bank robbery, the practices of criminal justice will be required to adapt to high-tech crimes of computer fraud. These changes, however, do not appear likely to change the criminal justice system in any fundamental way.

Computer crimes may pit justice system investigators skilled in systems analysis against offenders skilled in programming. Evidence at trials may come to be comprised of documents and disks more often than of hairs and weapons, but the process itself can continue in its present form. The type of crime and criminal may be different, but the basic response to crime can be maintained. Other effects of technology, however, pose a greater likelihood of altering the way in which criminal justice is accomplished.

In addition to the opportunities for crime that computers offer, computerized recordkeeping can aid the efforts of criminal justice officials. Tremendous amounts of information about almost every citizen are kept somewhere on computer records. If a suspected offender has ever applied for credit, or if he operates a motor vehicle, police can garner all sorts of information, quickly and easily, by requesting computer records. Credit applications generate data about employment, earnings, savings, debts, addresses, dependents, references, demographic characteristics (such as age, sex, race, education and marital status), and even height and weight. Access to a person's credit report can provide a tremendous amount of personal information about him or her. Operation of a motor vehicle provides similar background data, important identifying numbers (social security number, for example), as well as information about address and possible criminal record. It is possible to conduct a relatively thorough background check on the average American without ever leaving a computer terminal.

Credit card purchase records allow investigators to track travel patterns of individuals. Credit card purchasing and payment information exists on computer records which do not require a check on access (other than perhaps knowledge of a correct password); this means that personal data is potentially available to anyone. Consider what information about your private life could be learned by someone with access to computer records. If someone had unlimited access, could he discover your name, address, telephone number, income, age, sex, race, general whereabouts over the past month, courses you are taking, and your grade-point average? How difficult would it be for such a person to identify your friends, family, or taste in clothes or music? Of course, the more you use credit cards and electronic tellers, the more can be discovered about you. However, we are all known to some computer somewhere, and we would consider much of the available information to be "personal." Our right to be protected from unreasonable "searches and seizures" is increasingly at risk, and we are frequently unaware of the risk. The sheer availability of information about suspects, witnesses and offenders could lead to increased surveillance by the justice system. There is no doubt that much of this information would prove useful not only in criminal investigations, but also for what is called "intelligence gathering."

Yet another computer-generated technological change promises to alter the way in which criminal justice decisions are made. It is increasingly common for justice agencies to employ statistical models to assist in the determination of resource allocation and case processing decisions. Spelman and Eck (1987) reported on "smart policing," in which police reactions to crime problems (in the form of changing patterns of patrol, enlisting community assistance and selecting police problems for enforcement attention) are "incident driven." That is, crime reports are analyzed, and computer-generated patterns of police problems are then created to guide the deployment of police resources.

Some commentators call for increasing use of such models for making police decisions. They suggest that criminal complaints should be ranked according to solvability, and that detective and patrol officers should be assigned to respond to cases on the basis of the likelihood that the case can be solved (Greenberg & Wasserman, 1979; Cordner, et al, 1983). Therefore, the lower the probability that the case will be solved, the less should be the urgency for police response to the complaint.

Prosecutors' offices actually have begun to differentiate cases on the basis of factors associated with successful prosecution, or on other models of case importance. Cases are selected for special attention when an analysis of factors present in the case (witnesses, physical evidence, etc.) indicates a high probability of conviction. That is, prosecutorial resources are to be focused on those cases for which there is the greatest probability of successful prosecution.

The courts and parole authorities rely upon various analyses to assist in the determination of criminal sanctions. The tradition of research-generated guidelines for criminal justice decision-making is longest in parole and sentencing (Travis & O'Leary, 1979). Block and Rhodes (1987) assessed the new federal sentencing guidelines, noting that the Federal Sentencing Commission (author of the guidelines) does not expect federal judges to deviate from guideline sentences very often. William Wilkins, Chairman of the Commission, predicted that "if this effort at the Federal level is generally found to be successful, these guidelines will foster the development of guidelines by many States that do not already have them" (Wilkins, 1987:8).

As discussed in the previous chapter, probation and parole supervision levels in many states are determined with reference to risk and needs assessment measures.

Gettinger (1981) described the California system for assigning levels of supervision, referring to the system as "doing parole by the numbers." In that system, each case was assessed for risk, and determined to be either a "control case" or a "service case." Control cases received close supervision and an emphasis on crime prevention; service cases received counseling and assistance in receiving community services. Like the parolees, the parole officers were broken into classes of minimum supervision agents, who administered large caseloads of parolees requiring little attention; control officers, who served as "personal police" for dangerous parolees; and service agents, who arranged social services for parolees needing them.

Partially an outgrowth of research over the past three decades that identified inefficiencies in criminal justice processing, the use of these classification technologies is expected to insure that criminal justice resources are wisely expended on those cases for which they are most needed. The use of "problem-oriented policing," setting prosecution priorities, sentencing guidelines, and correctional classification also reflect the contemporary emphasis on career criminals (discussed in Chapter 2).

The problem posed by this new decision-making technology for criminal justice revolves around the question of *who* makes the decisions. To the extent that all of these classification and prediction technologies provide information and guidance to decision-makers, they do not alter tremendously justice system processing. These devices simply become another factor in the equation that produces criminal justice outcomes. The problem is that these technologies may actually alter the decisions themselves.

In regard to community supervision case classification, there is evidence that many jurisdictions simply adopted the National Institute of Corrections case management models, and that they did so without adjusting the models for local characteristics. Indeed, an evaluation of the application of the model system to several local departments indicated that the risk assessment instruments did not work very well at predicting risk in some places (Wright, et al, 1984). Nonetheless, classification decisions were made on the basis of an existing, though inappropriate, model; one could say that the model made the decisions.

In regard to prosecutorial guidelines, David Weimer (1980) found that a more effective use of prosecutorial resources would be obtained from focusing resources on cases with the lower probabilities of conviction. After all, cases with high probabilities of conviction do not need as much special attention. Further, lacking an effort to deal strongly with lower probability cases, and lacking continual evaluation of case decision-making and outcomes, the model becomes self-perpetuating. Nothing will change, because there will be no new information generated that will lead to change.

For sentencing decisions, guidelines are often stifling. Convicted offenders receive predetermined sentences because of factors that often are beyond their control. For example, to the extent that prior criminal record affects the severity of sentence, there is nothing the offender can do to alter his or her sentence. The prior record never gets better. When one considers that parole and sentencing guidelines are often based on past experience (what kinds of sentences were imposed in the past), the problem is more apparent. Arguably, one reason for the development of these models is to improve decision-making, but the models are based on the very decisions they are expected to improve (Gottfredson, et al, 1978).

For the foreseeable future, the tendency to adopt and use decision-making aids will probably continue and spread throughout the justice system. The effects of these models are presently unknown. By relieving decision-makers of responsibility for decisions, the guidelines allow decision-makers to claim that they were forced to decide a certain way. There will be a tendency toward uniformity in deci-

...ons. This uniformity will have the effect of masking differences between individual cases, which will result in less "humane" (or at least, less human) treatment of offenders. Further, it can be expected that such guidelines will further strengthen the justice system's ability to resist change. One long range result may well be a call for greater individualization in criminal justice case processing, which would return us, full cycle, to where these guidelines began.

CRIMINAL JUSTICE: A FINAL THOUGHT

Having come now to the end of our preliminary examination of American criminal justice, it seems appropriate to think of our future, and the future of the field. "Criminal Justice," as a title, seems paradoxical. Does it mean that justice is criminal, or that crime is just? We now know that it refers to how we define, detect and react to behaviors that we deem criminal. We should also have an appreciation for how complex a topic it really is.

We have seen how present practices reflect various mixes of historical, political, economic, social, philosophical and individual traits and factors. We can appreciate how the justice system, in balancing these many demands, is highly resistant to reform. There are so many places where reforms can be made, and so many levels at which reform can be stymied, that the justice process seems immune to change. Still, we have seen that changes have occurred in criminal justice over the years. Some changes have been more fundamental than others. Some appear to have been more long-lasting; others are not yet complete.

Through our examination of criminal justice, we have come to see that no single purpose does (or can) predominate. The central dilemma is that of controlling behavior in a free society. The tension is between individual liberty and the need for an orderly and predictable society. The pendulum shifts over the decades from an emphasis on one to an emphasis on the other. The result is the appearance that no change has occurred. However, criminal justice seems to proceed in a circular fashion, that is, it continually returns to earlier points. The effect is enough to make us despair in our hopes to achieve progress. That is not the intent of the study of criminal justice.

An understanding of criminal justice promotes an understanding of our society and culture. Similarly, it is not possible to grasp the intricacies of the justice system without understanding its larger context. The failure of past reforms can often be traced to either or both of two mistakes. First, we must be reasonable in our expectations for change. It is probably not possible to eliminate injustice or inefficiency, and it may not be desirable to do so. Second, change in the justice process is accomplished only by thorough planning and careful execution. As a system (or collection of separate systems), criminal justice is elastic and resists alteration. The would be reformer must anticipate reactions to change, and must prepare for them.

One thing that we can predict with confidence is that there will be a criminal justice process in the future. It is incumbent on us to try to understand it, and to work to improve it.

REVIEW QUESTIONS

1. Identify two ways in which an offender can receive a discharge from criminal justice custody.

2. What are collateral consequences of conviction? Identify five such consequences.

3. Describe a process by which an ex-offender may have his or her constitutional rights restored.

4. What are some of the problems in arriving at a definition of recidivism?

5. What are the implications of the concept of recidivism for criminal justice policy?

6. It is argued that there is a trend toward privatizing criminal justice. Summarize this argument, and tell whether or not you agree with it.

7. One recent trend in criminal justice has been the development and use of decision-making guidelines. Give three examples of such guidelines and discuss their possible effects.

REFERENCES

Allen, H. & C. Simonsen (1986), *Corrections in America: An Introduction, 4th.* (New York: MacMillan).

Beck, A & B. Shipley (1987), *Recidivism of Young Parolees.* (Washington, DC: U.S. Department of Justice).

Bennett, G. (1987), *Crime-warps: The Future of Crime in America.* (New York: Doubleday).

Block, M. & W. Rhodes (1987), "The impact of federal sentencing guidelines," *NIJ Reports* (September/October):2-7.

Braly, M. (1977), *False Starts: A Memoir of San Quentin and Other Prisons.* (New York: Penguin Books).

Bureau of Justice Statistics (1987), *Probation and Parole 1985.* (Washington, DC: U.S. Department of Justice).

Burton, V., F. Cullen & L. Travis (1987), "The collateral consequences of a felony conviction: A national study of state statutes," *Federal Probation* 51(3):52-60.

Camp, G. & C. Camp (1987), *Stopping Escapes: Perimeter Security.* (Washington, DC: U.S. Department of Justice).

Clinard, M. & P. Yeager (1980), *Corporate Crime.* (New York: Free Press).

Cordner, G., J. Greene & T. Bynum (1983), "The sooner the better: Some effects of police response time," in R. Bennett (ed.), *Police at Work: Policy Issues and Analysis.* (Beverly Hills, CA: Sage):145-64.

Cullen, F., W. Maakestad & G. Cavender (1987), *Corporate Crime Under Attack: The Ford Pinto Case and Beyond.* (Cincinnati, OH: Anderson).

Davidenas, J. (1983), "The professional license: An ex-offender's illusion," *Criminal Justice Journal* 7(1):61-96.

Davis, R. (1987), "Crime victims: Learning how to help them," *NIJ Reports* (May/June):2-7.

Duffie, H. & G. Graham (1986), "A paperless probation department?--Solutions to the endless paper chase," *Corrections Today* 48(1):46;50.

Finn, R. & P. Fontaine (1985), "The association between selected characteristics and perceived employability of offenders," *Criminal Justice & Behavior* 12(3):353-65.

Flanagan, T. (1985), "Questioning the 'other' parole: The effectiveness of community supervision of offenders," in L. Travis (ed.) *Probation, Parole, and Community Corrections: A Reader.* (Prospect Heights, IL: Waveland):167-83.

Forer, L. (1980), *Criminals and Victims: A Trial Judge Reflects on Crime and Punishment.* (New York: W.W. Norton).

Galaway, B. (1977), "The use of restitution," *Crime & Delinquency* 23(1):57-67.

Galaway, B. & J. Hudson (eds.) (1978) *Offender Restitution in Theory and Action.* (Lexington, MA: Lexington Books).

Gettinger, S. (1981), "Separating the cop from the counselor," *Corrections Magazine* 7(2):34-38.

Gottfredson, D., C. Cosgrove, L. Wilkins, J. Wallerstein & C. Rauh (1978), *Classification for parole decision policy.* (Washington, DC: U.S. Government Printing Office).

Gottfredson, M., S. Mitchell-Herzfeld & T. Flanagan (1982), Another look at the effectiveness of parole supervision," *Journal of research in Crime & Delinquency* 18(2):277-98.

Greenberg, I. & R. Wasserman (1979), *Managing Criminal Investigations.* (Washington, DC: National Institute of Justice).

Hoffman, P. & J. Beck (1984), "Burnout--Age at release from prison and recidivism," *Journal of Criminal Justice* 12(6):617-24.

Hoffman, P. & B. Stone-Meierhoefer (1979), "Post release arrest experiences of federal prisoners: A six-year follow-up," *Journal of Criminal Justice* 7(3):193-216.

Hoffman, P. & B. Stone-Meierhoefer (1980), "Reporting recidivism rates: The criterion and follow-up issues," *Journal of Criminal Justice* 8(1):53-60.

Homant, R. & D. Kennedy (1982), "Attitudes towards ex-offenders: A comparison of social stigmas," *Journal of Criminal Justice* 10(5):383-92.

Johnson, D. (1981), *American Law Enforcement: A History.* (St. Louis, MO: Forum Press).

Kelling, G., S. Edwards & M. Moore (1986), "Federally funded community crime control: Urban initiatives anti-crime program," *Criminal Justice Policy Review* 1(1):58-75

Latessa, E. & L. Travis (1987), "Citizen crime prevention: Problems and prospectives in reducing crime," *Journal of Security Management* 10(1):38-51.

Latessa, E., L. Travis, R. Oldendick, B. McDermott & S. Noonan (1988), *The Impact of Technology in Prisons: Final Report.* (Washington, DC: National Institute of Corrections).

Lundman, R. (1980), *Police and Policing: An Introduction.* (New York: Holt, Rinehart & Winston).

McGillis, D. (1986), *Community Dispute REsolution Programs and Public Policy.* (Washington, DC: National Institute of Justice).

Petersilia, J., S. Turner & J. Peterson (1986), *Prison Versus Probation in California: Implications for Crime and Offender Recidivism.* (Santa Monica, CA: Rand).

Pfuhl, E. & D. Altheide (1987), "TV mediation of disputes and injustice," *Justice Quarterly* 4(1):99-116.

Reed, J. (1979), "Civil disabilities, attitudes, and reentry: Or how can the offender reacquire a conventional status?" *Journal of Offender Rehabilitation* 3:219-28.

Rosenbaum, D., A. Lurigio & P. Lavrakas (1986), *Crime stoppers--A National Evaluation.* (Washington, DC: U.S. Department of Justice).

Schwartz, M., T. Clear & L. Travis (1980), *Corrections: An Issues Approach.* (Cincinnati, OH: Anderson).

Schwartz, R. & J. Skolnick (1962), "Two studies of legal stigma," *Social Problems* 10:133-42.

Sechrest, L., S. White & E. Brown (1979), *The rehabilitation of criminal offenders: Problems and prospects.* (Washington, DC: National Academy of Sciences).

Spelman, W. & J. Eck (1987), "Newport News tests problem-oriented policing," *NIJ Reports* (January/February):2-8.

Travis, L. & V. O'Leary (1979), *Changes in Sentencing and Parole Decision Making: 1976-78.* (Hackensack, NJ: National Council on Crime and Delinquency).

Umbreit, M. (1986), "Victim/offender mediation: A national survey," *Federal Probation* 50(4):53-56.

Vile, J. (1981), "The right to vote as applied to ex-felons," *Federal Probation* 45(1):12-16.

Walker, S. (1985), *Sense and Nonsense About Crime: A Policy Guide.* (Monterey, CA: Brooks-Cole).

Weimer, D. (1980), "Vertical prosecution and career criminal bureaus: How many and who?" *Journal of Criminal Justice* 8(6):369-78.

Wilkins, W. (1987), "Sentencing commission chairman Wilkins answers questions on the guidelines," *NIJ Reports* (September/October):7-9.

Wright, K., T.R. Clear & P. Dickson (1984), "Universal applicability of probation risk-assessment instruments: A critique," *Criminology* 22(1):113-34.

The following section presents an overview of the juvenile justice system. This chapter was prepared by John Whitehead and Steven Lab, who have written an introductory book on the juvenile justice system. Professors Whitehead and Lab have managed to succinctly summarize their work into the chapter which follows. Those readers interested in learning more about the juvenile justice system are encouraged to read the full treatment of this topic available in Whitehead and Lab, *Juvenile Justice: An Introduction* (Cincinnati: Anderson Publishing Co., forthcoming).

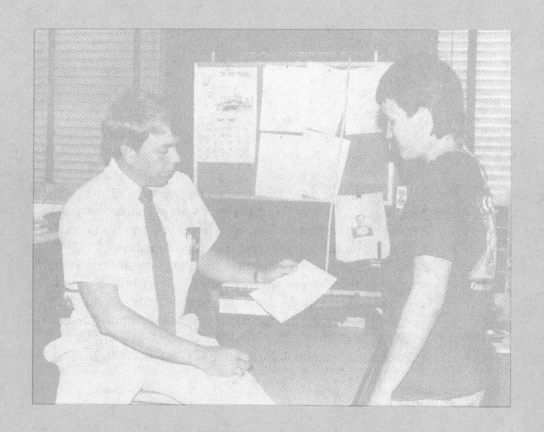

15 The Juvenile System

John T. Whitehead and Steven P. Lab

Misbehavior by juveniles poses special problems for agents of social control. Foremost among the concerns is the general societal belief that juveniles require handling different from that of adults. Indeed, we have an entire system of social control developed specifically for dealing with problem youths. The "juvenile justice system" operates under a different set of assumptions about deviant behavior than does the adult criminal justice system. The juvenile system also works somewhat independently of the adult system. This does not mean that there is no overlap between the adult and juvenile systems. There is a great deal of similarity in how the two systems operate. Some individuals claim that the differences are little more than semantic exercises. The aim of this chapter is to familiarize the reader with the problem of juvenile delinquency and the operations of the juvenile justice system. The chapter concludes with a discussion of the major issues now facing that system.

DEFINING DELINQUENCY

Perhaps the first point of departure between the adult and juvenile systems appears in the type of behavior that each system is charged with handling. Delinquency has been defined in a number of different ways. Many definitions reflect the same behavior outlined as criminal in the adult system. Such criminal law definitions often identify a delinquent as a juvenile that violates the criminal laws of the jurisdiction. For example, in Ohio, a delinquent is any child that violates any law of the state, the United States, or any ordinance or regulation of a political subdivision of the state, as long as the violation would be a crime if committed by an adult (Page's Ohio Revised Code, Anderson, 1987). The emphasis is on the same behavior that is prohibited for adults.

Besides adult criminal acts, the juvenile justice system intervenes in a variety of specific juvenile offenses. Such behaviors are usually referred to as *status offenses* because of their applicability to persons of a certain "status." Acts typically considered as status offenses include smoking, drinking, fighting, swearing, running away, being disrespectful to parents, and other actions that are allowable for adults. The statutes that outline status offenses are generally very vague, they leave the interpretation of what is not acceptable behavior to the reader's discretion, and they ensure that all youths could be subjected to intervention.

Implicit in the various definitions of delinquency is a definition of "juvenile." While some delinquency statutes provide a specific age, others simply refer to the age of majority or to another statute. Clearly, juveniles are young persons that are not yet considered adults. The legal definition, however, varies from place to place. For example, the courts of 38 states, the courts of the District of

Columbia and the federal courts identify individuals under the age of 18 as juveniles. Fifteen states recognize those that are age 15 or under as juveniles and eight states define juveniles as those that are under age 17. At the same time that an upper age limit is set, some states also set a lower age limit. These lower ages typically range from age six to age ten. A further age consideration deals with the "waiver" or "transfer" of youths to adult jurisdiction. While this issue will be dealt with later in the chapter, it is important to note that in some states juveniles as young as ten years old can be considered adults and handled by the adult criminal justice system. Disparity in maximum age, minimum age, and waiver provisions means that youths subject to the juvenile statutes in one location could be handled as adults in another jurisdiction.

SCOPE OF THE PROBLEM

How large is the delinquency problem? What characterizes the typical delinquent? Answers to both of these questions can present different images. The varied responses are attributable to the range of possible considerations in defining delinquents and the various methods used for measuring delinquency. Despite the potential variability, some common features about delinquency emerge.

Official Records

The most common source of information on delinquency is official records of the criminal and juvenile justice system. The Uniform Crime Reports (UCR), court records and correctional figures are among the varied official crime measures that present information concerning the level of juvenile misbehavior. Based on 1985 UCR data, youths under the age of eighteen accounted for roughly 17% of all arrests (approximately 1.7 million), 30% of the Index offenses, and 34% of the personal Index crimes (non-negligent homicide, rape, aggravated assault and battery) (FBI Uniform Crime Reports, 1986). The size of the juvenile problem appears even larger when you consider that youths between the ages of ten and seventeen (inclusive) make up roughly 12% of the total U.S. population (U.S. Bureau of the Census, 1986). Juveniles, therefore, are contributing more than their share to the arrest statistics. Indeed, arrests peak at age seventeen. Court and correctional figures present significantly smaller numbers of youths. This is because the police filter and screen many children away from the system. In 1983 the court handled roughly 1,275,000 delinquency cases (Flanagan & McGarrell, 1986), while the average one-day correctional count was about 72,000 youths (Nimick, Snyder, Sullivan & Tierney, 1987).

Official figures also provide a profile of delinquents. In terms of type of offense, youths confine most of their deviance to property offenses (89% of arrests). The sex distribution of juvenile offenders is heavily skewed; males represent 78% of all arrestees. Males and females, however, commit roughly the same portion of their offenses in the Index categories (non-negligent homicide, rape, aggravated assault, robbery, burglary, vehicle theft, larceny and arson) (33% of the female arrests and 38% of the male arrests). The racial breakdown in official figures shows an overrepresentation of minorities. Although blacks make up about 25% of youthful offenders, their population representation is only about 15%. The common view that deviance is highest in large cities does not appear in official figures. Arrest data show that the proportion of youths decreases as the size of the city increases. Finally, the trend in youthful crime has changed in recent years. Official records show a steady increase throughout the 1960s and mid-1970s, a leveling off in the late seventies, and a slight decline in the early 1980s. In summary, official statistics show that the delinquency problem mainly involves property offenses, is dominated by males, is overrepresented by minorities, is more prevalent in smaller cities, and shows signs of decreasing in recent years.

While the official records reveal much delinquency, these figures probably underrepresent the actual level of juvenile misbehavior in society. First, not everyone reports all the crimes he knows about to the police; thus, unreported deviant acts are not included. Second, official records do not adequately reflect status offenses. The police may ignore or simply fail to record youthful misbehavior that is not also an adult criminal act. The possibility that official records underreport delinquency has led to the use of other means of measuring deviance. The greatest advantage of the official methods lies in the fact that official data are collected on an ongoing basis and in a reasonably consistent fashion.

Self-Reports of Delinquency

Delinquency is also measured through self-report surveys. Self-reports ask the respondent what crimes he has committed. These methods have the potential of uncovering deviant acts that are not reported to the police. Indeed, self-report surveys were developed, in part, as a means of finding out about the criminal acts of which the police were unaware.

Self-report surveys have a fairly long history in juvenile justice. In fact, researchers designed the earliest such surveys specifically for the study of juvenile misbehavior. One well-known self-report scale is the Short-Nye Self-Report Delinquency Scale (1958). The items in the scale are dominated by status and minor offenses, such as defying parental authority, driving too fast, drinking alcohol, and committing petty theft. Such self-report scales typically uncover a great deal of delinquency. Indeed, various studies using these types of scales show that virtually every person is a delinquent. This can be directly attributed to the minor nature of the acts that are asked about in the questions.

Criticisms that the scales were dominated by trivial actions have prompted some researchers to construct scales that include more serious property and personal offenses. Hindelang, Hirschi and Weis (1981) and Elliott, Ageton, Huizinga, Knowles and Canter (1983) included acts such as felony assault, grand theft, sale of stolen items, and robbery in their surveys. One result of including more serious items is a reduction in the number of persons claiming to have participated in criminal acts. In fact, the level of offenses for the serious crimes is often close to that uncovered in official records. The level of minor offenses, however, remains high.

The demographic profile of offenders presented by self-report studies is somewhat different from the picture presented by official records. First, the peak age of offending appears around ages thirteen to fifteen. This earlier peak may be partly due to the use of minor and status offenses in the surveys. Second, the racial and social class distribution is much more similar in self-report surveys. Where racial differences appear for certain offenses, they are generally small. Similarly, differences between the social classes also appear to be minor (Elliott, et al, 1983; Hindelang, et al, 1981). The greatest similarity to official records appears in the sex distribution of offenses. Males again exceed females in the number of offenses. An interesting point to note is that, despite the numerical differences, males and females tend to commit similar types of offenses. That is, there do not appear to be any acts that are primarily committed by one or the other sex (Elliott, et al, 1983).

Comparing the Delinquency Measures

In general, both official and self-report measures show that delinquency is a widespread problem. Youths clearly commit more criminal acts than would be expected from the number of youths in society. The delinquency trend since the 1960s has been a steady increase with only minor decreases in the early 1980s. Males commit more offenses than females, but the two sexes participate in similar types of criminal acts. There is a clear diversity in the types of offenses that are committed; property and minor status offenses are the most prevalent. Racial and social class differences that appear in the official measures are not evident in the unofficial data. The self-report measures uncover greater amounts of juvenile misconduct than do the official statistics. This fact simply indicates that the already large numbers of juvenile offenses known to agents of social control do not reflect a complete picture.

GANG DELINQUENCY

The study of juvenile misbehavior consistently portrays delinquency as a group phenomenon (Erickson, 1971; Erickson and Jensen, 1977; Hindelang, 1971). Much of the interest in group delinquency revolves around the idea of juvenile gangs. One source of the public's concern about gangs may be the portrayal of gang behavior in the mass media. Movies and plays such as *The Blackboard Jungle*, *West Side Story* and *Colors* dramatize the lure of gangs for youths and the aggressive nature of these groups. While there has been much interest and research in the area of gang activity, no single definition of "a gang" has developed. A number of factors, however, are common to most definitions. Gangs are more common in poor, disorganized areas of the community, youths that are in gangs are recognized by themselves or others as a gang, members of gangs are involved in delinquent activities, the members claim a territory, and there is some degree of leadership and internal organization in gangs (Klein, 1971; Miller, 1975; Miller, 1980). The degree to which each of these factors is important is subject to debate.

The extent of gang criminal activity is also unclear. One study of gangs (perhaps the earliest conducted) identified 1,313, gangs with roughly 25,000 members, in Chicago (Thrasher, 1936). The gangs were comprised mostly of adolescent males and usually ranged in size from six to twenty members (although some were as small as two to three members and others numbered more than 100). The great number of gangs partly reflected the fact that Thrasher considered almost any consistent grouping of youths as a gang. One of the more recent examinations of gangs (Miller, 1975; 1980), using a conservative definition of the term, estimated that there were 760 gangs with more than 28,000 members in six major U.S. cities. A more liberal definition expanded the numbers to 2,700 gangs with 81,500 members.

Societal concern over gangs is based on the perception of gang violence. Most portrayals of gangs present a picture of constant violent confrontations, either gang against gang or gang against the general public. The gang fight, or rumble, is a key image associated with gangs. The common scenario of two groups of youths bedecked in leather jackets and wielding chains, knives or broken bottles coming together in a pre-arranged fight, however, is not the dominant form of behavior or violence undertaken by gangs. This is not to say that such "rumbles" do not take place. Rather, they are rare occurrences. Many gangs are involved in non-violent activities. Thrasher (1936) noted that many gangs supply leisure activities, a forum for talk or play, or an opportunity for gambling. Yablonsky's (1962) study explicitly excluded delinquent (property offending) and social (neither violent or delinquent) gangs from his study of violent gangs.

Gang violence in recent years does not conform to the image of a rumble. Rumbles have given way to "forays," in which one or two gang members attack a single rival gang member. The attack usually involves a weapon fired from a moving vehicle. The victim's gang then reciprocates against the transgressor's gang in a like fashion. There emerges a series of small, isolated attacks between gangs. Contrary to public perception, the forays typically are aimed at rival gang members and not at the public. Violence against the public mainly appears in accidental injuries to bystanders. One factor common to modern gang violence is the heavy use of firearms. Additionally, much of the violence appears to involve drug dealing.

Methods for dealing with gangs have revolved around use of detached workers. This approach places gang workers in the environment of the gang. The workers spend considerable time in the neighborhoods, maintain contact with the gangs, and provide assistance and input geared toward more acceptable activities. One key problem of these programs, however, has been the inadvertent strengthening of gangs by the worker's presence and the provision of activities (Klein, 1971). The impact of these programs on the level of deviance has been negligible. Despite the early failure of detached worker programs, this approach continues as the core of gang intervention techniques.

THE HISTORY OF JUVENILE JUSTICE

The history of juvenile delinquency and juvenile justice is relatively short. While deviance on the part of young persons has always been a fact of life, societal intervention and participation in the handling of juvenile transgressors has gained most of its momentum in the last 100 to 150 years. The reasons for this are easy to see. Throughout most of history, youthful members of society did not enjoy a distinct status as "child." The young were either property or people. The very young (from birth to age five or six) held much the same status as any other property. They were subject to being bought, sold and disposed of at the wishes of the owners (the parents). Once the individual reached the age of five or six, he became a full-fledged "adult" member of society subject to the same rules of conduct that governed adults.

This state of indifference toward youths can be seen as a result of the health and economic conditions that existed in society. The infant mortality rate typically exceeded 50%. The failure to develop a personal, caring attitude toward infants, therefore, was an emotional defense mechanism for reducing or eliminating any pain or sorrow attached to the death of a child. The economic conditions also meant that the birth of an infant was a financial burden on the family. Families lived from day to day on what they could produce. The very young were incapable of caring for themselves or contributing to the family. A child represented a drain on the family's resources.

A variety of practices were used over the centuries for dealing with unwanted or burdensome children. One common practice was *infanticide*, or the deliberate killing of an infant, usually by the mother. Infanticide was a common practice prior to the fourth century and appeared as late as the fourteenth century. A similar practice that gained prominence after the fourth century was *abandonment*. The abandoning of children was considered less offensive than outright infanticide, although the end result was the same. Children that survived the first few years of life were often subjected to new actions such as *apprenticeship* and *involuntary servitude*. These practices were nothing more than the sale of youths by families. They alleviated the need to care for the youth and brought an economic return to the family. In addition, these youths provided labor during the rise of industrialization.

Box 15.1
Milestones in the History of Juvenile Justice

Pre-1800s   Children Viewed as Property or "Little Adults"
Deviant youths handled in adult criminal system.

1825   Establishment of Houses of Refuge
View that youths could be saved through
education, moral training, hard work.

1838   *Ex parte Crouse*
Establishment of *parens patriae* as basis of
intervention with youths.

late 1800s   Move to "Cottage" Reformatories
Same rationale as houses of refuge, provided in
surrogate family set-up.

1869   Juvenile Probation Established in Massachusetts

1899   Juvenile Court Established in Chicago
Totally separate from adult court, heavy reliance
on *parens patriae* doctrine.

1905   *Commonwealth v. Fisher*
Court ruled that *parens patriae* and good
intentions are sufficient for intervention without
concern for due process.

1920-1960s   Various New Approaches to Treatment

1966   *Kent v. United States*
Justice Abe Fortas questions whether the juvenile
system is providing the benevolent treatment
promised by *parens patriae*, beginning of move
toward due process in juvenile court.

Once children entered the labor force, they were viewed as adults and subjected to the same rules and regulations as adults. A separate system for dealing with youthful offenders did not exist. At best, the father was responsible for controlling the child; the choices for punishment had no bounds. At the societal level, youths could be (and were) sentenced to the same penalties (including death) as were adults. While harsh punishments were permitted, there is little evidence that the youths actually received them (Faust & Brantingham, 1979; Platt, 1977).

Changes in the societal view of children did not really occur until the seventeenth and eighteenth centuries. It was during this time that medical advances were beginning to have a major impact on infant mortality and life expectancy. Additionally, scholars and religious leaders began to view the young as a means of attacking the ills of society. Reformers saw education and protection of the young as ways to create a moral society. Accompanying these views were changes in the discipline of youthful offenders.

Methods for dealing with problem youths grew out of the establishment of ways to handle the poor. A common method of dealing with the poor was the removal of children from the "bad influences" and "substandard training" of poor parents. The establishment of *Houses of Refuge* in the early 1800s conformed to this idea. The first such institution was established in New York in 1825. Key features of these institutions were the use of education, skills training, hard work and apprenticeships, which were all geared toward producing productive members of society. Despite the goals of the Houses of Refuge, various problems emerged. Among the concerns were the mixing of adults and juveniles, the mixing of criminals and non-criminals, overcrowding, the failure to supply the intended education and training, the use of harsh physical punishment, and the exploitative use of the clients for monetary gain.

The failure of the early Houses of Refuge gave rise to the establishment of "cottage" reformatories in the second half of the 1800s. These new institutions attempted to parallel a family, that is, surrogate parents provided the education and moral training for a small number of youths. Probation and the use of foster homes also emerged at the same time as did the reformatories. Unfortunately, like the earlier houses of refuge, these new alternatives suffered from many of the same problems.

In response to the failures of institutions to deal with problem youths and the call for new interventions, the juvenile court was first established in Chicago in 1899. In the late 1800s immigration by lower class Europeans continued at a high rate, delinquency was on the rise and there was an emerging body of sociological and psychological studies that attempted to explain the reasons for social ills. The new court reflected the general belief in the ability to alter youthful behavior through application of informal intervention and a desire to educate and train the child. Benevolent assistance, caring, training and guidance were the watch words of the new juvenile court. The mandate to help youths did not restrict the court to dealing with youths that committed criminal acts. Rather, the court could intervene in any situation in which a youth was in need of assistance. New laws placed status offenses under the purview of the court during this time. The growth of the court was phenomenal and, by 1920, almost every state had at least one juvenile court.

THE PHILOSOPHY OF THE JUVENILE SYSTEM

The underlying philosophy of the new juvenile court was the doctrine of *parens patriae*. *Parens patriae*, or the state as parent, was based on the actions of the English

Chancery Court, which supervised the financial affairs of orphaned juveniles. The court acted as guardian until the child was mature enough to assume responsibility. Early interventions with juveniles also relied on the *parens patriae* doctrine. For example, in the case *Ex parte Crouse*, the Pennsylvania Supreme Court ruled that the state had a right to intervene into a juvenile's life, against the wishes of the juvenile or his parents, if the state felt that the parents were not capable of properly caring for the youth (*Ex parte Crouse*, 1838). Similarly, the new juvenile court borrowed this idea of guardianship for the cornerstone of its operations. Debate over the *parens patriae* doctrine was largely settled in 1905, when the Pennsylvania Supreme Court ruled in *Commonwealth v. Fisher* that intervention based on protecting, caring for and training a youth was a duty of the state and did not violate the Constitution, regardless of the youth's actions (*Commonwealth v. Fisher*, 1905). The *parens patriae* philosophy stood largely unchallenged until the 1966 case of *Kent v. United States*. In this case, Justice Abe Fortas questioned the denial of due process for juveniles. The Justice noted,

> There is evidence...that there may be grounds for concern that the child receives the worst of both worlds: that he gets neither the protections accorded to adults nor the solicitous care and regenerative treatment postulated for children (*Kent v. U.S.*, 1966).

Despite this concern, *parens patriae* remains the dominant force behind intervention in juvenile cases.

THE JUVENILE COURT PROCESS

Once a police officer takes a youth into custody, it is fairly likely that the police will then refer that youngster to juvenile court. In 1987, 62% of the youths taken into custody were in fact referred to juvenile court, 30% were simply handled within the police department and released, 1% were referred to another police agency, 1% were referred to a welfare agency, and 5% were referred to adult criminal court (percentages do not add up to 100% due to rounding) (Federal Bureau of Investigation, 1988: 225). When police refer a youth to juvenile court, court personnel must then make one or more critical decisions: whether to detain (jail) the youth, whether to file a petition (charges) against the youth, whether to find (adjudicate) the youth a delinquent, and how to dispose of the petition. These decisions correspond to the adult court decisions of bail or jail, the filing of a formal charge versus dismissal, determination of guilt by plea or by trial, and sentencing. Several juvenile court actors, such as probation officers, defense attorneys, prosecutors and judges, are involved in these important decisions. While the judge is the primary decision-maker, other court personnel play important roles in deciding the fate of juvenile suspects.

This section will examine the critical decision points in the juvenile court process: detention, intake, waiver (transfer), adjudication, and disposition. We will look at the roles the various court personnel play and should play in the court process. We will describe what happens when a juvenile suspect goes through the juvenile court process, and we will compare the ideal with the reality. Finally, we will examine some of the controversial issues facing juvenile court today, such as the question of the extent to which attorneys in juvenile court should be adversarial and whether juveniles should have the right to a jury trial. It should be noted that, while we do not examine police decisions as to juveniles, many of the law enforcement issues raised earlier in the book (see chapters 5 and 6) apply to juveniles as well as to adults.

The Detention Decision

The first decision that juvenile court personnel must make is the detention decision. They must decide whether to keep a juvenile in custody or to allow the youth to go home with his or her parents and await further court action. The detention decision is the juvenile court counterpart of the bail decision in adult court. It is a very important decision because it concerns the freedom of the child and, therefore, resembles the disposition (sentencing) decision. In fact, children sent to detention may stay there for an extensive period of time; they may remain for even a longer time than do children that are sent to state training schools (youth prisons for juveniles determined to be delinquent). Most recently, youths sentenced to detention spent an average of twelve days in detention, even though they had not been adjudicated as delinquent (Sickmund & Baunach, 1986: 1).

Detention workers or probation officers usually make the initial detention decision, for which they have several options. *Releasing a child to the parents* is the most frequently used option and the preferred decision in most states (e.g., Alabama Code 12-15-59). *Secure detention*, which is placing a child in the juvenile equivalent of a local jail, is another alternative. This method involves placement in a locked facility for 10, 20, or more youths who are awaiting further court action or are awaiting transfer to a state correctional facility. *Non-secure detention* is another option in some places for youths involved in less serious crimes, youths that do not pose much threat to the community, and youths that are not a threat to themselves. Such youngsters may be placed in small group homes that are not locked or not locked as comprehensively as a secure detention facility. This type of detention is, therefore, called "non-secure." Youngsters in non-secure detention centers might even go to regular public school classes during the day. Alternatives to detention, such as *home deten-*

tion, have developed in the last few years. These alternatives are important in light of extensive overuse of detention in the past (McCarthy, 1987b).

Detention Statistics

Recent detention figures show that over 14,000 youths were detained in public juvenile facilities on February 1, 1985 (Sickmund & Baunach, 1986: 4). Most of these (90%) were being held in short-term institutional facilities, that is, traditional detention facilities. A total of 444 youths (3% of the total detained population) were being held in open short-term facilities, 760 (5%) were in public long-term institutional facilities, and 212 (1.5%) of all detained youths were being held in long-term institutional open facilities.

In 1984, the average cost of keeping a child in a short-term facility was $76 a day, and the average length of stay in short-term facilities (of children discharged from public facilities) was 12 days (Sickmund & Baunach, 1986: 5-6).

The Intake Decision

The second major decision point in juvenile court is the intake decision, which is analogous to the filing decision in adult court. At intake, a court official, either a probation officer or a prosecutor (or both), decides whether to file a court petition of delinquency, status offense, neglect, abuse or dependency in a particular case. Traditionally, a probation officer makes the intake decision. The *parens patriae* philosophy of the court dictates this approach because the philosophy's treatment orientation indicates that the probation officer, ideally a trained social worker, should consider the best interests of the child as well as the legal aspects of the case (as an adult court prosecutor might). That is, an intake probation officer is supposed to consider the welfare of the child and the legal demands of the police and victim, and then attempt to resolve every case in light of those considerations.

One frequent decision of the intake officer is not to file a petition alleging delinquency or a status offense, but instead to try to resolve the matter without resorting to a formal petition against the child. This action is usually called *adjustment at intake* or *informal adjustment*. It is important to note that such informal adjustment practices occur as frequently as 25% of the time (McCarthy, 1987a) and have been part of juvenile court since its inception.

The Prosecutor's Role

If an intake probation officer decides to file a petition against a child, that decision often requires the approval of an attorney, who usually is the prosecutor. The prosecutor's approval of the probation officer's decision to file a petition insures that a legally trained official has reviewed the legal criteria for a properly authorized petition. The prosecutor checks the legal wording of the petition, determines that enough evidence is available to establish the petition (so that the delinquent or status offender will be found "guilty"), and makes sure that the offense occurred in the court's jurisdiction and that the child was of proper age at the time of the offense.

Because of the importance of such legal criteria and because of the growing emphasis on more punitive juvenile models, some jurisdictions have turned away from the traditional probation officer model of intake to models in which the prosecutor is either the first or the sole intake decision-maker. Such models are more consistent with more legalistic views of juvenile court, in which the state has abandoned the traditional *parens patriae* philosophy. For example, Washington state has switched responsibility for the intake decision to the prosecutor for all felony charges and most misdemeanors. This action by Washington state represents a radical break from traditional juvenile court thinking and practice; the action is a close approximation of adult processing with its retributive emphasis.

The Waiver (Transfer) Decision

For some youths petitioned to juvenile court, the most critical decision point is the waiver or transfer decision. Many states allow the court to waive or transfer certain offenders (generally older offenders that commit serious crimes) to adult court. This is a crucial decision because the transfer to adult court subjects the transferred youth to adult penalties (such as lengthy incarceration in an adult prison) as opposed to juvenile penalties (perhaps a relatively short period of incarceration in a juvenile training school). Transfer also results in the creation of an adult criminal record, which is public and may hinder future opportunities for employment in certain occupations. A juvenile court record, on the other hand, is confidential, and therefore should not affect employment or other opportunities.

The waiver decision is made at a hearing that is analogous to the preliminary hearing in adult court. At a waiver hearing, the prosecutor must only show probable cause that an offense occurred and that the juvenile committed the offense. The prosecutor does not have to prove guilt beyond a reasonable doubt. Proof of guilt is reserved for the trial in adult court (if waiver is successful) or for the adjudication stage in juvenile court (if the waiver motion fails). The juvenile transfer hearing differs from an adult court preliminary hearing in that the prosecutor must also establish that the juvenile is not amenable to juvenile court intervention or is a threat to public safety. An example of nonamenability would be the case of a youth already on parole from a state training school for an earlier delinquent act who then commits another serious offense (e.g., armed robbery). If probable cause were established that the youth committed the robbery, then the judge would have to find that the juvenile court had a history of contacts with the youth dating back several years and that one more juvenile court effort to deal with the youth's problems, either through probation or a training school placement, would be futile. An example of a case involving a threat to public safety would be a murder case or an offender with a history of violent offenses.

Box 15.2
Selected Supreme Court Decisions on Juveniles

Breed v. Jones (1975): juveniles cannot be adjudicated delinquent in juvenile court and then waived to adult court for trial without violating double jeopardy.

Fare v. Michael C. (1979): trial court judges must evaluate the voluntariness of any confession obtained from a juvenile based on all the circumstances of the confession. There is no rule mandating that the police consult the child's parent or an attorney before they can question a juvenile suspect. The child can waive his or her privilege against self-incrimination and can waive the right to consult an attorney prior to interrogation.

In re Gault (1967): the fifth amendment privilege against self-incrimination (the right to remain silent) and the sixth amendment rights to adequate notice of the charges against oneself, to confront and cross-examine accusers, and to the assistance of counsel all apply in delinquency proceedings with the possibility of confinement as punishment.

In re Winship (1970): the standard of proof of guilty beyond a reasonable doubt applies to juvenile delinquency proceedings as well as to adult criminal trials.

Alternatives to Transfer

Because attitudes toward juvenile delinquents are indicating more of a willingness to punish, waiver will probably be used more frequently in the 1990s. Also, other methods to put delinquents into adult court and into incarceration for lengthier sentences will also be important. Examples of these methods are sentencing guidelines, statutory exclusion of certain offenses from juvenile court jurisdiction, and lowering the age of criminal court jurisdiction (Fagan, Forst & Vivona, 1987: 261).

Kent v. United States (1966): certain minimum safeguards apply to transfer (waiver) cases. The juvenile being considered for transfer to adult criminal court has the right to the assistance of counsel (an attorney), the right to a hearing, and a statement of the reasons for transfer if the judge decides to transfer the case to adult court.

McKevier v. Pennsylvania (1971): juveniles do *not* have a constitutional right to a jury trial.

New Jersey v. T.L.O. (1985): school officials can search a student based on reasonable suspicion that the search will result in evidence that the student is violating or has violated either a school rule or a law.

Schall v. Martin (1984): a juvenile that is awaiting court proceedings can be held in preventive detention if there is adequate concern that the juvenile would commit additional crimes while the primary case is awaiting further court action.

For a complete discussion of these cases, see *Juvenile Justice*, J.T. Whitehead & S.P. Lab (Cincinnati, OH: Anderson), forthcoming.

Adjudication and Disposition

For children not waived to adult criminal court, the next steps after the filing of a petition are *adjudication* and *disposition*. In these decisions, a judge determines whether there is enough evidence to establish the petition and then decides what to do if there is enough evidence. These decisions are comparable to the plea, trial and sentencing decisions in adult court.

Because the United States Supreme Court ordered that certain procedural rights apply to juveniles as well as to adults (see Box 15.2 for a summary of key Supreme Court decisions), the ideal is that the determination of the truth of the petition occurs in a rational fashion: the prosecutor, defense attorney and judge using their abilities and training to seek justice. Realistically, juvenile court sessions often are hectic, hurried and reflect the self-interests of the parties involved rather than the interests of justice or the interests of the child (Prescott, 1981).

Many attorneys in juvenile court back off from the zealous advocate approach that is (at least theoretically) the norm in adult criminal court, where the defense attorney gives his or her best effort in representing the defendant, even if the defendant admits to the defense attorney that he or she is factually guilty. Attorneys in adult criminal courts justify such zealous advocacy on the grounds that the system is adversarial and that the adversarial process is best for bringing out the truth. In juvenile court, some attorneys, parents and judges feel that the adult criminal court norm of zealous advocacy is inappropriate, especially if it teaches a child that he or she can "get off" despite being factually guilty of a delinquent action. These critics also worry that strong advocacy can result in an outcome in which a child that needs help will not get it because failure to establish the petition leaves the court with no jurisdiction over the child. Thus some attorneys act more like concerned adults than zealous advocates by encouraging youths to admit to petitions, whereas an adversarial approach might have resulted in the dismissal of the petition.

Attorney Effectiveness

Recent research has shown some interesting results concerning the effectiveness of defense attorneys in juvenile court. First, Michael Fabricant's 1983 study of juvenile court public defenders in Brooklyn and the Bronx, New York found that, contrary to stereotypes, public defenders were more effective, or at least as effective, as private attorneys in defending their juvenile clients. Specifically, the public defenders were very effective in obtaining adjournments, avoiding detention, and gaining dismissals. Such indicators of adversarial effectiveness led Fabricant to conclude that New York City public defenders were not inadequate. This is an impressive finding because public defenders represented roughly 75% of the delinquency and status offense defendants in New York City at the time of the study.

Stevens Clarke and Gary Koch (1980), however, found contrary evidence. Specifically, data from two North Carolina juvenile courts in the mid-1970s indicated that "the assistance of an attorney was on the whole not helpful (and may have actually been detrimental) with respect to reducing the child's chance of being adjudicated delinquent and committed" (Clarke and Koch, 1980: 307). The attorneys may have been more concerned with helping the youths to receive treatment than in helping them to "beat the rap." It should be noted that an alternative interpretation of the findings from North Carolina is that the attorneys studied were receiving the toughest cases, that is, they represented juveniles that judges had practically decided were going to wind up in youth prisons anyway. Finally, it is important to remember that juvenile court is often a low prestige assignment for new public defenders and new prosecutors; these new attorneys may very well "try to stay as briefly as possible" (Mahoney, 1987: 10). Such lack of experience may influence the effectiveness of both prosecutors and public defenders in juvenile court.

Thus, the current factual situation in America's juvenile courts appears to be that some attorneys are adversarial, some are still traditional and act as concerned adults, and some are in between the two extremes. This state of affairs raises the question of which is the best approach: zealous advocate, concerned adult, or some compromise between the two alternatives? The chief advantage of the "zealous advocate" model is that it is probably the best insurance that only guilty youths will come under court jurisdiction. Because the attorney does not pressure the child to admit to the petition (plead guilty), there is less danger that the court will attempt some type of intervention program with youths who are not really guilty. An added advantage is that this approach may generate the most respect from juveniles for the court system. Fewer youths may feel that they have been betrayed or tricked into something that some adult thought was best for them, despite their own wishes. The biggest danger of the zealous advocate approach is that it may contribute to what Fabricant called the contemporary version of benign neglect. That is, many youths appearing in juvenile court come from families racked with problems (low income, public assistance, broken homes), so that the youths need assistance. An adversarial approach may indeed prevent these children from being railroaded into juvenile prisons or other types of intervention due to insufficient legal defense. The adversarial approach, however, does nothing about the real problems that these kids face in their homes and their neighborhoods:

> It must be presumed that these youngsters' fundamental problems will neither be addressed nor resolved through a faithful adherence to process. Just as important, their

troubles are likely to be compounded by social indifference. Therefore, a policy of calculated nonintervention may, over time, cause severer and/or increased antisocial behavior from troubled youths who initially are ignored by the court or state (Fabricant, 1983:140).

The advantage of the "concerned adult" model is that it seeks to address the child's problems, which presumably led him into delinquency. This helping philosophy has been the rationale of the juvenile court since 1899; however, as David Rothman so aptly noted, the rhetoric of individualized attention has always far outstripped the reality of ineffective if not abusive programs (Rothman, 1980).

Jury Trials for Juveniles

As the U.S. Supreme Court has not mandated the right to a jury trial for all juveniles, only about a dozen states offer juveniles this right (Rossum, Koller & Manfredi, 1987: 112). Some commentators feel that it is critical for juveniles to have the right to a jury trial. For example, Barry Feld (1987b) argued that judges require less proof than juries and, therefore, it is easier to convict a youth in front of a judge than in front of a jury. The American Bar Association agreed that judges may be biased and thus called for jury trials in juvenile court (Institute of Judicial Administration: American Bar Association, 1980).

Having the right to a jury trial, however, may not make that much difference in juvenile court. In her study of a suburban juvenile court, Mahoney (1985) found that only seven cases out of the 650 she studied actually went to trial. For those seven youths, and for 87 other youths that initially requested a jury trial but later settled without a jury trial, setting (scheduling) the cases for trial had no impact on the respective outcomes.

The Recent Emphasis on Punitiveness

Traditionally, the disposition stage of juvenile court has represented the epitome of the *parens patriae* philosophy. With the advice of probation officers, social workers, psychologists, and psychiatrists, the judge has tried to act in the best interests of the child. Recently, however, disposition (sentencing) in juvenile justice has taken on an increasingly punitive character.

One indicator of this increasingly explicit focus on punishment is the revision of the purpose clauses of state juvenile codes. Forty-two states have such purpose clauses; virtually all of these clauses have some mention of what amounts to a focus on the best interests of the child. However, the last decade has seen eleven states amend their juvenile-code purpose clauses to include such goals as punishment, the protection of society or accountability (Feld, 1987a).

Parallel to the amendment of the purpose clauses, the states have taken more concrete measures to emphasize punishment. Three states (Washington, New Jersey and Texas) have adopted determinate sentencing statutes with an emphasis on proportionality. The law in such states limits the discretion of judges at disposition and attempts to set penalties that are proportionate to the seriousness of the offense. Some states have enacted mandatory minimum provisions. This means that if the judge commits a child to the state youth authority, the law dictates that the youth must serve a certain minimum amount of time. Some states have adopted dispositional guidelines or suggested sentences for most adjudicated delinquents. Unless a case has some unusual factors, judges are supposed to sentence within the ranges stipulated in the guidelines. Finally, there is the fear that the conditions of confinement have become more unpleasant or soon will deteriorate. This fear is based on the experience of the adult prison system, in which determinate sentencing has led to over-crowding and other negative consequences in the institutions (Feld, 1987a).

ISSUES IN JUVENILE JUSTICE

Modern juvenile justice is faced with a variety of concerns and issues. Many of these topics are interrelated and reflect different approaches and concerns. Among the issues are juvenile diversion, prediction of delinquency, the proper philosophy for juvenile justice, capital punishment for youths, and deinstitutionalization. Each of these is discussed in turn.

Diversion

One of the most significant movements in modern juvenile justice has been the adoption of diversion. While no single definition of diversion has emerged, diversion generally refers to programs that take youths out of the formal system of justice before they are subjected to total processing. This could mean immediate referral by the police to other agencies, referral at intake, or even treatment by a non-system related agency after adjudication.

The modern interest in diversion can be attributed to the 1967 President's Commission on Law Enforcement and the Administration of Justice. This commission critically evaluated the state of criminal justice in the United States and recommended that alternative means should be found for handling juveniles outside of formal justice system processing. The major goal of the commission was to eliminate the ineffective practices of the formal juvenile justice system. Despite the lack of a single definition for diversion, diversion programs exploded on the scene after the recommendations of the President's Commission. The reasons for the growth included the federal government's provision of funds for diversion, the overcrowded conditions of the formal juvenile system, and a belief that contact with the formal justice system led to further deviance.

Despite the move toward diversion, the approach has had questionable impact on delinquency and the juvenile justice system. The primary goal of reducing delinquency and recidivism has not been achieved. While a few studies provided positive results (Duxbury, 1973; Quay & Love, 1977; Regoli, Wilderman & Pogrebin, 1985), many others provided findings of no impact or increased levels of delinquency (Dunford, Osgood & Weichselbaum, 1982; Elliott, Dunford & Knowles, 1978; Florida, 1981; Klein, 1979; Lab and Whitehead, 1988; Lincoln, 1976; Osgood, 1983; Palmer & Lewis, 1980; Rausch, 1983; Severy & Whitaker, 1982). A second goal of reducing the number of youths having contact with agents of social control also has not been realized. Reviews of the evidence show that diversion has resulted in *net-widening*. This refers to the practice of handling youths who normally would have been left alone in the absence of the new program. Diversion appears to have engendered a totally new clientele (usually status offenders) that is normally funneled out of the system. Klein (1979) estimated that 45% of diversion clients are apprehended as a result of net-widening. At the same time that diversion is finding new clients, the formal system is dealing with at least as many youths as it did before the establishment of diversion.

Other problems add to the failure to reduce delinquency and the number of youths under social control. First, there is little evidence that processing youths through diversion programs is less stigmatizing than formally processing them. Youths in diversion programs perceive equal amounts of stigma from diversion and incarceration (Paternoster, Waldo, Chiricos & Anderson, 1979). Second, while proponents argue that diversion is less coercive, various programs coerce the client (Blomberg & Carabelo, 1979; Dunford, 1977; Palmer & Lewis, 1980) and family members into participating (Blomberg, 1979). Finally, reduced societal costs have not accompanied the growth of diversion. The costs of diversion vary greatly from study to study and often are equal to or greater than the costs of normal processing. Confounding these figures is the fact that diversion has increased the total number of youths that are under some form of intervention. While diversion may cost less, the diversion program itself is an additional cost to the already existing (and increasing) costs of juvenile justice. Diversion has not replaced past interventions; it has increased the number of programs being funded.

While most of the above results have not painted a rosy picture of diversion, neither have they been devastating. Proponents of diversion continue to point to the dismal record of formal system intervention, the potential of diversion to avoid many of the same problems, and the results that show equal (if not better) impact on clients as arguments in favor of continuing diversionary approaches. Support for diversion does not appear to be waning. Clearly, diversion is doing no worse than would the alternative of returning to full formal processing. Additionally, support for diversion is found in the dominant *parens patriae* philosophy underlying juvenile justice. At present, it appears that diversion will have a continuing role within juvenile justice.

Prediction in Juvenile Justice

Implicit in the philosophy and daily operations of the juvenile justice system is concern over the future behavior of youthful offenders. A key assumption underlying juvenile justice is the belief that, left unchecked or unaided, misbehaving youths will continue to commit delinquent acts and eventually will move on to adult criminality. Predicting future delinquency would allow early intervention both to help youths and protect society. The problem is in the *prediction* of future behavior for the different individuals: which individuals will continue to violate society's norms?

The two primary methods for making predictions are *clinical* and *actuarial*. Clinical predictions are made by a trained professional after examination of an individual or an individual's records. Conversely, actuarial prediction relies on known properties in the data. For example, insurance companies set their premiums according to knowledge about the class of individuals to which the person being insured belongs. In essence, the prediction of one person's behavior is based on the past actions of similar persons. Both of these methods have been used to predict future deviant activity.

Our current ability to predict future behavior is extremely limited. Use of either clinical or actuarial prediction methods result in a large number of false predictions. Monahan (1981), reporting on the results of a number of clinical predictions, noted that some predictions were wrong 99% of the time. None of the clinical studies is able to make correct predictions more than 46% of the time. The use of actuarial techniques has grown partly in response to the failures of the clinical approach. One of the most well-known actuarial instruments is the Gluecks' (1950) Social Prediction Table. Using data on parental supervision, parental affection, discipline, and family cohesiveness, the Gluecks claimed to be able to predict which youths will or will not become delinquent. Unfortunately, the predictions only apply to extreme categories of youths and are not applicable to the vast majority of youths. Burgess (1928) proposed another well-known form of actuarial prediction. This method entails providing one point for each predictive variable that is true about an individual and was also true of individuals who were successes in the past. Using 21 items in his scoring process, Burgess claimed to be able to identify good parole risks. Similar to the Glueck technique, however, this approach is best for the extremes and not for those individuals that score in the middle.

The failure of either the clinical or actuarial methods to make successful predictions in most situations suggests that these methods be used with caution in juvenile justice. This precaution becomes especially important for situations in which the decision is between intervention and leaving a youth alone. Any false prediction that the youth will continue delinquency could result in unnecessary intervention into a juvenile's life. The failure of these approaches, however, has not diminished attempts to uncover means of predicting future behavior.

Prediction research has shifted its focus from clinical and actuarial methods to a slightly different direction: research on the concept of *criminal careers*. The term criminal careers has variously been used to refer to longevity in offending, the number of deviant acts, specialization in offending, regularity in offending, or movement through different phases of offense behavior. In each of these conceptions, interest in criminal careers has been on identifying which individuals pose the greatest threat to society and which are in greatest need of intervention. Clearly not all delinquent youths become adult criminals. The trick is to identify those juveniles that will continue offending as adults. Criminal-career research attempts to identify these offenders.

As with clinical and actuarial predictions, research on criminal careers has failed to identify which juveniles will continue their offending. Studies have attempted to identify those juveniles that specialize in minor or status offenses and therefore pose little threat to society. As these youths are minor offenders, they can be left alone. Findings of specialization could also help to identify the proper intervention for different types of offenders. Unfortunately, studies fail to find much specialization among juve-

niles or adults (Cernkovich, 1978; Erickson, 1978; Petersilia, Greenwood & Lavin, 1978). Instead, individuals
commit a variety of different offenses throughout their careers.

Other studies recognize diversity in offending but propose that individuals may follow identifiable patterns over
time. Identification of patterns may reveal that some patterns lead to eventual desistance, prompting little need for
intervention, or a movement into certain behavior that is
best approached through a specific form of intervention.
Studies by Wolfgang, Figlio & Sellin (1972), Rojek & Erickson (1982), and Lab (1982; 1984) fail to find any clear
patterns in offending. There are a large number of possible
patterns in offending; few individuals follow the exact same
offense pattern (Lab, 1984). The most consistent finding in
the studies is that roughly two-thirds of all offenders cease
having contact with the police before committing a fourth
offense. Another clear result is that most youths commit
only minor offenses and few ever commit serious personal
or property crimes. Thus, there is a tendency for youths to
concentrate on minor offenses and to cease acting in deviant ways after only a few police contacts.

Attempts at developing successful prediction methods
in juvenile justice have been extremely disappointing. Most
attempts provide a large number of false predictions; some
make more errors than would be made by simply flipping a
coin. While actuarial prediction is superior to clinical prediction, the results are not good enough, in themselves, to
stand as authority upon which to base policy decisions.
Criminal career research presents similar questionable results and should likewise be used with caution. In sum, the
juvenile justice system should be prudent in its reliance on
prediction until further research can improve identification
of who will be deviant in the future and who will best benefit from different interventions.

The Philosophy of Juvenile Court

The fundamental issue facing juvenile justice policy-makers is the question of the philosophy and form of juvenile court. Some argue that juvenile court should be kept basically the same as it exists today, some call for substantial modifications in juvenile court, and still others call for the elimination of juvenile court. Each option has strong supporters and critics.

Retention of a Rehabilitation-Oriented Juvenile Court

The first option is to retain juvenile court as a rehabilitative institution for both delinquents and status offenders. This is a call for continuation of the traditional *parens patriae* philosophy court described above; this type of court looks beyond the offense to the troubled child and tries to offer whatever assistance is in the best interests of the juvenile. This position is the one taken by a national Task Force on Juvenile Justice and Delinquency Prevention (National Advisory Committee, 1976) and more recently by the National Coalition of State Juvenile Justice Advisory Groups (*Juvenile Justice Digest*, 1987).

A Just Deserts Model Juvenile Court

A second option is to retain juvenile court as a distinct court but to limit its jurisdiction to delinquency cases. There would be no jurisdiction over status offenses. Instead, voluntary community services, such as "crash pads" for runaways and alternative schools (schools with built-in work programs to make attendance attractive) for truants would be made available for status offenders. This model, called the "Just Deserts Model" by the Institute for Judicial Administration and by the American Bar Association, rests on a philosophy of dissatisfaction with the traditional juvenile court, a rejection of rehabilitation, and an emphasis on doing justice. The focus is on a court of law and fair proceedings and on the rejection of attempted but misguided benevolence. Such a court system would be a family court in that it would also exercise jurisdiction over abused and neglected children. There would be considerable discretion to divert children out of the juvenile justice system, but the prosecutor, not a probation officer, would decide whether to petition a child to court. Plea bargaining would be allowed. Children's rights would take precedence over parents' rights. In fact, under certain conditions, a child would have the right to sue his parents, have his own attorneys, and even establish his own residence. Dispositions would be determinate and proportional to the seriousness of the delinquent act, although there would be an emphasis on the use of the least restrictive alternative. Finally, if institutionalized, a child would have the right to refuse counseling and therapy (Institute of Judicial Administration: American Bar Association, 1982).

The state of Washington has actually implemented a new juvenile code that is based, at least to some extent, on the Just Deserts Model, but the results of Washington's new system have been mixed. Many desired changes did indeed occur, such as the involvement of the prosecutor in the intake and sentencing decisions, but there have been some less desirable results, such as differential treatment of males and females (Schneider & Schram, 1986) and the lack of any major impact on recidivism (Schneider, 1984).

Box 15.3
One Suggestion for Juvenile Court Reform

Strictly speaking, Alfred S. Regnery simply called for the modification of juvenile court, but his modification plan appeared to be more of a wrecking ball than a set of remodeling blueprints. Philosophically, he rejected rehabilitation and embraced deterrence. According to Regnery, rehabilitation has been "a vain search for... excuses...." because the juvenile justice system "must realize that ultimately crime is a matter of choice" (Regnery, 1985: 3). Furthermore, Regnery contended that concern for justice and for crime victims dictates that there should be little or no distinction in the handling of juvenile versus adult defendants:

> Criminals should be treated as criminals....Society may wish to be lenient with first offenders, particularly for lesser crimes, but there is no reason that society should be more lenient with a 16-year-old first offender than a 30-year-old first offender. Anyone familiar with the nature of juvenile crime will not make the argument that juvenile crimes differ in their magnitude or brutality than adult crimes; in many cases the reverse is true. So the current approach, which makes a radical distinction between criminals under 18 and those over 18, is often counterproductive (Regnery, 1985: 4).

One concrete example of the end of the "radical distinction between criminals under 18 and those over 18" is Regnery's suggestion that juvenile courts should not seal or destroy juvenile records because

> ...the most fertile age for crime, statistics show, is between 16 and 24. Thus many juvenile criminals are just getting started on a career of crime. To seal their records is to conceal from the police and prosecutor their previous actions, and crime prevention becomes more difficult (Regnery, 1985: 4).

Less strident were Regnery's calls for increased emphasis on restitution and for private initiatives in juvenile correctional programs such as parental and volunteer involvement in probation efforts. In summary, Regnery argued for an overhaul of the juvenile justice system that would result in a system with little resemblance to its predecessor.

The Call for the Elimination
of Juvenile Court

A third option is the elimination of juvenile court, which would entail the relegation of juvenile delinquents to adult court and status offenders to nonintervention or community alternatives. This was at least the implied position of such thinkers as Ernest van den Haag (1975) and James Q. Wilson (1985). Both of these writers stressed punishment, deterrence and incapacitation; thus, they had little room for the traditional *parens patriae* philosophy of juvenile court. Alfred S. Regnery, former administrator of the United States Justice Department's Office of Juvenile Justice and Delinquency Prevention (under President Reagan), also advocated an abandonment of juvenile court (see Box 15.3).

The Flexibility Option:
New York State

A fourth option is the flexibility option. This option would retain juvenile court jurisdiction over some youths and offenses but would grant adult court jurisdiction over selected youths and offenses. For example, New York State's Juvenile Offender Law of 1978 gives jurisdiction to the adult criminal courts in cases involving 13-year-old murderers and 14- and 15-year-olds committing very serious offenses, although the district attorney, grand jury or judge can waive such a child back down to Family Court. The law also requires mandatory confinement in a secure youth prison until release or until transfer to the adult prison system at age 21. Additionally, parole of juveniles is controlled by the Parole Board rather than by the New York State Division for Youth.

Capital Punishment for Juveniles

An issue related to the issue of the philosophy of juvenile court is the question of the appropriateness of the death penalty for juveniles. In early 1987, there were 34 death row inmates (out of a total of 1,874 death row inmates) who were younger than 18 at the time of their offenses. Between 1985 and 1987, three persons who were younger than 18 when they committed murder were executed. This has been possible because many of the 37 states that have death penalty statutes either set no minimum age for eligibility for execution or set minimum ages of 17 years or less (including Indiana, which set its minimum at age 10) (Criminal Justice Newsletter, 1987: 5).

As of the writing of this book, an Oklahoma case involving capital punishment for juveniles was decided by the U.S. Supreme Court, but the Court has not made a final determination on the constitutionality of capital punishment for minors (*Thompson v. Oklahoma*, 1988). Specifically, in June of 1988, the Supreme Court vacated the death sentence of William Wayne Thompson, who had been convicted of first-degree murder and sentenced to death for his active participation in a brutal murder when he was 15 years old. Four justices felt that the Constitution prohibits the execution of any person under 16 at the time of the offense for three reasons. First, the eighteen states that have set a minimum age for execution have set it at age 16. Second, no murderer less than 16 at the time of the offense has been executed since 1948. Third, these four justices felt that the inexperience and incomplete education of juvenile offenders render them less culpable than adult offenders. Three justices, however, saw no bar to the execution of juveniles. The specific ruling in the *Thompson* case hinged on the fact that Oklahoma did not specify any minimum age for death-penalty eligibility. The general issue of the constitutionality of the death penalty for juveniles may be decided in cases pending before the Court in its 1988-1989 term.

For adult murderers, capital punishment has been debated for years (see, e.g., van den Haag & Conrad, 1983, for two opposing viewpoints). The questions in the debate have been both philosophical and empirical. Some of the philosophical questions have focused on the issues of the morality of the state taking a human life and the morality of capital punishment in the face of the possibility of mistakes (i.e., executing someone who has been mistakenly convicted). The empirical questions include the issue of the deterrent impact of capital punishment (whether the death penalty prevents individuals from committing murder because they fear being put to death) and the issue of racial or class bias (whether the death penalty is more likely to be imposed on minorities than on whites). These questions and others are important considerations in the debate over capital punishment for juvenile murderers. (For further discussion, see Box 15.4.)

Jurisdiction Over Status Offenses

Also related to the fundamental issue of the philosophy and continued existence of juvenile court is the issue of divestiture: the elimination of juvenile court jurisdiction over status offenders. Assuming that a state chooses not to eliminate juvenile court, should it continue to exercise control over disobedient, runaway, and truant adolescents? Washington State has opted to continue juvenile court but to eliminate jurisdiction over status offenses. Maine is the only other state that has written full divestiture into law. Most states have retained jurisdiction but implemented policies of deinstitutionalization (stopped the confining of status offenders in state institutions). Additionally, these states have established diversion programs to handle status offenders, instead of relying on the juvenile justice system (Schneider, 1985).

Box 15.4
Death Penalty for Juveniles

The issue of the appropriateness of capital punishment for juveniles includes the same questions that apply to the issue of the appropriateness of the death penalty for adults, but additional issues appear. Victor Streib (1987) has written extensively about the death penalty for juveniles and detailed these issues. First, based on legal history and psychology, he has contended that juveniles are not mature enough to be subject to capital punishment. Second, Streib has argued that American and international "standards of decency reject the death penalty for juveniles and demand that we relegate the practice to our less civilized past" (Streib, 1987: 34). Third, opinion polls indicate that the majority of American citizens oppose the death penalty for juveniles, although not for adults. Fourth, the selection process for deciding which juvenile murderers have been sentenced to the death penalty has been "arbitrary and capricious" (Streib, 1987: 39). Finally, society has little to fear from sending juvenile murderers to prison and even paroling them eventually because "we know that juvenile murderers tend to be model prisoners and have a very low rate of recidivism when released" (Streib, 1987: 37). Thus, Streib has concluded that no person who committed murder while under age 18 should be subject to the death penalty. Age 18 is the appropriate limit because it is "the age commonly used for similar purposes" (Streib, 1987: 40).

Barry Feld (1987b) has agreed with Streib about prohibiting the death penalty for offenders that committed their crimes under age 18 and has provided two additional reasons for his opinion. First, Feld has noted that adolescents are much more susceptible to peer pressure than are adults. Second, he has contended that society is partially responsible for juvenile crime because juveniles are not afforded enough opportunities to become mature and responsible: "Indeed, even though the ability to make responsible choices is learned behavior, the dependent status of juveniles systematically deprives them of opportunities to learn to be responsible" (Feld, 1987b: 526).

Arguments for Ending Jurisdiction

There are several arguments in favor of complete divestiture. First, divestiture allows the juvenile court more time and resources to deal with juvenile delinquents, especially violent and chronic delinquents. As the court would not have to process or supervise status offenders, probation officers, prosecutors, public defenders, judges, and correctional program employees could focus on the more serious delinquents. Second, the elimination of status offense jurisdiction would prevent any possible violations of the due process rights of status offenders, such as the violation being prosecuted for very vague charges. For example, how disobedient does a child have to be before becoming "incorrigible," or how truant before becoming eligible for a truancy petition? Status offense statutes simply are unclear or vague about when youthful disobedience or adolescent rebellion turns into a status offense. Third, elimination of this jurisdiction recognizes the reality that juvenile courts are not adequately staffed and equipped to deal with status offenders. Most probation officers often have only bachelor's degrees and are not really qualified to do the social work and psychological counseling necessary to correctly assist troubled teenagers and their families. Thus, elimination of jurisdiction over status offenses would be an admission that private agencies with trained social workers and counselors are better equipped to handle the complex personal and interpersonal problems of status offenders by means of individual, group, and family counseling and other professional techniques. Furthermore, elimination of juvenile court jurisdiction and relegation of status offender intervention to community agencies would force any intervention to be voluntary, which some writers argue is the proper way to deal with status offenders.

Another argument for elimination is that juvenile court jurisdiction over status offenses has "weakened the responsibility of schools and agencies to arrange out-of-court interventive services and solutions" (Rubin, 1985: 63). What Rubin meant is that status offense laws have allowed schools to run inadequate and boring programs that promote truancy and, in turn, blame parents and children for the problem. Instead of petitioning youths to juvenile court, schools should be improving instructional programs or offering innovative approaches such as alternative schools, in which children attend school one-half day and then work half a day for pay. In other words, prosecuting status offenders often is a blame-the-victim approach that ignores the real causes of the problems: inferior schools, ineffective parents, and insensitive communities (see Rubin, 1985, and Schur, 1973, for further discussion of this issue).

Arguments for Continuing Jurisdiction

Some still feel, however, that juvenile court jurisdiction over status offenses is both desirable and necessary. Proponents of continued jurisdiction contend that parents and schools need the clout or authority of juvenile court to impress adolescents with the need to obey their parents, attend school, and not run away from home. Concerning truancy in particular, Rubin noted that "repeal will effectively eradicate compulsory education [and] children will be free to roam the streets with impunity" (Rubin, 1985: 65). Second, proponents of court jurisdiction argue that private agencies in the community could not handle, or could not be able to handle, all of the status offense cases if the juvenile court cannot intervene. Private agencies intervene only with willing clients, and proponents contend that many status offenders taken to such agencies would simply refuse assistance. In support of this claim, research in some jurisdictions that prohibited confinement of status offenders has found "that law enforcement officers and the agencies responsible for delivery of services on a voluntary basis simply were not dealing with these youths at all and that those most in need of services were not receiving them" (Schneider, 1985: vi).

Proponents also contend that status offenders are properly under juvenile court jurisdiction because these offenders often escalate into delinquent activity. Hence, early intervention can prevent much delinquency. This so-called escalation hypothesis, however, is controversial. Some percentage of status offenders do indeed escalate or progress, but most do not (Lab, 1984; Rojek & Erickson, 1982; Shannon, 1982). Therefore, it is questionable whether all status offenders should be subject to juvenile court jurisdiction. A similar argument is that many status offenders do get involved in very dangerous situations that may not result in a court referral but can cause serious harm to the child. For example, one study of runaways found that over 50% dealt drugs and about 20% (including 19% of the male runaways) engaged in acts of prostitution to support themselves while they were running (Miller, Miller, Hoffman & Duggan, 1980: 40). Proponents of court jurisdiction over status offenses feel that court jurisdiction would prevent some children from running and becoming involved in associated dangerous behaviors. A related argument is that state intervention to protect juveniles from the harmful consequences of their actions is consistent with state actions to prevent adults from the harmful consequences of their actions. Adults, for example, are not legally free to use any drugs that they wish (Ryan, 1987).

Another argument in favor of continued jurisdiction is that it prevents status offenders from being processed as delinquents. That is, where system processing of status offenders has been ended, there is some evidence that status offenders are treated as minor delinquents and thereby relabeled (Schneider, 1985). Finally, there is concern that total removal of status offense jurisdiction from juvenile court "changes the character of the court and may substan-

tially weaken attempts to consider the child status of delinquent" (Mahoney, 1987: 29). In other words, Mahoney
feared that removal of status offense jurisdiction and concentration only on delinquency might lead to, first, viewing
the juvenile court as only concerned with crime and, then,
to the belief that adult criminal courts can exercise the
function of crime control. Thus, removal of status offense
jurisdiction may be the beginning of the end of the juvenile
court.

A final comment on the status offense issue is Chesney-Lind's (1987) belief that status offenses are intricately
intertwined with the place of women in American society.
She argued that many female status offenders are not offenders but victims of neglect and abuse, especially sexual
abuse. Much of the concern, therefore, about status offenders is not so much for helping the children as for maintaining a patriarchal society:

> Routine horror stories about victimized youth, youthful
> prostitution, youthful involvement in pornography all ne-
> glect the unpleasant reality that most of these behaviors
> were often in direct response to earlier victimization, of-
> ten by parents, that officials ignored....What is really at
> stake here is not "protection" of youth so much as it is the
> right of young women to defy patriarchy. Such defiance
> by male youth is winked at, both today and in the past,
> but from girls such behavior is totally unacceptable
> (Chesney-Lind, 1987: 21).

Thus, Chesney-Lind questions the honorableness of the intentions of those concerned with the protection of status
offenders.

SUMMARY

This chapter has looked at the definition and extent of
delinquency, the history of juvenile justice, the juvenile
court process, and some of the key issues facing juvenile

justice, including diversion, the prediction of delinquency, the philosophy of juvenile court, capital punishment for juveniles, and the divestiture of status offense jurisdiction.

All of these topics have stirred considerable controversy and debate. As society has moved from neglect of juveniles to the *parens patriae* philosophy to calls for more punitive approaches to delinquents, more questions than answers accumulate. Hopefully, the next decades will see more satisfying answers than have been seen in the past.

REVIEW QUESTIONS

1. What is your philosophy of juvenile justice? Do you favor elimination of the juvenile justice system, retention of the system, or some other approach to handling juvenile misbehavior?

2. Do you favor capital punishment for juvenile murderers? Is your opinion about capital punishment for juveniles different from your opinion about capital punishment for adults?

3. Do think that diversion programs should be continued?

4. What lessons do we learn from the history of juvenile justice? Does the history of juvenile justice offer us any clues about some of the problems currently facing the system?

5. Do you think that status offenses should be under juvenile court jurisdiction? Is there a better method for handling the problem of status offenses?

REFERENCES

Blomberg, T.G. (1979), "Diversion from juvenile court: A review of the evidence," in F.L. Faust and P.J. Brantingham (eds.), *Juvenile Justice Philosophy: Readings, Cases and Comments* (2nd ed.) (pp. 415-29). (St. Paul: West).

Blomberg, T.G. & S.L. Carabelo (1979), "Accelerated family intervention in juvenile justice: An exploration and a recommendation for constraint," *Crime and Delinquency* 25:497-502.

Burgess, E.W. (1928), "Factors influencing success or failure on parole," In Bruce, A.A., A.J. Harno, E.W. Burgess & L. Landesco (eds.), *The Workings of the Indeterminate-Sentence Law and the Parole System in Illinois*. (Springfield, IL: State Board of Parole).

California, State of (1972), *Annotated Welfare and Institutions Code*. (St. Paul, MN: West).

Carroll, J.S., R.L. Weiner, D. Coates, J. Galegher & J.J. Alibrio (1982), "Evaluation, diagnosis, and prediction in parole decision making," *Law and Society Review* 17:199-228.

Cernkovich, S.A. (1978), "Delinquency involvement: An examination of the non-intervention strategy," *Criminal Justice Review* 3:45-51.

Chesney-Lind, M. (1987), "Girls' crime and woman's place: Toward a feminist model of female delinquency," Paper presented at the Annual Meeting of the American Society of Criminology in Montreal, Canada.

Clarke, S.H. & G.G. Koch (1980), "Juvenile Court: Therapy or Crime Control, and Do Lawyers Make a Difference," *Law and Society Review*, 14: 263-308.

Criminal Justice Newsletter (March 7, 1987: 5).

Dunford, F.W. (1977), "Police diversion: An illusion?" *Criminology* 15:335-352.

Dunford, F.W., D.W. Osgood & H.F. Weichselbaum (1982), *National Evaluation of Diversion Projects*. (Washington, DC: U.S. Department of Justice).

Duxbury, E. (1973), *Evaluation of Youth Service Bureaus*. (Sacramento: California Youth Authority).

Elliott, D.S., S.S. Ageton, D. Huizinga, B.A. Knowles & R.J. Canter (1983), *The Prevalence and Incidence of Delinquent Behavior: 1976-1980*. (Boulder, CO: Behavioral Research Institute).

Elliott, D.S., F.W. Dunford & B. Knowles (1978), *Diversion: A Study of Alternative Processing Practices*. (Boulder, CO: Behavioral Research Institute).

Erickson, M.L. (1971), "The group context of delinquent behavior," *Social Problems* 19:114-129.

Erickson, M.L. & G. Jensen (1977), "Delinquency is still group behavior: Toward revitalizing the group premise in the sociology of deviance," *Journal of Criminal Law and Criminology* 68: 262-73.

Fabricant, M. (1983), *Juveniles in the Family Courts*. (Lexington, Mass.: Lexington Books).

Fagan, J., M. Forst & T.S. Vivona (1987), "Racial determinants of the judicial transfer decision: Prosecuting violent youth in criminal court," *Crime and Delinquency*, 33: 259-286.

Farrington, D.P. (1985), "Predicting self-reported and official delinquency," in D.P. Farrington and R. Tarling (eds.), *Prediction in Criminology* (pp. 150-73). (Albany, NY: SUNY Press).

Faust, F.L. & P.J. Brantingham (1979), *Juvenile Justice Philosophy: Readings, Cases and Comments*. (St. Paul: West).

Federal Bureau of Investigation (1986), *Crime in the United States, 1985*. (Washington, DC: U.S. Government Printing Office).

_____ (1988), *Crime in the United States, 1987*. (Washington, DC: U.S. Government Printing Office).

Feld, B.C. (1987a), "The juvenile court meets the principle of the offense: Changing juvenile justice sentencing practices," Paper presented at the 1987 Annual Meeting of the American Society of Criminology.

_____ (1987b), "The juvenile court meets the principle of the offense: Legislative changes in juvenile waiver statutes," *The Journal of Criminal Law and Criminology* 78: 471-533.

Flanagan, T.J. & E.F. McGarrell (1986), *Sourcebook of Criminal Justice Statistics--1985.* (Washington, DC: U.S. Department of Justice).

Florida, State of (1981), *Evaluation of the Juvenile Services Project.* (Tallahassee, FL: Health and Human Services).

Glaser, D. (1962), "Prediction tables as accounting devices for judges and parole boards," *Crime and Delinquency* 8: 239-58.

Glueck, S. & E. Glueck (1950), *Unraveling Juvenile Delinquency.* (Cambridge, MA: Harvard Univ. Press).

Gottfredson, S.D. & D.M. Gottfredson (1985), "Screening for risk among parolees: Policy, practice and method," in D.P. Farrington and R. Tarling (eds.), *Prediction in Criminology* (pp. 54-77). (Albany, NY: SUNY Press).

Hindelang, M.J. (1971), "The social versus solitary nature of delinquent involvement," *British Journal of Criminology* 11: 167-75.

Hindelang, M.J., T. Hirschi & J.G. Weis (1981), *Measuring Delinquency.* (Beverly Hills: Sage).

Holland, T.R. & N. Holt (1980), "Correctional classification and the prediction of institutional adjustment," *Criminal Justice and Behavior* 7:51-60.

Institute of Judicial Administration: American Bar Association (1980), *Juvenile Justice Standards: Standards Relating to Adjudication.* (Cambridge, MA.: Ballinger Publishing Co.)

_____ (1982), *Standards for Juvenile Justice: A Summary and Analysis, Second Edition.* (Cambridge, MA: Ballinger Publishing Co.)

Juvenile Justice Digest (January 26, 1987: 5-7).

Klein, M.W. (1971), *Street Gangs and Street Workers.* (Englewood Cliffs, NJ: Prentice-Hall).

_____ (1979), "Deinstitutionalization and diversion of juvenile offenders: A litany of impediments," in N. Morris & M. Tonry (eds.), *Crime and Justice* (1: 145-202). (Chicago: Univ. of Chicago Press).

Lab, S.P. (1982), *The Identification of Juveniles for Non-Intervention*. Unpublished Ph.D. dissertation. (Tallahassee: Florida State Univ.).

_____ (1984), "Patterns in juvenile misbehavior," *Crime and Delinquency* 30:293-308.

Lab, S.P. & J.T. Whitehead (1988), "An analysis of juvenile correctional treatment," *Crime and Delinquency* 34:60-83.

Lincoln, S.B. (1976), "Juvenile referral and recidivism," in R.M. Carter and M.W. Klein (eds.), *Back on the Street: Diversion of Juvenile Offenders* (pp. 321-328). (Englewood Cliffs, NJ: Prentice-Hall.)

Mahoney, A.R. (1985), "Jury trial for juveniles: Right or ritual?," *Justice Quarterly*, 2: 553-565.

_____ (1987), *Juvenile Justice in Context*. (Boston: Northeastern University Press).

McCarthy, B.R. (1987a), "Case attrition in the juvenile court: An application of the crime control model," *Justice Quarterly* 4: 237-55.

_____ (1987b), "Preventive detention and pretrial custody in the juvenile court," *Journal of Criminal Justice* 15: 185-200.

Meehl, P.E. (1954), *Clinical vs. Statistical Prediction*. (Minneapolis: Univ. of Minnesota Press).

Miller, D., D. Miller, F. Hoffman & R. Duggan (1980), *Runaways-- Illegal Aliens in their Own Land: Implications for Service*. (New York: Praeger).

Miller, W.B. (1975), *Violence by Youth Gangs and Youth Groups as a Crime Problem in Major American Cities*. (Washington, DC: National Institute for Juvenile Justice and Delinquency Prevention).

_____ (1980), "Gangs, groups and serious youth crime," In D. Shichor and D.H. Kelly (eds.), *Critical Issues in Juvenile Delinquency* (pp. 115-138). (Lexington, MA: Lexington Books).

Monahan, J. (1981), *The Clinical Prediction of Violent Behavior*. (Rockville, MD: National Institute of Mental Health).

National Advisory Committee on Criminal Justice Standards and Goals (1976), *Juvenile Justice and Delinquency Prevention*. (Washington, DC: Law Enforcement Assistance Administration).

Nimick, E.H., H.N. Snyder, D.P. Sullivan & N.J. Tierney (1987), *Juvenile Court Statistics, 1983*. (Washington, DC: U.S. Department of Justice).

Osgood, D.W. (1983), "Offense history and juvenile diversion," *Evaluation Review* 7:793-806.

Page's Ohio Revised Code, Annotated (1987). (Cincinnati, OH: Anderson).

Palmer, T. & R.V. Lewis (1980), *An Evaluation of Juvenile Diversion*. (Cambridge, MA: Oelgeschlager, Gunn & Hain).

Paternoster, R., G.P. Waldo, T.G. Chiricos & L.S. Anderson (1979), "The stigma of diversion: Labeling in the juvenile justice system," in P.L. Brantingham & T.G. Blomberg (eds.), *Courts and Diversion: Policy and Operations Studies* (pp. 127-142). (Beverly Hills: Sage).

Petersilia, J., P.W. Greenwood & M. Lavin (1978), *Criminal Careers of Habitual Felons*. (Washington, DC: U.S. Department of Justice).

Platt, A.M. (1977), *The Child Savers: The Invention of Delinquency*. (Chicago: Univ. of Chicago Press).

Prescott, P.S. (1981), *The Child Savers: Juvenile Justice Observed.* (New York: Alfred A. Knopf).

Quay, H.C. & C.T. Love (1977), "The effect of a juvenile diversion program on rearrests," *Criminal Justice and Behavior* 4: 377-96.

Rausch, S. (1983), "Court processing versus diversion of status offenders: A test of deterrence and labeling theories," *Journal of Research in Crime and Delinquency* 20: 39-54.

Regnery, A.S. (1985), "Getting away with murder," *Policy Review* 34: 1-4.

Regoli, R., E. Wilderman & M. Pogrebin (1985), "Using an alternative evaluation measure for assessing juvenile diversion programs," *Children and Youth Services Review* 7:21-38.

Rojek, D.G. & M.L. Erickson (1982), "Delinquent careers: A test of the career escalation model," *Criminology* 20:5-28.

Rossum, R.A., B.J. Koller & C.P. Manfredi (1987), *Juvenile Justice Reform: A Model for the States.* (Claremont, CA: Rose Institute of State and Local Government and the American Legislative Exchange Council).

Rothman, D. (1980), *Conscience and Convenience.* (Boston: Little Brown).

Rubin, H.T. (1985), *Juvenile Justice: Policy, Practice, and Law, Second Edition.* (New York: Random House).

Ryan, C.M. (1987), "Juvenile court jurisdiction: Intervention and intrusion," In F.X. Hartmann (ed.), *From Children to Citizens: Volume II: The Role of the Juvenile Court*, pp. 56-64. (New York: Springer-Verlag).

Schneider, A.L. (1984), "Sentencing guidelines and recidivism rates of juvenile offenders," *Justice Quarterly*, 1: 107-124.

_____ (1985), *The Impact of Deinstitutionalization on Recidivism and Secure Confinement of Status Offenders*. (Washington, DC: U.S. Department of Justice).

Schneider, A.L. & D.D. Schram (1986), "The Washington State juvenile justice system reform: A review of findings," *Criminal Justice Policy Review*, 2: 211-235.

Schur, E.M. (1973), *Radical Nonintervention: Rethinking the Delinquency Problem*. (Englewood Cliffs, NJ: Prentice-Hall).

Severy, L.J. & J.M. Whitaker (1984), "Memphis-Metro Youth Diversion Project: Final report," *Child Welfare* 63: 269-77.

Shannon, L.W. (1987), *Assessing the relationship of adult criminal careers to Juvenile Careers*. (Iowa City, IA: Iowa Urban Community Research Center, University of Iowa).

Short, J.F. & I. Nye (1958), "Extent of unrecorded delinquency: Tentative conclusions," *Journal of Criminal Law, Criminology and Police Science* 49: 296-302.

Sickmund, M. & P.J. Baunach (1986), "Children in Custody: Public Juvenile Facilities, 1985," *Bureau of Justice Statistics Bulletin*. (Washington, DC: U.S. Department of Justice).

Streib, V.L. (1987), *Death Penalty for Juveniles*. (Bloomingtion, IN: Indiana University Press).

Thrasher, F.M. (1936), *The Gang*. (Chicago: Univ. of Chicago Press).

van den Haag, E. (1975), *Punishing Criminals: Concerning a Very Old and Painful Question*. (New York: Basic Books).

_____ & J.P. Conrad (1983), *The Death Penalty: A Debate*. (New York: Plenum).

Whitehead, J.T. & S.P. Lab (forthcoming), *Juvenile Justice*. (Cincinnati, OH: Anderson).

Wilbanks, W.L. (1985), "Predicting failure on parole," in D.P. Farrington & R. Tarling (eds.), *Prediction in Criminology* (pp. 78-95). (Albany, NY: SUNY Press).

Wilson, J.Q. (1985), *Thinking about Crime*. Revised Edition. (New York: Vintage Books).

Wolfgang, M.E., R.M. Figlio & T. Sellin (1972), *Delinquency in a Birth Cohort*. (Chicago: Univ. of Chicago Press).

Yablonsky, L. (1962), *The Violent Gang*. (New York: Macmillan).

TABLE
OF CASES

Breed v. Jones, 421 U.S. 519 (1975).

Commonwealth v. Fisher, 213 Pa. 48 (1905).

Ex parte Crouse, 4 Whart. (Pa.) 9 (1838).

Fare v. Michael C., 442 U.S. 707 (1979).

Gonzalez v. Mailliard, Civ. No. 50424 (N.D. Cal. Feb. 9, 1971), *appeal docketed*, No. 70-120 (Apr. 9, 1971).

In re Gault, 387 U.S. 1 (1967).

In re Winship, 397 U.S. 358 (1970).

Kent v. United States, 383 U.S. 541 (1966).

McKeiver v. Pennsylvania, 403 U.S. 528 (1971).

New Jersey v. T.L.O., 469 U.S. 325 (1985).

Schall v. Martin, 467 U.S. 253 (1984).

Thompson v. Oklahoma, 724 P.2d 780 (Okla. Crim. App. 1986), cert. *granted*, 107 S. Ct. 1281 (1987).

Subject Index

Name Index

Case Index